FOOD SAFETY LAW

This text was prepared as a general guideline for anyone involved in Food Safety. While every effort has been made to ensure the complete and total accuracy of the law cited, the reader must be aware that the law is a constantly evolving subject. The authors provide no warranty, either expressed or implied, as to the current law in the jurisdiction of the reader or does it contain an all encompassing review of the subjects covered. In addition, although suggestions are offered as to how to minimize or avoid litigation, the authors do not intend this text to provide specific counsel with regard to all possible circumstances the reader may face within his or her organization. Competent local legal counsel should be retained to assist the reader with regards to specific circumstances and situations.

This text is offered to food industry personnel in the hopes that a greater understanding and appreciation of the law as it applies to this area can be achieved. Given the growing complexity of the law, food industry personnel should understand the basic law and liabilities in this ever growing complex field. If knowledge is power, it is the authors hope that this text will play a small role in empowering food safety personnel within the legal arena.

FOOD SAFETY LAW

Michael S. Schumann
Thomas D. Schneid
B. R. Schumann
Michael J. Fagel

Appendix C is courtesy of
Dr. Worley Johnson

 VAN NOSTRAND REINHOLD
I(T)P® an International Thomson Company

New York • Albany • Bonn • Boston • Detroit • London • Madrid • Melbourne
Mexico City • Paris • San Francisco • Singapore • Tokyo • Toronto

I(T)P® an International Thomson Publishing Company
The ITP logo is a registered trademark used herein under license

Printed in the United States of America

For more information, contact:

Van Nostrand Reinhold
115 Fifth Avenue
New York, NY 10003

Chapman & Hall GmbH
Pappelallee 3
69469 Weinheim
Germany

Chapman & Hall
2-6 Boundary Row
London
SE1 8HN
United Kingdom

International Thomson Publishng Asia
221 Henderson Road #05-10
Henderson Building
Singapore 0315

Thomas Nelson Australia
102 Dodds Street
South Melbourne, 3205
Victoria, Australia

International Thomson Publishing Japan
Hirakawacho Kyowa Builiding, 3F
2-2-1 Hirakawacho
Chiyoda-ku, 102 Tokyo
Japan

Nelson Canada
1120 Birchmount Road
Scarborough, Ontario
Canada M1K 5G4

International Thomson Editores
Seneca 53
Col. Polanco
11560 Mexico D.F. Mexico

1 2 3 4 5 6 7 8 9 10 EDWAA 01 00 99 98 97

Library of Congress Cataloging-in-Publication Data

Food safety law / by Thomas D. Schneid . . . [et al.].
    p.   cm.
    Includes bibliographical references and index.
    ISBN 0-442-02216-6
    1. Food law and legislation—United States.   I. Schneid, Thomas D.
KF1900.F66   1996
344.73'04232—dc21
                                                                              96-40877
                                                                                 CIP

http://www.vnr.com
product discounts • free email newsletters
software demos • online resources

email: info@vnr.com

A service of I(T)P®

This text is dedicated to the hardworking men and women of the food service industry, to provide them guidance and assistance in their daily efforts.

Contents

Preface

Significant changes have occurred in the food industry in the twentieth century. Today in the United States consumers rely upon worldwide food sources instead of depending on local products. The nation's food is now mass-produced and nationally distributed, and the consumer increasingly depends upon governmental regulation to ensure the safety of the food supply.

Meat packers, poultry producers, and others in the food industry strive to achieve and maintain the highest quality in their products. However, food can be contaminated by organisms from soil, water, air, surfaces, other animals, insects, rodents, and even other people. Food can also be contaminated by chemicals such as pesticides, herbicides, fertilizers, and even contamination from the process itself. *Salmonella* is contained in 15 to 30% of all raw dressed poultry. *Clostridium perfringens* is cultured in up to 50% of red meat in stores, and there are other common contaminants such as *Salmonella aureus* in milk, eggs, and cheeses. In recent years, findings of *E. coli* have caused a major reemphasis on the need for food safety and improved sanitary conditions in production facilities and retail outlets.

In addition to focusing on product safety, it is important to realize that millions of people work in food-related industries. Providing for the safety and health of these individuals, who often work around equipment designed to cut and grind particular products, is imperative, and a matter of the highest priority in most food industry facilities. The safety of these workers, as well as the safety of the final product, is of utmost importance to the American household.

On July 6, 1996, President William J. Clinton announced the biggest change in regulations governing meat and poultry safety in the last 90 years. The new regulations add scientific methods to the tools federal inspectors utilize, and place the burden of compliance on the food industry. The hands-on system utilized by USDA inspectors, relying on sight, smell, and touch to detect spoiled products is being supplemented with new tests for *E. coli* and *Salmonella* bacteria. This significant change opens a new era in food safety in the United States.

The authors have prepared this text in hopes of expanding its readers' understanding and knowledge of not only the laws governing the food area but also the various rules and regulations pertaining to working in the food industry. Numerous federal and state agencies are responsible for various aspects of the U.S. food supply. Thorough knowledge of these rules and regulations will assist food producers, as well as consumers, in creating a safer and healthier work environment for employees and ensuring a safe food supply for the nation's population. This text is not all-inclusive; however, the authors, because of their respective backgrounds, have focused on the major areas of concern in the red meat industry and poultry industries. Moreover, the information contained in this book is very applicable to other food-related industries.

Special thanks are due to Dr. Worley Johnson, Professor of Environmental Health at Eastern Kentucky University for his advice and the use of his Food Service Sanitation Manual, reproduced in the Appendix.

The authors are particularly grateful to their families for their support and understanding during the writing of this text.

Chapter *1*

Overview

CHAPTER OBJECTIVES

The reader will:

1. *Acquire a basic understanding of the history of food safety in the United States.*
2. *Acquire an understanding of the wide range of potential diseases in food products.*
3. *Acquire a basic understanding of the status of food inspection laws and regulations.*

The United States has long been considered to have an exceptional food safety and inspection system. This system, ranging from meat to seafood to general food service was established early in the twentieth century and for many years has provided adequate results in protecting food sources from disease by relying primarily on the expertise of inspectors who identify spoiled products through their senses of smell, sight, and touch. However, in recent years a variety of well-publicized incidents—including the deaths of several children and numerous cases of illness due directly to the *E. coli* contamination of hamburgers at fast food establishments—have resulted in a public outcry for more stringent measures to safeguard food supplies.

Today's consumers are substantially different from their forebears. The U.S.

population today tends to consume more food prepared in restaurants or to purchase products substantially prepared at food service operations for fast consumption within the home. Because of labeling requirements consumers have been provided with more information than ever before, enabling them to evaluate products on the shelf prior to purchase. These consumers are highly concerned about *E. coli*, *Salmonella*, livestock antibiotics and growth hormones, pesticides and fertilizers, and various foodborne diseases and food toxins that have caused recent outbreaks of foodborne illnesses and deaths. The Centers for Disease Control and Prevention (CDC) have estimated that at least 9,000 people die and another 6.5 million become sick because of foodborne disease annually.[1] Fortunately, most foodborne illnesses are easily prevented.

Today, the U.S. food safety and inspection system is a highly complex regulatory network consisting of 12 federal agencies spending about one billion dollars annually to administer approximately 35 laws governing food safety and quality.[2] Unfortunately, the system is not perfect and has several problem areas, including fundamental differences in agency missions and approaches to inspections, as well as overlap in inspection processes, gaps in inspection systems, and inconsistent enforcement. Moreover, there are currently 21 agencies conducting food safety research with little or no coordination and a great deal of duplication of effort. Money spent on research in many cases is often wasted on nonessential issues, with efforts lagging in the development of new technology for controlling current concerns.

An ongoing problem involves the division of responsibility between the two primary agencies: the U.S. Department of Agriculture (USDA), which oversees meat and poultry inspection and regulations, and the Food and Drug Administration (FDA), which oversees almost all other food products. Food products under the FDA's jurisdiction can be marketed without preapproval by the FDA and are subject only to postmarketing surveillance and enforcement. Under the USDA, food products must be preapproved prior to marketing. For example, the food safety inspection service (FSIS), a branch of the USDA, conducts continuous inspection at meat packing plants and requires trained inspectors to be on duty to examine meat animals both before and after slaughter. The FSIS also inspects products prior to shipment to consumers. In contrast, the FDA inspects facilities on average once every three to five years. Clearly these two agencies' approaches are greatly different.

In 1993, the USDA, through the FSIS inspection program, oversaw approximately 6,100 slaughter and processing plants with a cost of approximately 660 million dollars.[3] The FSIS used about 7,800 inspectors, of whom 1,100 were veterinarians. In contrast, the FDA spent approximately 200 million dollars in food protection activities and oversaw approximately 53,000 food establishments. It has been estimated that the FDA has inspected less than one-fourth of these 53,000 establishments each year.[4]

To address many of the ongoing problems in the food safety inspection system, President Clinton announced, on July 6, 1996, the most sweeping changes ever proposed in the 90-year history of the laws governing food safety, focusing initially on meat and poultry products. These changes will maintain the best from the current system and interject new scientific measures to identify potentially dangerous bacteria, such as *E. coli* and *Salmonella,* at the slaughter and processing stages of product handling. These new stringent standards will place the major burden of food safety on the food industry and will provide oversight by the USDA.

With these broad changes as well as the current federal, state, and local food-related laws and regulations, today's food safety professionals must possess great knowledge and expertise to manage the myriad requirements. In the past, inspectors were sniffing and looking, and were most concerned about basic food contamination such as visible filth, spoilage, and mislabeling. Now, with these changes and the addition of scientific testing for bacteria and other contaminants normally unseen by the naked eye, food safety professionals must prepare themselves to address the requirements and regulations in their individual workplaces. Additionally, food safety professionals must deal with other issues—such as microorganisms, parasites, intentionally or unintentionally added chemicals, flavors and drug additives, animal drugs, industrial chemicals, and environmental contaminants—that were virtually unknown in the not-so-distant past.

Food safety often is taken for granted, and all too often it has been elevated to public attention by a catastrophic incident. Food safety professionals must know the rules and regulations and must work daily to ensure the safety of the food products entering the nation's food stream. Members of the American public depend on the food safety professional to ensure compliance with these regulations and to provide safe and healthful food products for their tables. Although there is too little recognition for a job well done, when food safety professionals do a "bad" job, the consequences can be brutal, for them and for the affected individuals. Loss of life or severe illness, medical costs, pain, and suffering, as well as financial devastation for the organization involved, may ensue. Knowing the rules and following them are essential to producing a safe food product for consumers.

NOTES

1. John V. Bennett et al., "Infectious and Parasitic Diseases," in *Closing the Gap: The Burden of Unnecessary Illness,* ed. Robert W. Amler and H. Bruce Dull (New York: Oxford University Press, 1987), 102–14.

2. *Food Safety and Quality: Who Does What in the Federal Government* (GAO/RCED-91-19A and 19B, Dec. 21, 1990).
3. See Geoffrey S. Becker, "Meat and Poultry Inspection: Background and Current Issues" (CRS-93-574 ENR, June 9, 1993).
4. *Comprehensive Needs Assessment: 1994–1997* (FDA, Dept. of Health of Human Services, 1990), p. B-18.

Chapter 2

Food and Drug Administration

CHAPTER OBJECTIVES

The reader will:

1. *Acquire an understanding of the historical significance of the Food and Drug Administration.*
2. *Acquire an understanding of food safety standards.*
3. *Acquire an understanding of the FDA's enforcement tools.*

OVERVIEW

The Food and Drug Administration (FDA) is one of the most necessary and vital agencies in the U.S. federal government. Falling under the jurisdiction of the Department of Health and Human Services (HHS), it is authorized by Congress to inspect, test, approve, and set safety standards for foods, food additives, drugs, chemicals, and cosmetics, as well as household and medical devices. This agency was first known as the Food, Drug, and Insecticide Administration when it was formed in 1927. It derives its regulatory power from four major laws: the Federal Food, Drug, and Cosmetic Act of 1938 (FFDCA);[1] the Fair Packaging and Labeling Act of 1966,[2] which requires standardized labeling of products and true honest information; the Radiation Control for Health and Safety Act of 1968,[3] which provides for consumer protection from possible excess radiation from X-ray machines, television sets, microwave ovens, and so on; and the Public Health Service Act of 1944,[4] which gives the FDA authority over vaccines and serums and allows the agency to inspect restaurants and travel facilities. Through the force of these and other major laws, the FDA regulates foods, drugs, cosmetics, and medical devices found in interstate commerce. In addition, the FDA is generally empowered to stop certain products from being sold in interstate commerce, and it has the authority to take legal action to stop the sale of any product involving a health or safety risk. Through the court system, the FDA has the right to seize products and prosecute persons or organizations responsible for the violation of these federal laws. The agency, whose authority is limited to products being sold in interstate commerce, cannot control prices or directly regulate advertising except for prescription drugs and medical devices.

One of the major challenges facing the FDA is its current attempt to develop a national, uniform, scientific, and risk-based inspection system to ensure a safe food supply. The Centers for Disease Control and Prevention (CDC) (within the U.S. Department of Health and Human Services) have estimated that at least 9,000 Americans die from foodborne illness each year, and that 6.5 million become sick from eating contaminated foods. As many cases go undiagnosed, it has been estimated by the FDA that the actual number is much higher—by some estimates, 24 million.[5] It should be noted that these numbers are only for *acute* illnesses. The extent of long-term disease as related to food is actually unknown. In addition, the social costs of foodborne illness such as medical expenses and lost productivity are estimated to reach between four billion and eight billion dollars annually.[6] Therefore, it is clear that the FDA's impact on food and food safety is enormous.

As most of the cases of foodborne illness can be attributed to meat, poultry, eggs, milk, fish, and shellfish, the FDA's involvement in food safety is critical. Today, when more meals than ever are being eaten outside of the home, and more of the meals being eaten at home are pre-prepared and pre-packaged, control over the raw food source and the supply of these meals is becoming more critical and burdensome on the FDA. Given this background, the FDA has taken major steps in reexamining its responsibilities and long-term agenda to become not only more efficient and streamlined but to have better coordination with the other federal agencies involved with food safety. Moreover, it has begun an effort to obtain greater enforcement authority in addition to introducing industrial control systems such as Hazard Analysis and Critical Control Point (HACCP) programs, to promote the production of wholesome, unadulterated food in the United States.

A current major concern of the FDA is that it has less authority to regulate foods than it does drugs and medical devices.[7] At this time, the FDA generally cannot "presume" that any single food production and processing company is engaged in interstate commerce; it must prove this. Thus, the FDA cannot require food firms to register with the agency, nor can it obtain access to the manufacturer's production and distribution records. Furthermore, it cannot impose civil penalties for violations or detain domestic products that violate food safety standards without obtaining the firm's voluntary cooperation or a court order. The impact of and resultant problems with these issues are more fully discussed later in this chapter.

HISTORICAL BACKGROUND

The origin of the FDA has been commonly traced to Mr. Harvey W. Wiley, the chief chemist of the Agricultural Department's Bureau of Chemistry during the early 1900s. Mr. Wiley had joined the Bureau in 1883 and became deeply involved in experimenting with food and drug adulteration. In fact, he became well known for his famed "Poison Squad," a group of human volunteers who took small doses of poisons. These poisons were identical to those found in food preservatives at that time. The Poison Squad generated great publicity and increased public awareness of the consumption of adulterated foods by the general populace. This publicity led Congress to enact the Food and Drug Act of 1906.

Thereafter, Mr. Wiley was put in charge of the Bureau of Chemistry in 1907, and he guided it for many years. Twenty years later, the administration of the Food and Drug Act was transferred to the Agricultural Department's newly created Food, Drug, and Insecticide Administration. In 1931, this department was renamed the Food and Drug Administration.

In 1938, with the passage of the Federal Food, Drug, and Cosmetic Act, the FDA's powers were greatly expanded. The most significant change in this legislation required manufacturers to test and prove the safety of any new drug before the FDA would grant approval to place the drug on the market. Unfortunately, like many laws, the FFDCA was not passed in response to a progressive and enlightened Congress but in response to the death in 1937 of over one hundred people who had taken what was considered to be a harmless elixir but was, in fact, contaminated.

In 1940, the Administration was transferred from the Agricultural Department to the Federal Security Agency (FSA). The FSA was then incorporated into the Department of Health, Education, and Welfare (HEW) when the latter was created in 1953.

In the 1950s there was great public concern regarding pesticides in food additives, which resulted in the 1958 amendments to the Food, Drug, and Cosmetic Act. These amendments expanded the FDA's regulatory powers to set limits on pesticides and to approve food additives. This concern also led the Eisenhower Administration to double the FDA's staff. The amendments, called the Delaney amendments for Congressman Delaney, required manufacturers to prove the safety of food additives. Also, the FDA had to prohibit the use of any food additive that produced cancer in humans or animals. The "Delaney Clauses" became quite controversial and generated much publicity over the ensuing years.

In addition, publication in 1962 of Rachel Carson's best seller *Silent Spring* generated great consumer anxiety about pesticides, and prompted the Kennedy Administration again to increase the FDA's size. There were also new amendments to the Food and Drug Act, which required drug manufacturers to prove the effectiveness as well as the safety of products before they could be placed on the market. This too was a reactionary move by Congress, after it was discovered that pregnant women who had taken the drug thalidomide ran a very high risk of giving birth to deformed children. Although thalidomide had been widely marketed in Europe, it had been kept off the U.S. market through the efforts of an FDA chemist who was convinced that the drug was unsafe.

Additional powers were given to the FDA in 1976 when Congress passed legislation requiring the regulation of complex medical devices and diagnostic products. Then, in 1979, Congress passed legislation that renamed HEW the Department of Health and Human Services. This action was, in part, a response to the educational functions of HEW being transferred to the new Department of Education.

RESPONSIBILITIES

As discussed in Chapter 1, the U.S. Department of Agriculture (USDA) has oversight responsibility for meat and poultry inspection and regulation in the United States. The FDA basically regulates all other food products, but this arrangement is not quite as simple as it sounds. For example, the two organizations share jurisdiction for egg products. In addition, the FDA is responsible for products containing less than 3% raw meat or poultry as well as those products containing less than 2% cooked meat or poultry. Both organizations monitor domestic and imported food for potentially harmful chemicals such as pesticides, animal drugs, and environmental contaminants.

The FDA generally regulates the composition, quality, safety, and labeling of food, food additives, colors, and cosmetics, and it carries out research in these areas. The FDA also regulates the composition, quality, safety, and labeling of all drugs for human use, as well as establishing scientific standards to carry out its oversight responsibilities. The agency evaluates applications and requests for new drugs, as well as premarket testing.

Further FDA responsibilities include the development of standards for the safety and effectiveness of over-the-counter drugs. The FDA also is responsible for gathering data on medical devices and setting standards for those devices. In addition, inspection and licensing of manufacturers of biological products, as well as requirements for premarket testing, fall under FDA jurisdiction. Finally, periodic inspections of drug manufacturing facilities in the United States as well as oversight of the facilities are FDA responsibilities.

STANDARDS FOR FOOD SAFETY

The 1938 Food, Drug, and Cosmetic Act gave the FDA broad authority to move against any chemicals and food that are unsafe for human consumption. This power was strengthened 20 years later with the passage of the Food Additives Amendment,[8] which required members of the food industry desiring to add a substance to food first to demonstrate its safety. The 1958 amendment, however, applied only to new additives. Hundreds of substances had been in common use in the food industry at that time, many of which had a long history of use and were considered safe. They were placed on what is known as the FDA's GRAS (generally recognized as safe) list.[9] This action, as well as growing concern over the identification of illnesses and disease attributed to substances' being foodborne, has caused the FDA to reexamine its efforts in the area of food safety.

Sections 401, 402, 403, 404, 406, 408, and 409 of the Federal Food and Drug Act set forth the basic standards for food safety, including food additives. Section 401 sets forth the basic standards for "food."[10] Section 402 outlines the prohibition against adulteration of food. Under the FDA's definition, set forth in Section 201, "food" is defined as (1) articles used for food or drink for humans or other animals, (2) chewing gum, and (3) articles used for components of any such articles.[11] The FDA also examines the intended use of the substance in judging whether the substance is a food and whether the food is adulterated or misbranded. Foods also are monitored to identify the process and the conditions that may cause the product to be unsafe. Under the FFDCA, certain foods must receive premarket approval before entering interstate commerce. Regulations promulgated under Section 404 require companies that produce low acid canned foods to register with the FDA before they can market their products. They must also comply with detailed goods manufacturing practice regulations in order to stay in business. Otherwise, foods currently do not need any further clearance before being sold in retail stores. In regard to "adulteration," according to the FDA a food is adulterated if it contains any poisonous or deleterious substance that may render it injurious to health. It should be noted that the term "adulterated" has another broad definition in the two other major laws that affect U.S. food and meat products. Under the Poultry Products Inspection Act (PPIA)[12] and the Federal Meat Inspection Act (FMIA),[13] the term "adulterated" is defined to include any meat or poultry product that is "unsound, unhealthful, unwholesome, or otherwise unfit for human food."[14] Meat and poultry products that bear or contain any poisonous or deleterious added substance that may render them injurious to health and meat and poultry products that bear or contain inherent substances in sufficient quantity to ordinarily render them injurious to health are also considered "adulterated" within the meaning of the Acts.[15]

The term "adulterated" is also defined to include meat and poultry products that have been "prepared, packed, or held under unsanitary conditions whereby [they] have become contaminated with filth or whereby [they] may have been rendered injurious to health."[16]

Section 403 of the FFDCA prohibits misbranding—that is, does not allow a food's labeling to be false or misleading. Section 406 allows some tolerances to be set for added poisonous ingredients in food, and Section 408 even provides tolerances for pesticide chemicals on raw agricultural products.[17] Section 409 provides for the premarket approval of food additives and requires that they be shown to be safe.

Title 21 of the Code of Federal Regulations (CFR) Parts 100–199, as well as Chapters 2, 3, 4, 7, and 8 of the FFDCA, the FDA's compliance policy guides, and the 1993 Model Food Code, provides guidance to food companies on the compliance issues that FDA inspectors look for and examine in this area. Therefore, by setting standards, the FDA indicates to companies what constitutes an adulteration violation, or the level of poisonous or deleterious substances that it considers when rejecting a product as adulterated.

FOOD LABELING AND WARNINGS

Labeling is an important feature of the FFDCA, especially as it controls the proper labeling of drugs. However, with regard to foods and food safety, the USDA has primary jurisdiction over meat and poultry products under the Federal Meat and Inspection Act and the Poultry Products Inspection Act. Both of these statutes contain general misbranding provisions.[18]

The FFDCA prohibits the adulteration and misbranding of foods, drugs, medical devices, and cosmetics before or during delivery in interstate commerce.[19] The Act sets forth a series of conditions that define when each of these types of products is determined to be misbranded.[20] For example, a drug or a medical device is considered misbranded unless its *label* bears "such adequate warnings against use in those pathological conditions or by children where its use may be dangerous to health, or against unsafe dosage or methods or duration of administration or application, in such manner and form as are necessary for the protection of users."[21]

In determining whether the labeling of a food, drug, device, or cosmetic is misleading, the Act specifies that consideration must be given to any "fail[ure] to reveal facts material . . . with respect to consequences which may result from the use of the article. . . ."[22] Under these provisions, the FDA enjoys broad authority to require that *warning statements* appear on products subject to its jurisdiction.

The Federal Food, Drug, and Cosmetic Act of 1938 was not the first federal legislation to require warning statements in the labeling of consumer products. It predecessor, the Federal Food and Drugs Act of 1906, prohibited interstate commerce in adulterated or misbranded food and drugs. Other than requiring that the presence of certain narcotic drugs be disclosed, however, the 1906 Act did not specifically mandate that warnings of product risks appear in labeling. Approximately 20 years later, Congress passed a Federal Caustic Poison Act, legislation requiring that the word "poison" and directions for treatment of accidental ingestion appear on the labels of a dozen enumerated chemicals.[23] The Federal Insecticide, Fungicide, and Rodenticide Act (FIFRA), enacted in 1947, mandated similar labeling disclosures for highly toxic chemicals—"poison" in red letters, accompanied by a skull and crossbones symbol—as well as warnings or cautions to reduce unreasonable risks associated with the use of pesticides. These requirements are currently enforced by the Environmental Protection Agency (EPA).[24]

Congress has delegated significant authority to administrative agencies to require that *warning labels* accompany consumer products. Pursuant to the FFDCA's broad prohibitions against misbranding, the FDA may mandate warnings for food, drugs, medical devices, and cosmetics. As it is the USDA that has the major labeling requirements for foods, the FDA's requirements generally refer to artificial flavorings, colorings, and chemical preservatives, as well as saccharin.[25]

The more interesting and current issues involve warning labels on food and food products. The FDA has historically mandated relatively few warnings for food products, one reason being, as stated above, that the USDA shares jurisdiction with the FDA over food products containing meat and poultry. The USDA generally has not required that any cautionary statements appear in the labeling of such products. However, in response to recent food poisonings traced to contaminated hamburger, and as part of a settlement reached with consumer groups, the USDA has mandated that safe handling instructions appear in labeling.[26]

The FDA has taken the position that the warnings on food products are appropriate only when based on sound scientific data with clear application to human health, stating that it "is unwilling to require a warning statement in the absence of clear evidence of a hazard."[27] In 1993, the FDA reiterated its position and stated that it "does not intend to require warning statements [on food labels] except in specific instances where there is scientifically based evidence of a potential health hazard."[28] Some food products and additives have been associated with chronic hazards, and is well recognized that potential carcinogens are nearly universally found in the human diet.[29] Although some occur naturally and others are introduced during processing, the FDA has never suggested that any food product containing a suspected carcinogen bear a warning statement. The FDA has stated that such warnings would be so numerous that they would confuse the public, would not promote informed consumer decision making, and would not advance the public health.[30]

The FDA has stated that if a chronic risk appears to be serious, then it will prohibit the use of the food or the food additive rather than require a warning label.[31] If the chronic health risk is not serious enough to justify a prohibition, the FDA also will not mandate that a warning appear on labels of food products. This hesitancy to demand precautionary labeling for either acute or chronic hazards associated with foods, partly to avoid overwhelming consumers with inconsequential information, stands in marked contrast to the FDA's apparent readiness to demand warnings of all sorts of risks or related safety information in the labeling of cosmetics. As a whole, the FDA's warning requirements applicable to food products are fairly mild.

ADMINISTRATIVE ENFORCEMENT

The FDA has a wide array of enforcement tools to assure compliance with the broad scope of the Federal Food, Drug, and Cosmetic Act. Table 2.1 provides a listing of the various enforcement tools available to the FDA by statute, showing their availability with respect to foods, drugs, devices, and cosmetics. The FDA may use such simple means as writing warning letters or other correspondence of a regulatory nature. It may detain or recall products. In many instances just the adverse publicity of an FDA action or threat of recall forces manufacturers and processors to comply with the Act. In other cases, products may be seized or imports detained, or the agency may even obtain injunctions when warranted. The FDA also uses an "import alert" list when there is a concern about a particular product that is being imported, and the FDA wants to give public notice of its concern for the imported product.

In other cases, the FDA may instigate prosecutions for misdemeanors and felonies to ensure that the regulated industries comply with the applicable standards.

Table 2.2 shows various federal agencies other than the FDA, when their basic authority was granted, and the various enforcement tools they can use. For example, the USDA was granted record inspection authority in 1967, OSHA and the DEA did not receive it until 1970, and the EPA was given this authority in 1988. Neither the USDA nor OSHA has the right to recall products, but the EPA gained recall authority in 1988. As to civil money penalties, the USDA still does

Table 2.1. Selected FDA Statutory Enforcement Authorities[a]

FDA Statutory Authorities	Foods	Drugs	Devices	Cosmetics
Inspection Authorities for:				
Container Manufacturers	No	No	No	No
Commercial Testing Laboratories	No	Limited[b]	Limited[b]	No
Records Inspection	Limited[c]	Limited[d]	Yes	No
Subpoena Authority	No	Limited[e]	Limited[f]	No
Establishment Registration	Limited[g]	Yes	Yes	No
Presumption of Interstate Commerce	No	No	Yes	No
Recall Authorities:				
Administrative Recalls	Limited[h]	No	Limited[i]	No
Recall Reporting to FDA	Limited[h]	No	Limited[i]	No
Temporary Detention/Embargo Authority (domestic)	No	No	Yes	No

(continued)

[a]The FDA also has jurisdiction over biological products (blood) and radiation-emitting products. This list of statutory authorities does not include all statutes for the listed articles.

[b]Limited authority is explicit for prescription drugs and restricted devices, whether FDA has this authority for other products is open to interpretation.

[c]This authority is limited to infant formula.

[d]FFDCA specifies which records can be inspected relative to prescription drugs, and authorizes inspection of records that are submitted under new reporting requirements.

[e]Subpoena authority is allowed in a hearing on drugs or in investigations that are relevant to abbreviated new drug application violations added under the Generic Drug Enforcement Act of 1992 (GDEA).

[f]Subpoena authority is permitted in a civil money penalty investigation which is carried out relevant to a violation of medical device regulations.

[g]This registration is limited to persons introducing new infant formula into interstate commerce.

[h]Infant formula recalls.

[i]This recall is used when the Secretary of Health and Human Services finds reasonable probability that the device would cause serious human adverse health consequences or death.

Table 2.1. Selected FDA Statutory Enforcement Authorities (*continued*)

FDA Statutory Authorities	Foods	Drugs	Devices	Cosmetics
Civil Money Penalties:				
Administrative Civil Money Penalties	No	Limited[j,k]	Limited[l]	No
Court Ordered Civil Penalties	No	Limited[j]	No	No
Court Ordered:				
Seizure	Yes	Yes	Yes	Yes
Injunction	Yes	Yes	Yes	Yes
Prosecution (misdemeanor and felony)	Yes	Yes	Yes	Yes

[j]This is permitted in the GDEA for abbreviated new drug application violations.

[k]For violations of the Prescription Drug Marketing Act (PDMA), as amended, the statute does not explicitly describe FDA's or the court's role in assessing civil money penalties, but FDA interprets the PDMA as authorizing these, subject to judicial review.

[l]Some restrictions are imposed on violations of device regulations subject to civil money penalties.

Source: Food and Drug Administration. Office of Enforcement. Prepared by Joan Davenport, May 12, 1994. (301) 443-7400.

not have the authority to issue such penalties, but OSHA received that authority in 1970 and the EPA in 1978 (see Table 2.2).

As stated earlier, one of the FDA's most important responsibilities is monitoring the marketplace. This is done by inspecting food establishments and import docks to ensure the quality of products, both foreign and domestic. Just as the threat of the USDA's resorting to formal court enforcement actions has a huge impact on the food industry, the FDA generally obtains compliance by threatening legal action. The food industry is highly competitive, and a company's reputation and brand name recognition are very important; so the mere threat of sanctions can have enormous consequences. In the vast majority of U.S. food companies, management has every intention of producing a high quality and wholesome product; so FDA notice of a problem gets a company's internal machinery working to resolve the issue. Also, the risk of product liability exposure provides a great incentive for food companies to comply with the FFDCA. In fact, the subject of

Table 2.2. Federal Agencies' Comparable Enforcement Authorities and Dates When Basic Authority was Granted.

	USDA	**CPSC**	**OHSA**	**EPA**	**DEA**	**NIHTSA**	**BATF**
Records Inspection	1967	1972	1970	1988	1970	1966	N.A.
Temporary Detention (Embargo)	1967	N.A.	N.A.	1972	1970	N.A.	1958
Civil Money Penalties	N.A.	1972	1970	1978	1988	1966	1988
Recall	N.A.	1972	N.A.	1988	N.A.	1974	N.A.
Subpoena	1968	1972	1970	1986	1970	N.A.	1954

USDA = U.S. Department of Agriculture

CPSC = Consumer Product Safety Commission

OSHA = Occupational Safety and Health Administration

EPA = Environmental Protection Agency

DEA = Drug Enforcement Agency

NIHTSA = National Institute for Highways and Traffic Safety Administration

BATF = Bureau of Alcohol, Tobacco, and Firearms

N.A. = Not Applicable

Source: Food and Drug Administration. Office of Enforcement. Prepared by Joan Davenport. (301) 443-7400.

product liability in the food industry is broad enough to warrant an entire text for its treatment.

Inspections

Probably the most important enforcement tool used by the FDA is its inspection process. FDA inspectors are authorized to enter and inspect at reasonable times any factory, warehouse, or establishment in which food, drugs, devices, cosmetics, or certain other electronic items are manufactured, processed, packaged, or held for the introduction for interstate commerce. However, prior to any inspection the FDA official must present his or her credentials and give a written notice to the owner or the agent in charge. If the official does not present his or her credentials, the organization can and should refuse entry.

Inspections basically cover the manufacturer's or processor's entire facility, including the physical plant, equipment, vehicles, and laboratories.[32] Failure of a company to permit an inspection is considered a criminal offense.

Section 704 of the Act requires that prior to leaving the premises the official leading the inspection shall give the owner, operator, or agent in charge a written report setting forth any condition or practice observed by the official that, in his or her judgment, indicates that a food, drug, device, or cosmetic in the establishment consists in whole or in part of any filthy, putrid, or decomposed substance, or has been prepared, packaged, or held under unsanitary conditions whereby it may have been contaminated with unsanitary matter.[33] If a sample of material is taken, the inspecting FDA official must give a receipt to the owner, operator, or agent in charge. The FDA official can request access to, copy, and/or verify records only for restricted medical devices and prescription drugs, not for foods.[34]

Warning Letters

A warning letter is issued by the FDA anytime a violation of the FFDCA is found. This letter comes from FDA headquarters or various district offices. It lists the inspector's findings of alleged violations and provides specific information regarding those violations. This is the only type of warning letter the FDA currently issues. Prior to 1991, the FDA sent two types of letters, one a notice of adverse findings and the other a regulatory letter. However, the information in these two letters has been combined since 1991. In the warning letter, the FDA notifies the manufacturer or the processor of its findings and requires a response within 15 working days stating that the violation will be corrected and telling what steps the organization will take to correct the violations and prevent their recurrence. If drugs or devices are involved, the warning letter generally places a hold on pending product or export approvals. It should be noted that if foods are involved, the statute does not authorize any temporary detention or embargo. Therefore, to stop the sale of a food product, the FDA generally asks state authorities to detain the product. Of course, as stated earlier, the publicity surrounding the warning letter generally puts a great deal of pressure on the organization to comply with the FDA's requests.

A major criticism of the FDA concerns its decreasing number of inspections. In 1988, the FDA conducted 19,192 inspections; in 1993, it conducted only 17,315 inspections. Much of the decrease is due to budget and resource constraints. A major issue, however, is the inspection of the nation's food supply. As the U.S. food system has grown increasingly complex and diversified, as well as becoming an extremely complicated distribution system, the FDA's capacity to inspect food and food facilities for compliance has dwindled. As of 1993, the

FDA apparently was inspecting the nation's approximately 50,000 domestic food establishments (e.g., manufacturers, processors, and warehouses), on average, once every 8 years.[35] Over a 12-year period, the number of FDA food safety inspections had been reduced by two-thirds, from 20,500 conducted in 1981 to about 6,600 in 1993.[36] By 1993, the FDA was inspecting less than 8% of the over one million entries of food imports per year.[37]

Recalls

The FDA has the authority to conduct voluntary recalls of products not in compliance with its regulations. Since 1988 the FDA has increasingly used this enforcement tool. For example, in 1988, the FDA conducted 1,526 recalls; in 1993, 2,375 recalls were issued (see Table 2.3).[38] To the FDA a "voluntary correction or recall" is defined by regulations to mean the correction or the withdrawal of a product that otherwise would be in violation of the FFDCA or other statutes administered by the agency. As can be seen from Table 2.1, the FDA has some limited authority in the areas of foods and devices. The FDA may begin formal judicial proceedings, but the threat of action, either implicit or explicit, generally brings about most voluntary recalls. Under the voluntary recall process, the FDA informs the organization that other enforcement actions may be taken if the recall is not commenced as soon as practicable. The FDA can also request an involuntary recall for food through the use of a court injunction.

Unfortunately, sometimes the inspection and judicial enforcement process of the Act can be greatly protracted. For example, in one case, a new ethnic food processing plant had repeated sanitation problems.[39] The FDA district office had been notified through a consumer complaint about the company's product labels. The FDA then conducted an inspection that revealed extremely poor sanitation in the food manufacturing facility. All five floors of the building showed evidence of active infestation with insects and rodents. There was active infestation on the floors, walls, and food production equipment and machinery. There was also contamination in the raw materials. Additionally, employees were found to be using poor sanitation practices, such as handling egg contents with their bare hands and washing their hands and faces in the same water that was used for washing the food.

In this case, FDA headquarters approved pursuing the case but requested an updated inspection by the district office. This inspection was conducted in October 1991 and revealed that conditions had not changed in the facility. The case was forwarded to the Department of Justice in November 1991 and subsequently forwarded to the U.S. Attorney, Southern District of New York. Another inspection was conducted on January 30, 1992. The facility again failed inspection. A complaint and an order to show cause were filed along with a Motion for Preliminary Injunction on February 10, 1992. The company, through its attorneys,

Table 2.3. FDA Regulatory Activities for Foods and Cosmetics,* Fiscal Years 1989–1993

	1988	1989	1990	1991	1992	1993
Establishment Inspections[a] (Adverse findings)	8,297 (3,075)	7,668 (2,927)	7,077 (3,044)	9,165 (3,490)	7,001 (2,828)	6,786 (2,766)
Domestic Samples Analyzed[b] (Adverse findings)	17,037 (2,446)	16,983 (2,216)	18,603 (2,163)	18,346 (2,508)	18,434 (2,558)	17,482 (2,248)
Import Wharf Examinations[c]	42,646	67,753	43,929	48,354	60,822	52,979
Import Samples Analyzed[d] (Adverse findings)	32,801 (11,648)	37,936 (14,294)	37,678 (15,080)	38,147 (13,487)	45,503 (21,926)	36,453 (16,900)
Warning Letters[a]	36	13	24	122	360	291
Recalls	470	570	725	566	569	663
Seizures	121	88	78	66	86	47
Injunctions	6	6	4	5	9	7
Criminal Prosecutions	13	5	5	2	12	2

*The data do not contain separate actions on cosmetics. Foods and cosmetics are lumped together. However, according to the FDA's Office of Enforcement which supplied the data, actions against food establishments and products make up more than 90 percent of these actions.

[a]The number of different inspections made in food or cosmetic establishments to determine if they are in compliance with FDA enforcement statutes. Adverse findings means the number of inspections which were classified as either "official or voluntary action indicated."

[b]The number of samples of products of domestic origin (or of foreign origin if collected in domestic channels of trade) analyzed to determine compliance with FDA enforcement statutes. Adverse findings means the number of analyzed samples which failed to meet established standards and policy guides, or would for other reasons support a regulatory action.

[c]The number of examinations made of products in import channels of trade that are sufficient in scope to determine whether the products are in compliance with FDA enforced statutes. By definition, all products accepted for import are in compliance.

[d]The number of examinations made of products of foreign origin in import channels of trade analyzed to determine whether the products are in compliance with FDA enforcement statutes. Adverse findings means the number of analyzed samples which failed to meet established standards and policy guides, or would for other reasons support a regulatory action.

[e]Until May 23, 1991, these numbers reflect only "regulatory letters" sent to companies after they had already received a "notice of adverse findings" letter describing the violations of the FFDCA. The numbers increase substantially after May 23, 1991, because FDA changed its policy and began issuing only one "warning letter" rather than two different letters: "notice of adverse findings" and "regulatory letters." Dr. Kessler decided that there was no need to alert companies who should comply with regulations without the first "notice of adverse findings" letter.

Source: Office of Planning and Evaluation. Planning and Management Communications Staff. Program Information and Analysis Group. U.S. Dept. of Health and Human Services. Public Health Service. Food and Drug Admin. FDA Quarterly Activities Report. Fiscal Years 1989, 1990, 1991, 1992, 1993.

agreed to a consent decree, which effected the total shutdown of the manufacturing plant on February 13, 1992. The company agreed, among other things, to do a complete sanitary cleanup, to make structural improvements in the building, and to fully educate the workforce in proper sanitation procedures. In March 1992, a follow-up inspection found the plant to be in satisfactory condition, and the company was allowed to resume operations.[40]

The above story indicates the difficulty that the FDA, as well as some other agencies, has in forcing a manufacturer or a food processor to comply with the law. This process can be extremely drawn out, and, in the meantime, public food safety is at risk.

Court Enforcement

If any "person" (i.e., individual or corporation) engages in or commits any prohibited act under the FFDCA, the FDA (through the Justice Department) is authorized to file a criminal suit against said person. Generally, the offense is a misdemeanor unless it is committed with the intent to defraud or mislead, or as a second offense after a prior conviction under the Act, in which case it is a felony. Pursuant to 21 U.S.C. § 335, the FDA first gives notice and opportunity to be heard prior to referring a criminal case to the Justice Department. If there is a conviction, the court can issue a fine and/or order the defendant's imprisonment.

This authority has come under great criticism, especially in the food industry. These criminal sanctions are possible even though the FDA need not prove knowledge or intent on the part of the person or the company committing the act.

In addition, the FDA (through the Justice Department) can file for an injunction to halt or prevent any violations of the Act. Thus, if a company continues to violate the Act while under a court-imposed injunction, criminal or civil contempt proceedings may be commenced. Although violations are limited to drugs and devices, the FDA also has the authority to seek civil monetary penalties. Some monetary penalties can be imposed by the FDA, but others can only be obtained through a federal court.

Finally, one of the more dramatic tools available to the FDA involves seizure and condemnation of articles that violate the Act. Again, this action must be brought before a federal court. Under Section 334, "any food, drug, device, or cosmetic condemned under this section ((d)(1)), shall, after entry of the decree, be disposed of by destruction or sale as the court may direct and the proceeds, if sold, less than the legal costs and charges, shall be paid into the U.S. Treasury."[41] No article shall be sold under decree contrary to the statutes or laws of the jurisdiction in which it is sold.

The court may also direct that the article be delivered to the owner. The expenses of supervision while such products are in storage must be paid by the person (as closed) obtaining the release of the article.

A critical issue in any seizure is that the Act authorizes seizure of a device regardless of any showing of a connection with interstate commerce. There is also no requirement of an interstate commerce connection in seizure actions against counterfeit drugs or oleomargarine, or any adulterated or misbranded article manufactured within the United States. However, for the large majority of seizure actions, the government must establish that the article has a tie to interstate commerce. This is generally easy for the FDA to prove. It has taken the position that a product satisfies the interstate commerce requirement if any component of the product has crossed state lines. Table 2.3 lists all of the regulatory actions taken for food and cosmetics over a six-year period (1988–1993). It should be noted that the FDA inspects far more domestic food manufacturing and processing establishments than import establishments, but collects more import samples than domestic samples (see Table 2.3).

PROPOSALS FOR EXPANDED ADMINISTRATIVE ENFORCEMENT "TOOLS"

In March of 1993, FDA Commissioner David A. Kessler prepared a memorandum to the Secretary of Health and Human Services, Donna Shalala, outlining the FDA's proposals for changes in the FDA's enforcement "tools" (see Table 2.4).[42] This list suggests nothing new; the FDA had sought these changes for several decades. Included in the proposals is the ability to order recalls other than just "voluntary recalls." In addition, civil money penalties would be available to "hurt the pocketbook" of companies in violation of the Act. Also, the FDA would have subpoena authority to gather evidence as part of its administrative hearings. As several other federal regulatory agencies have such authority, the FDA believes that it should have this authority and discretion. Finally, an important aspect would be the Hazard Analysis Critical Control Point System (HACCP), especially in the seafood industry.[43] The HACCP system is further described in Chapter 8 of this text.

SUMMARY

The FDA's responsibilities, assets, and shortcomings are too numerous to list in a single chapter. An entire text could be easily written on the FDA, about its history, experiences, and future. A discussion of lead and metallic poisoning in

Table 2.4. FDA's Proposals For Expanded Administrative Enforcement "Tools"

Enforcement Tool	Rationale	Criticism
Records Inspection FDA inspectors would review and copy food producers sources, processing, and distribution records without violating business trade secrets.	FDA would use these records to control a problem product. Records would show where the problem came from and to whom the product was delivered.	Records inspection should only be by court order for serious problems, to prevent administrative abuse and misuse and to protect trade secrets.
Registration of Food Processors FDA would require registration to establish an inventory of food purveyors.	Through such a registration, FDA would get an accurate inventory of whom they were regulating.	Registration creates an enormous and ineffective burden for FDA and an unnecessary interference with business.
HACCP/Quality Assurance System FDA on January 21, 1994 proposed for notice and comment a mandatory system which would require that the seafood industry establish a *H*azard *A*nalysis *C*ritical *C*ontrol *P*oint system. FDA could extend this plan to other facets of the food industry.	HACCP calls for a science-based analysis of potential hazards, determining where the hazards can occur in processing, instituting preventive measures to prevent problems, and taking corrective actions if they do occur. FDA saves money by monitoring HACCP records.	HACCP is already in existing FDA GMP regulations and is authorized by existing law. No new legislation is needed. FDA can adopt HACCP regulations where justified.
Presumption of Interstate Commerce FDA officials want to presume jurisdiction because most commerce involving food articles affect interstate commerce.	FDA could reduce its burden of proof before the courts and would no longer spend time and money processing records to prove to the courts that it had jurisdiction over a violative product.	FDA can easily prove its jurisdiction, and the issue is rarely contested, so new legislation is unnecessary.
Civil Money Penalties FDA wants to impose fines to seek punishment for offenders short of criminal action.	Such authority would allow FDA to take steps to "hurt the pocketbook" of the company in violation, particularly for acts which were committed without endangering public health, and after notice from FDA.	Such authority could easily be abused, especially if not imposed by a court after a full hearing. Existing sanctions are stringent and sufficient.

(*continued*)

Table 2.4. FDA's Proposals For Expanded Administrative Enforcement "Tools" (*continued*)

Enforcement Tool	Rationale	Criticism
Temporary (Domestic) Detention Authority (Embargo) FDA inspectors want to detain suspected violative foods until the foods can be seized under a court's order.	This tool would help prevent the violative product from reaching consumers while seizure is being initiated.	Detention would put excessive power in administrative officials, which could easily be abused. Only a court should be allowed to do this and only for a few days.
Recall Authority FDA currently asks for "voluntary recalls." FDA wants authority to order recalls when firms refuse prompt and effective voluntary recall.	No complaints would be filed with a court, and firms could defend their actions at an informal hearing. The voluntary recall process would remain as the initial recall approach.	The same criticism that only courts should have such power applies to recalls as to detention. Current FDA recall regulations work well.
Subpoena Authority FDA would issue subpoenas to gather evidence and as part of administrative hearings in connection with a violation of the FFDCA.	Several other federal regulatory agencies have such authority. FDA officials say that they have and will continue to abide by the law to protect the industry trade secret information (e.g., processing formulas), patient names, and other confidential information obtained as part of an investigation.	Administrative subpoena power would give unfettered discretion to FDA personnel. Only courts should have this enormous power. Companies will have no formal mechanism to object to a subpoena which is unduly burdensome or otherwise improper. Before records access is permitted, it must be subject to justification through judicial intervention, control, and review.
User Fees Domestic and foreign industries including foods could pay for services provided by FDA. Examples include preparation of product certificates for export, providing electronic clearance of imports, and foreign inspections conducted by FDA.	User fees would help support FDA's costs for services benefiting regulated industry, e.g., product certificates, faster product clearance. Fees also would allocate resources more efficiently because FDA would place its resources where there is the greatest client demand.	User fees would constitute a direct federal sales tax on all food products. User fees are not justified because FDA actions benefit the general public, not a particular company.

(*continued*)

Table 2.4. FDA's Proposals For Expanded Administrative Enforcement "Tools" (*continued*)

Enforcement Tool	Rationale	Criticism
Authority to Refuse Entry of Food Imports FDA wants to refuse foods offered for import where the food safety system of the country of origin is not equivalent to the U.S. system and food handlers have not registered with FDA. FDA has already proposed to implement HACCP for all U.S. seafood (domestic and imported) without new legislation. FDA also could act against products produced where there is no HACCP system or where FDA inspection of manufacturers has been refused.	This would enhance FDA's efforts to more effectively prevent entry into the United States of imported foods lacking assurance of safety.	Such treatment would greatly add to the cost of imported products, might be contrary to the new GATT agreement for lowering nontariff barriers, and could lead to retaliatory actions against U.S. products.

Source: Food and Drug Administration. Office of Enforcement. Prepared by Joan Davenport.

foods, food processing and packaging technologies, and seafood industry changes, as well as many other issues involving the FDA's responsibilities, could have been included here; but the basic review and the analysis of the FDA's responsibilities, shortcomings, and future in these areas would be similar to what this chapter has discussed. There is no question that the agency recognizes its shortcomings and has made an exhaustive study and analysis of the direction in which it needs to proceed. Budget constraints and administrative agendas will certainly have an impact on its future. The more likely it is that foodborne illnesses and outbreaks will occur, the more likely Congress is to grant the FDA further authority and better tools to fully enforce the Federal Food, Drug, and Cosmetic Act.

NOTES

1. Federal Food, Drug, and Cosmetic Act (FFDCA), 21 U.S.C. § 301 et seq., Pub.L.No. 717, Ch. 675, 52 Stat. 1040, June 25, 1938. (Selected sections

of the FFDCA v, dealing with food (§ 341 et al.), are included in Appendix E.

2. Fair Packaging and Labeling Act, Pub.L. 89-755, Nov. 3, 1966, 80 Stat. 1296 (Title 15, § 1451 et seq.).

3. Radiation Control for Health and Safety Act of 1968, Pub.L. 90-602, Oct. 18, 1968, 82 Stat. 1173 (Title 42, §§ 263b–263n).

4. Public Health Service Act, July 1, 1944, Ch. 373, 58 Stat. 682 (Title 42, § 201 et seq.).

5. John V. Bennett et al., "Infectious and Parasitic Diseases," in *Closing the Gap: The Burden of Unnecessary Illness,* ed. Robert W. Amler and H. Bruce Dull (New York: Oxford University Press, 1987), 102–14.

6. Tonya Roberts and David Smallwood, "Data Needs to Address Economic Issues in Food Safety," *American Journal of Agricultural Economics* (Aug. 1991): 935.

7. Memorandum from David Kessler, Commissioner, FDA, to the Secretary, H.A.S., "Food Safety Initiative—Decision," Mar. 31, 1993, in subcommittees files.

8. Pub.L.No. 85-929, § 1, Sept. 6, 1958, 72 Stat. 1784.

9. Chris Lecos, "Food Preservatives: A Fresh Report," *FDA Consumer* (Apr. 1984): 23–25.

10. FFDCA, 21 U.S.C. § 401 et seq.

11. Section 201 of the FFDCA.

12. 21 U.S.C. § 451 et seq.

13. 21 U.S.C. §§ 601 et seq.

14. 21 U.S.C. §§ 453(g)(3) and 601(m)(3).

15. 21 U.S.C. §§ 453(g)(1) and 601(m)(1).

16. 21 U.S.C. §§ 453(g)(4) and 601(m)(4).

17. The following laws also authorize the FDA's enforcement actions on foods: Fair Packaging and Labeling Act (15 U.S.C. §§ 1451–1461); Federal Anti-Tampering (18 U.S.C. § 1365); Key Importation Act of 1897 (KEA—Importation) (21 U.S.C. § 4150); Federal Import Milk Act (21 U.S.C. §§ 141–149).

18. Federal Meat Inspection Act (FMIA), 21 U.S.C. §§ 601–680 (1988); Poultry Products Inspection Act (PPIA), 21 U.S.C. §§ 451–470 (1988).

19. Federal Food, Drug, and Cosmetic Act, Ch. 675, § 301, 52 Stat. 1042 (1938) (codified as amended at 21 U.S.C. §§ 331(a)–(c) (1988)).

20. 21 U.S.C. §§ 343 (food), 352 (drugs and devices), 362 (cosmetics) (1988).

21. Id. § 352(f)(2).

22. Id. § 321(n).

23. Federal Caustic Poison Act, Ch. 489, § 2, 44 Stat. 1406–07 (1927). Although largely superseded by subsequent legislation, the FDA regulations implementing the statute are still in force. 21 C.F.R. §§ 1230.10–.16 (1993).

24. Federal Insecticide, Fungicide, and Rodenticide Act (FIFRA), Ch. 125, § 2(u), 61 Stat. 165 (1947) (codified as amended at 7 U.S.C. § 136(q)(2)(D)

(1980)). FIFRA was substantially amended in 1972 by the Federal Environmental Pesticide Control Act, Pub.L.No. 92-516, 86 Stat. 973 (1972).

25. 21 U.S.C. § 343.
26. 58 F.R. 52,000, 856 (1993) (9 C.F.R. Parts 317, 381).
27. 56 F.R. 28,592, 28,615 (1991).
28. 58 F.R. 2850, 2872 (1993).
29. 52 F.R. 5081, 5083 (1987). (Human nutrients such as selenium, chromium, and nickel have been found to be carcinogenic when isolated and given to laboratory animals in large quantities.)
30. 44 F.R. 59,509, 59,513 (1979).
31. See 42 F.R. 52,814 (1977).
32. Section 704(a) of the FFDCA [21 U.S.C. 374(a)] authorizes inspections at "reasonable times and within reasonable limits and within a reasonable manner." Section 301(f) states that a refusal to permit entry into or inspection of a regulated establishment is prohibited.
33. FFDCA 21 U.S.C. § 704(4)(b).
34. FFDCA 21 U.S.C. § 704(a)(1).
35. Edolphus Towns. Memorandum, Hearing, "Reinventing the Food Safety System: Review of FDA's Food Safety Programs," May 20, 1994.
36. Id.
37. Id.
38. Donna U. Vogt, CRS Report for Congress, *FDA's Enforcement Authorities for Foods: Are They Adequate?* (Congressional Research Services, May 1994), p. 385.
39. Source: U.S. Department of Health and Human Services, Public Health Service, Food and Drug Administration, Office of Regulatory Affairs, Office of Enforcement, *The Enforcement Story.* (1994).
40. Id.
41. 21 U.S.C. § 334.
42. David A. Kessler, Memorandum to the Secretary, U.S. Department of Health and Human Services, Subject: Food Safety Initiative-Action, Mar. 12, 1993.
43. On Dec. 18, 1995, the Final Rule on a Seafood HACCP program was published in the Federal Register. 21 C.F.R. Parts 123 & 1240. 65096 F.R. Vol. 60, No. 242, Dec. 18, 1995.

Chapter *3*

USDA Laws, Rules, and Regulations

CHAPTER OBJECTIVES

The reader will:

1. *Acquire a general understanding of the USDA laws.*
2. *Acquire an understanding of the USDA regulations and procedures.*
3. *Acquire an understanding of the required processes and procedures.*

The major law affecting food industry facilities is the Federal Meat Inspection Act,[1] a comprehensive statute that requires federal meat inspection of the vast majority of the meat consumed in the United States. The primary purpose of this Act was to protect the health and welfare of consumers by assuring that the meat and meat food products distributed to them were wholesome, not adulterated, and properly marked, labeled, and packaged.[2] The primary congressional purpose of the Federal Meat Inspection Act was to eliminate unwholesome, adulterated, or misbranded meat or meat food products that could be injurious to the public welfare or destroy markets for wholesome and properly labeled products—effects that could ultimately result in losses to livestock producers, processors, and consumers.[3]

The Federal Meat Inspection Act has been in effect since 1907 and endured with little change until the passage of the Wholesome Meat Act in 1967.[4] The Wholesome Meat Act, in essence, amended the existing Federal Meat Inspection

Act by expanding the scope and the number of topics covered and the jurisdiction of the Act. Since 1967, the Federal Meat Inspection Act has been amended several more times, by legislation including the Curtis Amendment,[5] the Humane Methods of Slaughter Act of 1978,[6] and the Agriculture and Food Act of 1981.[7] The Federal Meat Inspection Act is currently administered by the Food Safety and Inspection Service of the U.S. Department of Agriculture (USDA) (see Chapter 4 for additional details).

In addition to the Federal Meat Inspection Act,[8] states may maintain state inspection programs that are at least equal to or are more stringent than the Federal Meat Inspection Program. The primary focus of the Federal Meat Inspection Act is on actual in-plant operations and transactions that are in interstate commerce or in foreign commerce.[9]

In developing the Wholesome Meat Act legislation, Congress found that only 29 states imposed mandatory slaughter inspection of animals for interstate commerce and mandatory processing inspection of products for interstate commerce.[10] In this finding, Congress noted that 15% of all commercially slaughtered animals and 25% of the commercially prepared meat products were not federally inspected and were subject to often inadequate state or local inspections, or were not inspected at all.[11]

To address this concern for uninspected products, Congress created a federal–state cooperative program in which the federal government would assist the states in the development and administration of state meat inspection programs at least as strict as the federal programs. The Secretary of Agriculture was authorized to cooperate with the states in administering state meat inspection programs that imposed mandatory inspections, reinspections, and sanitation requirements that were at least equal to those of the federal programs.[12] In order to motivate states to become involved in this program, the federal government would fund up to 50% of the state program.[13] As a disincentive for states that did not wish to cooperate with this program, the Secretary was required to notify the particular state's governor, and then to designate the state by placing a notice in the Federal Register of its lack of or ineffective enforcement of the Act.[14] This designation program appears to be effective, given the fact that a substantial number of states that were "designated" in the Federal Register have elected to discontinue their own state meat inspection programs rather than pay at least 50% of the cost. These states are now back under federal inspection.[15]

Through the Federal Meat Inspection Act, various inspections of cattle, sheep, swine, goats, horses, mules, and other equines is required.[16] Inspection focuses on the wholesomeness, adulteration, and proper labeling of the product, whereas grading of products is concerned with the comparative quality of meat and meat food products. Grading services provided by the U.S. Department of Agriculture under the Agricultural Marketing Act of 1946 are voluntary in nature and are site-based programs elected by the packer or other entity.

Under the Federal Meat Inspection Act, all animals that are subject to the

Act must be inspected before they are allowed to enter any slaughtering, packing, meat canning, rendering, or similar establishment in which they are to be slaughtered.[17] Under the inspection program, animals whose disease status is suspect are set aside and slaughtered separately from the other animals to ensure that they receive a very careful inspection and examination.[18] The Federal Meat Inspection Act defines meat food product as meaning

> any product capable of use as a human food which is made wholly or in part from any meat or other portion of the carcass of any cattle, sheep, swine, or goat, exempting products which contain meat or other portions of the carcass only in a relatively small proportion or historically have been considered by consumers as products of a meat food industry, which are exempt from definition as a meat food product by the Secretary under such conditions as he may prescribe to assure that the meat or other portion of such carcass contained in such product is not adulterated and that such products are not represented as meat food products. This term as applied to food products of equines shall have a meaning comparable to that provided in this paragraph with respect to cattle, sheep, swine, and goats. [See 21 U.S.C. § 601(j)].

The slaughter of animals covered under the Federal Meat Inspection Act must be carried out in accordance with the Humane Slaughter Act (see Chapter 5). During and after slaughter, the carcass and various parts are provided a postmortem examination by USDA inspectors to determine if the product is adulterated. The Food Safety and Inspection Service has established a system of postmortem inspection procedures for cattle and other animals.[19] After inspection, all carcasses and parts found to be adulterated are marked "Inspected and Condemned."[20] These products are normally removed from the normal course of slaughter, and the Federal Meat Inspection Act requires the condemned carcasses and parts to be destroyed for human food purposes. Given that the Federal Meat Inspection Act is concerned only with human food, the U.S. Department of Labor has, by regulation, provided for various nonhuman food dispositions of the product, depending on the nature of the adulteration.[21] In most operations, the carcass or parts that have been determined to be condemned will be transferred to the inedible rendering area for use as pet foods, fertilizers, or other products that are not for human consumption. The USDA has set out specific rules to define which products can be used for animal foods[22] and to provide for specific labeling and denaturing of the products before they can be removed.[23]

In virtually all facilities, the inspectors will conduct the inspection and condemn the necessary carcasses and parts. However, it is the slaughtering facility that is responsible for the destruction of the condemned carcasses or parts. The disposal of the condemned carcasses and parts is subject to a withdrawal of inspection services for failure to destroy the condemned carcasses or parts in accordance with the inspection procedures.[24] In the event that a facility does not properly dispose of the condemned carcasses or parts, the USDA possesses the authority to withdraw the inspection services,[25] and the operator may be subject to other penalties or sanctions.

The Federal Meat Inspection Act also has provisions for inspection, similar to postmortem inspection, for the preparation of meat food products.[26] The edible meat products can be prepared only from carcasses and parts that have passed antemortem and postmortem inspections.[27] The USDA inspectors can normally take a reasonable sample of the product for evaluation. They are not liable to make payments to the operator for the sample.[28]

As a general rule, most slaughter operations have a veterinarian in charge as well as a number of inspectors on-site on a daily basis. Whenever slaughter operations are under way, a federal inspector usually is present and conducts antemortem and postmortem inspections on all animals slaughtered. The antemortem inspection is normally done visually in the yard area prior to commencement of the slaughter process. The postmortem inspection is normally conducted on the kill floor by a visual inspection of each carcass. Parts, such as the head, are removed from the carcass itself, and numbered tags normally are utilized to correlate the body parts with the carcass. If a defect is identified requiring condemnation of the carcass, the inspector normally identifies the carcass and parts for plant personnel, and the carcass is removed from the operation chain. The carcass is then normally marked with a dye or other substance and removed to an inedible rendering or other process for nonhuman use.

In the processing and meat food products area, a federal inspector's presence usually is required much less frequently than in the slaughter area. Companies often establish in-house quality control programs for the processing and meat food products area, and normally a small number of inspectors, often one, may be given sole responsibility for the area or for more than one establishment. If assigned responsibility for more than one establishment, the inspector normally visits the establishment at least once a day but concentrates his or her efforts on facilities and establishments that may require additional inspection.[29] It should also be noted that the USDA would like to propose mandatory quality control programs in the future, but believes that the Act does not presently provide statutory authority for such mandatory programs.

In most circumstances, the USDA inspector makes the final determination of the acceptance or the rejection of a carcass or a meat food product. In most circumstances, the determination is made in accordance with objective standards as set forth by the USDA in its inspection procedures. However, in certain circumstances, an appeal may be filed to the inspector in charge, for reevaluation of the determination made by the inspector. Given that the carcass or meat food products are perishable in nature, a longstanding appeal on a particular carcass or product normally is not feasible. If there is continual conflict about the inspection procedures, the inspector in charge and often the regional inspector can provide avenues of appeal. Other avenues of appeal are set forth in the Food Safety Inspection Service Regulation, including, but not limited to, appeal to the FSIS in Washington.

In most slaughtering operations, the packer follows these procedures:

1. Stockyards area: herding and inspection, as well as antemortem inspection.
2. Chute area: singling the cattle through a drive to the knocking pen.
3. Knocking operation: with cattle, use of a knocking gun that stuns the cattle, normally utilized in a restraint to prevent the cattle from thrashing and to safeguard employees, and to prevent bruising of animal. For hog operations, electrical shock is utilized to stun the hogs.
4. Shackle area: in meat and cattle operations, use of a chain to hoist the stunned cow to a vertical overhead rail for transport through the disassembling operation. A similar shackling operation is utilized for hogs.
5. Sticker area: as required by the Act, laceration of the carotid artery of the animal to permit the blood to flow from the animal while it is suspended vertically from the rail.
6. Hoof/hock and hide removal: through a number of skinning operations, removal of the hooves of the animal and the hide. This operation can be performed manually or may be assisted by the use of a down puller, up puller, or side puller to remove the hide. For hogs they go through a dehairing machine unless they are a large boar or sow, which is skinned.
7. Head removal: process in which the removal head is tagged and inspected by the USDA inspector.
8. Viscera area: removal of the internal organs.
9. Trim area: removal of possible contamination on carcasses.
10. Shroud or wash area: washing of the carcass and placement of a shroud on it (beef). Hogs go through a dehairing machine prior to final wash.
11. Hot box or chill area: use of the cooler area to lower the carcass's body temperature.

INSPECTION SERVICES

Although most food processing facilities have already established USDA inspection procedures, new products and industries are emerging that may require voluntary or mandatory inspection. One such emerging industry involves the slaughter and processing of ostrich, emu, and other ratites. Food products derived from other such "exotic" animals (such as bison) are normally exempt from the Federal Meat Inspection Act.[30] The process of applying for inspection by the USDA is set forth in 9 C.F.R. § 304.1.

The initial steps needed for a slaughter and processing facility to apply for a grant of inspection normally include completing specific application procedures as set forth by the USDA. Accompanying the application itself, there must be detailed blueprints, drawings, and certifications. Normally, the application for inspection requires a submission of at least two sets of complete drawings, which contain specific information such as floor plans, room schedules, dimensions, and a minimum of four sets of specifications.[31] The applicant for inspection services is required to achieve and to maintain compliance with detailed facilities, equipment, and sanitation requirements as set forth in 9 C.F.R. § 307.1.

The USDA ensures compliance with the specific facility equipment and sanitation requirements through examination of the facility before the inspection service is provided, and thereafter through the on-site inspection service. During the initial compliance inspection, if the facility is found not to meet the USDA requirements, the application can be denied. If the application is approved, an inspector will be assigned to the plant to check for compliance on a daily basis. If at any time the on-site inspector (under a mandatory program) believes that the facility is not in compliance, the inspector can stop the operation or pull the inspection service.

For existing facilities, any changes in the facility or in any equipment or utensils being used therein require prior approval from the USDA. This includes changes in the structural facility such as expansion of the processing area, changes in equipment, and even changes in such utensils as knives, hooks, or personal protective equipment. The USDA is permitted to conduct any and all necessary sanitation inspections to ensure that the facility and the operation are adhering to sanitation rules and regulations as set forth in 21 U.S.C. § 608. Additionally, an inspection is conducted prior to the start of any operating shift and continuously throughout the operating day. When a USDA inspector finds that the conditions are not sanitary and operators are not adhering to the regulations so that products are becoming adulterated, the inspector may refuse to allow the products to be denominated as inspected in the past, and even may go so far as to withdraw the inspection service. Withdrawal of inspection services is set forth in 21 U.S.C. §§ 608 and 671 and under 9 C.F.R. § 305.5.

Specifically, a USDA inspector possesses the ability to refuse or to withdraw inspection services under the Federal Meat Inspection Act for failure to maintain sanitary conditions as set forth in Section 335.13.

In many facilities, a product rejected during the initial inspection may be reinspected by the inspector. This often happens if the carcass may have been contaminated with hair, fecal material, or other such contamination during the initial inspection. The Act permits reinspection of product within the operating facility as often as the inspector deems necessary.[32] In many facilities, there is a "rail off" area in a slaughter operation that permits carcasses that may be rejected at initial inspection to be trimmed or otherwise cleaned and replaced on the operating chain for reinspection.

USDA inspectors have the ability to enter the plant at all times, day or night, whether the plant is operating or is shut down.[33] USDA inspectors are not required to comply with company rules and regulations if they could hinder the inspection process. This often occurs when USDA safety and health regulations are substantially different from the safety and health policies required of plant personnel. For example, many facilities require their employees to wear hearing protection if working in an area above 85 decibels. The USDA inspector is required to comply with the USDA safety regulations which may not parallel those set forth for plant employees.

In plant operations that are transporting products from other inspections, the carcass or the meat food product is subject to reinspection upon entry into the plant.[34] Additionally, products being returned to a plant must be held for reinspection.[35] This procedure often happens in facilities that are processing substantially more animals than the capacity of the in-house slaughter facility. Satellite slaughter facilities may be utilized to transport the swinging carcasses to the processing area for further disassembly. All of the products entering, leaving, or reentering the facility are subject to reinspection. The USDA also is authorized to limit the entry of any materials into inspected facilities under any conditions set forth by the Secretary, in order to ensure consistency for statutory purposes.[36]

The cost of the inspection service depends on the type of inspection obtained from the USDA. For voluntary inspection, the operating facility normally bears all costs. For mandatory inspection, the cost of inspection is normally borne by the federal government except for overtime and holiday pay, which is billed to plant operations.[37] The plant management group is responsible for scheduling the operation with the USDA to ensure that inspectors are on site during all operating hours.[38]

If at any time the inspector on-site or the USDA perceives that the required sanitary conditions are not being achieved and/or the plant facility is not meeting compliance standards, the inspection may be pulled from the facility. In addition, civil and criminal penalties are prescribed under the Act for individuals and operations that try to circumvent the Act or specified regulations. Also, the Secretary of Agriculture has the authority to make rules and regulations that are deemed necessary to effect the execution of the provisions of the Act at any time.[39] One last note, the main slaughter provisions of the Act are inapplicable for ritual slaughter requirements, in order not to interfere with individuals' freedom of religion.[40]

IMPORTED PRODUCTS

Under 21 U.S.C. § 620; 9 C.F.R. § 327, carcasses, parts, and meat and meat food products may not be imported into the United States unless they have been slaughtered and prepared only in foreign plants that are, in all respects, at least equal to federally inspected facilities in the United States. Additionally, meat products that are imported into the United States are subject to reinspection, sanitation requirements, species verification, residual standards, and other standards applied to products produced in the United States.[41] (See below, section on "Importing and Exporting Meat and Meat Food Products.")

ADULTERATION OF MEAT PRODUCTS

Identification and elimination of adulterated meat and meat food products constitute an essential component of the Federal Meat Inspection Act. The basic purpose of the inspection service is to prevent the U.S. consumer from receiving adulterated or misbranded meat and meat food products. USDA-approved and inspected facilities and facilities that are exempt from inspection are still required to meet the adulteration requirements. The primary reason for the USDA to regulate not only the inspection process but also inedible operations, such as inedible rendering, is to prevent adulterated meat and meat food products from reentering the edible product chain somewhere in the process.

Under 21 U.S.C. § 601(m), meat or meat food products are considered adulterated if they meet one of nine stated circumstances. The circumstances cover a wide variety of possible defects in the meat or meat food product and include a catchall provision: "for any other reason unsound, unhealthful, unwholesome or otherwise unfit for human food."[42] Although the regulations are specific about certain diseases and conditions that would constitute adulteration in meat or meat food products, the judgment of the inspector on-site is heavily relied upon in making the final determination. The inspector's determination is often subjective but is substantiated in law under catchall provisions. The Federal Meat Inspection Act provides great discretion to the inspectors to make such determinations, and, in most cases, the courts generally are reluctant to overrule the on-site inspectors.[43] In most circumstances, the decision of the on-site inspector is final, unless there is an on-site appeal to the on-site veterinarian, or the product can be maintained while an appeal is ongoing.

Of particular interest in most food operations is the issue of certain additives that have been found unsafe by the Food and Drug Administration.[44] Meat and meat food products that contain the specified additives are automatically considered adulterated under the Federal Meat Inspection Act. However, a determination by the Food and Drug Administration is not binding on the USDA. Conversely, if an additive is found to be safe by the Food and Drug Administration, the USDA has the authority to further evaluate the additive with regard to meat and meat food products, and to consider the product to be adulterated under USDA regulations.[45] The Secretary of Agriculture possesses the authority to promulgate processing standards directed to the issue of taste quality.[46] The FDA can regulate the process and any methodology utilized that could affect the taste quality of the product.[47]

An area of frequent confusion and conflict in a meat processing or slaughter operation is the adulteration of meat and meat food products where the defect is only economical without any requisite health consequences to the consumer.[48] In most cases, the product is considered adulterated; however, in a criminal circumstance, this type of adulteration is not the basis for a felony conviction, absent a showing of intent to defraud the consumer.[49] Cases often arise in which meat or meat food products have been enhanced through the use of additives or other products to improve the shelf life or the visual appearance of the product.

The most common circumstance for adulteration of product outside of the slaughter or processing area occurs with products that have been prepared, packed, or held in insanitary conditions, causing them to become contaminated or rendering them injurious to the health of the public.[50] This type of contamination may occur in freezer areas or in material handling storage areas within larger operations. USDA inspectors are authorized to prevent the use of any packaging materials that may lead to adulteration of the product, and, in most organizations, the packaging products must be approved beforehand by the USDA. Packaging materials must be safe for their intended use and must conform with FDA requirements. Meat packers and others are normally required to possess a guarantee or written assurances from the box manufacturer or other packaging material manufacturer that the materials provided on a consistent basis meet FDA standards.[51] In these circumstances, there is no requirement of a showing of actual product contamination required to support a finding that a product is in fact adulterated and thus must be rejected.[52]

In most circumstances, adulteration of the product is straightforward and visible to the USDA inspector. The USDA is currently implementing rules for additional testing, such as testing for *E. coli* bacteria, which may be instituted in the inspection process to supplement the current visual inspection of meat and meat food products. In most circumstances the condemnation of a carcass or meat food product by the inspector normally is not challenged by the plant operation because of the visual evaluation, which can be conducted by all parties. When a product is determined to be adulterated, it normally is appropriately marked and immediately removed from the production or slaughter areas to the inedible area for further processing as inedible food products, or transferred outside of the operation facility for disposal.

LABELING OF MEAT AND MEAT FOOD PRODUCTS

A frequent source of confusion in meat and meat food product operations is the labeling provision of the Federal Meat Inspection Act. Under 21 U.S.C. §§ 610 and 611, Congress enacted laws specifically addressing the labeling, branding, and other identification of meat food products and, conversely, adulterated meat products. Congress identified 12 different circumstances in which a product can be considered misbranded.[53]

A product can be considered misbranded "if its labelling is false or misleading in any particular circumstances."[54] In addition to the requirements set forth under the Act, the FSIS has issued interpretations of the labeling requirements and has published them as forms. The specific interpretations of the regulations can be acquired from the Printing and Distribution Section, Paperwork Management Branch, Administrative Service Division, Food Safety and Inspection Service, United States Department of Agriculture, Washington, DC 20250.

A label is defined under 21 U.S.C. § 601(o) as a "display of written, printed, or graphic material upon the immediate container (not including package liners) of any article." In order not to confuse the word "label" with "labeling," labeling is defined under 21 U.S.C. § 601(p) to mean "all labels and other written, printed, or graphic material (1) upon any article, container, or wrapper, or (2) accompanying such article."[55] Labeling information often requires inspection legends,[56] the proper name of the product,[57] the net quantity of the contents of the container,[58] a list of ingredients in the container,[59] the name of the manufacturer, packer, or distributor,[60] and other information that the USDA may require as set forth in 21 U.S.C. § 601(n)(12). Packers and other food product manufacturers should be aware that the regulations in this area are extensive in nature, as they relate to the labeling of various products and ingredients.[61] Specific adherence to each and every requirement is essential in order to ensure compliance with these extensive labeling and branding regulations.

The Act defines three different types of product names to be used on meat and meat food products: (1) the name specified in a description or standard of identity or composition prescribed by a regulation,[62] (2) a common or usual name,[63] and (3) a descriptive name.[64]

Over the years, the USDA has promulgated more than 50 of these definitions and standards of identity or composition for meat and meat food products.[65] The basic reason for prescribing the definitions and standards is to ensure that the integrity of the meat or meat food product can be maintained on a consistent basis.[66] Additionally, the USDA is authorized to prescribe, by regulation, definitions and standards for identification or composition of any meat or meat food product that it deems necessary to protect public safety.[67] For example, by definition meat stews such as "beef stew" cannot contain less than 25% meat of the species named on the label, as computed from the weight of the fresh meat product. Other products such as "potted meat food products" or "deviled meat food products" cannot contain cereal, vegetable flour, nonfat dry milk, or similar substances. Water added to these products must be limited to that necessary to replace the moisture lost during processing.[68]

With the exception of new meat and meat food products that may not have been defined by USDA regulations, an article must bear its common or usual name if there is one.[69] Common or usual names are usually associated with products in normal usage over a period of time. The USDA normally does not create these names but merely recognizes their existence for food products. However, the USDA can prescribe regulations to assure that a product conforms to its name and to modify the name if there is any deviation from the recognized product.[70]

If a product is not addressed or defined, and there is no general standard for the product and no common or usual name associated with it, a product name must be created by the operator or the packer.[71] This type of product name is generally known as a descriptive or fanciful name, and such names created by manufacturers must be approved by the USDA to ensure that they are not false or misleading and are not inconsistent with the products. Such names are often used for new products or for heavily processed products with a limited or exclusive market.

The Federal Meat Inspection Act also provides that if an article is an imitation of another food product, it must be labeled with the product name of the other food followed immediately by the word "imitation."[72] This application of the word "imitation" has been controversial for a number of years.[73] Now the USDA appears to agree with the FDA's position regarding the "imitation" issue.[74] FDA regulations basically require that an article that simulates another be labeled as an "imitation" if it is nutritionally inferior to the basic food product that it is imitating.[75] If the imitation is not nutritionally inferior to the basic product, the FDA regulations allow the product to be labeled with a descriptive or fanciful name of its own.[76]

It is important to operations that will be adding a new product line or will be starting a new operation that the USDA is authorized to review all labeling materials *before* their use and to refuse the use of proper labeling or require modifications to such labeling.[77] Any disputes regarding labeling decisions are normally resolved through the use of an administrative adjudicative process.[78] Rules for such administrative hearings are set forth in 9 C.F.R. § 335 (Rules of Practice Governing Procedures under the Federal Meat Inspection Act) and 9 C.F.R. § 335.1 (Scope and Application of These Rules).

In applying for labeling approval, the procedures require that the proposed label be submitted first in sketch form and later in final form, with the actual printed label attached to the final application submission.[79] The labels must be approved by the administrator of the Food Safety and Inspection Service (FSIS) or the administrator's delegate. The application must contain information about how the product is prepared and the formulation and the use of the product. In some circumstances, samples of the product also are required for evaluation of the proposed label. This is done to ensure that the product conforms to the product name on the proposed label and to ensure that the label contains the required information and is not false or misleading in any respect. The determination of whether a product is false or misleading is normally a question of fact and falls to the discretion of the Secretary of Agriculture. The determination of the Secretary is not reviewable by a court if it is not arbitrary and is supported by substantial evidence.[80] The USDA additionally is not bound by the fact that the particular product name has been in use or by the economic value provided to the operator. Also, the USDA is not bound by the fact that an operation has registered the trademark or the tradename of the particular product.[81]

IMPORTING AND EXPORTING MEAT AND MEAT FOOD PRODUCTS

Carcasses, parts of carcasses, meat, and meat food products may not be imported into the United States unless they have been slaughtered and prepared in a foreign plant that possesses an inspection service equal to or greater than that of federally inspected plants in the United States.[82] Meat products that are imported into the United States are subject to inspection, sanitation requirements, species verification, and residue standards applied to products produced in the United States under USDA regulations.[83] The USDA normally makes detailed evaluations of the foreign inspection service to ensure that the particular inspection service meets or exceeds the federal inspection requirements of the United States.[84] The USDA also provides inspection standards for imported meat products that are the same as the standards for domestic products. Failure to follow the proper standard or the use of counterfeit USDA import inspection stamps warrants withdrawal by the FSIS of the import privileges for the offending foreign meat packing producer or operation.[85]

When a foreign country certifies that a particular plant possesses inspections that are at least equal to those of the United States,[86] federal inspection personnel normally review the foreign operation and report their findings to Congress on a yearly basis.[87] If continued violation of meat inspection laws or regulations is found, the USDA may withdraw the import privilege, or imported meat can be held on arrival at a U.S. port for reinspection by federal inspectors before it is allowed to enter.[88] The FSIS has adopted an import inspection procedure utilizing a central computer system to provide random sampling techniques to ensure foreign plant compliance. The computer program also contains a compliance history, information on the nature and the volume of shipments, and other data used to determine sample frequency.

With regard to exports from the United States, the USDA requires that an export certificate accompany meat and meat products being exported.[89] Operations that intend to export products from the United States must arrange for issuance of the proper official inspection documents to accompany meat and meat food products under the jurisdiction of the USDA. The regulations for the export of meat and meat food products from the United States are set forth in 9 C.F.R. § 312.8.

EXEMPTIONS FROM INSPECTION

Inspection requirements that have been set forth are applicable to most slaughter and processing facilities for commercial use in the United States.[90] The USDA regulations in the Act provide for three types of exceptions from inspection: custom exceptions, territorial exceptions, and retail store and restaurant exceptions.

The custom exception provides that inspection services are not required for the slaughter by a person of animals "of his own raising" or for the preparation of carcasses, meat products, or other products thereof and their transport and commerce, if the articles are "exclusively for the use of him and the members of his household and for his non-paying guests and employees."[91] This exemption from inspection is normally allowed for the slaughter by any person, firm, or corporation of cattle, sheep, swine, and goats delivered by their owner for slaughter and preparation by slaughter and the transport and commerce of a carcass, meat products, or other food products that are to be used by the owner or a member of the owner's household.[92] It should be noted that this is the only custom exemption provided by the Wholesome Meat Act of 1967.[93]

Territorial exceptions are provided by the USDA to territories not possessing an organized legislative body.[94] The Secretary of Agriculture must find that the inspection is impracticable within appropriate funding limits, and that the exemption would otherwise facilitate enforcement of the Act.

A third exemption from the Act is the retail store and restaurant exemption, whereby regulations limit certain retail stores and restaurants to certain clearly defined types of processing operations.[95] These retail stores may sell only to their customers, and their sales for nonhousehold customers may not exceed either 25% of the dollar value of the total sales or specified dollar limits per calendar year as set forth in 9 C.F.R. § 303.1(d)(2)(iii)(B). The dollar limitations are automatically adjusted during the first quarter of each calendar year, and the administrator of the FSIS publishes a notice in the Federal Register announcing the adjustment and new dollar limitations. As a general rule, only federally inspected products may be handled or processed at an exempt retail store. Exempt restaurants may use products prepared at exempt retail stores, and such restaurants may only sell products as meals to individual customers and in a very limited catering operation.[96]

There is some controversy about the use of central meat-cutting establishments or central kitchen facilities, as found in grocery stores or chain restaurants. At this time, restaurants utilizing central kitchen facilities are considered to be restaurants if the central kitchen prepares meat or meat food products ready to eat when they leave the facility, and the restaurant and the central kitchen facilities are under the same ownership.[97] For most central meat-cutting facilities and central kitchen facilities, the USDA inspection service is required. These retail store and restaurant exemptions only apply to the inspection requirements under the USDA regulations; the sanitation, adulteration, and mislabeling requirements of the Act are applicable to these exempt facilities.[98]

CIVIL AND CRIMINAL PENALTIES

The Federal Meat Inspection Act sets forth a number of criminal penalties and civil penalties under 21 U.S.C. § 676(a). In the vast majority of circumstances, the USDA utilizes the civil sanctions against operators and reserves the criminal sanctions for the most egregious types of situations.

The USDA possesses two types of civil actions: injunctive relief and product seizure or condemnation. Under the sanction of injunctive relief, the U.S. District Courts are vested with jurisdiction to enforce and prevent violations of the Act.[99] In most of these situations, there is no known public health problem, and the violator had not applied for federal inspection services. For example, if operators believed that they were exempt from the inspection service because of one of the known exemptions, but their repeated failure to comply with a requirement forced the USDA to take action, an injunction might be acquired from the local U.S. District Court ordering them to cease and desist, to stop the operation. The USDA also possesses the ability to go to U.S. District Court for seizure and condemnation of particular meat or meat products.[100] The USDA normally re-quests that the court authorize or order the particular meat or meat products to be destroyed or sold, with the proceeds to be paid to the U.S. Treasury. The USDA must prove that the animal or article was: (1) transported in commerce, (2) being held for sale after transportation in commerce, or (3) subject to Title I or Title II of the Act.[101]

The USDA also must prove that the meat or meat food product being subjected to condemnation or seizure: (1) is or has been prepared, sold, trans-ported, or otherwise distributed or offered or received for distribution in violation of the Act; (2) is capable of being used as human food and is adulterated or misbranded; (3) is in any other way in violation of the Act.[102]

More often utilized is the USDA's ability to detain meat or meat food products on premises for up to 20 days if there is a reason to believe that a seizure or condemnation action will be brought. This detention is not required for a seizure and condemnation action, and it is within the USDA's authority to retain such products in federally inspected establishments.[103] Additionally, the USDA possesses the ability to withdraw, deny, or suspend inspection services to establishments under five basic types of circumstances: for failure to destroy condemned meat or meat products, for insanitary conditions, for convictions, for assault, or for inhumane slaughter procedures. Additionally, the USDA possesses the ability to ban particular operators from obtaining federal government contracts such as contracts under the National Safety Lunch Act.[104]

Inspections may be suspended or withdrawn because of threats of forceful assaults, intimidation, or interference with the USDA inspector on account of the inspector's performance of his or her duties. In most circumstances, the owner or the operator of a facility is given the opportunity to justify such incidents and to take effective steps to prevent their reoccurrence and provide assurances of no reoccurrence prior to the suspension.[106] If the service is suspended, the owner or the operator of the facility is entitled to an administrative hearing as set forth under the USDA regulations.[107] The USDA inspector also can deny or temporarily suspend an inspection service if an animal is not being treated in accordance with the humane slaughter requirements.[108] The suspension of inspection services is normally terminated if the owner or the operator of the establishment takes effective steps in preventing reoccurrence and provides satisfactory assurances of no reoccurrence.[109] An administrative hearing is permitted if the owner or the operator wishes to contest the merits or the validity of the suspension.[110]

The Federal Meat Inspection Act also contains criminal provisions that provide for "any provision of this Act for which no other criminal penalty is provided by this Act." Under this provision, violations are considered to be misdemeanors carrying a maximum penalty of one-year imprisonment, a thousand-dollar fine, or both. However, violations that involve either the intent to defraud or the attempt to distribute adulterated articles are considered felonies punishable by a maximum of a three-year imprisonment, a fine of ten thousand dollars, or both. It should be noted that such felonies are considered strict liability crimes; thus there is no proof required by the government of knowledge or intent to defraud.

In situations where a corporation commits a criminal violation, its employees who are responsible for the business process can also be held individually liable. In the case of *U.S. v. Park*,[112] the U.S. Supreme Court found that "the Defendant had by reason of his position in the corporation, responsibility and authority either to prevent the first occurrence, promptly to correct the violation complained, and that he failed to do so." With sufficient evidence, authorities could prosecute the corporation official. However, the general criminal provisions normally exclude individuals who in good faith receive product in violation of the Federal Meat Inspection Act, if they identify the source and furnish the necessary documentation upon request by the USDA.[113] This provision does not exclude from prosecution individuals who, even if acting in good faith, have already transported the product in violation of the Act.

Two other provisions of the Federal Meat Inspection Act that are applicable to most operations involve assaults on USDA employees and bribery of a USDA official. Under the assault section, there is a felony violation if any person "forcibly assaults, resists, opposes, impedes, intimidates, or interferes with any person while engaged in or on account of the performance of his/her official duties."[114] The maximum penalties for violation of this section include up to three years of imprisonment, a fine of five thousand dollars, or both. If the assault involves the use of a deadly or dangerous weapon, or if the USDA official is killed, more severe penalties of a criminal nature are applicable.

Within the bribery section of the Federal Meat Inspection Act, both the giver and the receiver may be liable. The major issue in most cases concerns the intent of the individual. An individual who gives or offers to give a thing of value to a government employee must intend to influence the government employee in the discharge of his or her duties to be in violation. However, USDA inspectors and other employees may violate the Act by accepting anything of value from a person engaged in commerce, whatever the purpose or the intent of the giver. The Act provides that if the gift is sufficient to constitute a bribe, then the bribe would be considered a felony offense for both the giver and the receiver; but it should be noted that in the Department of Justice Memorandum of Understanding with the Department of Agriculture, items of very trivial value do not constitute "things of value" within the meaning of the Act.[115]

ADDENDUM

On July 6, 1996, President Clinton announced the most sweeping changes in the meat and poultry inspection system since its creation approximately 90 years earlier. The proposed new rules call for more inspections and controls by meat and poultry producers and provide for new sanitation controls and scientific testing specifically focused on *E. coli* and *Salmonella* bacteria. (See Appendix E).

The new plan, which directly impacts meat and poultry producers as well as the USDA, requires:

1. Each meat and poultry plant to establish a plan and demonstrate the effectiveness of the plan in addressing sanitation issues. The FSIS service within the USDA will verify the results of each plan.
2. Every slaughterhouse to conduct microbiological tests of raw meat and poultry for *E. coli* bacteria to ensure that efforts to reduce fecal contamination are effective.
3. All slaughterhouse facilities to ensure that the rate of *Salmonella* contami-

nation is below the current national baseline. The USDA will begin testing to enforce the new standard.

4. Every facility to adopt and carry out a written sanitation plan to ensure that the locations where meat and poultry products are handled are as clean as possible.

These changes in the meat and poultry regulations are to be phased in over a specified period of time. President Clinton stated that these regulations can be accomplished without micromanagement or excessive government red tape.

NOTES

1. 21 U.S.C. § 201 et seq.
2. 21 U.S.C. § 602 (Congressional Statement of Findings). See also *U.S. v. Mullens,* 583 F.2d 134, 139 (5th Cir. 1978); *G. A. Portello and Co. v. Butz,* 345 F. Supp. 1204 (D.D.C. 1972).
3. Id.
4. Wholesome Meat Act of 1967, Pub.L.No. 90-201, 81 Stat. 584 (1967).
5. Curtis Amendment, Pub.L.No. 91-342, 84 Stat. 438 (1970), codified as 21 U.S.C. § 623(a) (expanding the scope of custom exemptions in § 23 of the Act).
6. Humane Methods of Slaughter Act of 1978, Pub.L.No. 95-445, 92 Stat. 1069 (1978) (adding provisions to §§ 3, 10, and 20 of the Act).
7. 21 U.S.C. § 620(f), added by Pub.L.No. 97-98, § 1122, 95 Stat. 1273 (1981) (requiring all meat imports into the United States to be subject to the same meat inspection standards as applied to products produced in the United States).
8. 34 Stat. 1260–1265 (1981).
9. The term "commerce" is used in most provisions of the Act and is defined as "between any state, any territory, or the District of Columbia and any place outside thereof; or within any territory not organized with a legislative body or the District of Columbia." 21 U.S.C. § 601(h).
10. S. Rep. No. 799, 90th Cong., 1st Sess., U.S. Code Cong. & Admin. News 2188, 2190.
11. Id.
12. 21 U.S.C. § 661(a).
13. 21 U.S.C. § 661(a)3.
14. 21 U.S.C. § 661(c)1, 3.
15. Through Sept. 1990, 26 states and territories had been designated under 21 U.S.C. § 661(c).

16. See also Poultry Product Inspection Act (21 U.S.C. § 441 et seq.) (Chapter 6).
17. 21 U.S.C. § 603; 9 C.F.R. § 309 (Antemortem Inspections).
18. Id.
19. Streamline Inspection System for Cattle, 7 C.F.R. 310 as amended, 53 F.R. 48, 262 (1988).
20. Id.
21. 9 C.F.R. § 314 (Handling and Disposal of Condemned or Other Inedible Products of Official Establishments).
22. 9 C.F.R. § 301.2.
23. 9 C.F.R. § 325.
24. 21 U.S.C. §§ 604, 671; 9 C.F.R. § 305.5.
25. See *Wyszynski Provision Co. v. Secretary of Agriculture,* 538 F. Supp. 361 (E.D. Pa. 1982).
26. 21 U.S.C. § 606.
27. 21 U.S.C. § 604.
28. See *Chipsteak, Inc. v. Hardin,* 353 F. Supp. 438 (N.D. Cal. 1973), affirmed 502 F.2d 764 (9th Cir. 1974) cert. denied, 420 U.S. 926 (1975). (Taking of product sample does not violate due process so long as the sample is not excessive in nature.)
29. The USDA has published voluntary quality control programs for preparation facilities. See 44 F.R. 53526 (1979).
30. *U.S. v. Articles of Food, Buffalo Jerky,* 456 F. Supp 207 (D. Neb. 1978). (Court held that food products derived from bison meat were not within the coverage of the Federal Meat Inspection Act.).
31. See 9 C.F.R. § 304.2(a).
32. 21 U.S.C. § 604.
33. 21 U.S.C. § 606. (See also 21 U.S.C. § 609.)
34. 21 U.S.C. § 605; 9 C.F.R. § 318.2.
35. 21 U.S.C. § 605; 9 C.F.R. § 318.1.
36. 21 U.S.C. § 605; 9 C.F.R. § 318.
37. 21 U.S.C. § 695.
38. 9 C.F.R. § 307.4 (Schedule of Operations).
39. 21 U.S.C. § 621 (Provisions Related to Examination by Inspectors, Appointment and Duty of Inspectors, Promulgation of Regulations by the Secretary).
40. See Humane Methods of Slaughter Act of 1978, Pub.L.No. 95-445 §§ 6, 9 Stat. 1069. (See also Chapter 5 of this text.)
41. 21 U.S.C. § 620(f).
42. 21 U.S.C. § 601(m)(3).
43. See, for example, *G. A. Portello and Co. v. Butz,* 345 F. Supp. 1204 (D.D.C. 1972); *Bubb Davis Packing Co. v. U.S.,* 443 F. Supp. 589 (W.D. Tex., 1977), affirmed on other grounds, 584 F.2d 116 (5th Cir. 1978), cert. denied, 441 U.S. 931 (1979).

44. 21 U.S.C. § 601(m)(2).
45. 21 U.S.C. § 601(m)(8); see also *U.S. v. 2623 pounds, more or less, of veal and beef,* 336 F. Supp. 140 (N.D. Cal. 1971), supplemented 332 F. Supp. 1091 (N.D. Cal. 1971). (This case noted that adulterated product within the meaning of the Federal Meat Inspection Act includes not only one not fit to be eaten but also one in which almost anything has been added or extracted to make the product seem better than it actually is for the consumer.)
46. *Tennessee Valley Ham Company, Inc. v. Berglind,* 493 F. Supp. 1007 (W.D. Tenn. 1980).
47. Id.
48. 21 U.S.C. § 601(m)(8).
49. 21 U.S.C. § 676(a).
50. 21 U.S.C. § 601(m)(4).
51. 9 C.F.R. § 317.20.
52. *G. A. Portello and Company v. Butz,* 345 F. Supp. 1204 (D.D.C. 1972).
53. 21 U.S.C. § 601(n).
54. 21 U.S.C. § 601(n)(1).
55. See *Kordel v. U.S.,* 335 U.S. 345, 69 S.Ct. 106, 93 L.Ed. 52 (1948).
56. 21 U.S.C. § 601(n)(12).
57. 21 U.S.C. § 601(n)(5).
58. 21 U.S.C. § 601(n)(5).
59. 21 U.S.C. § 601(n)(7), (9).
60. 21 U.S.C. § 601(n)(5).
61. 9 C.F.R. § 317.
62. 21 U.S.C. § 601(n)(7).
63. 21 U.S.C. § 601(n)(9).
64. Id.
65. 21 U.S.C. § 607(c).
66. *Armour & Co. v. Ball,* 468 F.2d 76 (6th Cir. 1972), cert. denied, 411 U.S. 981 (1973).
67. 21 U.S.C. § 607(c).
68. See, e.g., 9 C.F.R. §§ 319.304, 319.761.
69. 21 U.S.C. § 601(n)(9); 9 C.F.R. §§ 317.2(c), 319.9.
70. See, e.g., 9 C.F.R. §§ 317.5, 317.8.
71. 9 C.F.R. § 317.2(c) and (e).
72. 21 U.S.C. § 601(n)(3).
73. See, e.g., *Armour & Company v. Freeman,* 304 F.2d 404 (D.C. Cir.) cert. denied, 370 U.S. 920 (1962).
74. See *In re Castleberry's Food Company,* FMIA Docket No. 36 (1980); *Grocery Manufacturers of America, Inc. v. Gerace,* 581 F. Supp. 658 (S.D.N.Y. 1984) (USDA and FDA not required to conduct rulemaking before USDA adopts definition of "imitation" as applied to food products).

75. 21 C.F.R. § 101.3.
76. See *Federation of Homemakers v. Schmidt,* 536 F.2d 740 (D.C. Cir. 1976).
77. 21 U.S.C. § 607(d) and (e).
78. 21 U.S.C. § 607(e); 9 C.F.R. § 335.1.
79. 9 C.F.R. § 317.5.
80. See *Houston v. St. Louis Packing Company,* 249 U.S. 479, 39 S.Ct. 332, 63 L.Ed. 717 (1919); *Brougham v. Blant Manufacturing Company,* 249 U.S. 495, 39 S.Ct. 363, 63 L.Ed. 725 (1919).
81. *Brougham v. Blant Manufacturing Co.,* supra.
82. 21 U.S.C. § 620; see generally 9 C.F.R. § 327.
83. 21 U.S.C. § 620(f).
84. 9 C.F.R. § 327.2.
85. *Grenadera Industrial, S.A. v. Block,* 727 F.2d 1156 (D.C. Cir. 1984).
86. 9 C.F.R. § 327.2.
87. 21 U.S.C. § 620(e).
88. 21 U.S.C. § 620.
89. 21 U.S.C. §§ 612, 613, 614, 616, 617, and 618.
90. 21 U.S.C. §§ 603, 604, 606, 610, and 661.
91. 21 U.S.C. § 623(a).
92. Wholesome Meat Act, Pub.L.No. 90-201, 81 Stat. 584 (1967).
93. Id.
94. 21 U.S.C. § 623(b).
95. 21 U.S.C. § 661(c)(2); 9 C.F.R. § 303.1(d)(2)(i), (iii), (iv).
96. 9 C.F.R. § 303.1(d)(2)(iv).
97. Pub.L.No. 98-487, § 1, 98 Stat. 2264 (1984).
98. 21 U.S.C. § 623(c); 9 C.F.R. § 303.1(e).
99. 21 U.S.C. § 674.
100. 21 U.S.C. § 673.
101. Title I of the Act governs inspection, adulteration, and misbranding as set forth in §§ 601 to 624 of Title 21 of the U.S. Code. Title II governs meat processors and related industries as set forth in §§ 641 to 645 of Title 21 of the U.S. Code.
102. See 21 U.S.C. §§ 601(m), 601(n), and 673(a).
103. 21 U.S.C. §§ 606, 604, 605, 606, and 608.
104. See *Stanko Packing Company v. Berglind,* 489 F. Supp. 947 (D.D.C. 1980).
105. 9 C.F.R. § 305.5(b).
106. 9 C.F.R. §§ 305.5(b), 335.1, 335.20, and 335.21.
107. 21 U.S.C. § 603(b).
108. See Humane Method of Slaughtering Act of 1978, Pub.L. 95-445, 92 Stat. 1069. Also see Chapter 5 of this text.
109. 9 C.F.R. § 305.5(c).
110. 9 C.F.R. §§ 305.5(c), 335.1(c), 335.30, 335.31, and 335.32.
111. 21 U.S.C. § 676(a).

112. 421 U.S. 658, 95 S.Ct. 1903, 44 L.Ed. 2d 489 (1975).
113. 21 U.S.C. § 676(a).
114. 21 U.S.C. § 675.
115. Memorandum of Understanding between the Secretary of Agriculture and the Attorney General, July 6, 1976. Also see *United States v. Mullins,* 583 F.2d 134 (5th Cir. 1978).

Chapter 4

Food Safety and Inspection

CHAPTER OBJECTIVES

The reader will:

1. *Acquire an understanding of the federal food inspection service.*
2. *Acquire an understanding of the process of obtaining a grant of inspection and of the processes that occur thereafter.*
3. *Acquire an understanding of the enforcement provisions of the Food Inspection Act.*
4. *Acquire an understanding of the difference between meat and poultry inspection.*

OVERVIEW AND HISTORY

The United States has long been considered to have one of the best food safety inspection programs in the world. However, with the recent outbreaks of illness and deaths resulting from foodborne pathogens, this system has been called into question. Today's consumer is educated and cautious about *Salmonella, E. coli,* livestock antibiotics and growth hormones, pesticides, fertilizers, and other food-related concerns connected with outbreaks of illness and death. As noted in Chapter 1, Centers for Disease Control and Prevention (CDC) estimate that over nine thousand people die and several million more become sick each year because of foodborne diseases.[1] Fortunately, the vast majority of foodborne illnesses are controllable and preventable. The question is, "What are we doing wrong and what can we do to eliminate this illness and death?"

Currently, the U.S. food safety and inspection system is a highly complex regulatory network; its 12 federal agencies spend about one billion dollars annually in administering approximately 35 laws governing food safety and quality.[2] Unfortunately, this system is replete with problems, involving fundamental differences in the various agencies' missions and approaches to food inspection, as well as overlaps in inspection processes, gaps in inspection systems, and highly inconsistent enforcement. Moreover, each presidential administration has set forth a different agenda for handling food safety, compounding the problems. Also, 21 agencies are conducting food safety research, with little or no coordination between them and much duplication of effort. The money spent on research in many cases is wasted on trivial issues, and researchers are behind the times in developing new technology to control the problems.

The division of responsibility between the two primary agencies that govern food and drug inspection in the United States is particularly problematic. The U.S. Department of Agriculture (USDA) oversees the meat and poultry inspection program, and the Food and Drug Administration (FDA) oversees nearly all other food products. The food products under the FDA's jurisdiction can be marketed without preapproval by the FDA, subject only to postmarket surveillance and enforcement; but under the USDA, meat and poultry products must be preapproved prior to marketing. The Food Safety and Inspection Service (FSIS), a branch of the USDA, conducts continuous inspection of meat packing plants, requiring its inspectors to be on duty from the preslaughter process through postslaughter and processing. The FSIS also inspects products prior to shipment to the consumer. In contrast, the FDA inspects facilities on an average of once every three to five years. Obviously, the approaches of these two agencies differ greatly and thus have contributed to public concern about food safety and have made mutually beneficial coordination between these agencies difficult to achieve.

This chapter first discusses the Food Safety and Inspection Service (FSIS) and its responsibilities and oversight, and then reviews two of the major federal laws that govern food safety in the United States, the Federal Meat Inspection Act[3] and the Poultry Products Inspection Act.[4] (The Egg Products Inspection Act[5] is very important, as eggs are used in many U.S. food products, but a discussion of its requirements is beyond the scope of this chapter.) A discussion of obtaining a grant of inspection for slaughter facilities is included, as well as a review of general labeling requirements in food inspection. A comparison of the meat and poultry regulations shows some significant differences in substantive regulatory requirements between the two major regulations governing the inspection of meat and poultry products.

FOOD SAFETY AND INSPECTION SERVICE

The Food Safety and Inspection Service (FSIS) of the U.S. Department of Agriculture (USDA) is responsible for inspecting all meat and poultry products shipped in interstate commerce and for assuring consumers that meat and poultry products are wholesome and not adulterated. The FSIS also must ensure that all meat and poultry products are properly marked, labeled, and packaged. Both the Federal Meat and Inspection Act (FMIA) and the Poultry Products Inspection Act (PPIA) provide the USDA with this mandate.[6]

In 1993, the FSIS provided oversight and inspection to approximately 6,100 slaughter and processing facilities in the United States, at a cost of nearly 660 million dollars.[7] The FSIS used nearly 7,800 inspectors, 1,100 of them trained veterinarians. In contrast, the FDA spent approximately 200 million dollars in 1993 for food protection activities while overseeing approximately 53,000 food establishments. It has been estimated that the FDA inspects less than one-fourth of these establishments each year.[8]

In addition to supervising the quality of meat and poultry products, the FSIS inspects egg products under the Egg Products Inspection Act.[9] All plants processing liquid, dry, or frozen egg products are subject to mandatory inspection under the Act, which also covers shell eggs, which may contain deleterious strains of bacteria.[10]

THE FEDERAL MEAT INSPECTION ACT

The Federal Meat Inspection Act (FMIA) is a fairly comprehensive statute that requires the federal government to inspect the vast majority of the meat slaughtered, processed, and consumed in the United States.[11] The general purpose of the Act is to protect the health and welfare of consumers by assuring a wholesome meat product. Meat and meat food products must be free from adulteration and properly marked, labeled, and packaged.[12] The Fifth Circuit Court of Appeals, in *United States v. Mullins,* stated that the purpose of the Meat Inspection Act was to ensure a high level of cleanliness and safety in meat products.[13] The term "meat food product" is defined in the Act [14] (see Chapter 3 for the full definition).

The first federal law dealing with meat inspection was passed in 1907.[15] In 1967, the Wholesome Meat Act was passed, and it greatly expanded the scope of the existing legislation.[16] Basically, the Wholesome Meat Act designated the 1907 Act, with all of its amendments, as the Federal Meat Inspection Act. However, since 1967, the FMIA has been amended several times. These amendments added provisions such as preventing inhumane slaughtering of animals and requiring that all meat imported into the United States be subjected to the same meat inspection standards as are applied to products produced in the United States.[17] The Federal Meat Inspection Act is currently administered by the FSIS.

Inspection Requirements

The Federal Meat Inspection Act requires that all animals subject to the Act be inspected before they are allowed to enter any slaughtering, packing, meat canning, rendering, or similar establishment in which they are to be slaughtered.[18] Government inspectors examine the animals prior to slaughter, and any animal suspected of being diseased is segregated from the other animals and further examined. After slaughter, all animal carcasses and parts are examined for disease, adulteration, contamination, and so on, prior to being approved for human consumption.[19] Any carcass or part found to be adulterated is marked "condemned" by the FSIS inspector and is not allowed to be used for human consumption.

It should be noted that, in practice, not every carcass that goes through a federally inspected plant is personally examined by a federal inspector. In the larger facilities that slaughter and process up to 200 or more carcasses per hour, there are many federal inspectors present, who examine each and every carcass on the production line. However, a federal inspector may be assigned to four or five of the smaller establishments, visiting each of them at least once a day but usually concentrating his or her efforts on the facility having the most problems that day. The inspector then spotchecks various carcasses and parts to assure their wholesomeness and quality.

Obtaining a Grant of Inspection

If an organization wishes to request a grant of inspection from the USDA, the process and procedures are the same for everyone. However, the process can be quite intensive, and the application is highly scrutinized by the USDA. Initially an organization submits to the regional director, in the area where the facility is to be located, an application for federal inspection. The application must be accompanied by blueprints, drawings, and certifications.[20] Figure 4.1 shows the Application for Federal Meat, Poultry, or Import Inspection. Figure 4.2 is a blueprint checklist, outlining some of the specifications required, such as plant construction, location of facility, water supply, plant drainage, and equipment plans. The full regulation for a grant of federal inspection is provided in Appendix E.[21]

Upon receiving an approval for grant of inspection and beginning slaughter and production, a facility must allow a federal FSIS inspector to review all facets of compliance with the FMIA. The inspector is authorized to conduct all necessary

Collection of this information is voluntary. It is needed before Federal inspection of meat and poultry is granted. It is used by FSIS to determine whether the applicant should be issued a grant of inspection. (9 CFR-304.1 and 9 CFR-381.16) FORM APPROVED OMB 0583-0015

U.S. DEPARTMENT OF AGRICULTURE FOOD SAFETY AND INSPECTION SERVICE **APPLICATION FOR FEDERAL MEAT, POULTRY, OR IMPORT INSPECTION**	**INSTRUCTIONS:** Submit this application to the Area Supervisor, Meat and Poultry Inspection Operations, or Import Inspection Division Director, Food Safety and Inspection Service, U.S. Department of Agriculture for applicable inspection requests. If application is for Inspection Services at facilities not previously providing such services, also submit two sets of plans and four sets of specifications of plant. Complete all sections. If a section is not applicable enter "N/A" or "None." If additional space is needed for any item, attach sheet and number the item.

SECTION I *(to be completed for Import or Domestic Inspection Activities)*

1. DATE OF APPLICATION	2. TYPE OF APPLICATION ☐ NEW ☐ CHANGE OF OWNER ☐ CHANGE OF LOCATION ☐ OTHER *(Specify)*	3. TYPE OF INSPECTION REQUIRED ☐ MEAT ☐ IMPORT ☐ POULTRY	4. EXEMPTED ACTIVITIES *(specify)*

5. FORM OF ORGANIZATION ☐ INDIVIDUAL ☐ COOPERATIVE ASSOCIATION ☐ PARTNERSHIP ☐ CORPORATION ☐ OTHER *(specify)*	6. IF CORPORATION; NAME OF STATE WHERE INCORPORATED
	7. DATE INCORPORATED *(Month and Year)*

8. NAME OF APPLICANT *(Company Name)* AND MAILING ADDRESS *(Include ZIP Code)*	FEDERAL EMPLOYER IDENTIFICATION NO. *(As assigned by Internal Revenue Service)*	9. AREA CODE AND TELEPHONE NUMBER

10. LOCATION OF PLANT AND MAILING ADDRESS IF DIFFERENT FROM ITEM 8 *(Include ZIP Code)*	11. AREA CODE AND TELEPHONE NUMBER

12. NAME AND ESTABLISHMENT NUMBER OF OTHER ESTABLISHMENTS LOCATED IN THE SAME FACILITY.	13. OTHER NAMES *(if any)* UNDER WHICH BUSINESS WILL BE CONDUCTED.

14. DAYS PER YEAR PLANT WILL OPERATE		15. HOURS PER WEEK PLANT WILL OPERATE		16. HOURS PER DAY PLANT WILL OPERATE		17. MONTH AND YEAR WHEN PLANT WILL BE READY TO OPERATE UNDER INSPECTION PROGRAM	
EXEMPT	NON-EXEMPT	EXEMPT	NON-EXEMPT	EXEMPT	NON-EXEMPT	EXEMPT	NON-EXEMPT

SECTION II *(to be completed for Domestic Inspection Activities)*

SLAUGHTER

18. ANIMALS TO BE SLAUGHTERED WHEN INSPECTION IS INAUGURATED *(SLAUGHTER ONLY)*

☐ CATTLE	☐ CALVES	☐ SHEEP	☐ GOATS	☐ SWINE	☐ EQUINES
☐ YOUNG CHICKENS	☐ MATURE CHICKENS	☐ TURKEYS	☐ GEESE	☐ DUCKS	☐ GUINEAS

19. FRESH MEAT OR READY-TO-COOK POULTRY TO BE DISPOSED OF IN COMMERCE 1/ *(COMMERCE ONLY)*

☐ BEEF	☐ VEAL	☐ LAMB OR MUTTON	☐ GOAT MEAT	☐ PORK	☐ EQINE MEAT
☐ YOUNG CHICKENS	☐ MATURE CHICKENS	☐ TURKEY	☐ GOOSE	☐ DUCK	☐ GUINEA

1/ Also include product distributed to Government purchasing agencies or others under circumstances that would indicate that the product will subsequently move in commerce.

PROCESSING

20. PREPARED OR PROCESSED WHEN INSPECTION IS INAUGURATED

TYPE OF PRODUCT
☐ MEAT
☐ POULTRY
☐ BOTH

a. ☐ BREAKING/CUTTING *(carcasses, primal cuts, whole poultry, poultry parts etc.)*
b. ☐ BONING *(manual boning meat/poultry)*
c. ☐ MECHANICAL DEBONING *(mechanical deboning meat/poultry)*
d. ☐ FABRICATING *(roast, steaks, chops, ground beef, hamburger etc.)*
e. ☐ CURING *(pork cuts, beef cuts, turkey, ham etc.)*
f. ☐ FORMULATING *(fresh/cured sausages, loaves, poultry rolls, pattie mix etc.)*
g. ☐ COOKING/SMOKING *(pork cuts, beef cuts, sausage, loaves etc.)*

h. ☐ CANNING *(shelf stable, perishable, cans, pouches, glass)*
i. ☐ DRYING *(pork cuts, beef cuts, sausage, dehydrated products)*
j. ☐ CONVENIENCE ITEMS *(entrees, dinners, pies, pizzas etc.)*
k. ☐ SLICING *(bacon, luncheon meats sausage etc.)*
l. ☐ FATS/OILS *(lard, tallow, shortening, margarine etc.)*
m. ☐ OTHER *(specify)*

FSIS FORM 5200-2 (9/86)   REPLACES MP FORM 401 (3/83), WHICH IS OBSOLETE.

(continued)

Figure 4.1. Application for federal inspection.

FSIS FORM 5200-2 (REVERSE)

SECTION III *(to be completed for Import Inspection Activities)*

21. IMPORT INSPECTION ACTIVITIES

a. CARCASSES
- ☐ BEEF
- ☐ VEAL
- ☐ SWINE
- ☐ SHEEP
- ☐ GOATS
- ☐ EQUINE

☐ VENISON
☐ OTHER *(describe)*

b. FRESH
- ☐ CUTS
- ☐ BONELESS MFG MEAT

c. FROZEN MFG. MEATS
- ☐ CUTS
- ☐ BONELESS MFG MEAT

d. COOKED BEEF
- ☐ RESTRICTED
- ☐ UNRESTRICTED

e. CONTAINERS
- ☐ PERISHABLE
- ☐ SHELF STABLE

f. PROCESSED PRODUCTS
- ☐ FRESH/FROZEN
- ☐ HEATED
- ☐ DRIED/SEMI-DRIED

g. POULTRY (Whole Carcass)
- ☐ RAW
- ☐ COOKED

h. POULTRY (Parts)
- ☐ RAW
- ☐ COOKED
- ☐ OTHER POULTRY *(describe)*

SECTION IV *(to be completed for Import and Domestic Inspection Activities)*

22. List all persons responsibly connected with the applicant. Include all owners, partners, officers, directors, holders or owners of 10 per centum or more of voting stock, and employees in a managerial or executive capacity in the business. Notify the Area Supervisor of any changes in the listing given.

NAME TITLE *(Indicate if partner, manager)*	SOCIAL SECURITY NUMBER	DATE OF BIRTH	PLACE OF BIRTH *(City and State)*	PRESENT HOME ADDRESS *(Street and Number, City, State, Zip Code)*	HOLDER OF 10 OR MORE VOTING STOCK *(If Corp.)*
					YES / NO

23. Enter the name of each person listed under Item 22 who has been convicted in any Federal or State court of any felony. Enter the name of each person listed under Item 22 who has been convicted in any Federal or State court of more than one violation of any law, other than a felony, based upon the acquiring, handling, or distributing of unwholesome, mislabeled, or deceptively packaged food or upon fraud in connection with transactions in food. Include the nature of the crime, the date of conviction and the court in which convicted. If none write "None."

24. List each conviction against the applicant *(person, firm or corporation)* in any Federal or State court of any felony. List each conviction against the applicant *(person, firm or corporation)* in any Federal or State court of more than one violation of any law, other than a felony, based upon the acquiring, handling, or distributing of unwholesome, mislabeled, or deceptively packaged food or upon fraud in connection with transactions in food. Include the nature of the crime, the date of conviction and the court in which convicted. If none write "None."

25. APPLICANT HAS BEEN PROVIDED WITH A COPY OF THE PRIVACY ACT NOTICE *(Check)*   ☐ YES   ☐ NO

AGREEMENT AND CERTIFICATION: If inspection is granted under the application, I (we) expressly agree to conform strictly to the Federal Meat Inspection Act *(21 U.S.C. 601 et seq.)*, the Regulations Governing the Meat Inspection of the United States Department of Agriculture *(9 CFR Part 301 et seq.)*, or the Poultry Products Inspection Act *(21 U.S.C. 451 et seq.)*, and the Poultry Products Inspection Regulations *(9 CFR 381 et seq.)*, or both I CERTIFY that all statements made herein are true to the best of my knowledge and belief.

WARNING: Persons willfully making false, fictitious, or fraudulent statements or entries are subject to $10,000 fine or imprisoned not more than five years or both as prescribed by Title 18 U.S. Code 1001.

This is an Equal Opportunity Program. If you believe you have been discriminated against because of race, color, religion, sex, national origin, age or handicap, write immediately to the Secretary of Agriculture or the Administrator, FSIS, Washington, D.C. 20250.

26. TYPED NAME OF PERSON SIGNING APPLICATION	SIGNATURE AND TITLE OF OWNER, PARTNER, OR AUTHORIZED OFFICER MAKING THIS APPLICATION	
	27. SIGNATURE	28. TITLE
29. OFFICIAL NUMBER ASSIGNED/RESERVED EST. _____ / P. _____ I. _____		30. IS THIS PLANT PRESENTLY UNDER STATE INSPECTION *(Completed by Regional Office or Import Inspection Div. Dir.)* ☐ Yes ☐ NO

TO BE COMPLETED BY USDA

31. DATE RECEIVED	32. DATE REVIEWED	33. SIGNATURE OF AREA SUPERVISOR OR IMPORT FIELD OFFICE SUPERVISOR	
34. THIS PLANT TO BE UNDER TALMADGE-AIKEN ACT ☐ YES ☐ NO		35. SIGNATURE OF REGIONAL DIRECTOR OR IMPORT INSPECTION DIVISION DIRECTOR	36. DATE

Figure 4.1. Application for federal inspection. *(continued)*

Blueprint Checklist

I. **Description of Plans**
   A. MP Form 423 completed?
   B. Name and address on all specifications and prints?
   C. Prints 34″ × 44″ or smaller?
   D. Two complete copies of drawings?
   E. Plot plan of entire premises included in drawings? Official premises indicated?
   F. Plot plans not less than 1/32-inch per foot?
   G. Drawings done to 1/8-inch per foot scale? (EXCEPTIONS: Complicated layouts, red meat kill floors, 1/4-inch.)
   H. Specifications sheets included and do they reflect the type of operation (slaughter, processing, poultry, etc.)?
   I. Four copies of specifications?
   J. Floor plan of each floor submitted?
   K. Floor plan illustrates facilities as they will exist in operation?
   L. Work positions indicated and the number of employees for each position shown?
   M. Drawings legible with clear, sharp lines, good contrast in all areas?
   N. Symbols used understandable? Legends provided?
   O. Space provided for approval stamp?
   P. Paster drawings drawn to same scale?
   Q. Pasters do not obscure essential data?
   R. Pasters on background similar to original drawings?

II. **Location of Establishment**
   A. Establishment separate from unofficial establishment or building?
   B. Retail meat business indicated on print?
   C. Inedible products, catch basins for grease indicated?
   D. Dustproof accessways to connect shipping, receiving areas to street?
   E. Rail spur for establishment shipping by rail?
   F. Loading area hard-surfaced and drained?

G. North point of compass shown on each print?

III. **Water Supply, Plant Drainage, Sewage Disposal System**
   A. Potable hot and cold water provided?
   B. Nonpotable water kept separate from potable supply?
   C. Approved cross-connection between potable and nonpotable supply?
   D. All floors where wet operations conducted well-drained?
   E. Drainage lines from toilets not connected with other drainage lines within plant?
   F. Drainage lines of proper diameter?
   G. Floors properly sloped to drainage inlets?
   H. Acceptable method of disposing of plant wastes shown?
   I. Catch basins for grease recovery separate from edible areas?
   J. Origin of water supply?
   K. Back-flow effectively prevented?
   L. Floor drains properly trapped?

IV. **Plant Construction**
   A. Building materials impervious, easily cleanable, resistant to wear and corrosion (must be USDA-MPI accepted)?
   B. Floors of durable water-resistant materials?
   C. Ceilings of acceptable height?
   D. Coves installed at juncture of floors and walls in all rooms?
   E. Window ledges sloped 45° or more?
   F. Doors, doorways wide enough?
   G. Doors of rust-resistant metal, other approved materials?
   H. Adequate insect, rodent control?
   I. Stairs impervious, with solid treads, closed risers, and side curbs?
   J. Exposed wood surfaces properly treated?
   K. Retaining compartments provided?
   L. Doors of toilet rooms and dressing room solid and self-closing?
   M. Room finish schedule for each area (walls, floors, ceilings)? *(continued)*

Figure 4.2. Blueprint checklist.

V. Plant Lighting, Ventilation, and Refrigeration
  A. Adequate artificial lighting provided?
  B. Light fixtures equipped with shatterproof devices?
  C. Adequate ventilation in workrooms, welfare rooms, scalding areas, equipment wash rooms, and picking rooms?
  D. Sufficient space refrigerated and maximum cooler temperature shown?
  E. Type of refrigeration indicated?
  F. Ice supply indicated on poultry drawings?

VI. Equipment
  A. Equipment listed in MPI-2 or approved in letter from Equipment Branch of MPITS?
  B. Stationary or not readily movable equipment installed away from walls and ceilings?
  C. Permanently mounted equipment far enough above floor for cleaning/inspection or sealed watertight to floor?
  D. Water-wasting equipment discharges into drainage system without overflowing on floor?
  E. Separate wash area for cleaning curing vats, hooks, handracks, utensils, containers, etc.?
  F. Chutes for transfer of product easily cleanable?
  G. All equipment shown with identifying codes or properly labeled and drawn to scale?
  H. Mechanical boning room temperature indicated on drawings?
  I. All containers and portable equipment shown?

VII. Handwashing Facilities, Drinking Fountains, Sanitizers, and Connections for Cleanup Hoses
  A. Each processing area equipped with adequate handwashing facilities?
  B. Sanitizers adjoin lavatories in slaughtering departments?
  C. Sanitary drinking fountains provided in large workrooms and dressing rooms?
  D. Device for hanging or storing hose when not in use?

  E. Location of all lavatories, sanitizers, drinking fountains, similar features shown?
  F. Each lavatory supplied with hot and cold water?
  G. Lavatories pedal-operated?
  H. Liquid soap and sanitary towels provided in lavatories?
  I. Meat-washing equipment shown?

VIII. Facilities for Processing Edible Product
  A. Meat preparation and processing department of sufficient size?
  B. Processing department arranged so that product flows without congestion or backtracking?
  C. Raw product areas separate from fully cooked product areas (describe how)?
  D. Incubation room provided?
  E. Sufficient and suitable dry storage space for supplies?
  F. Truckways adequate and designated on drawings?
  G. Truck, railroad access areas illustrated on drawings?
  H. Cooking vats, etc., provided with overflow pipes?
  I. Separate spice area?

IX. Design, Equipment, and Operation of Slaughtering Departments and Related Areas
  A. Adequate livestock pen capacity with water?
  B. Pens, ramps, unloading chutes, and runways paved, curbed, drained, and with clean-up connections?
  C. Antemortem inspection area under watertight roof with adequate light?
  D. Holding and shackling pens adequately separated from slaughtering department?
  E. Proposed maximum slaughter rate and species (class for poultry) indicated?
  F. Drawings indicate if more than one species slaughtered simultaneously?
  G. Specifications indicate if ritual slaughtering will be done?
  H. Adequate space and facilities for separating and handling viscera?
  I. Suitable facilities for holding edible organs and parts under refrigeration?

Figure 4.2. Blueprint checklist. *(continued)*

sanitation inspections and prescribe sanitation rules and regulations.[22] Where sanitary conditions are such that products are rendered adulterated, the inspector may refuse to allow products to be designated as inspected and passed, and the department, upon full review, may withdraw the grant of inspection.[23] The cost of the inspection service is paid by the United States, except for overtime and holiday pay, which is billed to the facility by the USDA.[24] In addition, the facility must notify the inspector of its scheduling of overtime and working on holidays.[25]

Exemptions from Inspection

There are three major exemptions from the inspection requirements of the Act: the custom exemption, the territorial exemption, and the retail store and restaurant exemption (see also Chapter 3 discussion).

The custom exemption[26] provides that inspection services are not required for the slaughter of animals by a person who raised the animals, or for the preparation of carcasses, parts, and products thereof and their transportation in commerce if such products are for the exclusive use of the person and members of his or her household. Basically, this means that any livestock raiser, (i.e., rancher, farmer, etc.) may slaughter and process his or her own animals raised for meat purposes. This also means that the person who raised the animal can either slaughter the animal him- or herself or have it slaughtered at a facility if the meat products are returned to the person for consumption by him- or herself, members of his or her household, and nonpaying guests and employees.

The territorial exemption[27] provides that the Secretary of Agriculture may allow slaughter and processing in any territory not organized with a legislative body if the products are to be solely distributed within the territory. However, to create such an exemption, the Secretary of Agriculture must first make a determination that inspection is impracticable within the appropriate funding limits and that the exemption will otherwise facilitate enforcement of the Act.

The third exemption has been called the retail store and restaurant[28] exemption. Prior to the Wholesome Meat Act, there was a significant "retail dealers and butchers" exemption.[29] As the Act specifically states that any slaughtering, meat canning, salting, packing, rendering, or other similar establishment falls within the scope of the Act, without the exemption the Act could be easily interpreted to require inspection at virtually every grocery store and restaurant located near state borders or in the District of Columbia, as the Act applies to interstate commerce. By opinion from the U.S. Attorney General, who found that the inspection provisions of the Act were not intended to apply to retail establishments such as grocery stores, meat markets, and restaurants, whether operating in interstate commerce or intrastate commerce, the exemption applies.[30]

Since the Attorney General's opinion, the Department of Agriculture has been applying the exemption provision and implementing the regulations for all establishments regardless of their location.[31] The Act and regulations limit exempt retail stores to certain clearly defined types of processing operations.[32] Retail stores may sell only to consumers, and their sales to nonhousehold consumers must not exceed either 25% of the dollar value of their total sales or a specified dollar limitation per calendar year.[33]

Generally, only federally inspected products may be handled or processed at an exempt retail store. Exempt restaurants may also use products prepared at exempt retail stores. Such restaurants may only sell products as meals to individual consumers at the restaurant, except for some limited catering operations.

Adulteration

The true focus of the Federal Meat Inspection Act is the protection of the consumer from adulterated meat products and misbranded or mislabeled products. Meat or a meat product is adulterated under any of the following circumstances:[34]

1. If it bears or contains any poisonous or deleterious substance that may render it injurious to health, etc.
2. If it bears or contains any added poisonous or added deleterious substance that may make it unfit for human food, etc.
3. If it consists in whole or in part of any filthy, putrid, or decomposed substance, etc.
4. If it has been prepared, packaged, or held under unsanitary conditions where it may have become contaminated.
5. If it is, in whole or in part, the product of an animal that has died otherwise than by slaughter.
6. If its container is composed, in whole or in part, of any poisonous or deleterious substance that may render the contents injurious to health.
7. If it has been intentionally subjected to radiation, etc.
8. If any valuable constituent has been in whole or in part omitted or abstracted therefrom, etc.
9. If it is a margarine containing animal fat and any of the raw material used therein consists in whole or in part of any filthy, putrid, or decomposed substance.

As can be seen, these conditions cover a whole range of possible defects. The Act even contains a general statement covering most other issues, through the wording "or any other reason unsound, unhealthful, unwholesome, or otherwise unfit for human food."[35] Within the guidelines of the regulations, which specify certain diseases and conditions that render meat and meat products adulterated, the inspectors in the plants are given considerable discretion in determining whether a product is adulterated.[36] There is overlap between the USDA and the

FDA when products contain certain additives found unsafe by the FDA. If a meat or meat product contains certain additives deemed unsafe by the FDA, it is automatically considered adulterated by the USDA and the FSIS.[37] However, the fact that an additive has been found safe by the FDA does not bind the USDA to approve it as an additive for meat and meat products; the USDA has the authority to further evaluate the additive with regard to meat products and to outlaw or limit its use.[38]

Another area of adulteration is the situation in which additives are added that may improve "taste quality" but not cause any harmful health problems. In this case, the Secretary of Agriculture has the power to promulgate processing standards.[39]

The authority and the power of the FSIS are such that it can claim adulteration of a product even though there is no actual showing of product contamination. For example, if a product has been prepared, packed, or held under unsanitary conditions, the FSIS may declare that it "may have become" contaminated with filth or "may have been" rendered injurious to health.[40]

Labeling Concerns and Misbranding

A very important aspect of the inspection process of FSIS inspectors is that of proper labeling of meat and meat products. The Federal Meat Inspection Act lists 12 different circumstances in which an article is misbranded.[41] Probably most important is the definition that states an article is misbranded "if its labeling is false or misleading in any particular."[32] Of great importance and a current issue today, especially with concerns about misleading information, is that the Act requires specific information on labels. It is important to note that the Act and the regulations distinguish between the terms "label" and "labeling." The Act defines a label as "a display of written, printed, or graphic matter upon the immediate container (not including package liners) of any article."[43] The Act defines labeling to mean "all labels and other written, printed, or graphic matter (1) upon any article or of its containers or wrappers, or (2) accompanying such article."[44] The U.S. Supreme Court, in *Kordel,* under an identical provision in the Federal Food, Drug, and Cosmetic Act, concluded that the phrase "accompanying such article" is not limited to material packaged with the product, but also includes material related to the product that is shipped under separate cover either before or after the product. The courts stressed three factors: (1) both the product and the literature were shipped in interstate commerce; (2) both the product and the literature had a common origin and common destination; (3) the literature was designed for, and used in, distribution and sale of the product.[45] Among the required information on a label are the inspection legend, the proper name of the product, the net quantity of the contents, a listing of ingredients, the name of the manufacturer, packer, or distributor, and other information that the Secretary of Agriculture may by regulations require.[46]

The Secretary has promulgated extensive regulations regarding proper labeling of meat and meat products. The full text of the labeling regulations falls under 9 C.F.R. Part 317.

The regulations for labeling, marking devices, and containers are extensive and very detailed. They outline when labels are required and give many specific requirements for proper labeling.[47] Size, color, abbreviations, and type of ink are even noted within the regulations. All labels must be preapproved by the Department of Agriculture before use.[48] Even names used on labels for certain terms having geographical significance (i.e., with reference to a locality) are controlled by the regulations.[49]

Subpart B of Part 317 presents the regulations for nutrition labeling. Part 317.300(a) states that nutrition labeling shall be provided for all meat products except single-ingredient, raw products, in accordance with requirements of Part 317.309. This nutrition information must appear on the label's principal display panel or the information panel, except as specifically provided. Matters such as number of servings, nutritional content, and added ingredients are all covered in Part 317. Finally, and of current interest, are regulations regarding the nutrient content claims for "light" or "lite," as set forth in Part 317.356. The regulations also establish requirements for nutrient content claims for sodium content, calorie content, and fat, fatty acids, and cholesterol content of meat products.[50]

ENFORCEMENT PROVISIONS OF FEDERAL MEAT INSPECTION ACT

The FMIA has given the USDA fairly strong enforcement provisions. Criminal penalties as well as civil administrative sanctions are provided under the Act. (See also Chapter 3 discussion of this topic.) As to criminal penalties, violations of the Act include misdemeanors, punishable by a maximum of a one-year imprisonment, a thousand-dollar fine, or both.[51]

However, if a violation involves either "intent to defraud" or any distribution or attempted distribution of an adulterated product, then it is a felony punishable by a maximum of three years of imprisonment, a fine of ten thousand dollars, or both.

Violations of the Act are considered strict liability crimes and require no proof of knowledge or intent. Although there are currently no reported decisions regarding the legality of the strict liabilities standard under the Act, such a standard has been upheld by the Supreme Court under the provisions of the Federal Food, Drug, and Cosmetic Act.[52] Therefore, when an organization such as a corporation commits criminal violations, its employees who share management responsibility are equally liable and can be prosecuted even though individuals may not be conscious of the organization's wrongful acts. In one case, *United States v. Park,*[53] the president of the company, a large grocery chain, was found to have, by reason of his position in the corporation, the ability either to prevent in the first instance or promptly to correct the violation complained of. His failure to do so made him responsible, and thus a prima facie case was established.

Additional criminal penalties provided for in the Act cover bribery and assaults. The bribery section applies to both givers and receivers.[54] This generally involves a situation where government inspectors or other officers are given bribes or gifts. The statute provides that a giver may be imprisoned from one to three years and fined from $5,000 to $10,000. The recipient (i.e. the government inspector) may be discharged and imprisoned from one to three years and fined $1,000 to $10,000. Although this is not required, it appears that the gift usually must bear some connection to or arise out of the performance of the government inspector's official duties.[55] Concern has been expressed among federal inspectors about the value limit of a gift. For example, the question came up of whether receiving a free cup of coffee from a plant employee would constitute a "thing of value" and subject the inspector to a violation of the Act. In a Memorandum of Understanding, the Department of Justice and the Department of Agriculture have taken the position that certain specified items of trivial value do not constitute "things of value" within the meaning of the Act.[56]

The assault section generally involves situations where individuals assault, resist, oppose, impede, intimidate, or interfere with any person while they are engaged in or on account of the performance of their official duties.[57] The maximum penalties are three years of imprisonment, a fine of five thousand dollars, or both. More severe penalties are available if a deadly or dangerous weapon is used, or if the person is killed.

As to civil sanctions, the Act provides two types of civil enforcement powers: injunctive relief and product seizure and condemnation. The Act provides and vests the U.S. District Courts with jurisdiction to enforce, prevent, or restrain violations of the Act. There have been numerous cases of the Department of Agriculture's seeking injunctive relief. Most of the cases have involved situations where there was no known public health problem, and the violator was not receiving federal inspection service.

A proceeding under seizure and condemnation of products is provided under 21 U.S.C. § 673 et al. A court has the authority to order that the product be destroyed, returned to its owner under certain limited conditions, or sold with the proceeds paid to the U.S. Treasury. However, the government must prove certain facts in order to prevail. First, it must be shown that the livestock or meat product: (1) is being transported in commerce; (2) is being held for sale after transportation in commerce; or (3) is otherwise subject to Titles 1 or 2 of the Act.[58]

A second category of proof requires the government to establish that: (1) the livestock or meat product has been prepared, sold, transported, or otherwise distributed or offered or received for distribution in violation of the Act; (2) it is capable of use as human food and is adulterated or misbranded; or (3) it is in any other way in violation of the Act.[59]

ADMINISTRATIVE SANCTIONS

One of the major enforcement tools used by the Secretary of Agriculture is the threat and power of withdrawal, denial, or suspension of the inspection service. If a facility has lost its grant of inspection, then it is basically out of business with respect to slaughter, processing, or shipping meat or meat products through interstate commerce.

The Act authorizes the Secretary of Agriculture to refuse to provide, or to withdraw, inspection service upon the determination that the applicant, or the recipient of, inspection service is unfit to engage in business because the applicant or the recipient has been convicted in any federal or state court of either a felony or more than one nonfelony resulting from the acquisition, handling, or distribution or unwholesome, mislabeled, or deceptively packaged food products.[60] Since the mid-1970s, there have been a large number of proceedings by the USDA for administrative sanctions. Crimes that have been the basis for these actions have included bribery of federal meat inspectors and meat graders, food stamp fraud, transactions involving adulterated and misbranded meat food products, and receiving highjacked meat.

Suspensions of inspections have been used in situations of forcible assault and intimidation, as well as in interference in the performance of an employee's official duties. This is provided for under the regulations.[61] After the inspection service has been suspended, the meat plant operator is entitled to an administrative adjudicated hearing under the regulations.[62] The operator of the inspected establishment is given the opportunity to justify the incident, to take effective steps to prevent a reoccurrence, or to provide acceptable assurance that there will be no reoccurrence. Finally, the Act also authorizes the denial or the suspension of inspection services to establishments that slaughter animals if the animals are not slaughtered within the Humane Slaughter Act requirements.[63] The suspension then terminates if the operator takes effective steps to prevent a reoccurrence or provides satisfactory assurance that no reoccurrence will happen. Again, an administrative adjudicatory hearing is available under the regulations.[64]

POULTRY PRODUCTS INSPECTION ACT

In 1957, Congress passed the Poultry Products Inspection Act (PPIA) (hereafter "Poultry Act").[65] The reason why the Poultry Act was not passed until this late date was that until then poultry was not commonly shipped interstate, but was locally grown, slaughtered, and consumed. There was federal inspection prior to 1957, but it was conducted on a voluntary fee basis only.

However, by 1957 poultry and poultry products were becoming an important source and percentage of the total U.S. food supply. The purpose of the Act was to protect the health and the welfare of consumers by assuring that, like meat and meat products, poultry products would be distributed in a wholesome manner, not adulterated, and properly marked, labeled, and packaged.[66]

The Act defines poultry as "any domesticated bird, whether live or dead." The term includes chickens, turkeys, ducks, geese, and guineas.[67] In general, the Act requires federal inspection of poultry and poultry products that can be used as human food and processed at any approved establishment engaged in interstate or foreign commerce.[68] Appendix E has an outline of the Regulations under the Poultry Act.[69] (See also Chapter 6, which is devoted to the PPIA.)

Concurrent Jurisdiction and Federal Preemption

Although the Poultry Act allows states to exercise concurrent jurisdiction with respect to federally inspected products or imported products in state-inspected plants, the Act also provides an express preemption clause that prohibits a state from adding to or making different the requirements set forth in the Poultry Act regarding labeling, packaging, and ingredients. However, states may enact extensive health laws "consistent with requirements under the Act," which also regulate poultry and poultry products.[70]

The Federal Food, Drug, and Cosmetic Act (FFDCA) and the Poultry Act have been construed to be complementary.[71] Therefore, in situations where drugs given to poultry during the growing stage have been denied approval by the FDA, this action has not been held to preempt the FDA's jurisdiction over the drug.

Any state that has enacted a state poultry inspection law governing intrastate operations that is at least equal to the regulations set forth in the Poultry Act shall have the full and complete cooperation of the USDA. Thus, there is federal and state cooperation in protecting the consuming public from adulterated or misbranded poultry products.

Inspection Provisions

As with the Federal Meat Inspection Act, the cornerstone of the Poultry Act is the mandatory inspection program conducted by the U.S. Department of Agriculture. The Poultry Act has many provisions similar to those of the FMIA, but there are some significant differences, as pointed out in this section.

Inspection under the Poultry Act is required unless specifically exempted. Some of the exemptions granted are for retail dealers, religious dietary laws, territorial exemptions, personal use, custom operations, and poultry producers' own poultry.[72]

Again, similarly to the FMIA, the Poultry Act requires that all poultry carcasses and poultry products found to be adulterated be condemned and destroyed for purposes of human food.[73] However, product initially found to be defective can be reprocessed if so approved by the inspector, and subsequently reexamined.[74]

Both ante- and postmortem inspections are authorized by the Poultry Act. Government inspectors examine carcasses for disease, abnormal conditions, filth, and contamination with feces. The postmortem inspection consists of government inspectors' examining the exterior, the interior of the body cavity, and the exposed viscera of the carcass of each bird processed. However, under current line speeds, it is practically impossible for an inspector to examine birds, as they move down the production line with speeds of up to 90 birds per minute. In recent years, two new methods, the Stream Line Inspection System, and the New Line Inspection System, have been approved for the inspection of broilers and Cornish game hens.[75] In addition, the regulations provide for the New Turkey Inspection (NTI) System, available only for the inspection of turkeys.[76]

Adulteration

The Poultry Act broadly defines the term "adulterated" to apply to poultry or a poultry product under one or more of the following circumstances:[77]

(1) If it bears or contains any poisonous or deleterious substance which may render it injurious to health; but in case the substance is not an added substance, such articles shall not be considered adulterated under this clause

if the quantity of such substance in or on such article does not ordinarily render it injurious to health;

(2) (A) If it bears or contains (by reason of administration of any substance to the live poultry or otherwise) any added poisons or added deleterious substance (other then one which is (i) a pesticide chemical in or on a raw agricultural commodity; (ii) a food additive; or (iii) a color additive)[78] which may, in the judgment of the Secretary, make such article unfit for human food;

(B) If it is in whole or in part, a raw agricultural commodity and such commodity bears or contains a pesticide chemical which is unsafe within the meaning of 21 U.S.C. § 346a;

(C) If it bears or contains any food additive which is unsafe within the meaning of 21 U.S.C. § 348;

(D) If it bears or contains any color additive which is unsafe within the meaning of 21 U.S.C. § 376: provided, that an article which is not otherwise deemed adulterated under clause (B), (C), or (D), shall nevertheless be deemed adulterated if use of the pesticide chemical, food additive, or color additive in or on such article is prohibited by regulations of the Secretary in official establishments;

(3) If it consists in whole or in part of any filthy, putrid, or decomposed substance or is for any other reason unsound, unhealthful, unwholesome, or otherwise unfit for human food;

(4) If it has been prepared, packaged, or held under unsanitary conditions whereby it may have become contaminated with filth or whereby it may have been rendered injurious to health;

(5) If it is, in whole or in part, the product of any poultry which has died otherwise than by slaughter;

(6) If its container is composed, in whole or in part, of any poisonous or deleterious substance which may render the contents injurious to health;

(7) If it has been intentionally subjected to radiation, unless the use of the radiation was in conformity with the regulation and exemption in effect pursuant to 21 U.S.C. § 348;

(8) If any valuable constituent has been in whole or in part omitted or abstracted therefrom; or if any substance has been substituted, wholly or in part therefor; or if damage or inferiority has been concealed in any manner; or if any substance has been added thereto or mixed or packed therewith so as to increase its bulk or weight or reduce its quality or strength, or make it appear better or of greater value than it is.[79]

Grant of Inspection

Any facility that wishes to become approved for the slaughter or processing of poultry or poultry products must seek approval through the USDA and must maintain its premises, facilities, and equipment within the requirements of the Act and its regulations.[80] Of course, any establishment that fails to meet the statutory requirements may be refused a grant of inspection or have its grant of inspection withdrawn by the Secretary.[81]

Prohibited Acts

Section 9 of the Poultry Act makes several types of activities unlawful. They include:

1. The slaughter of any poultry or processing of any poultry products capable of use as human food not in compliance with the Poultry Act.[82]
2. The sale, transportation, offer for sale or transportation, or receipt for transportation, in commerce, of any poultry products that are capable of use as human food and are adulterated or misbranded, or any poultry products that are required to be inspected under the Act and have not been inspected.[83]
3. The doing of any act, with respect to any poultry products capable of use as human food, while the products are being transported in commerce or held for sale after transportation, that is intended to cause or has the effect of causing the products to be adulterated or misbranded.[84]
4. The sale, transportation, or offer for sale or transportation, in commerce or from an official establishment, of any slaughtered poultry from which certain parts, such as blood, feathers, etc., have not been removed.[85]
5. The use or disclosure, except as authorized, of any information acquired under the authority of the Act, that is entitled to protection as a trade secret.[86]

In addition, activities such as unauthorized use of official devices, official marks, or official certificates used in the inspection of products are strictly prohibited by the Act.[87] In addition, Section 9 strictly prohibits knowingly making any false statement in a shipper's certificate representing that an article has been inspected and passed when it has not, or detaching, defacing, or destroying any official device, mark, or certificate contrary to the regulations, etc.[88] Violations of Section 9 subject the violator to fine, imprisonment, or both.[89]

Administration and Enforcement

The administration of the Poultry Act is given to the Secretary of Agriculture. The Act contains several broad enforcement mechanisms in addition to the criminal penalties noted above. As mentioned earlier, the most important enforcement tool that the Secretary of Agriculture is empowered with is the authority to refuse or withdraw inspection service. There are three major grounds upon which the Secretary may refuse or withdraw inspection service. The first is for any applicant or recipient, or "anyone responsibly connected with the applicant or recipient," to have been convicted in any federal or state court within the previous ten years of:

(1) Any felony or more than one misdemeanor under any law based upon the acquiring, handling, or distributing of adulterated, mislabeled, or deceptively packaged food or fraud in connection with transactions in food; or
(2) Any felony, involving fraud, bribery, extortion, or any other act or circumstances indicating a lack of the integrity needed for the conduct of operations affecting the public health.[90]

A person is deemed to be "responsibly connected" with a business if he or she was a partner, officer, director, holder, or owner of 10% of more of its voting stock or an employee in a managerial or executive capacity.[91]

The Secretary's refusal or withdrawal of inspection service based upon unfitness is a very severe sanction. In many cases, it can put a company out of business. This is probably one of the strongest deterrents in the industry to prevent the type of activities noted herein.

The second basis for withdrawal of inspection is for an establishment to fail to destroy condemned poultry products as required under the Act.[92]

Finally, the third grounds for an inspection to be withdrawn is for an establishment to fail to comply with the sanitation requirements set forth in the Poultry Act.[93] In addition, the Poultry Products Inspection Regulations do provide for the temporary suspension of inspection service if there is an assault or a threatened assault on any federal inspector.[94] Anytime there is a contemplated refusal or withdrawal of inspection service, the Secretary of Agriculture must provide the organization an opportunity for a formal adjudicatory hearing. The process is governed by the rules of practice for formal adjudicatory proceedings instituted by the Secretary[95] and by the rules of practice for proceedings under the Poultry Products Inspection Act.[96] Appeals from a decision by the Administrative Law Judge must be made within 30 days and filed directly with the appropriate U.S. Court of Appeals or the U.S. Court of Appeals for the District of Columbia.[97]

Criminal Penalties

Violation of any specified provisions of the Poultry Act subject the person to a maximum fine of one thousand dollars, imprisonment for up to one year, or both.[98] However, if the violation involves an intent to defraud, or any distribution or attempted distribution of an adulterated product, except an economically adulterated product, the violator may be subject to a fine of up to ten thousand dollars, imprisonment for up to three years, or both.[99] Thus, these penalties imply that the distribution or the attempted distribution of an adulterated product is a felony. If an economically adulterated product is involved, the violation is considered a misdemeanor unless intent to defraud is shown. With intent to defraud, it is considered a felony.

Like the Federal Meat Inspection Act, the Poultry Act provides that any person who forcibly assaults, resists, opposes, impedes, intimidates, or interferes with any government inspector or agent engaged in his or her official duties is subject to a maximum fine of five thousand dollars, imprisonment of three years, or both.[100] If one of these activities also involves the use of a deadly or dangerous weapon, the violator may be fined up to ten thousand dollars, imprisoned for up to ten years, or both.[101]

Comparison of Meat and Poultry Regulations

In June of 1993, the Research Triangle Institute and three independent consultants (hereafter R.T.I.) reviewed Title 9, Code of Federal Regulations, Subchapters A (mandatory meat inspection [Parts 301–335]) and C (mandatory poultry products inspection [Part 381])[102] to identify the significant differences, if any, between the substantive regulations of these two Acts. This analysis was made because of industry concerns about differences in the regulations for meat and poultry inspection that might benefit or harm one segment of the industry compared to the other. In response, the FSIS administrator requested this comprehensive comparison of the regulations.[103] The researchers found that, in general, the regulations covering meat and poultry were designed with the same intent, to protect the health and welfare of consumers by assuring that meat and meat food products (or poultry products) are wholesome, not adulterated, and properly marked, labeled, and packaged.[104] However, even though the intent of these regulations was the same, the requirements were quite different. Although many of the regulatory differences were deemed minor, mainly because of different species requirements and the dates of enactment of the regulations (the FMIA was enacted in 1907 and the PPIA in 1957), there were many significant differences.

The specific significant regulatory differences between the meat and poultry regulations, as determined by R.T.I., are listed in the following paragraphs.[105]

1. Carcass chilling procedures:

Meat C.F.R.	Poultry C.F.R.
none	§ 381.66(d)(1)–(6)

The major difference between meat chilling and poultry chilling is the difference between cold air and cold water immersion. Poultry carcasses are normally immersed in chilled water and ice, a process that allows poultry to absorb 8% or more water by weight into the carcass. Meat carcasses are chilled by exposure to cold air, and a gain in carcass weight is not allowed. Many processing plants do spray-chill carcasses, but they are not allowed to gain weight through the process.

2. Humane slaughter:

Meat C.F.R.	*Poultry C.F.R.*
§ 3.13.1, .2, .5, .15, .16, .30, .50	none

Although there are numerous regulations pertaining to the humane slaughter of livestock, there are no comparable or corresponding laws or regulations regarding humane slaughter for poultry. The basis for the difference is statutory; the FMIA has requirements for humane slaughter, but the PPIA does not have such requirements.

3. Poultry reprocessing:

Meat C.F.R.	*Poultry C.F.R.*
none	§ 381.91(b)(1), (2)

In the meat packing plant, contamination of carcasses is considered adulteration, and the only method of removing the contamination is trimming, as contaminated meat may not be washed. On the other hand, poultry carcasses can be reprocessed by washing the contaminated area with chlorinated water. The FMIA has no such provision for reprocessing.

4. Poultry slaughter modernization:

Meat C.F.R.	*Poultry C.F.R*
none	§ 381.76(b)(3)(i)(a)–(d), (g), (h)
	§ 381.76(b)(3)(iv)(c)

Several new poultry inspection procedures, based upon the modernization of poultry slaughter technologies, have been adopted in poultry; but similar procedures have not been developed for meat. These innovations include the use of: quality control (QC) concepts and the cumulative sum (CUSUM) technique in establishing and controlling product nonconformities; plant-operated QC programs and personnel for the purpose of obtaining maximum production potential; and finished product standards (FPS), as published in the regulations. Although many meat plants have voluntarily implemented these or similar concepts, they are not provided for in the meat regulations.

5. Exemptions:

Meat C.F.R.	Poultry C.F.R.
§ 303.1(d)(2)(i)(C)	§ 381.10 et seq., § 381.11(a), § 381.2

The R.T.I. researchers found that, in general, the regulatory exemptions from inspections were more liberal for poultry than for meat. For example, the meat regulations permit uninspected slaughter and processing of livestock for household use only, whereas the poultry regulations permit uninspected slaughter, processing, and sale of limited quantities of poultry and poultry products to consumers. In addition, the poultry regulations exempt from inspection certain products containing certain amounts of poultry that would otherwise receive inspection under the meat regulations.[106] Finally, the researchers found that the basis for most of the exemption differences was statutory. (See 21 U.S.C. §§ 464 and 463.)

6. Sanitation:

Meat C.F.R.	Poultry C.F.R.
§ 308.3(d)(4)	§ 381.50(b)
§ 308.8(c)	§ 381.58(a)

An interesting difference in the regulations regarding meat and poultry slaughter is the mandatory use of 180°F water to clean and disinfect slaughter equipment for meat. There are no such requirements in the poultry regulations.

7. Mechanically separated product:

Meat C.F.R.	Poultry C.F.R.
§ 318.18	none
§ 319.5(a)	§ 381.117(d)
§ 319.15(c), § 319.300,	
§ 319.301, § 319.302,	
§ 319.303, § 319.305,	
§ 319.311, § 319.312,	
§ 319.5(e)(1)–(2),	
§ 319.6, § 319.105(b)	

8. Cooking temperatures:

Meat C.F.R.	Poultry C.F.R.
§ 318.17(a)–(c)(3)	§ 381.150
§ 318.17(d)(1)–(k)	none

The researchers found regulatory requirements concerning the time/temperature cooking relationships for killing *Salmonella* in beef and trichina in pork. There were no similar temperature requirements for poultry other than for cooking poultry rolls, which require cooking poultry to 160°F, or 155°F if it is cured in smoke. The basic difference is that certain meat products are eaten rare by consumers, but poultry products generally are not eaten rare.

9. Use of skin:

Meat C.F.R.	Poultry C.F.R.
§ 319.15(b)	§ 381.160
none	§ 381.168

In meat, the only product allowed to have attached skin is pork jaws, if there is a proper label declaration. However, the poultry regulations allow poultry carcasses, cuts, and products to contain skin, the permitted amounts ranging from 8% to 20%. Poultry skin may be added to a product without a label declaration. In addition, the poultry regulations permit the use of skin in natural proportions in poultry burgers and patties. Hamburger must be made of beef, with no skin allowed.

10. Chilling and freezing requirements:

Meat C.F.R.	Poultry C.F.R.
none	§ 381.66(b)–(c)(5)
none	§ 381.66(e)–(f)(6)

Basic industry practices control this area. Poultry regulations contain numerous requirements concerning time/temperature relationships for the chilling and freezing of poultry carcasses and poultry parts. Inspectors are required to review these products and assure compliance. There are no such comparable requirements for meat carcass chilling or freezing.

11. Standards of industry:

Meat C.F.R.	Poultry C.F.R.
§ 319.300	§ 381.167
§ 319.301	§ 381.167
§ 319.302	§ 381.167
§ 319.304	§ 381.167
§ 319.305	§ 381.167
§ 319.311	§ 381.167
§ 319.312	§ 381.167
§ 319.313	§ 381.167

This comparison deals with standards of identity regarding percentage of meat or poultry in a particular product. For example, meat hash must contain 35% fresh meat, whereas poultry hash must contain 30% cooked deboned meat.

12. Moisture limitations in processed products:

Meat C.F.R.	Poultry C.F.R.
§ 319.140	none
§ 319.180	none
§ 319.104	none
§ 319.105	none
§ 318.19(a)(5)	none
§ 327.23	none

Through examination of the regulations, the R.T.I. researchers found that moisture limitations in processed products tend to favor poultry.[107] For example, fresh meat sausage must have plus or minus 3% added water; fresh poultry sausage has no limit. Cooked meat sausage must have plus or minus 40% combined fat and water, whereas cooked poultry sausage has no limit. Pork ham is protein fat-free (PFF) controlled for both domestic and foreign imports, but turkey ham has no PFF control. Finally, meat roast must have a label declaration for any added moisture, whereas poultry roasts may contain no more than 10% added moisture without a label declaration.

This chapter's short review of the history and current focus of the FSIS is a mere tip of the iceberg with respect to the scope and the number of proposals and changes for the food safety inspection service in the United States. Recently, there have been major changes in how the FSIS conducts its oversight activities, including inspections, in the food industry, with significant analysis and major recommendations made by both government and industry. The Department of Agriculture has published an extensive rule to implement a Hazard Analysis and Critical Control Point (HACCP) system for all meat and poultry plants in order to reduce the occurrence of harmful pathogens that have caused many of the severe outbreaks of foodborne illness and death in the United States. (A full discussion of this rule is presented in Chapter 8 of this text.)

There is no question that both government and industry recognize that change is needed. Unfortunately, the size of the federal government and the strength of the various interest groups with their differing agendas will slow the implementation of this much needed change. Hopefully, improvements in the national food, safety, and inspection program will be made before any further serious outbreaks of foodborne disease and illness occur.

NOTES

1. John V. Bennett et al., "Infectious and Parasitic Diseases," in *Closing the Gap: The Burden of Unnecessary Illnesses,* ed. Robert W. Amler and H. Bruce Dull. (New York: Oxford University Press, 1987), 102–14.
2. *Food Safety and Quality: Who Does What in the Federal Government* (GAO/RCED-91-19A and 19B, Dec. 21, 1990).
3. 21 U.S.C. § 601 et seq.
4. Pub.L.No. 85-172, approved Aug. 28, 1957, 71 Stat. 441, as amended by the Act of June 25, 1962, 76 Stat. 110, and the Wholesome Poultry Products Act of Aug. 18, 1968, Pub.L.No. 90-492, 82 Stat. 791–808 (1968). For the legislative history and purpose of the Poultry Products Inspection Act as originally enacted, see 1957 U.S. Code Cong. & Admin. News 1630 et seq.
5. 21 U.S.C. § 1031 et seq.; 15 U.S.C. § 1031 et seq.; 15 U.S.C. § 633, 636.
6. See notes 3 and 4 supra.
7. See Geoffrey S. Becker, "Meat and Poultry Inspection: Background and Current Issues" (CRS-93-574 ENR, June 9, 1993).
8. Comprehensive Needs Assessment: 1994–1997 (FDA, Dept. of Health and Human Services, 1990), B18.
9. See note 5 supra.
10. Egg Products Inspection Act, 21 U.S.C. §§ 1031–1056.
11. 21 U.S.C. § 601 et seq.
12. 21 U.S.C. § 602.
13. *United States v. Mullins* 583 F.2d 134, 139 (5th Cir. 1978).
14. 21 U.S.C. § 601(j). It has been held that food products derived from bison meat are not within the coverage of the Federal Meat Inspection Act. The *United States v. Articles of Food, Buffalo Jerky* 456 F. Supp. 207 (D. Neb. 1978).
15. Act of Mar. 4, 1907, Ch. 2907, 34 Stat. 1260–1265.
16. Wholesome Meat Act, Pub.L.No. 90-201, 81 Stat. 584 (1967). For the legislative history and purpose of the Wholesome Meat Act of 1967, see 1967 U.S. Code Cong. & Adm. News 2188 et seq.
17. 21 U.S.C. § 620(f) added by Pub.L.No. 97-98, § 1122, 95 Stat. 1273 (1981).
18. 21 U.S.C. § 603; 9 C.F.R. Part 309 (antemortem inspection).
19. 21 U.S.C. § 604: 9 C.F.R. Part 310 (postmortem inspection). See also "Streamlined Inspection System—Cattle," 7 C.F.R. Part 310, as amended, 53 F.R. 48,262 (1982).
20. 9 C.F.R. § 304.1 (Application for Inspection), 9 C.F.R. § 304.2. This regulation requires the applicant for inspection to submit two sets of complete drawings (containing specified information such as floor plans and a room

schedule) and four sets of specifications (containing certain specified statements). § 304.2(a).

21. Authority: 21 U.S.C. 601–695; 7 C.F.R. 2.17, 2.55. See also 9 C.F.R. Part 304 (full regulation on application for inspection; grant or refusal of inspection).
22. 21 U.S.C. § 608.
23. 21 U.S.C. §§ 608, 671; 9 C.F.R. §§ 305.5 (withdrawal of inspection), 335.13 (refusal or withdrawal of inspection service under the FMIA for failure to maintain sanitary conditions).
24. 21 U.S.C. § 695. 9 C.F.R. §§ 307.5 (overtime and holiday inspection service), 307.6 (basis of billing for overtime and holiday services).
25. 9 C.F.R. § 307.4 (schedule of operations).
26. 21 U.S.C. § 623(a).
27. 21 U.S.C. § 623(b).
28. 21 U.S.C. § 623(c).
29. Act of June 29, 1938, Ch. 810, 52 Stat. 1235.
30. 42 O.A.G. 459 (1972).
31. 21 U.S.C. § 661(c)(2); 9 C.F.R. § 303.1(d).
32. 21 U.S.C. § 661(c)(2); 9 C.F.R. § 303.1(d)(2)(i), (iii), (iv).
33. The dollar limitations are automatically adjusted during the first quarter of each calendar year when the Consumer Price Index indicates a change of at least $500, upward or downward, in the stated dollar limitation. Whenever adjustments are indicated in the Consumer Price Index, the administrator of the Food Safety Inspection Service publishes a notice in the Federal Register announcing the adjustment and new dollar limitation. 9 C.F.R. § 303.1(d)(2)(iii)(B).
34. 21 U.S.C. § 601(m).
35. 21 U.S.C. § 601(m)(3).
36. See regulations 9 C.F.R. Parts 309–311. *G.A. Portello & Co. v Butz* 345 F. Supp. 1204 (D.D.C. 1972). See also *Bubb Davis Packing Co. v. U.S.* 443 F. Supp. 589 W. Tex. (1977), affirmed on other grounds, 584 F.2d 116 (5th Cir. 1978, cert. denied, 441 U.S. 931 1979) (showing the courts are generally reluctant to overrule the discretion of FSIS inspectors).
37. 21 U.S.C. § 601(m)(2).
38. *Chips Date Co. v. Hardin* 332 F. Supp. 1084 (N.D.Cal. 1971), affirmed 467 F.2d 481 (9th Cir. 1972), cert. denied, 411 U.S. 916 (1973).
39. *Tennessee Valley Ham Co. v. Berblend* 493 F. Supp. 1007 (Tenn. 1980). Although not specifically authorized by statute, the court found that the authority was authorized under the intent and congressional policies of the Federal Meat Inspection Act.
40. *G. A. Portello & Co. v. Butz* 345 F. Supp. 1204 (D.D.C. 1972).
41. 21 U.S.C. § 601(m).
42. 21 U.S.C. § 601(m)(1).

43. 21 U.S.C. § 601(o).
44. 21 U.S.C. § 601(p).
45. *Kordel v. U.S.* 335 U.S. 345, 69 S.Ct. 106, 93 L.Ed. 52 (1948).
46. See 21 U.S.C. § 601(n)(3–12).
47. 9 C.F.R. Part 317.1.
48. 9 C.F.R. 317.3.
49. 9 C.F.R. 317.8.
50. 9 C.F.R. Part 317.354–.369.
51. See 21 U.S.C. § 676 et al.
52. *United States v. Dotterwich* 320 U.S. 277, 64 S.Ct. 134, 88 L.Ed. 48, rehearing denied, 320 U.S. 815 (1943).
53. *United States v. Park* 421 U.S. 658, 673–674, 95 S.Ct. 1903, 44 L.Ed.2d 489 (1975).
54. 21 U.S.C. § 622.
55. *United States v. Seuss,* 474 F.2d 385 (1st Cir.) cert. denied, 412 U.S. 928 (1978), *United States v. Mullins,* 583 F.2d 134 (5th Cir.) (1978).
56. Memorandum of Understanding between the Secretary of Agricultural and the Attorney General, July 6, 1976.
57. See 21 U.S.C. § 675, outlining the felony violations for interfering with a government official.
58. Title 1 of the Act, governing inspection requirements, adulteration, and misbranding, consists of §§ 601–624 of Title 21, U.S. Code. Title 2 of the Act, governing meat processors and related industries, consists of §§ 641–645 of Title 21.
59. 21 U.S.C. §§ 601–673.
60. 21 U.S.C. § 671. 9 C.F.R. § 305.1 et seq.
61. 9 C.F.R. § 305.5(b).
62. 9 C.F.R. § 335.1, 335.20, 335.21.
63. 21 U.S.C. § 603(b).
64. 9 C.F.R. §§ 305.5(c), 335.1(c), 335.30, 335.31, 335.32.
65. Pub.L.No. 85-172, approved Aug. 28, 1957, 71 Stat. 441, as amended June 25, 1967, 76 Stat. 110, and amended by the Wholesome Poultry Products Act, Aug. 18, 1968, Pub.L.No. 90-492, 82 Stat. 791–808 (1968).
66. *Specific Meat Co. v. Otagaki,* 47 H.A.W. 652, 394 P.2d 618, 621 (1964). See also *Canton Poultry, Inc. v. Conner,* 278 F. Supp. 822 (N.D. Fla. 1968).
67. 21 U.S.C. § 453(e). See also 9 C.F.R. § 381.1(b)(40).
68. 21 U.S.C. § 453 et seq.
69. Title 9 C.F.R. Subchapter C. Mandatory Poultry Products Inspection Part 381. (See Appendix E.)
70. 21 U.S.C. § 467(e). See also *Swift & Co. v. Wickham,* 364 F.2d 241, 244 (2d Cir. 1966), cert. denied, 385 U.S. 1036, 87 S.Ct. 776, 17 L.Ed.2d 683 (1967).

71. *Bell v. Goddard,* 366 F.2d 177 (7th Cir. 1966).
72. 21 U.S.C. § 464 et seq. See also 9 C.F.R. § 381.10 et seq.
73. 21 U.S.C. § 455(c).
74. 21 U.S.C. § 455(c).
75. 9 C.F.R. §§ 381.36, 381.76.
76. 9 C.F.R. § 381.76.
77. 21 U.S.C. § 453 (g).
78. The terms "pesticide chemical," "food additive," and "raw agricultural commodity" are given the same meanings under the Poultry Products Inspection Act and the Federal Food, Drug, and Cosmetic Act. 21 U.S.C. § 453(y).
79. This last issue regards economic adulteration, which is not subject to the same penalties as those imposed by the Act. See 21 U.S.C. § 461(a).
80. 21 U.S.C. § 453 et seq. See also 21 U.S.C. § 456 et seq.
81. 21 U.S.C. § 456(b).
82. 21 U.S.C. § 458(a)(1).
83. 21 U.S.C. § 458(a)(2).
84. 21 U.S.C. § 458(a)(3).
85. 21 U.S.C. § 458(a)(4).
86. 21 U.S.C. § 458(a)(5).
87. See 21 U.S.C. § 453 et seq.
88. 21 U.S.C. § 458(c) et seq.
89. 21 U.S.C. § 461.
90. 21 U.S.C. § 467(a). See also 9 C.F.R. §§ 381.21, 381.29.
91. 21 U.S.C § 467(a).
92. 21 U.S.C. §§ 455, 467.
93. Id.
94. 9 C.F.R. § 381.29(d).
95. 7 C.F.R. § 1.130.
96. 9 C.F.R. § 381.230 et seq.
97. 21 U.S.C. §§ 457, 467(c).
98. 21 U.S.C. § 461(a).
99. 21 U.S.C. § 461(a).
100. 21 U.S.C. § 461(c).
101. Id.
102. 9 C.F.R. Parts 301–335, and 381, respectively; revised as of Jan. 1, 1992, with ancillaries.
103. Donald W. Anderson and Brad J. Bowland, "Comparison of USDA Meat and Poultry Regulations Title 9 C.F.R. Subchapter A, Subchapter C." R.T.I. Project No. 5461-1, pp. 490–503, June 1993, published in *Reinventing the Federal Food Safety System,* Human Resources and Intergovernmental Regulations Subcommittee, Vol. 1, June 16, 1994, Joint Hearing.

104. 21 U.S.C. §§ 602, 451.
105. See note 104 at 495–499.
106. See note 104 at 496.
107. Id. at 499.

Chapter 5

Humane Slaughter Act

CHAPTER OBJECTIVES

The reader will:

1. *Acquire an understanding of the Humane Slaughter Act.*
2. *Acquire an understanding of the requirements of the Act.*
3. *Acquire an understanding of the methodology of the Act.*

T he method used to humanely slaughter livestock is often controversial. Addressing the particular methodology utilized, Congress set forth in 48 C.F.R. §§ 1901 through 1906 methods to be used for the humane slaughter of livestock to prevent needless suffering of the animals. Additionally, the methods utilized were designed to provide safer and better working conditions for individual employees, to improve the products provided through the slaughtering process, and to produce other benefits for producers, processors, and consumers. All livestock animals slaughtered in the United States must undergo prescribed procedures as set forth in the Act. The general requirements include humane methods of slaughter,[1] postmortem inspections,[2] and other regulations. Under the Humane Methods of Livestock Slaughter Act, only two methods for slaughtering and handling of livestock are authorized as humane: (1) for cattle, calves, horses, mules, sheep, swine, and other livestock, all animals are to be rendered insensible to pain by a single blow or gunshot or by an electrical, chemical, or other means that is rapid and effective, before being shackled, hoisted, thrown, cast, or cut; and (2) for slaughtering in accordance with the ritual requirements of the Jewish religion or other religious faith that prescribes a method whereby the animal suffers less consciousness, anemia of the brain is induced by instantaneous severance of the carotid artery with a sharp instrument in the slaughtering process.[3] In practice, the method utilized to stun the particular livestock animal may vary. With beef cattle, the animal is normally driven from the yards area to a chute area and ultimately into a restraint normally known as a "knocking pen." Then the animal is rendered insensible through the use of a knocking gun, which is normally a gunpowder-charged instrument that drives a boltlike object into the skull of the animal, making the animal insensible to pain. Normally, the animal is then released from the knocking pen area and hoisted onto a chain or a rail for further disassembly. At the next stage of the operation, the carotid artery of the animal is severed and bled, thus providing death as required by law.

For hogs, the use of electrical shock is normally prescribed. Utilizing the appropriate voltage, an instrument containing live electrical current is placed upon the spinal column of the hog to stun the animal in order that it be insensible to pain. The hog is then normally hoisted or transported to the next area, at which time the carotid artery is severed to permit the animal to be bled.

Specific regulations have been adopted under 9 C.F.R. § 313.1 and 313.2 with regard to the method of transporting the livestock from the pen area to the plant facility. Livestock pens, driveways, ramps, and other means of transporting the animal must be maintained in good repair and free of any sharp or protruding objects. Loose boards, broken planking, unnecessary openings, and other areas must be free from any danger to the animal. The USDA inspector in charge normally evaluates the pen and ramp areas to ensure that the animal cannot be injured, or that these areas will not cause any pain to the animal prior to its entry into the kill floor area.

The floors of livestock pens, ramps, and other areas must be constructed and maintained so as to provide good footing for the animals. Slip-resistant or waffled floor surfaces, cleated ramps, sand during winter months, and other means are often utilized to comply with this law. Additionally, the livestock pens and yards area must be arranged in such a way that sharp corners are removed and so that the animal being driven to the area may not reverse direction.

Animals that are labeled as suspect[4] and animals that have been identified as dying, diseased, or disabled must be provided a covered pen area that is sufficient to protect them from adverse weather conditions. Diseased and suspect animals normally are retained in a separate area while they await disposition by the inspector.

The handling and the driving of livestock from the yards area to the plant operations also are governed by law.[5] The driving of the animals from the yards to the plant operation must be done with a "minimum of excitement and discomfort to the animal."[6] The livestock may not be forced to move any faster than their normal walking speed, and electric prods and other devices to drive the animals shall be used as little as possible in order to minimize excitement or injury. If an inspector believes that the use of the prod is excessive, the inspector possesses the right to prohibit such use. Electric prods that are permitted must have the a/c house current reduced by a transformer so that it does not exceed 50 volts a/c. The use of pipes, sharp or pointed objects, or other instruments that may cause injury or unnecessary pain to the animal is not permitted.

For "downed" animals in the yard area or other animals that have been disabled, a method must be provided to transport them to the appropriate USDA suspect area. Disabled animals who are unable to be separated from normal ambulatory animals can be placed in the appropriate area. The dragging of disabled animals who are unable to move, while conscious, is normally prohibited. In practice, these animals are normally stunned before being dragged to the appropriate area. If the operation possesses the appropriate equipment for moving the animal, a disabled animal unable to move may be moved while conscious.

In many operations, the animals are transported to the yards area a day or more prior to initiation of the process. Animals kept in holding pens longer than 24 hours must have access to feed and water. Additionally, there must be sufficient room in the holding pen for an animal being held overnight to lie down. Animals in holding areas should always have access to water.[7]

Sheep, calves, and swine may be humanely slaughtered through the use of carbon dioxide gas.[8] The gas must be administered in a chamber so it can provide surgical anesthesia before any hoisting, shackling, or cutting of the animal. The animal must be exposed to the gas in a way that accomplishes the anesthesia quickly and calmly, with a minimum of excitement or discomfort to the animal.[9] As with livestock pens and driveways, driving or moving of the animals to the gas chamber must be done in a manner that minimizes excitement or discomfort. This is especially important when carbon dioxide is used so that the initial phase of the anesthesia is less violent for the animal. Any electrical shocks or prodders employed in this process should be used as little as possible and at the lowest possible voltage to minimize excitement in the animal. Upon completion of the process in the carbon dioxide chamber, the animal must be in a state of surgical anesthesia before any shackling, sticking, or bleeding is done. Asphyxia or death from any causes must not be produced in the animal before the sticking or bleeding process.[10]

Two types of chambers, based on the same principal, are commonly used for carbon dioxide anesthesia: a "U" type and a "straight line" chamber. Both of these chambers are based upon the principal that the carbon dioxide gas has a higher specific gravity than air. In both the U and the straight line type, the chamber is open at both ends, for entry and exit of the animals, and there is a depressed central section in which the gas is administered. The animals are normally driven from the holding pens along a pathway to enter the chamber. Then they are compartmentalized and moved on a conveyor, by impellers synchronized with the conveyor or by other methods of preventing crowding among the animals. Either mechanically or manually, a gate is opened to permit the animal to move into the chamber. After being administered carbon dioxide gas in the chamber, the anesthetized animal is moved from the other end of the conveyor so that the slaughter process can begin.

The number and the flow of the animals through the carbon dioxide chamber depend on the operation. Operators must be highly skilled, attentive, and aware of their responsibilities. They must be aware of what they are doing so that the animals are not overdosed with carbon dioxide, which could cause them to die prematurely.[11]

There are several special requirements for gas chambers and the auxiliary equipment used to perform carbon dioxide anesthesia. The equipment must be in good working order and functioning at maximum efficiency according to the design of the chamber. Pathways, gas chambers, and all the equipment must be designed to accommodate the particular species of animal properly, and the animal must be free of pain-producing restraining devices. Sharp objects, exposure to wheels and gears, V-belts, and unnecessary holes in the flooring and other areas must be eliminated so that the animal is not injured during this process. The carbon dioxide gas must be maintained in a uniform concentration and distributed properly to the carbon dioxide chamber to produce the required surgical anesthesia. Concentrations must be kept uniform so that the exposure to all animals will be constant. If necessary, the USDA inspector may acquire a sample of the gas for analysis; and appropriate recordkeeping is required for each day's operation.

In addition to the recordkeeping requirements, each day before the carbon dioxide chamber is utilized for anesthesia purposes, precautions are required to ensure an adequate mixture of carbon dioxide and air within the chamber. The gas-producing equipment and the control equipment must be kept in good operating condition, and all instruments must be available for inspection by a USDA inspector. Additionally, a suitable exhaust system must be provided to eliminate possible overdose due to mechanical failure, as well as danger to employees who must enter the chamber for specific purposes.

For cattle, horses, mules, and other larger animals, a captive bolt mechanism, often known as a "stun gun" or a "knocker," normally is utilized to stun the animal. The knocker is a captive bolt that is applied to the head of the animal to produce immediate unconsciousness before it is shackled, hoisted, or cut. With all other processes, the yards and the driveway area must be free of any objects or processes that might injure the animal. The animal must be delivered to the area in a calm condition to ensure accurate placement of the stunning equipment in the appropriate area of the animal's skull. Captive bolt stunning instruments may be either skull-penetrating or nonpenetrating.

In many slaughter operations for cattle, a knocking gun utilizing a captive bolt and a gunpowder charge is often used. In operations providing a substantial number of head of cattle per day, a restraint system with an air-powered knocking mechanism is often employed. The latter is often described as a concussion or mushroom type stunner.

The captive bolt stunning operation normally delivers a bolt, of varying diameter and length, into the skull and the brain of the animal. Unconsciousness is immediately produced in the animal by physical brain destruction and a combination of changes in intracranial pressure and the accelerated concussion.

Nonpenetrating or mushroom stunners immediately deliver a flattened circular head against the external surface of the animal's skull over the brain. The diameter of the striking surface of this type of stunner may vary, depending upon the conditions. Unconsciousness is produced immediately in the animal by a combination of accelerated concussions and a change in intracranial pressure within the animal. Combination stunners, utilizing both the penetrating and the nonpenetrating principles of the above devices, can also be used.

In utilizing either type of captive bolt stunner, it is important to ensure uniform unconsciousness with the animal with every blow. With air-compressed stunners, the gauges must be easily readable and conveniently located for the stunner operator and the inspector. For safety purposes, the stunners must be equipped with appropriate safety features to prevent injury from accidental discharge, and the stunning equipment must be kept in good repair.

For the animal, several different types of restrainers are utilized. In many organizations, a knocking box area is utilized to restrain the animal in a small space while the stunning operation is under way. For larger-scale operations, a restrainer, which may lift the animal off its feet and immobilize it during the stunning process, often is used. No matter which type of operation is utilized, the operator of the stun gun must be well trained and experienced. The stunning mechanism must be accurately placed on the animal to ensure immediate unconsciousness. Appropriate detonating charges or air pressure must be utilized, with regard to the specific kind, breed, size, age, and sex of the animal, to produce the desired results. Young swine, lambs, and calves usually require less stunning force than mature animals of the same kind. Bulls, rams, and boars usually require skull penetration to produce immediate unconsciousness.[12]

In addition to captive bolt stunning operations, firearms are often used in smaller operations to stun the animal. When used for stunning purposes, the firearm is required to deliver a bullet or a projectile into the animal so as to produce immediate unconsciousness with a single shot before shackling, hoisting, or cutting. The shooting should be done in an area of minimal excitement and discomfort for the animal. Immediately after the firearm is discharged, the animal must be in a complete state of unconsciousness, and it must remain in that condition throughout the shackling, sticking, and bleeding operation.

It is important for the firearm to use a minimal charge to prevent ricochet or other damage to the animal. The bullet may vary in size and diameter, but it must produce appropriate results. The firearm used should be properly aimed and discharged, with the projectile producing immediate unconsciousness in the animal.[13]

To produce appropriate unconsciousness in the animal on every discharge of a small-bore firearm, it is normally necessary to use hollow point bullets, fragmentable iron plastic composition bullets, or gun powdered iron missiles. Firearms must be kept in good condition, and the muzzle of the firearm should be in close proximity to the skull of the animal when it is fired. This closeness is necessary to protect other employees, inspectors, and others from ricochet or other injurious incidents. Individuals working in the area should be provided all of the safety equipment necessary to be protected. The operator utilizing the firearm should be experienced and well trained to produce the appropriate results. The choice of firearms and ammunition should correspond to the age, sex, and type of animal.

Another method approved by the USDA for the humane slaughter of animals is electronic stunning. As with the captive bolt and other processes, electrical current stunning must be administered so as to produce a minimum, surgical anesthesia in the animal. The animal must be appropriately anesthetized prior to any shackling, hoisting, or cutting. Drive areas and yard areas used in conveying the animals to the stunning area must be appropriately free of any sharp objects, and so on, in order to avoid injury to the animal. With electric current stunning, each animal must be given a sufficient application of electrical current to ensure surgical anesthesia. Suitable timing, voltage, and current control devices must be utilized so that the proper and necessary electrical charge is administered to produce immediate unconsciousness. Electrical current should also be used to prevent any hemorrhages or tissue changes that could interfere with the inspection process.

Electrical current stunning is often used in hog operations. Often a hand-held electrical stunner is placed upon the spinal column of the animal to immediately render it unconscious. Varying quantities of current and voltage are normally used, depending on the type, size, and other characteristics of the particular animal. Electric stunning should render the animal completely anesthetized, and the animal should be free of any pain-producing restraining devices during this process. As with the captive bolt and other mechanisms, the animal is often restrained through the use of a knocking box or restraining mechanism.

In the event that a USDA inspector observes an incident of inhumane slaughter or improper handling in connection with the slaughter, the inspector is authorized to take the necessary steps to prevent reoccurrence.[14] If the operator fails to take such action or fails to properly assure the inspector that the appropriate actions will be taken, the inspector may attach a USDA rejected tag to the process, with the tag to remain there until the process is made acceptable to the inspector. Or the inspector may attach a USDA rejected tag to the entire operation, prohibiting the operation from running while the tag is in place. Along with other aspects of a USDA-inspected operation, the USDA inspector will evaluate the method and procedures that the operator is following to ensure the humane slaughter of the particular livestock in the operation. Failure to follow the prescribed procedures also can result in the operation's being tagged, or in further measures being taken to ensure that humane slaughter of the animals results.

NOTES

1. 9 C.F.R. § 313.1 et seq.
2. 9 C.F.R. § 310.1 et seq.
3. 9 C.F.R. § 1902; also See, Pub.L.No. 85-765, § 2, Aug. 27, 1958, 72 Stat. 862; Pub.L.No. 95-445, § 5(a), Oct. 10, 1978, 92 Stat. 1069.
4. 9 C.F.R. § 301.2.
5. 9 C.F.R. § 313.2.
6. 9 C.F.R. § 313.2.
7. See 9 C.F.R. § 313.2.
8. See 9 C.F.R. § 313.5.
9. See 9 C.F.R. § 313.5.
10. Id.
11. 9 C.F.R. § 313.5(ii).
12. 9 C.F.R. § 313.15.
13. 9 C.F.R. § 313.16.
14. 9 C.F.R. § 313.50.

Chapter 6

Poultry Products Inspection Act

CHAPTER OBJECTIVES

The reader will:

1. *Acquire an understanding of the requirements of the Poultry Products Inspection Act.*
2. *Acquire an understanding of the history and basis of the Act.*
3. *Acquire an understanding of the procedural aspects of the Act.*

T he Poultry Products Inspection Act[1] was originally passed by Congress on August 28, 1957 although it did not become effective until two years later. The Act has been amended on several occasions since its inception, including the major Amendment for the Wholesome Poultry Products Act in 1968. Prior to 1957, federal poultry inspection was conducted in the United States, but it was performed on a voluntary fee-paid basis. The primary congressional purpose of the Poultry Products Inspection Act was to ensure that all poultry and poultry products were wholesome, not adulterated, properly marked, properly labeled, and properly packaged.[2] Congressional investigators concluded that "unwholesome, adulterated, or misbranded poultry products impair the effective regulation of poultry products in interstate or foreign commerce, are injurious to the public welfare, destroying markets for wholesome, not adulterated, and properly labeled and packaged products, and result in sundry losses to poultry producers and processors of poultry and poultry products, as well as injury to the consumer."[3]

In general, the Act requires federal inspection of poultry, poultry products, and other related items capable of use as human food, which must be processed and inspected at an approved official establishment. In essence, the Act granted the USDA jurisdiction over all poultry and poultry products unless they are specifically exempted from the rule. Under the Act, poultry is defined as "any domesticated bird, whether live or dead," and includes chickens, turkeys, ducks, geese, and guineas.[4] Poultry products are defined as "any poultry carcass or part thereof; or any product which is made wholly or in part from any poultry carcass or part thereof, exempting products which contain poultry ingredients only in a relatively small portion or historically have not been considered by consumers as products of the poultry food industry which are exempt by the Secretary from the definition as a poultry product under such conditions as the Secretary may prescribe to ensure that the poultry ingredients in such products are not adulterated and that such products are not represented as poultry products."[5] Processed poultry is defined as meaning "slaughtered, canned, salted, stuffed, rendered, boned, cut up, or otherwise manufacturer processed."[6]

An area that often causes confusion is the distinction between state inspection and federal inspection. Within the federal Act, an express preemption clause is included that prohibits a state from imposing on federally inspected products markings, labels, packaging, ingredients requirements, or other requirements in addition to those prescribed under the Act.[7] Additionally, states may not establish requirements beyond those of the Act concerning facilities, operations, inspection procedures, or products, or other requirements beyond those set forth in the act. States are able to enact extensive health laws "consistent with the requirements of the Act," which also may regulate poultry or poultry products.[8]

The USDA, however, may cooperate with state agencies in the development and the administration of state poultry product inspection programs.[9] The USDA may additionally cooperate with the states in enacting state poultry inspection laws governing interstate operations and transactions that are "at least equal to" those set forth in the Act.[10] In these cooperative efforts, the USDA may provide advisory assistance, technical or laboratory assistance, training, and financial assistance to the states.[11] In these circumstances, the USDA is required to appoint an advisory committee consisting of representatives of the appropriate state agency to consult with the USDA with regard to federal and state poultry programs.[12]

The USDA is also authorized to designate a specific state for federal inspection if the Secretary of Agriculture determines that the state has failed to develop or is not effectively enforcing the Act.[13] In these circumstances, the Secretary is required to notify the governor of the state and to publish this notice in the Federal Register. The Secretary is authorized to designate establishments that are producing adulterated poultry products which are "clearly endangering the public health,"[14] and to take appropriate actions.

Of additional importance to employers is the Federal Food, Drug, and Cosmetic Act, which is often regarded as complementary to the Poultry Products Inspection Act.[15] In essence, the Poultry Products Inspection Act has been determined not to be construed so as to deprive the Food and Drug Administration of jurisdiction to withhold approvals for drugs given to poultry during the growing stages.[16]

For most employers, the essence of the Poultry Products Inspection Act is the mandatory inspection program established for poultry slaughter and production of products. The primary purpose of the federal inspection program is to conduct inspections to protect the health and welfare of consumers and prevent the introduction into commerce of adulterated or misbranded products.[17]

Inspection of all poultry and poultry products is required unless specifically exempted under Section 66.1 of the Act. The Secretary of Agriculture has some discretion with respect to the inspection process, but the Act requires the inspection process to assure that poultry products are not adulterated or misbranded. The inspection process normally consists of antemortem, postmortem, and process inspections of poultry and poultry products at an official establishment. The terms "adulterated" and "misbranded" are specifically defined in the Act and possess specific meaning. The cost of the inspection, with the exception of overtime and holiday pay, is normally borne by the USDA. (See also Chapter 4 discussion of this inspection process.)

In the inspection process, the USDA inspectors are normally stationed at the operation. All poultry carcass and poultry products "found to be adulterated" by an inspector must be condemned and otherwise destroyed, to be kept out of food.[18] The Act does provide for an appeal of the inspector's determination and authorizes the reprocessing of any product that the inspector can subsequently determine is not adulterated following the processing.[19] The appeals procedure prior to an actual condemnation is set forth in Section 455 (c) of the Act.

One misconception is that the USDA inspects poultry and poultry products that are *not* intended for human consumption. The Act prohibits inspection at any establishment for the slaughtering of poultry or processing products if the products are not intended for use as human food.[20] Any poultry or poultry products not meant for use as human food must be denatured or otherwise identified. The methods for denaturing and identifying a product not intended for human food are specifically outlined in the USDA procedures. The Act itself prohibits the purchase, sale, transport, offer for sale or transport, receipt for transport, or importation of any products that are not intended for human food and have not been denatured or otherwise identified as required by the Secretary's regulations.

The first step in most inspection procedures is the antemortem inspection, an inspection of the poultry prior to entry into the particular establishment (normally a kill floor) used for the slaughter of the birds. At this stage, the animals are examined to detect any diseases or any abnormal conditions. An antemortem inspection normally is made on the day of the intended slaughter of the birds at the particular operation or establishment.

The USDA inspectors normally conduct a postmortem inspection of each poultry carcass processed whenever there is a quarantine, segregation, or processing inspection as deemed necessary by the Secretary. In a postmortem inspection, inspectors normally examine the interior and the exterior of the body cavity and exposed viscera on the body of the carcass of each bird processed. In most facilities, the inspection is performed in a standardized manner with the birds moving on an assembly line in front of the inspectors. Postmortem inspections normally are of four types: the traditional method of examination, two methods of streamlined inspection, and the new line inspection system. The streamlined inspection systems and new line inspection system have been approved for inspection on broilers and Cornish game hens.[21]

For turkeys, the New Turkey Inspection (NTI) system has been approved, whereby two inspectors perform the whole bird inspection and one inspector monitors the application of the approved partial quality control program.[22]

One of the major issues under the Poultry Products Inspection Act is whether a product is adulterated. Under the Act, the term "adulterated" applies to any poultry product in one or more of any of the following circumstances:[23]

(1) if it bears or contains any poisonous or any deleterious substance which may render it injurious to health; but in case the substance is not an added substance, such article shall not be considered adulterated under this clause if the quantity of such substance in or on such article does not ordinarily render it injurious to health;

(2)(A) if it bears or contains (by reason of administration of any substance to the live poultry or otherwise) any added poisonous or any added deleterious substance (other than one which is (i) a pesticide chemical in or on a raw agricultural commodity; (ii) a food additive; or (iii) a color additive) which may, in the judgement of the Secretary, make such article unfit for human food [the terms pesticide chemical, food additive, and raw agricultural commodity are provided the same meaning as in the Federal Food, Drug, and Cosmetic Act (21 U.S.Code Section 301 et seq.)];

(B) if it is, in whole or in part, a raw agricultural commodity and such commodity bears or contains a pesticide chemical which is unsafe within the meaning of 21 U.S.C. Section 346a;

(C) if it bears or contains any food additive which is unsafe within the meaning of 21 U.S.C. Section 348;

(D) if it bears or contains any color additive which is unsafe within the meaning of 21 U.S.C. Section 376: *Provided,* That an article which is not otherwise deemed adulterated under clause (B), (C), or (D) shall nevertheless be deemed adulterated if use of the pesticide chemical, food additive, or color additive in or on such article is prohibited by regulations of the Secretary in official establishments;

(3) if it consists in whole or in part of any filthy, putrid, or decomposed

substance or is for any other reason unsound, unhealthful, unwholesome, or otherwise unfit for human food;

(4) if it has been prepared, packed, or held under unsanitary conditions whereby it may have become contaminated with filth, or whereby it may have been rendered injurious to health;

(5) if it is, in whole or in part, the product of any poultry which has died otherwise than by slaughter;

(6) if its container is composed, in whole or in part, of any poisonous or deleterious substance which may render the contents injurious to health;

(7) if it has been intentionally subjected to radiation, unless the use of the radiation was in conformity with a regulation or exemption in effect pursuant to 21 U.S.C. Section 348;

(8) if any valuable constituent has been in whole or in part omitted or abstracted therefrom; or if any substance has been added thereto or mixed or packed therewith so as to increase its bulk or weight, or reduce its quality or strength, or make it appear better or greater value than it is.[24]

The Secretary of Agriculture is authorized to prescribe regulations as to the buying, selling, storing, freezing, transporting, or importing of poultry products. Violation of these prescribed regulations is prohibited, and the Secretary is provided broad rulemaking authority to carry out these provisions. The propagation of these rules is virtually identical to that followed in the other Acts discussed in this book.

The issue of improper labeling or misbranding of a product is an important component of the Act, as the USDA determines whether a product is misbranded or mislabeled. A product is considered misbranded in any of the following circumstances:

(1) if its labeling is false or misleading in any particular;

(2) if it is offered for sale under the name of another food; or

(3) if it is the imitation of another food, unless its label bears, in type of uniform size and prominence, the word "imitation" and immediately thereafter the name of the food imitated; or

(4) if its container is so made, formed, or filled as to be misleading;

(5) unless it bears a label showing (A) the name and place of the business of the manufacturer, packer, or distributor; and (B) an accurate statement of the quantity of the product in terms of weight, measure, or numerical count: *Provided,* That under clause (B) of this subparagraph (5), reasonable variations may be permitted, and exemptions as to small packages or articles not in packages or other containers may be established by regulations prescribed by the Secretary;

(6) if any word, statement, or other information required by or under authority of this Act to appear on the label or other labeling is not prominently

placed thereon with such conspicuousness (as compared with other words, statements, designs, or devices in the labeling) and in such terms as to render it likely to be read and understood by the ordinary individual under customary conditions of purchase and use;

(7) if it purports to be or is represented as a food for which a definition and standard of identity or composition has been prescribed by regulations of the Secretary under section 8 of this Act unless (A) it conforms to such definition and standard, and (B) its label bears the name of the food specified in the definition and standard and, insofar as may be required by such regulations, the common names of optional ingredients (other than spices, flavoring, and coloring) present in such food;

(8) if it purports to be or is represented as a food for which a standard or standards of fill of container have been prescribed by regulations of the Secretary under section 8 of this Act, and it falls below the standard of fill of container applicable thereto, unless its label bears, in such manner and form as such regulations specify, a statement that it falls below such standard;

(9) if it is not subject to the provisions of subparagraph (7), unless its label bears (A) the common or usual name of the food, if any there be, and (B) in case it is fabricated from two or more ingredients, the common or usual name of each such ingredient; except that spices, flavorings, and colorings may, when authorized by the Secretary, be designated as spices, flavorings, and colorings without naming each: *Provided,* That to the extent that compliance with the requirements of clause (B) of this subparagraph (9) is impracticable or results in deception or unfair competition, exemptions shall be established by regulations promulgated by the Secretary;

(10) if it purports to be or is represented for special dietary uses unless its label bears such information concerning its vitamin, mineral, and other dietary properties as the Secretary, after consultation with the Secretary of Health and Human Services, determines to be, and by regulations prescribes as, necessary in order to fully inform purchasers as to its value for such uses;

(11) if it bears or contains any artificial flavoring, artificial coloring, or chemical preservative, unless it bears labeling stating that fact: *Provided,* That to the extent that compliance with the requirements of this subparagraph (11) is impracticable, exemptions shall to established by regulations promulgated by the Secretary; or

(12) if it fails to bear on its containers, and in the case of nonconsumer packaged carcasses (if the Secretary so requires) directly thereon, as the Secretary may by regulations prescribe, the official inspection legend and official establishment number of the establishment where the article was processed, and unrestricted by any of the foregoing, such other information as the Secretary may require in such regulations to assure that it will not have false or misleading labeling and that the public will be informed of

the manner of handling required to maintain the article in a wholesome condition.[25]

Additionally, the Act imposes certain recordkeeping requirements, including:

1. Recordkeeping as specified by the Secretary.
2. Access by an authorized representative of the Secretary, at all reasonable times and with notice, to the place of business.
3. An opportunity, at all reasonable times and with notice, to examine the facilities, inventory, and records and to copy the records.
4. An opportunity to take reasonable samples of the inventory upon payment of the fair market value of the inventory.

These requirements apply to any person who, in or for commerce, does any of the following:

1. Engages in the business of slaughtering poultry or processing, freezing, packaging, or labeling of any poultry or poultry products for use in human food or animal food.
2. Engages in the business of buying, or selling (as poultry products brokers, wholesalers, or otherwise), or transporting, storing, or importing poultry products.
3. Engages in business as a renderer, or is in the business of buying, selling, transporting or importing dead, dying, disabled, or diseased ("4-D") poultry.

The following persons conducting business in or for commerce must register their name, address, and trade name with the Secretary as prescribed in the poultry products inspection regulations:

1. Poultry product brokers.
2. Renderers.
3. Animal food manufacturers.
4. Wholesalers.
5. Operators of public warehouses storing poultry or poultry products.
6. Any persons buying, selling, transporting, or importing dead, dying, disabled, or diseased poultry.[26]

Another common source of problems for organizations is the prohibited acts. Specifically, Section 9 of the Poultry Products Inspection Act prohibits the following acts from being conducted:

1. The slaughter of any poultry or the processing of any poultry products

capable of use as human food at any establishment processing any such articles for commerce, except in compliance with the Act.

2. The sale, transportation, offer for sale or transportation, or receipt for transportation, in commerce, of any poultry products that are capable of use as human food and are adulterated or misbranded, or any poultry products that are required to be inspected under the Act and have not been inspected.

3. The commission of any act, with respect to any poultry products capable of use as human food, while the products are being transported in commerce or held for sale after transportation, that is intended to cause or has the effect of causing the products to be adulterated or misbranded.

4. The sale, transportation, offer for sale, or transportation, in commerce or from an official establishment, of any slaughtered poultry from which certain parts (blood, feathers, etc.) have not been removed.

5. The use or disclosure, except as authorized, of any information acquired under the authority of the Act that is entitled to protection as a trade secret.[27]

Employers should be aware that, under certain circumstances, they may be exempt from the Act or from specific provisions of the Act. These exemptions are very complicated and apply to:

1. Poultry processors under specific circumstances (i.e., facilities slaughtering less than one thousand poultry animals per year[28]); specific conditions must be met, including the poultry processors' not buying or selling poultry products other than those produced on their own farm, and the poultry product sales must be limited to intrastate commerce.

2. Retail dealers.

3. Religious dietary laws.

4. Territorial exceptions.

5. Personal use.

6. Custom operations.

7. Poultry producers' own poultry.

8. Small poultry producers' distribution to specific receivers.

9. Small enterprise exceptions.[29]

As with most USDA regulations, the Act provides that any person who violates specific provisions of the Act is subject to a maximum fine of one thousand dollars, imprisonment for up to one year, or both.[30] Additionally, violations involving the intent to defraud, or any distribution or attempt to distribute articles of adulterated product, may subject violators to a maximum fine of ten thousand dollars, imprisonment for up to three years, or both.[31] It should be noted that there are not provisions for civil penalties in violation of the Act although there are other enforcement tools available to ensure compliance.

With regard to USDA inspectors, "any person who forcibly assaults, resists, imposes, impedes, intimidates, or interferes with any person while engaging in or on account of the performance of his official duties under the Act" is subject to a maximum fine of five thousand dollars, maximum imprisonment of three years, or both.[32] In the event that a deadly weapon or dangerous weapon is utilized, the violator may receive a maximum fine of ten thousand dollars, imprisonment for up to ten years, or both.[33] The Act also provides a penalty for killing a person while "engaged in or on account of his official duties under the Act."[34]

NOTES

1. Pub.L.No. 85-172, approved Aug. 28, 1957, 51 Stat. 441, as amended by the Act of June 25, 1962, 76 Stat. 110, and the Wholesome Poultry Products Act of Aug. 18, 1968, Pub.L.No. 90-492, 82 Stat. 791 (1968).
2. 21 U.S. Code § 451. Also see *Canton Poultry, Inc. v. Conner,* 278, F. Supp. 822 (N.D. Fla. 1968).
3. 21 U.S. Code § 451.
4. 9 C.F.R. § 381.1(b)(40).
5. 21 U.S. Code § 453 (f); 9 C.F.R. § 381.1(b)(41), (42).
6. 21 U.S. Code § 453(u).
7. 21 U.S. Code § 467(e).
8. *Swift and Company v. Wickham,* 367 7.2d 241 (2d Cir. 1966).
9. 21 U.S. Code § 454(a).
10. 21 U.S. Code § 454(a)(1).
11. 21 U.S. Code § 454(a)(3).
12. 21 U.S. Code § 454(a)(4).
13. 21 U.S. Code § 454(c)(1).
14. 21 U.S. Code § 454 (c)(1).
15. 21 U.S. Code § 301 et seq.
16. *Bell v. Goddard,* 366 F.2d 177 (7th Cir. 1966).
17. See, e.g., Barry, *An Overview of Meat and Poultry Inspection Programs,* 33 Food, Drug, and Cosmetic Journal 44 (1978).
18. 21 U.S. Code § 455(c).
19. 21 U.S. Code § 455(c).
20. 21 U.S. Code § 460(a).
21. 9 C.F.R. § 381.36, 381.76.
22. 9 C.F.R. § 381.76.
23. 21 U.S. Code § 453(g).

24. Poultry Products Inspection Act, § 66.03(3). Also see, Agricultural Law, Volume 9.
25. Poultry Products Inspection Act, Agricultural Law, Vol. 9, 66.06, 66-18 to 66-20.
26. Poultry Products Inspection Act, Agricultural Law, Vol. 9, 66.08, 66-26 to 66-27.
27. Poultry Products Inspection Act, Agricultural Law, Vol. 9, 66.09, 66-29.
28. 21 U.S. Code § 464(c).
29. 21 U.S. Code § 464(c) et seq.
30. 21 U.S. Code § 461(a).
31. 21 U.S. Code § 461(a).
32. 21 U.S. Code § 461(c).
33. Id.
34. 21 U.S. Code § 461(c).

Chapter 7

Managing Facility Safety and Sanitation Programs

CHAPTER OBJECTIVES

The reader will:

1. *Acquire an understanding of the maintenance of the employee and food safety program.*
2. *Acquire an understanding of the sanitation function.*
3. *Acquire an understanding of the management of the safety and sanitation functions.*

T he maintenance of a food processing plant involves much more than just fixing equipment, patching walls, or resurfacing the floor; maintenance is first and foremost a safety issue. Providing a safe and sanitary work environment for employees is a key element in any food industry sanitation program. Food processing is by its very nature a high risk industry. The types of equipment that must be utilized to perform the various job functions often present an ongoing hazard. Many studies, as well as the OSHA injury and illness record for the food industry, paint a vivid picture of the risks inherent in the industry. From large, powerful saws and extremely sharp knives to grasping hooks and heavy lifting, the food industry has greater potential for injuries than almost any other industry.

Focusing specifically on the red meat industry, the Bureau of Labor Statistics estimates that there are over 100,000 people employed in the meatpacking industry. In recent years, the meatpacking industry has had the highest injury/illness rate of any industry in the United States. OSHA has placed special emphasis on the red meat industry to address many of the identified hazards, such as cumulative trauma disorders.[1]

Workers in the meatpacking industry can be injured while moving and stunning animals and during hoisting operations, as well as during the butchering and maintenance processes. Severing fingers or hands on machines that are improperly locked-out or not adequately guarded is not uncommon in the meat-packing industry. Thus sanitation and maintenance are of vital importance.

Maintenance is, by definition, the work of keeping something in proper condition; and a well-thought-out maintenance plan that is carried out to the letter can help to reduce some of the risks inherent in the food industry. Sanitation is defined as the daily cleaning and inspection of the equipment to eliminate or minimize contamination.

Safety during maintenance and sanitation procedures involves common sense. A key question that should be at the core of any maintenance and sanitation plans is: "If my own family members were the workers in my plant, what would I do to keep them as safe as possible?"

MAINTENANCE

The maintenance of a plant begins with the design of the facility; the plant must be designed in such a way as to allow for reasonable maintenance. The purchase and the placement of equipment must be considered with regular maintenance in mind. The USDA must approve the blueprint for the construction of any food processing plant, as its scrutiny of the design of the buildings takes into consideration both sanitation and maintenance issues. The Occupational Safety and Health Administration (OSHA) guidelines for safety are another key element in determining how best to lay out a food processing plant, as maintenance plays an important role in the safe operation of the plant.

Contamination must be a primary consideration in any maintenance plan. Mechanics may need to move from one area of the plant to another to repair equipment, and special precautions must be taken to ensure that the quality of the food products is not jeopardized by their moving from the "hot side" to the "cold side" of the plant. The mechanics, after all, may have been working on equipment in the slaughtering end of the operation and may thus have been exposed to fecal matter or ingesta. If they are called to repair a piece of equipment in the packaging area, obviously something must be done to keep the fecal matter or ingesta from entering the food processing area and causing contamination.

Suppose that one of the bolts that holds a machine in place is sheared off. The remaining portion of the bolt must be drilled out to prepare the area for a replacement bolt, but drilling causes debris. Here precautions must be taken in the food processing plant to ensure that the debris caused by the drilling does not get into the processed food. There must be a plan for accomplishing even the simplest procedure when the potential for contamination exists.

Anyone who has studied Continuous Quality Improvement (CQI) or Total Quality Management (TQM) has heard time and again about "doing right things right." That could not be more necessary than in the maintenance of a food industry operation, where shortcuts always come back to haunt the perpetrators. Managers responsible for maintenance who think they can take a shortcut or do something just because the inspector is not looking undoubtedly will get caught. This brings to mind the old adage "Pay now or pay later."

It behooves an employee to take the time and do something right the first time to avoid having to redo it later. This includes using the best parts or equipment for the job. Choosing the least expensive part in the interest of saving money is not always wise. One should check to be certain that the part that costs less meets the same specifications as the more expensive one. Often a part is priced less because the materials used to manufacture it are not of as high a grade as those in the more expensive alternative. Additionally, substituting a "similar" part might provide a temporary solution, but it might also cause an injury. There is no substitute for using the "right" part and doing the job "right" the first time.

Another adage by which to guide maintenance activities is: "If there's enough time to do over, then there was enough time to have done it right the first time." Employees should not do what they do not know how to do or have not been properly trained to do. People with just a bit of mechanical knowledge often think they can fix anything. For the protection of themselves and others, employees must not do what they do not know how to do, no matter how simple it seems. The cost of getting an expert to do the job is probably far less than the cost of harming an employee or of causing further, and perhaps more extensive, damage to already broken equipment.

Maintenance Checklist

It is very helpful to survey the plant and make a checklist of equipment and other items that need to be maintained on a regular schedule, such as the following:

1. Are all V-belt drivers guarded?
2. Are all pinch points guarded?
3. Are all boning or processing table sprockets and other sprockets guarded?

4. Are all handrails in place where needed?
5. Are all toeguards in place where needed?
6. Are emergency cables on all boning or processing tables?
7. Are emergency stops on tables, machinery, etc.?
8. Are guards being replaced after cleaning and maintenance?
9. Have moving parts on all machinery been analyzed for guarding purposes?
10. Are all augers guarded?
11. Are all open pits, manholes, etc., guarded?
12. Are all trailers jacked and chocked?
13. Are all extended shafts cut off to specification or properly guarded?
14. Are guardrails and railing in place and sturdy?
15. Are the rubberized cushioned floor mats in place, or is the nonskid flooring material in good condition?
16. Is the electrical wiring in good condition? Are there any signs of cracking, fraying, or defects? Is all electrical equipment properly grounded?
17. Are all necessary machine guards in place and in good repair? Do any need to be replaced or tightened?
18. Is the ventilation system working properly?

Lockout/Tagout

As indicated in Chapter 9, an alarming number of accidents are caused by machines or tools being turned on by one person while another person is trying to repair or service them. The Occupational Safety and Health Administration (OSHA) has responded to this problem by enacting legislation in reference to power lockouts. The legislation reads:

> Devices such as padlocks shall be provided for locking out the source of power at the main disconnect switch. Before any maintenance, inspection, cleaning, adjusting or servicing of equipment (electrical, mechanical or other) that requires entrance into or close contact with the machinery or equipment, the main power disconnect switch or valve, or both, controlling its source of power or flow of material, shall be locked out or blocked off with a padlock, blank flange or similar device.[2]

The following is a sample lockout/tagout procedure:

Plant safety policy is to eliminate all potential dangers to employees as a result of unexpected movement of objects as maintenance or service is performed on machinery, equipment, or processes.

1. To achieve this objective all potentially dangerous sources of energy shall be neutralized before work is performed.
   (a) The following sources of energy shall be considered:
      (1) Electrical.
      (2) Steam and condensate systems under pressure.
      (3) Hydraulic fluids under pressure.
      (4) Compressed air.
      (5) Energy stored up in springs, hydraulic accumulators, or electrical capacitors.
      (6) Potential energy from suspended parts.
      (7) Any other source that might cause unexpected mechanical movement.
   (b) Only qualified personnel shall be permitted to neutralize any of the previously mentioned sources of energy.
2. To effectively neutralize the various sources of energy, the following steps should be taken:
   (a) Electrical: open the main power source switch.
      (1) Lock out that switch with a safety padlock.
      (2) Tag the machine control panel.
      (3) Pull the main power source fuses if lockout is not possible.
   (b) Steam and condensate systems under pressure:
      (1) Close the main source control valve.
      (2) Bleed all lines to relieve any stored-up energy.
      (3) Lock out the main source control valve.
      (4) Tag the main source control valve (as a minimum).
   (c) Hydraulic fluids under pressure:
      (1) Close the main source control valve or pump motor.
      (2) Bleed all accumulators to relieve any stored-up energy.
      (3) Lock out the main source control valve or pump motor.
      (4) Tag the main source control valve or pump motor (minimum).
   (d) Compressed air:
      (1) Close the main source control valve on the compressor.
      (2) Bleed all lines to relieve any stored up energy.
      (3) Lock out the main source control valve on the compressor.
      (4) Tag the main source control valve (as a minimum).
   (e) Energy stored up in springs:
      (1) Release spring tension if possible.
      (2) Block movable objects properly (as a minimum).
   (f) Potential energy from suspended objects:
      (1) Secure loose or freely movable objects.
      (2) Block movable objects properly (as a minimum).
   (g) Other potential energy sources:

    (1) Restrain any movable objects to immovable objects with rope, chain, or cable.

    (2) Block movable objects properly (as a minimum).

3. As a precaution against unexpected actuation of the neutralized controls, such controls shall be tagged and locked out before work is performed.

  (a) Each craftsperson shall be provided with a company-approved safety padlock for his or her exclusive use.

    (1) The user's name, identification number, section, and shift shall be attached to each safety padlock.

    (2) Each safety padlock shall be key-coded so that removal of that padlock can be done only by the person protected by that lock-out device.

    (3) Safety padlocks shall not be used for any purpose other than to lock out neutralized controls.

    (4) If work being performed is to be carried over to the succeeding shift, the person leaving the job will replace his or her lock with a warning tag. The follow-up craftsperson shall replace the previous person's warning tag with his or her personal padlock.

    (5) If continuation of work is to be delayed for a long period, safety padlocks may be removed, provided that:

      a. Main electrical power source fuses are pulled; and

      b. Each potentially dangerous source of energy is properly tagged at the controls.

  (b) Each craftsperson shall be provided with warning tags.

    (1) The appropriate warning tags shall be placed on each particular control once that control has been neutralized.

      a. This shall be done before any work is done.

      b. This shall also be done, without fail, even though lockout devices may subsequently be used.

    (2) Warning tags, properly filled out, shall be placed on all controls that could possibly cause danger to employees if accidentally actuated.

    (3) When machinery, equipment, or processes are properly restored for normal use, the warning tag shall be removed.

4. Whenever an eminent danger exists, the following steps shall be taken by the supervisor responsible for the machinery, equipment, or process:

  (a) Immediately instruct employees not to operate such machinery, equipment, or process.

  (b) Alert Plant Engineering of the urgent need for corrective action:

    (1) Personal contact shall be made (phone or face-to-face).

    (2) Call in for a repair ticket once personal contact is made.

(c) See to it that a proper warning tag is placed in a conspicuous location on or near controls that could cause injury to any employee:

    (1) The appropriate craftsperson shall attach the warning tag if an immediate response by Plant Engineering is possible.

    (2) The supervisor responsible for the machine, equipment, or process shall attach a warning tag as soon as possible if an unreasonable delay in the craftsperson's response is anticipated for any reason.

    (3) As a minimum precaution: when in doubt, tag it out!

Maintenance as Every Employee's Job

Maintaining a safe and healthy work environment is not just the job of the maintenance engineer; it is the responsibility of every employee. Employers should provide both enough time and appropriate equipment and supplies for work areas to be kept clean and safe, and should encourage their employees to adopt such maintenance as a regular part of their duties.

Employers and managers need to educate their employees about the safety aspects of good maintenance. Safety precautions might include:

1. Immediate cleaning of water, blood, or grease spills on floors where they could cause falls.
2. Checking for wet conditions near electrical equipment as potential sources of electrocution.
3. Checking for equipment such as knives that might be left lying about on counters or in sinks.
4. Checking for worn equipment (e.g., dull knives).
5. Checking refrigeration systems for leaks.
6. Ensuring that hazardous materials are identified and appropriately labeled.

Proper Training for Safety and Maintenance

Injuries and illnesses in the meat packing and food industries are often due to inadequate training and education. It is imperative for both employee safety and the survival of the business that employers develop, implement, and maintain a training program for all employees.

Statistics have shown that new and younger employees are at the greatest risk of injury, primarily because they are not adequately trained for their responsibilities. Experienced workers are not at much less risk simply because they have been performing their job for a period of time, and it has become routine.

A sound training program should educate workers about existing safety and health hazards, the proper use and maintenance of any equipment, preventive measures, and how to deal with emergency situations.

Training and education are not one-time experiences. Employees should receive training at least annually; and additional training may be necessary when new equipment or materials are purchased, or when procedures are altered or updated.

Maintenance as the Key to Loss Prevention

Maintaining equipment and machinery in good working order and keeping the physical plant in tip-top shape can not only keep the business running but can actually save the company money by preventing injuries and reducing lost workdays.

The key to reducing lost workdays is prevention. A sound safety program that includes proper education and training of employees and creates a safe working environment can prevent accidents from happening.

Developing a safety audit for a particular plant can help one to assess the plant's deficiencies. By identifying these crucial areas, one can make immediate corrections. The goal of such an audit is to compare one's own plant to the "ideal" plant.

A Safety and Health Audit Instrument has been provided in Appendix B to assist readers in developing programs for their facilities.

SANITATION PROGRAMS

Sanitation is one of the most crucial functions in the food processing industry. In fact, sanitation begins long before the first food products arrive in the plant. Achieving sanitary conditions really begins when the plant is designed. The architect must design a food processing plant with sanitation in mind.

A good food processing plant is designed from top to bottom with cleanliness as a primary goal. Architects who specialize in food processing plant design know that from the light fixtures to the floor, everything in the plant must be designed for sanitation. The USDA must review and approve all food plant site blueprints to ensure that the agency's guidelines are met.

Sanitation means different things to different people. To some, a clean-looking plant exemplifies sanitary conditions. But looks can be deceiving; sanitation demands much more scrutiny than a casual look. In this age of product recall and gross contamination, just looking clean could cause major public health problems and destroy a business.

The food processing industry can no longer rely on the USDA and the FDA to be its quality control agents. The industry cannot assume that these agencies will do, much less do well, the job of quality control. Each plant must be responsible for its own quality control. Every manager and every supervisor must assume responsibility for the safety, cleanliness, and wholesomeness of the environment in which food products are produced. In short, the best way to assure quality control and sanitation is for management at each plant to assume the responsibility for meeting and even exceeding government and industry guidelines.

This responsibility includes not only cleaning the physical areas but also setting standards and guidelines for the cleanliness of those persons who process the food. This includes such matters as clean clothes, clean shoes, and personal hygiene. It involves maintenance of a segregated process; in other words, employees and equipment from one area should not be allowed to cross over into another area or from the "hot side" to the "cold side." Any movement of employees or equipment between areas must be carefully controlled to avoid cross contamination.

One of the most effective ways to ensure sanitation within a plant is to develop a regular inspection protocol. The goals of this protocol should be to determine if:

1. The process is effective.
2. The cleaners used are appropriate for the job.

Sanitation Checklist

Developing a checklist for sanitation inspection can be very helpful. Such a checklist might be divided into areas, beginning with the ceiling, and include the following:

1. Ceiling:
   - Are there any exposed beams or other areas where dust and bacteria could reside?
   - Of what materials are these exposed areas composed?
   - Can these areas be sanitized adequately?
2. Support areas:
   - Are there exposed columns that support the structure?
   - Of what materials are these columns made?
   - Are they rusty? Do they need to be painted?
   - Are these areas that could harbor bacteria?
3. Pipework and electrical conduit:
   - Are there exposed pipes and electrical conduit?
   - Are pipes insulated, and, if so, with what sort of material (asbestos, fiberglass, etc.)?

- Are there loose particles that could fall and enter the food process?
4. Wiring:
    - Are all wires encased in conduit?
    - Are there any exposed wires?
    - Can these areas be safely cleaned and sanitized?
5. Fixtures:
    - Are there ceiling fans? If yes, is there a buildup of grease and dust that could contaminate food products?
    - Is the ventilation system cleaned on a regular basis?
    - What kind of light fixtures are present?
    - Are there exposed light bulbs or glass lamp shades that could break, allowing glass to enter the food process?
    - Are there any exposed wires?
6. Wall surfaces:
    - Are wall surfaces impervious and easily sanitized?
    - Are there any gaps at wall joints?
    - Are there any loose rivets?
    - Are there refrigeration or air-handling units that need to be cleaned on a regular basis?
    - Are there any wall-mounted fans that could harbor dust?
7. Control switches:
    - Are control switches cleaned regularly?
    - Are switches rusty, in need of painting or replacing?
    - Could switches harbor bacteria or dust?
8. Equipment:
    - Is equipment well maintained?
    - Is equipment suspended from the ceiling so that there are upper areas that could harbor dust and bacteria?
    - Is equipment bolted to the floor, where extra effort should be made to clean around bolted areas?
9. Floors:
    - Of what material is the floor made?
    - Is it easily sanitized?
    - Are there steel gratings that need to be clean and sanitized?
    - Are there any fixtures on the floor that might be rusting and in need of painting or replacing?
10. Mobile equipment:
    - Is mobile equipment kept within the same area of the plant?
    - Is all equipment inspected on a regular basis?
    - Is equipment allowed to be moved from one area of the plant to another?

Staff members responsible for the sanitation of food processing plants bear a great burden. They have the public's trust, as consumers believe that every precaution has been taken to ensure the safety and the quality of the food they consume. Probably the best guideline for sanitation engineers in the food industry is to treat the sanitation of the plant as though the lives of their own families depended on it.

SANITATION SAFETY RULES AND USE OF CHEMICALS

The next most important step in the sanitation process is to ensure the safe use of the sanitizing chemicals. Each facility's safety manual should include a comprehensive section on the safe use of chemicals, covering such topics as mixing, usage, handling, and storage.

The following pages contain examples of such sections from a facility safety manual.

Sanitation Safety Rules for Chemical Mixing and Use

1. High-caustic-based cleaners:
   - Add chemicals to water *slowly*—never fast.
   - Never add water to chemicals.
   - Use water at maximum of 140°F for mixing.
   - Use rubber-type gloves, apron, face mask, and goggles when mixing chemicals.
   - If a chemical comes in contact with the skin or eyes, immediately rinse the affected area with water for 15 minutes.
2. General purpose cleaners:
   - Add the chemical to water *slowly*.
   - If a chemical comes in contact with the skin or eyes, rinse the affected area with water as soon as possible.
   - *Warning:* These chemicals will burn if left on the skin.
3. Wetting agents:
   - These chemicals are relatively harmless, but very expensive. Use as directed.
4. Acid:
   - Use only at the direction of the foreperson.
   - Use rubber-type gloves and eye protection (goggles and face shield).
   - If acid comes in contact with skin, rinse the skin immediately with cold water. If burning persists, report to the first aid station.
   - If acid comes in contact with the eyes, rinse the eyes immediately with water for at least 15 minutes, and report to the first aid station.

5. Chlorine—concentrated bleach and sanitizer:
   - Wear rubber-type gloves, face shield, and goggles.
   - *Never* mix chlorine and acid.
   - *Never* use acid and chlorine in the same room at the same time (deadly chlorine gas can be generated).
6. General rules:
   - Never mix any chemicals without the approval of the foreperson.
   - Never use any chemical unless directed to do so.
   - Never fail to follow the dilution instructions of the foreperson.
   - Never spray chemicals or acids through oilers.
   - Always wear eye protection, protective footwear, hard hat, and other protective equipment.
   - Use spray guns for oil only.
   - Always use lockouts when working in or around equipment.
   - Always rinse tanks and buckets before using them.
   - Know where the eyewash stations are.
   - Consult your foreperson for proper instructions.

There is a provision in the OSHA regulations allowing a chemical's manufacturers to withhold specific chemical identity provided that they can support the claim that a trade secret is involved. They must still disclose information on the Material Safety Data Sheet (MSDS) about the effects of the chemical, and they must provide health professionals with the specific chemical identity in cases of emergency. There are also provisions in the OSHA standard requiring health professionals to maintain trade secrets. All employees must work together to ensure their compliance with all the provisions for using chemicals. When new chemicals are purchased, they must be added to the list of hazardous chemicals and substances, and new Material Safety Data Sheets are needed. When outside contractors or other outside people are on the premises, the plant safety director needs to notify them of any hazardous chemicals or substances they may come in contact with while they are there. Following the procedures of this policy should ensure that employees are kept fully informed about all the hazardous chemicals and substances they work with, and that they are well trained in the safe handling and use of these substances. The single purpose of this policy, and of the related regulations and laws, is to prevent injuries to employees using hazardous chemicals and substances.

Chemical Safety Precautions and Tips

All workers should follow these practices:

1. Be aware of potential chemical hazards. Develop a healthy respect for all chemical cleaners and sanitizers.

2. Precautionary statements are printed on all chemical cleaner container labels; so read all chemical cleaner labels carefully. All end-use containers must have proper labels at all times to identify their contents.
3. First aid instructions are found on chemical container labels, as well as Material Safety Data Sheets and marketing sheets. Read them, and be aware of the location of first aid materials.
4. Follow all chemical use instructions carefully.
5. Avoid breathing of chemical fumes. Replace lids or caps on chemical containers after using products.
6. Store chemicals in a neat, organized manner with labels turned so that they can be easily read.
7. Protect your eyes with safety glasses or goggles when handling concentrated chemicals.
8. Don a rubber apron, boots, gloves, and a face shield before working with cleaning chemicals.
9. Do not smoke or eat in chemical storage or use areas.
10. Do not use chemical containers for stools, ladders, shelves, etc.
11. Wipe up chemical spills promptly.
12. Do not switch drum pumps or scoops from one chemical container to another.
13. Do not mix chemicals unless specifically instructed in writing to do so.
14. Never mix an acid cleaner with a chlorinated cleaner. Mixing acid and chlorine-bearing compounds will produce dangerous chlorine gas.
15. Slowly add the chemical cleaner to cold water. Do not add water to the cleaner.
16. In case of chemical burns, immediately rinse the skin with cool water for at least 15 minutes. Follow first aid instructions. Notify the supervisor, and seek medical aid if necessary.
17. For chemical splashes in the eyes, immediately wash the eyes thoroughly at the eyewash station with cool, flowing water for at least 15 minutes. Seek medical attention, and notify the supervisor.
18. Chemical safety is no accident: work defensively, work smart, and stay safe.

Safety Rules for Chemical Cleaners

Many detergent products contain ingredients that could be harmful. Understanding and applying the safety techniques required for these products is essential to their safe use. With proper handling and applications, these products will give the desired results without harming personnel, equipment, or the user's product. You should always follow these safety rules when working with chemical cleaners:

1. Know the product. Read the container label. Make sure you have the

right product for the cleaning job. Keep a file of the Material Safety Data Sheets for all the products used in the plant.

2. Protect yourself:
   - Use your safety glasses. Wear the proper gloves, aprons, and boots when working directly with chemicals.
   - When water or chemical solutions are spilled or drain onto smooth-surface floors, they create very slippery conditions. Work and walk with extreme care in these areas.

3. Avoid improper mixing:
   - Many products, especially caustics and some acids, give off heat when mixed with water. Always add these products slowly and carefully to water, with agitation, to avoid a violent reaction.
   - Chlorinated compounds will react violently with acids, organic matter, or very hot water. With acids, they produce a toxic gas that can be lethal. Strong chlorinated or oxidizing compounds may produce a fire with organic compounds.
   - Be careful not to contaminate chlorinated compounds with even small amounts of other materials, such as might be found on a dirty scoop or in a drum previously used to handle or store other products.
   - Mixing acids with alkalies gives off large amounts of heat. In some combinations these substances react violently and may give off undesirable gases. Follow the directions and avoid improper mixing. A good general rule is not to mix chemicals without the approval of the supervisor.

4. Store chemicals in a clean, dry area. Many products require special attention for storage; read the Material Safety Data Sheets. If possible, store chemicals in a locked area. Never store chemical products next to food products such as salt or sugar. Avoid eating or smoking in chemical storage areas.

5. Emergency measures: The best first aid treatment for eyes and chemical skin burns is the immediate application of cold, running water for at least 15 minutes. If a hazardous material is involved, the product label gives the necessary antidote. Get medical attention immediately.

6. Your responsibility: Only you can protect yourself. Follow instructions for product application, mixing procedures, and container handling, and always wear protective clothing.

Chemical Handling Policies

1. Handle chemicals, including acids, solvents, and caustic solutions, with special caution and in accordance with the manufacturer's label instructions.
2. Wash your hands after using chemicals, especially before eating.

3. Wear adequate eye protection devices while handling chemicals, including acids, solvents, and caustic solutions.
4. If your skin comes in contact with any chemical, including acids, solvents, and caustic solutions, flush the skin with large amounts of water, and report to the first aid station. Report the incident to your supervisor.
5. Never place any chemical in an unmarked container. All containers must be properly marked to identify their contents. Refer to Chemical Safety Act, SARA, and Title III manuals for the complete policy.

The foregoing are just a few examples of policies that a food processing plant should have in place to protect the public, its employees, and its future.

PERSONAL PROTECTIVE EQUIPMENT

The use of chemicals and/or steam can pose a safety threat to the sanitation engineer. In all industries, safety should be job one. Some of the policies previously covered dealt with using the appropriate use of chemicals. The use of personal protective equipment is also of vital importance.

Personal protective equipment can include aprons, glasses, goggles, gloves, boots, and respiratory gear. Chemicals can cause irritations of the eyes, skin, and lungs; so it is extremely important that the each sanitation task be evaluated as to the exposure to certain chemicals so that the appropriate type of protective gear can be supplied and used.

Some chemicals react differently with various types of gloves and aprons, depending upon what material the gloves and aprons are made from. After careful evaluation and study, the most effective protective gear possible should be specified for use.

For example, there are different types of gloves. Cotton or fabric gloves can be used for handling slippery objects or for protecting against low levels of heat or cold. For use with corrosives, gloves made of rubber, neoprene, or vinyl are best. Lined or leather gloves would be appropriate for hot or rough surfaces. Special cut-resistant gloves work best with sharp objects, whereas aluminized fabric is good for jobs involving intense heat. There are even gloves with an insulated lining for electrical work.

Protecting the Eyes

Employees can offer pretty trivial excuses for not wearing safety goggles or glasses, especially when the absence of such personal protective equipment can result in blindness. The proper use of eye protection devices significantly reduces one's chances of eye injury; at the very least, these protective devices can reduce the severity of the injury if there is an accident.

Contact with chemicals in the clean-up operation and in production processes is a cause of work-related eye injuries. Almost 60% of reported eye injuries are due to employees' not wearing protective equipment. A vast majority of accidents could be avoided by following safety precautions and wearing protective equipment.

There are various types of eye safety equipment. Safety glasses with polycarbonate lenses are light and impact-resistant, and they can be ordered with special coatings to prevent fogging of the lenses. These glasses also can be purchased with side shield guards that protect the eyes from the sides. Goggles, another form of eye protective equipment, are similar to safety glasses but provide additional protection from splashing liquids, vapors, dust, and fumes. Goggles can be worn over prescription eyeglasses.

Safety glasses and goggles should be cleaned and maintained regularly. One's vision can be reduced by cracks, scratches, or dirt. Remember that replacing damaged safety glasses or goggles is easy and inexpensive, but eyes cannot be replaced.

Contact lenses should not be worn without safety glasses or goggles, especially in situations where chemical fumes, vapors, and splashes might be encountered. Redness, blurring of vision, and pain are signals that contacts should be removed from the eyes immediately.

Foot Protection

Protecting the feet is also an important aspect of safety in the sanitation process. A wide variety of protective devices are available to prevent injury to the toes, ankles, and feet. Protection against oil, water, acids, corrosives, and other industrial chemicals can be provided by rubber or plastic safety boots. Some boots are even puncture-resistant. These boots are usually made to be worn over safety shoes, which give a second level of protection.

SANITATION IS MORE THAN CLEANING

It should be evident from the foregoing discussion that sanitation of a food processing plant involves more than just cleaning. It involves the design of the building, inspections for cleanliness, and adherence to safety measures. Safety is the key concept, whether for preventing contamination of food products or in preventing injuries to employees.

Safety involves commitment, from the CEO all the way down to the newest employee. Safety is an attitude and must always have top priority. Management is responsible for training each sanitation engineer in the correct procedures to follow when using sanitizing substances. The sanitation engineer is responsible for following the guidelines developed by management and specified during training.

Employees should be responsible for monitoring the condition of their own personal protective equipment. For example, employees should be responsible for making certain that their gloves are clean and do not have any rips or holes in them. They should make sure that their safety equipment is well maintained by rinsing off pieces such as gloves to prevent damage and contamination. After removing protective equipment, employees should wash their hands thoroughly with soap and water. Strong solvents such as gasoline or turpentine should not be used because they could react with even the slightest residue of chemicals from the sanitation process that might remain on the employees' hands.

Employees should understand that problems with chemicals are not always immediately evident. Injuries such as burns might be noticeable right away, but development of an allergy-type sensitivity to a chemical might take months or years of exposure.

NOTES

1. OSHA, *Ergonomic Guidelines for the Red Meat Industry* (1985).
2. 29 CFR 1910.147.

Chapter 8

Foodborne Illness, Microbiological Testing, and HACCP

CHAPTER OBJECTIVES

The reader will:

1. *Acquire an understanding of some of the major foodborne illnesses.*
2. *Acquire an understanding of the need for the Hazard Analysis and Critical Control Point (HACCP).*
3. *Acquire an understanding of the major principles of HACCP and its requirements for seafood, meat, and poultry.*

OVERVIEW

Until recently, the food industry itself governed and monitored the testing of raw and processed food products for dangerous microbes that cause spoilage and/or foodborne illness. The government agencies responsible for food safety had no formal mechanisms in place to monitor or test for dangerous microorganisms. In the food industry, the common theory was that it made good business sense to provide a safe and healthy food product as well as longer shelf life. The companies with good sanitation practices and quality control not only had more satisfied customers but were able to keep their products on the shelf or in the meat case for longer periods of time than less well-managed competitors, all of which resulted in greater economic benefits. In the seafood industry, historically there has been little, if any, inspection of seafood prior to packaging. In the area of beef and poultry slaughter, except for gross visual inspection for bruised, abscessed, or contaminated raw products, government inspectors have had no responsibility for monitoring or conducting microbiological testing. However, with the advent of sophisticated and high speed processing facilities and a surge of growth in processed food consumption, such as frankfurters, frozen dinners, pizza, and sausages, the government recently has recognized the need to educate the public on the dangers of foodborne microbes and to monitor slaughter and processing of meat products for pathogens.

In December 1995, the FDA issued its Final Rule on the "Procedures for the Safe and Sanitary Processing of Importing of Fish and Fishery Products."[1] The Rule was implemented to establish specific requirements relating to the processing and importing of seafood for commercial distribution in the United States. The requirements involve the application of the Hazard Analysis and Critical Control Point (HACCP) principles by processors and importers to ensure food safety to the maximum extent possible. HACCP is a system by which food processors evaluate the kinds of hazards that can affect their products, institute proper controls to prevent these hazards from occurring or to significantly minimize their occurrence, monitor the performance of those controls, and maintain records of this monitoring. In addition, the Food Safety and Inspection Service (FSIS), on July 25, 1996, published its Final Rule implementing HACCP regulations for the meat and poultry industry. Along with the HACCP, the regulations of the FSIS include a clarification of the responsibilities of companies for sanitation compliance, antimicrobial treatments during the slaughter process and prior to the chilling of carcasses, observing requirements for prompt chilling of carcasses and meat parts, establishing targets for pathogen reduction, and doing daily microbial testing in slaughter facilities and establishments. Finally, the FSIS announced an intention to initiate joint rulemaking with the Food and Drug Administration (FDA) to establish federal standards for safe handling of food during transportation, distribution, and storage prior to delivery to retail stores.

BACKGROUND—FSIS

Brief History of the FSIS Program

The following paragraphs give a brief history of the FSIS program, explaining its purpose and its function in meat inspection in the United States. (See Chapter 4 for additional discussion of the FSIS.)

1890s–1940s

In the 1890s, European countries raised questions about the safety of U.S. beef. In response, Congress gave the U.S. Department of Agriculture (USDA) the responsibility for ensuring that beef exports met European standards. In 1891, Congress also provided that the USDA would conduct both antemortem (predeath) and postmortem (after death) inspection of livestock slaughtered in the United States and intended for distribution in the United States. The Food Safety and Inspection Service is a branch of the USDA.

In 1906, Upton Sinclair's novel *The Jungle* graphically told of the terrible and unsanitary conditions in meat slaughter plants in the United States. It described diseased carcasses and even human body parts in the food products. According to the novel, mice, rats, and general filth were prevalent throughout American slaughterhouses. American consumers protested vigorously, and over the years Congress responded to their concerns by passing meat inspection laws, which led in 1967 to the Federal Meat Inspection Act (FMIA).[2] (See Chapter 4 for further discussion.) The legislation established sanitary standards for slaughter and processing facilities and mandated preslaughter inspection of livestock, as well as postmortem inspection of all carcasses.

The meat inspection laws also required that government inspectors monitor all slaughter facilities as well as manufacturing facilities, and that they perform online inspections. In addition, the USDA implemented a Bureau of Animal Industry, which provided for veterinarians to oversee inspection in the slaughter plants. Their job was to do the antemortem as well as the postmortem inspections of live animals and carcasses for signs of disease.

The major focus of the veterinarians and USDA inspectors was to prevent diseased animals from entering the food supply. Inspectors would view lots of live animals and segregate those with obvious signs of disease or abscesses. These animals were either prevented from entering the slaughterhouse or tagged for future inspection in the carcass stage. Condemned product did not enter the processing area but went straight to the inedible rendering department.

These inspectors had only sight, smell, and touch as their primary means of inspection. Modern microbial testing procedures were not available then, nor were they required under the law.

Congress passed the Federal Food and Drug Act of 1906 as companion legislation to the meat inspection laws. A different group from the USDA, the Bureau of Chemistry, was responsible for implementation of the Food and Drug Act, which covered all food products except meat and poultry. However, the Act did not require the continuous inspection of food product production, as meat inspection regulations did.

1940–1970

The 1950s saw enormous growth of meat and poultry processing facilities. The sale of ready-to-eat products such as processed hams, sausages, soups, hot dogs, frozen dinners, and pizza rose dramatically. In part, World War II had a significant impact on this change, with increasing numbers of women in the workforce, and consumption of fast foods become commonplace. In addition, new ingredients, new technology, and specialization added to the complexity of the slaughter and processing industry. Small slaughterhouses turned into huge, high speed facilities that could slaughter and process thousands of animals per day.

These changes had a great impact upon the federal meat inspection program. Food technology and microbiology became important tools in the growth of this industry. Specialized skills were necessary for both manufacturers and the FSIS. As the industry grew, more inspectors were necessary. Today there are more than 7,000 FSIS inspectors, who are responsible for the compliance of inspection laws and regulations in over 6,000 meat and poultry facilities nationwide.

With this growth, it became impossible to continue inspecting each production unit (i.e., each carcass). In the high speed processing facilities, inspectors could only focus on the production line for compliance. In contrast, in slaughterhouses, inspectors were required to do carcass-by-carcass inspection to prevent contaminated or diseased animals from passing through the system.

In 1957, the Poultry Products Inspection Act (PPIA)[3] was passed by Congress. Requiring mandatory inspection of all poultry products intended for distribution throughout the United States, it generally followed the guidelines of the FMIA.

In the early sixties, the public became aware of the harmful effects of pesticides and other chemical contaminants in the food chain, in part because of Rachel Carson's book *Silent Spring*. By 1967, the USDA established the National Residue Program to determine the presence and the level of chemicals in meat and poultry and to control any chemical that presented a public health hazard.

In addition, the Wholesome Meat Act of 1967[4] was enacted to give the USDA regulatory authority over food brokers, animal food manufacturers, and freezer storage facilities, as well as transporters and retailers of food products. (See discussion in Chapter 4.) The Wholesome Poultry Products Act[5] of 1968 gave the USDA additional ammunition to govern poultry inspection. Both of these Acts incorporated adulteration and misbranding prohibitions into the agency's area of responsibility. Moreover, both Acts provided greater enforcement authority, including the withdrawal or refusal of inspection services, the detention of food products, injunctions, and further investigatory authority.

1970 to the Present

By the early 1970s, the FSIS's inspection program was quickly becoming very outdated. Automation and industry expansion were overwhelming the ability of the FSIS to do good-quality continuous inspection, especially in the poultry industry. In the past, many meat slaughter facilities had used a bed system, whereby individual animals were laid on a "bed" (consisting of stainless steel rods) and completely butchered one at a time. With automation, animals were hung upside down from a rail on movable trolley hooks and made to slide down the line automatically. The line or chain speeds, in the early seventies, had increased to several hundred head per hour in the beef industry and up to a thousand head per hour in the pork industry. In the poultry industry, inspectors began facing line speeds as high as 90 birds per minute. These speeds made it extremely difficult if not impossible for inspectors to examine individual carcasses. In addition, congressional budget cuts made it even more difficult for FSIS inspectors to handle the increased slaughter rate.

In September of 1976, the management consulting firm of Booz, Allen, and Hamilton, Inc., was hired to perform an in-depth study to find less costly ways to inspect meat and poultry without affecting consumer protection.[6] Among other things, the study recommended that FSIS:

1. Use quality control mechanisms to shift responsibilities from inspectors to the slaughter facility, giving inspectors oversight and verification responsibility.
2. Establish microbiological criteria for finished products.
3. Explore substitution of air chilling for water chilling of poultry carcasses because of potential contamination with bath chilling.
4. Require chlorination of chilling water for poultry.
5. Expand the food safety education of consumers and food handlers.[7]

Although the study generally elicited a negative response from consumer groups, which were concerned that the recommendations would cause the FSIS to turn over too much control to the industry, it did help the agency focus on change. As part of this change, the agency issued its own report, *Added Strength in Meat and Poultry Inspection Program.*[8] The report emphasized that the poultry postmortem system had been designed before the vertical integration of the poultry industry and the increased attention to production control. With the introduction of high speed production lines, the traditional system had become severely stressed, and inspectors were "forced to work at speeds well over those at which peak effectiveness is expected."[9] Scientific evidence indicated that with improvements in animal health, antemortem inspection of carcasses was less necessary than in previous years.

In 1980, the agency established a voluntary Total Quality Control (TQC) program. This allowed the FSIS flexibility in tailoring inspection programs to the specific establishments' needs. It also gave those facilities the ability to examine their production needs and processes, which in many cases led to overall improvement in facilities' compliance efforts.

In the mid-1980s, the FSIS introduced what became known as the Streamlined Inspection System (SIS) in high speed poultry slaughter operations. This system shifted routine tasks that controlled for quality, rather than safety, from inspectors to the individual establishments' employees. Thus, under the SIS system, establishment employees perform detection and trimming of carcass defects that affect the quality but not the safety of the product.

Today, inspection occurs in two phases, antemortem and postmortem. During antemortem inspection, the inspectors observe meat animals both at rest and in motion, segregating any abnormal animals before they enter the slaughter facility. A veterinarian medical officer (VMO) then inspects the segregated animals and either condemns them or allows them to be slaughtered under special handling.

Because of the large number of chickens and turkeys slaughtered daily, FSIS inspectors conduct their inspections on a flock or lot basis. Birds found to be abnormal are then condemned by flock or lot. It should be noted that over six billion chicken and turkeys are slaughtered annually.

One problem with this type of system is that many diseases cannot be detected through antemortem inspection. During the postmortem phase, viscera and carcasses are examined on the processing line. Because many of the bacteria implicated in cases of foodborne illnesses live in the intestinal track of meat animals and poultry, physical removal and examination of heads and viscera are required. An inspector generally performs a sequence of observations, palpitations, and incisions of the tissue to determine whether the animal is diseased.

Currently, the prevention of ingesta and fecal contamination of beef and poultry carcasses is the focal point of the inspection system. This is so because harmful bacterial pathogens, such as *Salmonella Campylobacter*, and *E. coli 0157:H7* can contaminate meat through the feces and ingesta. However, drug residues and pathogenic microorganisms cannot always be seen through a visual inspection, especially an inspection that is only looking for gross evidence of contamination.

In 1993, 384,543 (or 0.3%) of the 129,831,110 million meat animal carcasses inspected were condemned for disease, contamination, or adulteration during ante- or postmortem inspection. Of the 7,085,491,852 poultry carcasses inspected, 63,926,693 (or 0.9%) were condemned.[10]

FOODBORNE ILLNESS

There is no doubt that foodborne illness is a major cause of morbidity and mortality in the United States. However, estimates of the incidence of foodborne illness vary widely. In the past, many food-related illnesses went undetected, with no knowledge of the etiology of the pathogen(s) involved. Etiologies are still unknown for approximately 50% of acute foodborne illness occurrences.[11] However, with improved analytical techniques, we are now able to narrow the scope and determine the cause of many foodborne illnesses. Unfortunately, research has demonstrated that microorganisms are highly adaptable and rather unpredictable. They can also quickly change and evolve in order to survive. In addition, as the food industry has expanded globally, and new foods and new food ingredients have been introduced, the potential for foodborne illness has increased substantially. In many food production facilities that have grown in size to very large and complex operations, minor mistakes can cause tremendous outbreaks of foodborne illness. The 1985 Chicago outbreak of milk-related illness certainly underscores this point. Thousands of people suffered from the *Salmonella* contamination in one milk processing facility.

Food can be contaminated by microorganisms not only from animals, insects, and people but also from the air, soil, and water. In addition, chemicals from pesticides, herbicides, fertilizers, and radionuclides contaminate foods. Contamination can occur not only during processing of food, as evidenced by an outbreak of botulism from vacuum-packed tuna fish, but during any stage of production, transportation, storage, preparation, and serving.

Even raw foods contain dangerous microorganisms. Some 15 to 30% of raw dressed poultry contains *Salmonella*. *Salmonella aureus* is present in many pooled milk supplies and in approximately 20% of cheddar cheeses. *Clostridium perfringens* is cultured in 50% of red meat in grocery stores. *Salmonella* is found in 15 to 30% of commercial egg products, with *S. enteritidis* now a very serious problem. Seafood, such as shellfish, is contaminated with organisms causing infectious hepatitis and cholera.[12]

Some Major Pathogens

Some of the major pathogens have been recognized for many years, whereas other pathogens that have only recently been discovered have caused some serious outbreaks of foodborne illness. For example, *Campylobacter jejuni* was first described as an agent of human disease in the late 1970s, and it is now recognized as the leading cause of foodborne bacterial diarrhea.[13] There are other campylobacters, which may be more difficult to culture (and thus identify), that also cause gastritis and gastric ulcers.[14]

Listeria monocytogenes has been known as a foodborne pathogen for a number of years. It had been thought that refrigeration would be an adequate barrier to the growth of this microorganism, but investigators now have learned that refrigeration alone does not prevent this pathogen from being a very serious threat to health.[15] Of course, more common known pathogens are *Clostridium, Botulinum* (which causes botulism), and *Salmonella* spp. (the last a common cause of severe stomach cramps and acute gastroenteritis). *Salmonella* can get into the bloodstream of some infected patients, particularly the very young and the very old. These bloodstream infections can have serious complications, including death. *Salmonella* infections can also trigger pneumonia and phenomena such as reactive arthritis, which may result in long-term disability.

A fairly newly discovered pathogen, *E. coli 0157:H7* (commonly called *E. coli 0157*) is a very dangerous type of *E. coli*. Healthy cattle carry the bacteria, which are transferred from animal to animal, animal to human, and person to person through close contact or food. This pathogen can survive refrigeration and freezer storage. Thorough cooking to 160°F is recommended, as it generally kills *E. coli 0157*, which was the culprit in a western states illness outbreak in January of 1993. The national Centers for Disease Control and Prevention (CDC) estimate that *E. coli 0157* may cause 20,000 illnesses per year.

It is still very difficult to get accurate data on the incidence of foodborne illness in the United States. Most of the information gathered by the CDC is passively collected and depends upon doctors submitting cultures. That is, if a patient does not see a doctor, or the doctor does not collect a stool culture, the case does not enter the CDC's reporting system. Furthermore, of the major foodborne pathogens, laboratory-based surveillance is available only for *Salmonella*. Even with these deficiencies, several groups of investigators have attempted to estimate actual rates of disease occurrence, drawing on CDC databases and extrapolating from population-based studies in specific geographic areas. In some cases, the data suggest that foodborne pathogens account for up to 7 million cases of foodborne illness each year, and up to 7,000 deaths. Meat and poultry products contaminated with pathogenic microorganisms account for nearly 5 million cases of illness and more than 4,000 deaths.[16]

Although the health concerns of foodborne illness are paramount, the actual costs of foodborne illnesses also have a significant impact on society. Not only are the direct costs of medical treatment important, but other issues such as time lost from work, pain and inconvenience, and the burden on families and coworkers should be taken into account. The food industry also suffers significant costs due to foodborne illness, involving product recalls, plant closings and cleanup, higher premiums for product liability insurance, and, probably most important, loss of reputation and reduced product demand.

It has been estimated that 300 million dollars is spent on microbial foodborne diseases annually by the federal public health sector. It also has been estimated that federal costs average about 200 thousand dollars per foodborne illness outbreak. The USDA's Department of Economic Research Service and the CDC estimated that the costs of all foodborne illnesses in 1993 were between 5.6 and 9.4 billion dollars. Meat and poultry products accounted for 4.5 to 7.5 billion dollars of that cost, with the remaining 1.1 to 1.9 billion dollars attributed to nonmeat and poultry sources.[17]

There is a general consensus that change is needed in the U.S. food inspection service. Given the higher speed, higher volume, and more sophisticated slaughter and processing systems, as well as the increased risk of foodborne illness, change must come. Basically, the current federal food safety system is obsolete because it has failed to keep pace with changes involving the new foodborne threats. More people than ever are consuming commercially processed or commercially prepared foods. According to the FDA, consumer demand for "fresh" foods in convenient, ready to cook or eat forms has fostered the development of sophisticated processing and packaging systems that significantly increase product shelf life.[18] Back in 1983, FSIS requested the National Academy of Sciences (NAS) to evaluate its inspection system and recommend a modernization program. The resulting report, *Meat Poultry Inspection: The Scientific Basis of the Nation's Program,* was issued in 1985.[19] The NAS recommended that the FSIS focus on pathogenic organisms and require that all official establishments operate under a Hazard Analysis and Critical Control Point (HACCP) system to control pathogens and other safety hazards. Unfortunately the HACCP system was not initiated at that time. Two later NAS studies reinforced these earlier recommendations for both poultry and cattle inspection.[20] (*Note:* The HACCP system was developed by the Pillsbury Company and first presented at the 1971 National Conference on Food Protection. Pillsbury's main focus on food safety came about when the company was asked to design and produce foods to be used in space. Concerns about bacterial and viral contaminants and the result of illness in space were paramount in the successful production of safe and healthy food products for the early astronauts.)

THE HACCP APPROACH

Basically, the Hazard Analysis and Critical Control Point (HACCP) process has two parts. The hazard analysis portion of HACCP consists of the identification of sensitive ingredients, sensitive areas in the processing of the food or ingredients, problems involving people control, and so forth, from which critical safety points can be identified for monitoring. The critical control aspect of HACCP is concerned with those areas of food production (in going from raw materials to the finished product) where the loss of control may result in an unacceptable safety risk. Many company managers will be surprised to find that many, if not most, of the controls in an HACCP system are already in place and operating in their plants. This is especially true if they have written specifications for products and good quality control programs. The primary distinction of HACCP is that, rather than having isolated quality control checkpoints throughout the process, these controls are all put together in an interrelated and interlocking system. Thereafter, each point that must be monitored is checked and data are recorded by a designated individual. The frequency of monitoring must be established, and pertinent information is recorded in a log, along with the time of the recording.

In applying HACCP principles to foods, the following issues must be addressed:[21]

1. Description of the product and its intended use. The description should include those characteristics of the food product that may affect microbial growth, the intended shelf life, the type of packaging used, and other issues such as storage, distribution, preparation, and cooking procedures.
2. Preparation of flow diagrams.
3. Analysis of hazards. General microbiological risk assessments should be developed for each microbial, chemical, and physical hazard associated with the specific food and type of processing system.
4. Identification of critical control points. The critical control points are selected to eliminate or at least minimize any of the hazards associated with the product. The critical control points in the manufacturing and distribution flow diagrams can be incorporated into these tools.
5. An effective monitoring system. Matters such as recordkeeping, record review, corrective actions, and appropriate procedures when dealing with deviation should be incorporated into this system. In addition, test methods and sampling plans can be established.
6. Verification and control. This is an oversight function used to ensure that the HACCP program is effective. Individuals in various levels of management can review procedures to ensure that critical control points and the monitoring systems are appropriate and up-to-date.

The Implementation of HACCP

Seafood—Final Rule

As stated above, on December 18, 1995, the FDA issued its Final Rule on the Procedures for Safe and Sanitary Processing and Importing of Fish and Fishery Products. The procedures evolved from the FDA's proposed rule, issued on January 28, 1994.[22] The FDA also published a Notice of Availability of Draft Guidelines on how to develop HACCP controls for specific types of processing.[23] Thereafter, there were several requests for extensions of the comment period, which were granted by the FDA.

The FDA stated in its preamble to the proposed rule five principal reasons for the creation of these regulations: (1) to create a more effective and efficient system for ensuring the safety of seafood than currently exists; (2) to enhance consumer confidence; (3) to take advantage of the developmental work on the application of HACCP-type preventive controls for seafood that had already been undertaken by industry, academia, some states, and the federal government; (4) to respond to requests by seafood industry representatives that the federal government institute a mandatory, HACCP-type inspection system for their products; and (5) to provide U.S. seafood with continued access to world markets, where HACCP-type controls are increasingly becoming the norm.[24]

It should be noted that the safety of seafood presents special challenges both to industry and to the regulator. Seafood consists of hundreds of edible species from around the world, and contaminants such as bacteria and viruses, toxic chemicals, natural toxins, and parasites present special concerns. In addition, the harvesting of previously underutilized species can be expected to create new sources of process hazards that must be identified and controlled. Moreover, unlike beef and poultry, seafood is predominantly a wild-caught flesh food that frequently must be harvested under difficult conditions and at varying distances from processing, transport, and retail facilities. An additional complicating factor in ensuring the safety of seafood is the fact that no other flesh food is imported in as great a quantity, or from as many countries, as seafood. Over 55% of the seafood consumed in the United States is imported from approximately 135 countries.[25]

During the comment period before the issuance of the final rule, there were a number of comments addressing the legal basis for the new FDA regulations on seafood. The FDA issued its HACCP regulations for seafood under various sections of the Federal Food, Drug, and Cosmetic Act, including most significantly Sections 402(a)(1) and (a)(4) and 701(a).[26] Section 402(a)(1) of the Act states that a food is adulterated if it bears or contains any poisonous or deleterious substance that may render the food injurious to health.[27] Section 402(a)(4) of the Act states that a food is adulterated if it has been prepared, packaged, or held under unsanitary conditions whereby it may have been contaminated with filth, or whereby it may have been rendered injurious to health. It is important to recognize that Section 402(a)(4) of the Act addresses conditions that may render food injurious to health, rather than conditions that have actually *caused* the food to be injurious.[28] The question thus is whether the conditions in a plant are such that is reasonably possible that the food may be rendered injurious to health. The FDA stated that, if a seafood processor does not incorporate certain basic controls into its procedures for preparing, packaging, and holding food, it is reasonably possible that the food may be rendered injurious to health and, therefore, adulterated under the Act. Section 701(a) of the Act authorizes the agency to adopt regulations for the efficient enforcement of the Act.

One of the commentors questioned whether the FDA had met its responsibility for presenting the shortcomings in the existing law when attempting to demonstrate the need for these new regulations. In general, the Act provides a broad statutory framework for federal regulations to ensure that human food will not be injurious to health and to prevent commerce in adulterated foods. Given these concerns and its responsibility, the FDA stated it had concluded that it was necessary to require that firms incorporate certain basic measures into the way they process seafood. The agency also concluded that failure to incorporate these measures into a firm's processing procedures would mean that the firm would be producing the product under insanitary conditions whereby it could be rendered injurious to health.[29] Another commentor questioned whether the FDA had authority to issue the regulations because Congress had considered similar legislation but had not enacted it. The FDA stated that the fact that Congress had considered the issue but had not passed any bills did not preclude the FDA from implementing a mandatory seafood HACCP Program. The effect of legislation that was never enacted on a federal agency's initiatives was considered in *National Confectioner's Association v. Califano,* a case involving a challenge to the FDA's statutory authority to issue good manufacturing practice regulations for candymaking. The Court rejected the argument that the existence of legislation that was not enacted, which would have given the FDA express authority to require some of the things that the agency included in its regulations, indicated that Congress intended to exclude such authority from the Act as it was then written. The Court upheld the validity of the regulations by considering whether the statutory scheme as a whole justified the promulgation of the regulations. In addition, the fact that the 101st Congress did not pass any seafood bills did not necessarily amount to a refusal on the part of Congress to authorize a mandatory HACCP program.[30]

Another legal issue dealt with whether Section 402(a)(4) of the Federal Food, Drug, and Cosmetic Act was an appropriate authority upon which to base a mandatory HACCP program. Most of the concern hinged on whether the failure to have an HACCP Plan or to keep HACCP records could really be considered an "insanitary" condition under Section 402(a)(4) of the Act.[31] In addition, some commentors questioned whether safety issues relating to chemical or physical hazards, or to pesticides, unapproved additives, and drug residues, as included in the proposed regulations, could be deemed to have been the result of insanitary conditions. Two commentors expressed the view that Section 402(a)(4) of the Act is not concerned with food safety generally but only with safety problems caused by insanitary conditions.

In response, the FDA stated that the relevant case law supports a broad reading of the term "insanitary." In the *Nova Scotia* case cited above, the Court read "insanitary" to cover a wide set of circumstances necessary to ensure that food was not produced under conditions that could render it injurious to health. Specifically, the Court concluded that the FDA's regulations mandating time–temperature–salinity requirements for smoked fish products were within the agency's statutory authority under Section 402(a)(4) of the Act.[32] The Court rejected the argument that "insanitary" limited coverage under Section 402(a)(4) of the Act only to bacteria that could enter the raw fish from equipment in the processing environment and not to proper processing to kill bacteria that enter the processing facility in the raw fish itself.

As the Court noted, acceptance of a restrictive reading of Section 402(a)(4) of the Act would probably invalidate several existing FDA regulations, including those relating to the thermal processing of low-acid canned food in Part 113 (21 C.F.R. Part 113). The Court then concluded that, when dealing with public health, the statute should not be read too restrictively but should be consistent with the Act's overall purpose to protect the public health.[33] Finally, it should be noted that in all the comments received by the FDA regarding the seafood HACCP regulations, the supporters outnumbered the opponents by over ten to one. In fact, many of the strongest supporters were Seafood Trade Associations and seafood processors.

Summary of the Regulations

The FDA regulations for ensuring safe and sanitary processing of fish and fishery products (i.e., seafood) are outlined below, according to the appropriate sections of the regulations. The citations for the regulations are given as they appear in the Code of Federal Regulations, 21 C.F.R. Parts 123 and 1240.[34]

Section 123.3. Definitions

- *Critical control point:* a point, step, or procedure in a food process at which control can be applied, and a food safety hazard can as a result be prevented, eliminated, or reduced to acceptable levels.
- *Critical limit:* a maximum or a minimum value to which a physical, biological, or chemical parameter must be controlled at a critical control point to prevent, eliminate, or reduce to an acceptable level the occurrence of the identified food safety hazard.
- *Fish:* fresh or saltwater fin fish, crustaceans, other forms of aquatic animal life, including, but not limited to, alligator, frog, aquatic turtle, jellyfish, sea cucumber, and sea urchin and the roe of such animals (other than birds or mammals), and all mollusks where such animal life is intended for human consumption.
- *Fishery products:* any human food product in which fish is a characterizing ingredient.
- *Food safety hazard:* any biological, chemical, or physical property that may cause a food to be unsafe for human consumption.
- *Processing:* with respect to fish or fishery products, handling, storing, preparing, heading, eviscerating, shucking, freezing, changing into different market forms, manufacturing, preserving, packing, labeling, dockside unloading, or holding.

Section 123.6. Hazard Analysis and Hazard Analysis Critical Control Point (HACCP) Plan

- *Hazard Analysis:* Every processor shall conduct, or have conducted for it, a hazard analysis to determine whether there are food safety hazards that are reasonably likely to occur for each kind of fish and fishery product processed by that processor and to identify the preventive measures that the processor can apply to control those hazards. Such food safety hazards can be introduced both within and outside the processing plant environment, including food safety hazards that can occur before, during, and after harvest. A food safety hazard that is reasonably likely to occur is one for which a prudent processor would establish controls because experience, illness data, scientific reports, or other information has provided a basis for concluding that there is a reasonable possibility that it will occur, in a particular type of fish or fishery product being processed, in the absence of those controls.
- *The HACCP Plan:* Every processor shall have implemented a written HACCP Plan whenever a hazard analysis reveals one or more food safety hazards that are reasonably likely to occur, as described in paragraph (a) of this section. A HACCP Plan shall be specific to:
  (1) Each location where fish and fishery products are processed by that processor; and
  (2) Each kind of fish and fishery product processed by the processor. The Plan may group kinds of fish and fishery products together, or group kinds of production methods together, if the food safety hazards, critical control points, critical limits, and procedures required to be identified and performed in paragraph (c) of this section are identical for all fish and fishery products so grouped or for all production methods so grouped.[35]

The Contents of the HACCP Plan

- *Effective Date:* Although the FDA proposed that the final regulations be in force one year after their date of publication in the Federal Register, more than 60 comments were received by the FDA regarding the effective date. Based on the concerns of the commentors, the FDA agreed to implement the regulations two years after publication of the proposed rule; so, the effective date became December 18, 1997.

The regulations require that the HACCP shall, at a *minimum*, list the food safety hazards that are reasonably likely to occur, with consideration given to whether any food safety hazards are likely to occur as a result of the following:

1. Natural toxins.
2. Microbiological contamination.
3. Chemical contamination.
4. Pesticides.
5. Drug residues.
6. Decomposition in toxin-forming species.
7. Parasites.
8. Unapproved use of direct or indirect food or color additives.
9. Physical hazards.

In addition, critical control points designed to control food safety hazards that could be introduced in the processing plant environment must be included in the plan. Furthermore, the plan must include critical control points designed to control food safety hazards outside the plant before, during, and after harvest. Critical limits must be listed at each of the critical control points, and procedures (with a listing of the procedures and the frequency thereof) must be used to monitor each of the critical control points to ensure compliance with the critical limits.

Verification and recordkeeping procedures must be implemented in accordance with the regulations. Finally, the HACCP Plan must be signed and dated by the most responsible individual on-site at the processing facility or by a higher level official of the processor.[36]

Section 123.8. Verification. The regulations provide that every processor must verify that the HACCP Plan is adequate to control food safety hazards that are reasonably likely to occur, and that the plan is being effectively implemented. Verification shall include, at a minimum, a reassessment of the HACCP Plan whenever a change occurs that could affect the hazard analysis or alter the HACCP Plan in any way, or at least annually. In addition there is a requirement for ongoing verification activities. Moreover, at least within one week after critical control points are monitored and documented, a review shall occur. Corrective actions must also include reviewing records to ensure their completeness and to verify that appropriate corrective actions were taken in accordance with Section 123.7.

Section 123.9. Records. The recordkeeping requirement of the regulations requires that the name and the location of the processor or the importer be given, the date and the time of the activity that the record reflects be recorded, the signature initials of the person performing the operation be included, and, where appropriate, the identity of the product or the production code, if any, be recorded. All records must be retained at the processing facility or the importer's place of business in the United States for at least one year after the date when they were prepared, in the case of refrigerated products, and for at least two years after they were prepared in the case of frozen, preserved, or shelf-stable products.

Section 123.10. Training.   At a minimum, the regulations require that individuals be trained at least to the level of USDA curriculum to perform the functions of reviewing HACCP Plans, understanding and reviewing corrective actions, and performing records review. The trained individual need not be an employee of the processor.

Section 123.11. Sanitation Control Procedures.   The regulations require that each processor have and implement a written Sanitation Standard Operating Procedure (SSOP) or similar *document* that is specific to each location where fish and fishery products are produced. The SSOP should specify how the processor will meet the requirements for the sanitation conditions and practices that are to be monitored in accordance with the regulations. There must be monitoring of the following: the safety of the water that comes into contact with the food or food surfaces; conditions and cleanliness of the food contact surfaces, including utensils, gloves, and outer garments; prevention of cross contamination from insanitary objects; maintenance of hand-washing, hand-sanitizing, and toilet facilities; protection of food, food packaging materials, and food contact services from adulteration with lubricants, fuel, pesticides, cleaning compounds, sanitizing agents, and so on; proper labeling, storage, and use of toxic compounds; employee health conditions that could result in microbiological contamination of food; and exclusion of pests from the food plant. Sanitation control records must be maintained to monitor and to document the monitoring and the corrective measures of the sanitation program.

Meat and Poultry

On July 25, 1996, the Food Safety Inspection Service published in the Federal Register its Final Rule for "Pathogen Reduction; Hazard Analysis and Critical Control Point (HACCP) Systems." Basically, the Rule contains a series of regulatory changes to improve the safety of food products at every step, from the slaughter process through the manufacturing process, for meat and poultry. This is one of the first steps in what the FSIS calls its farm-to-table approach. Several significant changes will be made in the inspection system, as the new regulations require: (1) that each establishment develop and implement written sanitation standard operating procedures (sanitation SOPs); (2) regular microbial testing by slaughter establishments to verify the adequacy of process controls for the prevention and removal of fecal contamination and associated bacteria; (3) establishment of pathogen production performance standards for *Salmonella*, which slaughter establishments and the establishments producing raw ground products must meet; and (4) that all meat and poultry establishments develop and implement a system of preventive controls designed to improve the safety of their products, that is, an HACCP Plan.[37]

Effective Dates

The effective date of the new rule was July 25, 1996. However, there are specific applicability dates for the various components of the rule. The HACCP regulations, which are set forth in 9 C.F.R. Part 417, as well as the related provisions set forth in 9 C.F.R. 304, 327, and 381, have applicability dates as follows:

- In *large* establishments, defined as all establishments with 500 or more employees, an applicability date of January 26, 1998.
- In *smaller* establishments, defined as all establishments with 10 or more employees but fewer than 500, an applicability date of January 25, 1999.
- In *very small* establishments, defined as all establishments with fewer than 10 employees or annual sales of less than 2.5 million dollars, an applicability date of January 25, 2000.

The *E. coli* process control testing regulations, set forth in 9 C.F.R. 310.25(a) and 381.94(a), were applicable on January 27, 1997. Also, the Sanitation SOP regulations, set forth in 9 C.F.R. 416, were applicable on January 27, 1997. Finally, the *Salmonella* pathogen reduction standards regulation, set forth in 9 C.F.R. 310.25(b) and 9 C.F.R. 381.94(b), will be applicable simultaneously with the applicability dates of the HACCP.[38]

On February 3, 1995, the FSIS had published its proposed rule for pathogen reduction and HACCP in the meat and poultry industries. It is interesting to note the significant changes between the proposed rule and the final rule. One of the most important changes is that the proposed rule required *Salmonella* testing by the establishments themselves. Many of the subsequent comments received by FSIS considered *Salmonella* less useful then generic *E. coli* testing as an indicator of whether process control and slaughter establishments are effective in preventing microbial contamination. Based upon these public comments, FSIS modified its approach to establishing microbial performance standards; it agreed with the critics and decided to require that slaughter establishments conduct testing only for generic *E. coli* to verify their process controls. In addition, rather than setting regulatory standards, the FSIS established performance criteria based on national microbial baseline surveys for evaluating *E. coli* test results. Those test results that do not meet the performance criteria will indicate that the slaughter establishments may be maintaining inadequate process controls for fecal contamination. These results will be used in conjunction with other information to evaluate and make appropriate adjustments to ensure adequate process controls. The FSIS has not ruled out testing for *Salmonella*, but its investigators will do the *Salmonella* testing themselves.

In addition, the proposed rules set forth three near-term measures for raw meat and poultry products as part of its overall strategy for pathogen reduction: sanitation SOPs, antimicrobial treatments, and carcass cooling standards. However, based on the comments to the proposed rule, the FSIS reconsidered its approach to these near-term measures, which had been meant to help in the transition to the HACCP, and not necessarily to continue as mandatory elements of an HACCP-based system.

The FSIS did decide on and adopt in its Final Rule a mandatory sanitation SOP program, in the belief that mandating near-term sanitation SOPs would facilitate the transition to HACCP. However, the FSIS decided not to mandate antimicrobial treatments in slaughter establishments. Although the agency expects that antimicrobial treatments will play an important role in the design of slaughter HACCP plans as establishments institute controls to effectively reduce pathogens, as well as in meeting FSIS performance standards, it decided not to mandate the specific controls that establishments must adopt in their HACCP plans. The FSIS considers that the necessary improvements in food safety are better served by providing establishments the incentive and the flexibility to incorporate antimicrobial treatments in any manner that the food companies judge most effective for their particular operations, instead of having mandatory treatments.

As to the carcass cooling standards in the proposed rule, the FSIS, while continuing to consider appropriate performance standards necessary for the cooling of carcasses and raw meat, concluded that the specific time and temperature combinations it proposed were too restrictive, and that further review of this issue was necessary. Therefore, the FSIS extended the rulemaking process to consider alternative approaches to performance standards for carcass cooling within establishments. Concurrently, the FSIS stated in its Final Rule that it intends to develop rules covering the adoption of standards for the cooling of raw products during transportation, storage, and retail, restaurant, or food service sale.[39]

Finally, the timetable for implementing these programs was changed from that of the proposed rule. Basically, the time requirements were lengthened to give the FSIS time to implement its own transition program and to train inspectors and agency employees, as well to give the industry a chance to begin voluntary implementation of these programs.

With respect the implementation of HACCP programs, roughly 75% of the meat and poultry producers in the United States will be required to implement an HACCP Plan within 18 months of publication of the Final Rule, rather than the 30 months originally proposed. At the same time, very small establishments (those with fewer than ten employees or annual sales of less than 2.5 million dollars) will be provided an additional six months beyond the originally proposed three years to implement HACCP.

The Seven HACCP Principles

Although not explicitly listed as such in the codified regulatory text, the following seven HACCP Principles, first identified in 1992 by the National Advisory Committee on Microbial Criteria for Food (NACMCF), are embodied in the regulatory requirements for an HACCP Plan.[40]

Principle I. A *hazard analysis* of each process must be carried out. The purpose of the analysis is to identify and list the food safety hazards reasonably likely to occur in the production process for a particular product, and the preventive measures necessary to control the hazards. A food safety hazard is any biological, chemical, or physical property that may cause a food to be adulterated or otherwise unsafe for human consumption. A listed hazard must be of such a nature that its prevention, elimination, or reduction to acceptance levels is essential to the production of a safe food.[41]

Some questions to consider in a hazard analysis under Principle I include:

1. What potential hazards may be present in the animals to be slaughtered or the raw materials to be processed?
2. What may cause or lead to the contamination of finished products with pathogenic microorganisms or hazardous chemicals?
3. What is the likelihood of such contamination, and how can it be prevented?
4. Does the process include a controllable step that destroys pathogens?
5. What product safety devices may enhance consumer safety (metal detectors, filters, thermocouples)?
6. Is the product epidemiologically linked to a foodborne disease?[42]

Principle II. *Critical Control Points* (CCPs) of each process must be identified. A CCP is a point, step, or procedure where control can be applied and a food safety hazard prevented, eliminated, or reduced to an acceptable level. It is important to identify all the hazards and the steps in the process where they may be found. It is particularly important to identify CCPs for controlling microbial hazards throughout the production process because these hazards are the primary cause of foodborne illness. A CCP decision tree may be useful in this identification process. (A CCP decision tree developed by the NACMCF is set forth in the FSIS Final Rule on HACCP.[43])

Principle III. *Critical limits* for preventive measures associated with each critical control point must be established. A critical limit is the maximum or the minimum value to which a process parameter must be controlled at the critical control point in order to prevent, eliminate, or reduce to an acceptable level an identified physical, biological, or chemical food safety hazard. Process parameters used as guidelines to set critical limits include time, temperature, physical dimensions, humidity, moisture level, water activity, pH, salt concentration, chlorine, preservatives, or survival of target pathogens. These critical limits should be based upon applicable FSIS regulations or guidelines, FDA tolerances, and action levels, as well as scientific and technical literature and studies.

Principle IV. *Monitoring* of critical control points is necessary. An integral part of any HACCP program, monitoring consists of observations or measurements taken to assess whether parameters are within the established critical limits. Continuous monitoring is preferable, but when that is not feasible, the monitoring frequencies must be sufficient to ensure that the critical control points are under control.

Principle V. The use of *corrective actions* must be included when monitoring indicates that there is a deviation from a critical limit at a critical control point. Although the implementation of an HACCP Plan should preclude situations where correction is required, no guarantees exist. Therefore, a corrective action plan must be in place for the disposition of potentially unsafe or noncompliant products, as to well as identify and correct the cause of any deviation.

Principle VI. *Recordkeeping* is an essential aspect of any HACCP system. Consistent and reliable records must be generated during operations, and those records must be maintained and available for review.

Principle VII Finally, in any valid HACCP system there must be systematic *verification.* After the initial validation of the HACCP system, it is essential that there be periodic verification that the system is working correctly and effectively with respect to hazards. This verification involves the use of methods, procedures, or tests, in addition to those used for monitoring, to determine whether the HACCP system is in compliance with the HACCP Plan. The NACMCF recommends four processes to be used in the verification program: (1) a scientific and technical process known as validation, which determines that the CCPs and associated critical limits are adequate and sufficient to control likely hazards; (2) a process of ensuring, initially and on an ongoing basis, that the entire HACCP system functions properly; (3) documented periodic reassessments of the HACCP plan; and (4) definition of the FSIS's responsibility for certain actions (government verification) to ensure that the establishment's HACCP system is functioning adequately. The FSIS adopted Principle VII in its final rule on HACCP, thus making the establishments responsible for the first three processes and itself responsible for the fourth.[44]

Inspection under HACCP

In its background material for the Final Rule, the FSIS stated that it plans to make significant changes in its approach to overseeing the safety of meat and poultry products. Under the new approach using HACCP, the FSIS will rely less on after-the-fact detection of product and process defects and more on verification of the effectiveness of an establishment's processes and process controls designed to ensure food safety. With this in mind, beginning on the appropriate effective date for a particular establishment, FSIS personnel will carry out a general review of the establishment's HACCP Plan to determine its conformance with the seven HACCP principles. Thereafter, special teams of FSIS personnel will work in conjunction with the assigned inspectors to conduct in-depth reviews on a regular basis, to verify the plan's validity and adequacy in preventing food safety hazards. Then, anytime that the establishment's HACCP Plan is revised or amended, FSIS personnel will review the plan to confirm its conformance with the regulatory requirements.

In addition, the FSIS will also carry out its own verification activities through FSIS inspectors. These verification activities may include reviewing the establishment's monitoring records, reviewing particular production lots, direct observation of CCP controls, collecting samples for FSIS laboratory analysis, or confirming the establishment's verification activities for a particular process.

Although numerous commentors expressed concern about whether the FSIS planned to eliminate carcass-by-carcass inspection, the FSIS specifically stated that carcass-by-carcass inspection is a legal requirement that binds both the FSIS and industry (and it also addressed nonsafety considerations of inspections that are not part of the HACCP program). The FSIS will continue its carcass-by-carcass examination program.[45] However, it plans to examine its current tasks related to carcass inspection and to determine what changes, if any, can improve the effectiveness of the inspection process.

Small Business Concerns

A major concern of small slaughter/processing companies is their lack of familiarity with the HACCP program, whereas many larger establishments have already implemented and refined their HACCP programs. The FSIS has stated that it is planning an array of assistance activities that will facilitate the implementation of HACCP in small and very small establishments.[46]

The FSIS stated that it is developing 13 generic HACCP models for the major process categories, which will be available in draft form for public comment, and in final form at least six months before HACCP implementation is mandated for small businesses.[47]

In addition, the FSIS indicated that it would conduct HACCP demonstration projects for small and very small establishments during the two-year period following the promulgation of the Final Rule, with each project to be conducted at various sites to demonstrate how HACCP systems can work for various products under actual operating conditions. Finally, the FSIS included guidance materials in Appendices to the Final Rule to give additional guidance to small and very small establishments. These guidance materials include "Guidebook for the Preparation of HACCP Plans" (Appendix C to the Final Rule) and a "Hazards and Preventive Measures Guide" (Appendix D of the Final Rule).[48]

Sanitation Standard Operating Procedures

In its proposed rule, the FSIS stated that all meat and poultry establishments should be required to develop, maintain, and adhere to written sanitation standard operating procedures. This proposal was based upon the FSIS's belief that effective establishment sanitation is an essential factor in overall food safety and in the successful implementation of an industry-wide HACCP Plan. Insanitary facilities or equipment, poor food handling practices, improper personnel hygiene, and similar insanitary practices create an environment conducive to contamination.

The FSIS also determined that sanitation SOPs would improve the utilization of FSIS inspectors and resources by refocusing sanitation inspection activities on a program consisting mainly of oversight of establishments' activities. The FSIS reasoned that after sanitation SOPs were in place, FSIS inspection personnel could spend less time enforcing sanitation requirements and directing the correction of problems after they occurred. Instead, the FSIS inspectors could focus on oversight of the establishments' implementation of their own sanitation SOPs. Although many commentors questioned placing additional responsibility on the food establishments, the FSIS disagreed with them and mandated sanitation SOPs in the Final Rule. Thus, all inspected establishments must develop, implement, and maintain written sanitation SOPs, which must describe all procedures and activities conducted daily that the establishments will use to prevent direct contamination and adulteration of products. An important point that the FSIS clarified in the Final Rule is that each establishment must identify the establishment employee(s) responsible for the implementation and maintenance of each procedure in the sanitation SOP.[49]

Although the employee responsible for implementation and maintenance of the procedures of the sanitation SOP may be the person who actually performs such activities, he or she instead may be the employee in charge of ensuring that the sanitation procedures are carried out. All that is required is that the sanitation SOP identify the employee who is responsible for implementation and maintenance of the procedures in the sanitation SOP. The Final Rule does require the establishment to identify the employee(s) who will actually perform the sanitation procedures. In addition, more than one employee may be responsible for implementation and maintenance of the sanitation procedures. For example, one employee may be responsible for preoperational procedures and another for operational procedures. The rule allows such flexibility.

It is important to note that the FSIS clarified in the Final Rule that establishments must explicitly identify preoperational sanitation procedures in their written sanitation SOPs and distinguish them from sanitation activities to be carried out during operations. This requirement is designed to assist both the establishment and the FSIS in identifying which sanitation procedures are to be carried out each day before start-up of operations.

The FSIS is also requiring that sanitation SOPs be signed and dated by the individual with overall authority on-site or a higher level official of the establishment. In addition, the signee must indicate that the establishment will implement the sanitation SOPs. The Final Rule specifies that sanitation SOPs must be signed upon initiation and upon any modification.

Not surprisingly, the format and the content of sanitation SOPs are not specified in the final regulation, as many types of inspected establishments achieve their required sanitary compliance in different ways. The Rule allows the establishments flexibility to customize their own sanitation plans. For those facilities with no experience in establishing standard operating procedures for sanitation, the FSIS has published, as Appendix A to the Final Rule, a sample guideline for developing an SOP for sanitation.[50]

Summary of Regulations—Meat and Poultry

The following discussion gives a detailed summary of the critical regulations set forth in the Final Rule for HACCP and Pathogen Reduction.

Application for Inspection; Grant or Refusal of Inspection. Before being granted a federal inspection, an establishment shall have developed written sanitation standard operating procedures (SOPs), conducted a hazard analysis, and developed and validated an HACCP Plan.[51] A conditional grant of inspection shall be issued for a period not to exceed 90 days, during which the establishment must validate its HACCP Plan.[52]

Before producing new products for distribution and commerce, an establishment shall have conducted a hazard analysis and developed an HACCP Plan applicable to that product in accordance with Section 417.2. During a period not to exceed 90 days after the date when the new product is produced for distribution in commerce, the establishment shall validate its HACCP Plan.[53]

Sanitation. Both the Federal Meat Inspection Act and the Poultry Products Inspection Act are amended to include 9 C.F.R. Part 416 for the implementation of sanitation SOPs.[54] The new Rule requires that each official establishment develop, implement, and maintain written standard operating procedures for sanitation. The sanitation SOPs shall describe all procedures an official establishment will conduct daily, before and during operations, sufficient to prevent direct contamination or adulteration of product(s).[55] The sanitation SOPs shall be signed and dated by the individual with the overall authority on-site or a higher level official of the establishment. This signature signifies that the establishment will implement the sanitation SOPs as specified and will maintain them in accordance with the regulations. Procedures that are to be conducted prior to operations shall be identified as such and shall address, at a minimum, the cleaning of food contact surfaces of facilities, equipment, and utensils.[56] In addition, sanitation SOPs shall specify the frequency with which each procedure is to be conducted, and shall identify the establishment employees responsible for the implementation and maintenance of such procedures.[57]

Section 416.13 and 416.14 require that each official establishment conduct the proportional procedures in the sanitation SOPs before the start of operations, conduct all other procedures in the sanitation SOPs at the frequency specified, and conduct such daily monitoring as set forth in the SOPs. In addition, each official establishment must routinely evaluate the effectiveness of its SOP procedures to prevent direct contamination or adulteration of products.[58] Furthermore, the regulations state that each establishment must take the appropriate corrective actions determined by the FSIS or the establishment sanitation SOPs when the SOPs fail to prevent direct contamination or adulteration. Corrective actions include procedures to ensure appropriate disposition of product that may be contaminated, restore sanitary conditions, and prevent the reoccurrence of direct contamination or adulteration.[59]

Section 416.16 sets forth the recordkeeping requirements of the sanitation SOP Program. Each official establishment must maintain daily records sufficient to document the implementation and monitoring of the sanitation SOPs as well as any corrective action taken. The person identified as responsible in the sanitation SOPs must authenticate these records with his or her initials and the date.[60] The records required by this regulation may be maintained on computers if the establishment implements appropriate controls to ensure the integrity of the data. Records must be maintained for at least six months and made accessible to the FSIS. All such records must be maintained at the official establishment for 48 hours following their completion, after which time they may be maintained off-site, provided that they can be made available to FSIS within 24 hours of a request.[61]

Agency Verification.   The regulations also provide that the FSIS shall verify the adequacy and the effectiveness of the sanitation SOPs and the procedures used therein. Such verification may include: (a) reviewing the sanitation SOPs; (b) reviewing the daily records, and documenting the implementation of the sanitation SOPs and the procedures specified therein as well as any corrective action taken; (c) direct observation of the implementation of the sanitation SOPs ; and (d) direct observation or testing to assess the sanitary conditions in the establishment.[62]

Postmortem Inspection.   Postmortem Inspection is found at 9 C.F.R. Part 310 under the title "Meat Inspection, Microbial Testing."[63]

As part of the required postmortem inspection and criteria for verifying

Table 8.1.   Evaluation of *E. coli* Test Results

Slaughter Class	Lower Limit of Marginal (*m*)	Upper Limit of Marginal (*M*)	Number of Samples Tested (*n*)	Maximum Number Permitted in Marginal Range (*c*)
Steers/heifers	Negative*	100 cfu/cm^2	13	3
Cows/bulls	Negative*	100 cfu/cm^2	13	3
Market hogs	10 cfu/cm^2	10,000 cfu/cm^2	13	3

*Negative is defined by the sensitivity of the method used in the baseline study with a limit of sensitivity of at least 5 cfu/cm^2 carcass surface area.[68]

process controls, each official establishment that slaughters cattle and/or hogs shall test for *Escherichia coli* Biotype I (*E. coli*) and shall: (a) collect samples in accordance with the sampling techniques, methodology, and frequency set forth in the establishment's written specimen collection procedures; (b) obtain analytical results; and (c) maintain records of such analytical results.[64]

The establishment shall collect random samples from carcasses by sponging three sites on the selected carcass. On cattle carcasses, the samples must be taken from the flank, brisket, and rump. On swine carcasses, the samples must be taken from the ham, belly, and jowl areas.[65]

Samples shall be taken at a frequency proportional to the slaughter establishment's volume of production, at the following rates:

- Bovines: one test per 300 carcasses.
- Swine: one test per 1,000 carcasses.[66]

Establishments with very low volumes—that is, slaughtering no more than 6,000 bovines, 20,000 swine, or a combination of bovines and swine not exceeding 6,000 bovines and 20,000 animals total—shall collect one sample per week starting the first full week of June and continuing through August of each year. An establishment slaughtering both species shall take samples from the species it slaughters in larger numbers. Weekly samples shall be collected and tested until the establishment has completed and recorded one series of tests that meets the criteria set forth in Table 1 of the regulations (shown here as Table 8.1).[67]

Once the establishment meets the requirements listed above, weekly sampling and testing are optional unless changes are made in establishment facilities, equipment, personnel, or procedures that may affect the adequacy of existing process control measures as determined by the establishment or the FSIS.[69]

With regard to the analysis of samples, the establishment may employ any laboratory that uses any quantitative method for analysis of *E. coli,* as approved by the Association of Official Analytical Chemists International, or approved by a scientific body, and runs collaborative trials against the three-tube most probable number (MPN) method, in agreement with the 95% upper and lower confidence limits of the appropriate MPN Index.[70]

Recording of Test Results. The regulations require that establishments maintain accurate records of all test results in terms of cfu/cm^2 of surface area sponged. Results must be recorded on a process-controlled chart or table showing at least the 13 most recent test results, by class of livestock slaughtered, permitting evaluation of laboratory results in accordance with the criteria set forth in the regulations. These records shall be retained for a period of 12 months and made available to the FSIS upon request.

Criteria for Evaluation of Test Results. An establishment is considered operating within the criteria when the most recent *E. coli* test result does not exceed the upper limit (*M*), and the number of samples, if any, testing positive at levels above the limit is 3 or fewer out of the most recent 13 samples taken (see Table 8.1).

Failure to Meet Criteria. Test results that do not satisfy the above criteria are an indication that the establishment may not be maintaining process controls sufficient to prevent fecal contamination. The FSIS shall take further action as appropriate to ensure that the provisions of the law are being meet. If the establishment fails to test and record results, inspection shall be suspended in accordance with the rules adopted by the FSIS.[71]

Pathogen Reduction Performance Standard—Salmonella. As stated above, establishments are not required to sample and test for *Salmonella*; but the FSIS will sample and test for *Salmonella* within the criteria set forth in the regulations. The sampling and the testing of raw meat products in any individual establishment will be on an unannounced basis to determine the prevalence of *Salmonella* in such products and compliance with the standard.

The most significant difference between the proposed rule and the Final Rule is that in the latter the FSIS is not relying on *Salmonella* to be a process control indicator as well as a target organism for the Pathogen Reduction Performance Standards. Establishments will not be required by the Final Rule to test for *Salmonella* as had been previously proposed. Instead, the FSIS will obtain samples from slaughter establishments and establishments producing raw ground product or fresh pork sausage and test those samples for *Salmonella* to ensure that the Pathogen Reduction Performance Standards are being meet.

The *Salmonella* Pathogen Reduction Performance Standards are not lot-released standards, and the detection of *Salmonella* in a specific lot of raw products will not by itself result in the condemnation of that lot. The performance

Table 8.2.   *Salmonella* Performance Standards

Class of Product	Performance Standard (Percent Positive for Salmonella)[a]	Number of Samples Tested (n)	Maximum Number of Positives to Achieve Standard (c)
Steers/heifers	1.0%	82	1
Cows/bulls	2.7%	58	2
Ground beef	7.5%	53	5
Hogs	8.7%	55	6
Fresh pork sausages	N.A.[b]	N.A.	N.A.

(a) Performance Standards are FSIS's calculation of the national prevalence of *Salmonella* on the indicated raw product based on data developed by FSIS in its nationwide microbiological data collection programs and surveys.

(b) Not available; values for fresh pork sausage will be added upon completion of data collection programs for those products.

standards and the FSIS's enforcement approach are intended to ensure that each establishment is consistently achieving an acceptable level of performance with regard to controlling and reducing harmful bacteria on raw meat and poultry products.

The Pathogen Reduction Performance Standards for *Salmonella* are meant to complement the process control performance criteria for fecal contamination in *E. coli* testing.

The FSIS has stated that, in the future, it may develop Pathogen Reduction Performance Standards for a number of pathogens. *Salmonella* is one of the enteric pathogens, which, as a group, cause most preventable illnesses associated with meat and poultry. The FSIS stated that it has selected *Salmonella* because: (1) it is the most common bacterial cause of foodborne illness; (2) FSIS baseline data show that *Salmonella* colonizes a variety of mammals and birds, and occurs at frequencies that permit changes to be detected and monitored; (3) current methodologies can recover *Salmonella* from a variety of meat and poultry products; and (4) intervention strategies aimed at reducing fecal contamination and other sources of *Salmonella* on raw product should be effective against other pathogens.[72] Table 8.2 shows the *Salmonella* Performance Standards initially set forth by the FSIS and published in the Final Rule.

The FSIS will sample and test raw meat products in individual establishments on an unannounced basis. The frequency and the timing of such testing will be based upon an establishment's previous test results and other information concerning the establishment's performance. When the FSIS determines that an establishment has not met a performance standard, the FSIS will require it to take immediate action to meet the standard. If the establishment fails to meet the standard on the next series of tests, it will be required to reassess its HACCP Plan for the product and to take appropriate corrective measures. Failure to act in accordance with this rule, or failure to meet the standard on the third consecutive series, will constitute failure to maintain sanitary conditions and failure to maintain an adequate HACCP Plan. This will cause the FSIS to suspend inspection services until such time as satisfactory written assurance detailing the action taken to correct the HACCP system, or some other measure to reduce the prevalence of pathogens occurs.

Poultry Products.   Basically, the regulations applying to poultry products are very similar to the regulations for beef and pork establishments. Poultry plants must develop and implement written sanitation standard operating procedures (SOPs), conduct a hazard analysis, and develop and validate an HACCP Plan.[73] An important aspect of the pathogen reduction standard in testing for *E. coli* is that samples taken at random from carcasses shall be collected by taking a whole bird from the end of the chilling process, after the drip line, and rinsing it in an amount of buffer appropriate for the type of bird being tested.[74]

Samples will be taken at a frequency proportional to a slaughter establishment's volume of production, at the following rates:

- Chickens: one sample per 22,000 carcasses.
- Turkeys: one sample per 3,000 carcasses.

As in the meat industry, the regulations allow for alternative sampling in establishments slaughtering in very low volumes. An establishment annually slaughtering no more than 440,000 chickens, 60,000 turkeys, or a combination of chickens and turkeys not exceeding 60,000 turkeys and 440,000 birds total shall collect one sample per week starting in the first full week of June and continuing through August of each year. An establishment slaughtering both chickens and turkeys shall collect samples from the species it slaughters in larger numbers. Weekly samples shall be collected and tested until the establishment has completed and recorded one series of 13 tests that meets the criteria shown in Table 8.3.[75]

As in the beef and pork industry, the analysis of the samples and the recording of test results are set forth in the regulations, under the same type of criteria. Failure to meet the criteria indicates that an establishment may not be maintaining process controls sufficient to prevent fecal contamination. The Final Rule also sets forth FSIS testing for *Salmonella* similar that for beef and pork. Table 8.4 gives the *Salmonella* Performance Standards for poultry products.

The FSIS will sample and test raw poultry products in an individual establish-

Table 8.3. Evaluation of *E. coli* Test Results

Slaughter Class	Lower Limit of Marginal (*m*)	Upper Limit of Marginal (*M*)	Number of Samples Tested (*n*)	Maximum Number Permitted in Marginal Range (*c*)
Broilers	100 cfu/mi	1,000 cfu/mi	13	3
Turkeys	N.A.[a]	N.A.	N.A.	N.A.

(a) Not available; values for turkeys will be added upon completion of data collection program for turkeys.

Table 8.4. *Salmonella* Performance Standards

Class of Product	Performance Standard (Percent Positive for *Salmonella*)[a]	Number of Samples Tested (*n*)	Maximum Number of Positives to Achieve Standard (*c*)
Broilers	20.0%[b]	51	12
Ground chicken	44.6	53	26
Ground turkey	49.9	53	29
Turkeys	N.A.[b]	N.A.	N.A.

(a) Performance Standards are FSIS's calculation of the national prevalence of *Salmonella* on the indicated raw products based on data developed by FSIS in its nationwide microbiological baseline data collection programs and surveys.

(b) Standard is based on partial analysis of baseline survey data; subject to confirmation upon publication of baseline survey report.[76]

ment on an unannounced basis to determine the prevalence of *Salmonella*. Non-compliance will constitute failure to maintain sanitary conditions and ultimately result in the suspension of inspection services.[77]

Hazard Analysis and Critical Control Point (HACCP) Systems. Under 9 C.F.R. Part 417, the FSIS has set forth its Final Rule regarding the implementation of HACCP for the beef, pork, and poultry industries. As required by the Final Rule, the first step in implementing an HACCP System is to conduct a hazard analysis.[78] The establishment can conduct the hazard analysis itself or have another party do it. The hazard analysis is designed to discover the food safety hazards reasonably likely to occur in the production process and to identify preventive measures that the establishment can apply to control those hazards. The hazard analysis must include food safety hazards that may occur before, during, or after entry into the establishment. In addition, a hazard analysis must be conducted for any particular type of product being processed. Food safety hazards might be expected to come from the following sources: (1) natural toxins, (2) microbiological contamination, (3) chemical contamination, (4) pesticides, (5) drug residues, (6) zoonotic diseases, (7) decomposition, (8) parasites, (9) unapproved use of direct or indirect food or color additives, and (10) physical hazards.[79]

In addition, every establishment must develop and implement a *written* HACCP Plan covering each product of the establishment whenever a hazard analysis reveals one or more food safety hazards that are reasonably likely to occur. The plan must cover products in the following processing categories:

1. Slaughter/all species.
2. Raw products/ground.
3. Raw products/not ground.
4. Thermally processed/commercially sterile products.
5. Not heat-treated/shelf-stable products.
6. Heat-treated/shelf-stable products.
7. Fully cooked/not shelf-stable products.
8. Heat-treated but not fully cooked/not shelf-stable products.
9. Products with secondary inhibitors/not shelf-stable.[80]

The rule provides that a single HACCP Plan may encompass multiple products within a single processing category if the food safety hazards, critical control points, critical limits, and procedures are essentially the same. HACCP Plans for thermally processed/commercially sterile products do not have to address the food safety hazards associated with microbiological contamination if the products are made in accordance with the requirements of Part 318, Subpart G, or Part 381, Subpart X.[81]

Contents of the HACCP Plan.   The HACCP Plan at a minimum must contain the following:
1. List of food safety hazards that must be controlled for each process.
2. List of critical control points for each of the identified food safety hazards.
3. List of critical limits that must be met at each of the critical control points.
4. List of procedures that will be used to monitor each of the critical control points to ensure compliance.
5. All corrective actions to be followed in response to any deviation from a critical limit at a critical control point.
6. A recordkeeping system that documents monitoring of the critical control points.
7. List of the verification procedures and the frequency at which they will be performed.[82]

Finally, the HACCP Plan must be signed and dated by the responsible establishment individual.[83]

Training. The Final Rule states that only an individual who has successfully completed a course of instruction in the application of the seven HACCP principles for meat or poultry processing, including the segment on the development of an HACCP Plan for a specific product, will be permitted to develop an HACCP Plan. The individual need not be an employee of the establishment. In addition, only a trained individual can reassess and modify the HACCP Plan according to the Rule.[84]

CONCLUSION

The establishment of a federal microbiological inspection program is an extremely important step toward improving the national food safety system. Those organizations that have voluntarily established an HACCP program in their facilities have shown the benefits of this type of program.

The FDA and USDA are jointly working on rulemaking to improve food safety inspection programs. Some of the problems of these programs, such as inefficient inspection overlap, differing enforcement tools, and a general lack of coordination, should be eliminated with this new course of action. Hopefully, the United States is entering a new era of food safety inspection, with better and safer products for its consumers.

NOTES

1. FDA, Procedures for the Safe and Sanitary Procedures and Importing of Fish and Fishery Products: Final Rule, 60 F.R. No. 65,096, 242, Dec. 1995.
2. Federal Meat Inspection Act. Pub.L.No. 90-201, Dec. 1967, 21 U.S.C. § 601 et seq.
3. Poultry Products Inspection Act (PPIA). 21 U.S.C. § 451 et seq. Pub.L.No. 85-172, Aug. 28, 1957, 71 Stat. 441, as amended.
4. Wholesome Meat Act of 1967. Pub.L.No. 90-201, § 1, 81 Stat. 584, Dec. 15, 1967.
5. Wholesome Poultry Products Act. Pub.L.No. 90-492, Aug. 18, 1968, 82 Stat. 791, as amended.

6. Booz, Allen, and Hamilton, Inc. *Study of the Federal Meat and Poultry Inspection Program, Volume 1—Description of the Meat and Poultry Inspection Program, June 1977; Volume 2—Opportunities for Change—and Evaluation of Specific Alternatives, June 1977; Volume 3—Executive Summary, July 1977.*

7. Id.

8. FSIS, *Added Strength in Meat and Poultry Inspection Program* (1978).

9. Id.

10. FSIS, Pathogen Reduction; Hazard Analysis and Critical Control Point (HACCP) Systems, Proposed Rule, 60 F.R. No. 23, 6774, Feb. 3, 1995.

11. Douglas L. Archer, "The Need for Flexibility in HACCP," *Food Technology* (May 1990): 174–78.

12. See Herman Koren, *Handbook of Environmental Health and Safety* (Boca Raton, FL: CRC Press, 1996).

13. M. J. Blaser, I. D. Berkowitz, F. LaForce, J. Cravens, I. Reller, and W-L.L. Wang, "Campylobacter Enteritis: Clinical and Epidemiological Features," *Ann. Intern. Med.* 91 (1979).

14. D. Y. Graham, "*Campylobacter pylori* and Peptic Ulcer Disease," *Gastroenterology* 96 (Suppl. 2) (1989): 615.

15. B. G. Gellin and C. V. Broome, "Listeriosis," *J. Am. Med. Assn.* 216 (1989): 1313.

16. FSIS, Pathogen Reduction; Hazard Analysis and Critical Control Point (HACCP) Systems, 60 F.R. No. 23, 6774, Feb. 3, 1995.

17. Id.

18. Edolphus Towns, Memorandum—Hearing, "Reinventing the Food Safety System: Review of FDA's Food Safety Programs," May 20, 1994.

19. NRC, Committee on the Scientific Basis of the Nation's Meat and Poultry, Inspection Program, *Meat and Poultry Inspection: The Scientific Basis of the Nation's Program* (Washington, DC: Food and Nutrition Board, Committee on Life Science, National Research Council, National Academy Press, 1985).

20. NRC, Committee on Public Health Risk Assessment of Poultry Inspection Programs, *Poultry Inspection: The Basis for Risk-Assessment Approach* (Washington, DC: Food and Nutrition Board, Commission on Life Sciences, National Research Council, 1987). See also NAS, Committee on Evaluation of USDA Streamlined Inspection System for Cattle (SIS), *Cattle Inspection* (Washington, DC: Food and Nutrition Board, Institute of Medicine, National Academy of Sciences, National Academy Press, 1990).

21. K. E. Stevenson, "Implementing HACCP in the Food Industry," *Food Technology* (May 1990): 179–80.

22. FDA, Procedures for the Safe and Sanitary Processing and Importing of Fish and Fishery Products; Proposed Rule, 59 F.R. 4142, Jan. 28, 1994.

23. FDA, Fish and Fishery Products Hazards and Control Guide, 59 F.R. 16655, Apr. 7, 1994.
24. FDA, Procedures for the Safe and Sanitary Processing and Importing of Fish and Fishery Products; Final Rule, 60 F.R. 65097, Dec. 18, 1995.
25. Id.
26. Federal Food, Drug, and Cosmetic Act, 21 U.S.C. 342(a)(1) and (a)(4) and 371(a).
27. Id.
28. See *U.S. v. One-Thousand Two-Hundred Cans, Pasteurized Whole Eggs, etc.,* 339 F. Supp. 131, 141 (N.D.Ga. 1972).
29. Id. at 65099; see *U.S. v. Nova Scotia Food Products Corp.* 568 F.2d 240, 247 (2d Cir. 1977).
30. Id.
31. Id. at 65099.
32. *U.S. v. Nova Scotia Food Products Corp.,* 568 F.2d 240 (2d Cir. 1977).
33. See also *U.S. v. Bacto-Unidisk,* 394 U.S. 784, 798 (1969); *U.S. v. Dotterweich,* 320 U.S. 277, 280 (1943).
34. 21 C.F.R. Parts 123 and 1240.
35. 21 C.F.R. Part 123.
36. Id. at 65,198.
37. FSIS, Pathogen Reduction; Hazardous Analysis and Critical Control Point (HACCP) Systems Final Rule, 61 F.R. 38805, July 25, 1996.
38. Id.
39. Id. at 38,812.
40. Id. at 38814–17.
41. Id. at 38815.
42. Id.
43. Id. at 38816—See Figure 1.
44. Id. at 38816–17.
45. Id. at 38818.
46. Id. at 38819–20.
47. Id.
48. The Appendices to the Final Rule are included in Appendix E of this book.
49. Id. at 38830.
50. Final Rule—Appendix A—Guidelines for Developing a Standard Operating Procedure for Sanitation (Sanitation SOP's) in Federally Inspected Meat and Poultry Establishments. See Appendix E to this book.
51. 9 C.F.R. Part 304 (§ 304.3/Conditions for Receiving Inspection).
52. Id. at § 304.3(b).
53. Id. at § 304.3(c).
54. 9 C.F.R. Part 308, 9 C.F.R. Part 416, authority: 21 U.S.C. §§ 601–695; 7 C.F.R. 2.18, 2.53; 21 U.S.C. 451–470, 601–695; 7 U.S.C. 450, 1901–1906.
55. 9 C.F.R. Part 416.11, § 416.12(a).

56. 9 C.F.R. § 416.12.
57. Id. at § 416.12(d).
58. Id. at § 416.13 and 416.14.
59. Id. at § 416.15(b).
60. Id. at § 416.16(a).
61. Id. at § 416.16(b)(c).
62. Id. at § 416.17.
63. Authority: 21 U.S.C. 601–695; 7 C.F.R. 2.18, 2.53. Part 310 is amended by adding a new § 310.25.
64. Id. at § 310.25(a).
65. Id. at § 310.25(2).
66. Id. at (a)(2)(iii).
67. Id. at § 310.25(v)(A).
68. Id.
69. Id. at (a)(2)(v)(B).
70. Id. at (a)(3).
71. Id. at (a)(v)(b)(6), (7).
72. 61 C.F.R. 144 at 38846 (July 25, 1996).
73. Id. at 38866, 9 C.F.R. Part 381.
74. See Appendix G of the Final Rule/Guidelines for *E. coli* Testing for Process Control Verification in Poultry Slaughter Establishments. The entire guideline for *E. coli* testing for poultry plants is set forth in the Appendix to the Final Rule (see Appendix E of this book).
75. 61 F.R. No. 144, 38867 (1996).
76. Id.
77. Id. at 38868.
78. 9 C.F.R. § 417.2.
79. Id. at 38869 (9 C.F.R. 417.2).
80. 9 C.F.R. 417.2(b).
81. 9 C.F.R. 417.2(b)(3).
82. 9 C.F.R. 417.2(c).
83. Id. at 38869 and 38870.
84. 9 C.F.R. § 417.7.

Chapter 9

Related Regulations

CHAPTER OBJECTIVES:

The reader will:

1. *Acquire a basic understanding of some other laws and regulations applicable to the food industry.*
2. *Acquire a general understanding of other applicable health and safety regulations.*
3. *Acquire a basic understanding of environmental requirements applicable to the food industry.*

In addition to the myriad food-related federal and state regulations for which the food industry must ensure compliance, a variety of related laws and regulations, in peripheral areas such as safety and health, the environment, employment discrimination, and others, also must be addressed. In most food-related industries, an extensive labor force is utilized to complete the essential functions of the job. Thus, a substantial number of additional employment-related laws normally are applicable in this setting. Although most of these laws are directed at the workforce producing the food product rather than the food product itself, these laws and regulations play a major role in the methodology and practices of the food producers. This chapter discusses several selected areas of the law that directly impact food industry personnel.

OCCUPATIONAL SAFETY AND HEALTH ACT

Before the Occupational Safety and Health Act (OSH Act) of 1970 was enacted,[1] safety and health was limited to specific industry safety and health laws and laws that governed federal contractors. In the years before the OSH Act, Congress gradually began to regulate the safety and health of the American workplace through such laws as the Walsh–Healey Public Contracts Act of 1936, the Labor Management Relations Act (Taft–Hartley Act) of 1947, the Coal Mine Safety Act of 1952, and the McNamara–O'Hara Public Service Contract Act of 1965.

With the passage of the controversial OSH Act, federal and state government agencies became actively involved in managing health and safety in the food industry. Employers were placed on notice that unsafe and unhealthful conditions and acts no longer would be permitted. In many food industry circles, the Occupational Safety and Health Administration (OSHA) became synonymous with the "safety police," and a number of food industry employers were forced under penalty of law to address safety and health issues in their workplaces during the early years of the OSH Act.

The OSH Act covers virtually every food industry workplace that has one or more employees and engages in a business that in any way affects interstate commerce.[2] The Act covers employment in every state, the District of Columbia, Puerto Rico, Guam, the Virgin Islands, American Samoa, and the Trust Territory of the Pacific Islands.[3] The Act does not, however, cover employees where other state or federal agencies have jurisdiction that requires the agencies to prescribe or enforce their own safety and health regulations.[4] It also does not cover federal,[5] state, and local governments[6] and Native American reservations.[7]

The OSH Act requires every food industry employer engaged in interstate commerce to furnish employees "a place of employment . . . free from recognized hazards that are causing, or are likely to cause, death or serious harm."[8] To help employers create and maintain safe work environments and to enforce laws and regulations to ensure safe and healthful work environments, the OSH Act created the Occupational Safety and Health Administration, a new agency under the direction of the Department of Labor. The most widely known enforcement agency, OSHA has been granted broad regulatory powers to promulgate regulations or standards, investigate, inspect, issue citations, and propose penalties for violations.

The OSH Act also established an independent agency to review OSHA citations and decisions, the Occupational Safety and Health Review Commission (OSHRC). The OSHRC is a quasijudicial, independent administrative agency composed of three commissioners, appointed by the president, who serve staggered six-year terms. It has the power to issue orders, to uphold, vacate, or modify OSHA citations and penalties, and to direct other appropriate relief and penalties.[9]

The educational arm of the OSH Act is the National Institute for Occupational Safety and Health (NIOSH), which was created as a specialized educational agency of the existing National Institutes of Health.[10] NIOSH conducts occupational safety and health research and develops criteria for new OSHA standards. It can conduct workplace inspections, issue subpoenas, and question employees and employers, but it does not have the power to issue citations or penalties.[11]

Notwithstanding OSH Act enforcement through the above federal agencies, OSHA encourages individual states to take responsibility for OSHA administration and enforcement within their own respective boundaries.[12] A state may request and be granted the right to adopt state safety and health regulations and enforcement mechanisms. In Section 18(b), the Act provides that any state "which, at any time, desires to assume responsibility for development and the enforcement therein of occupational safety and health standards relating to any . . . issue with respect to which a federal standard has been promulgated . . . shall submit a state plan for the development of such standards and their enforcement."[13] For a state plan to be placed into effect, the state must develop and submit the proposed program to the Secretary of Labor for review and approval. The Secretary must certify that the state plan's standards are "at least as effective" as the federal standards, and that the state will devote adequate resources to administering and enforcing standards.[14] In most state plans, the agency develops more stringent safety and health standards than OSHA[15] and usually develops more stringent enforcement schemes.[16] The Secretary of Labor has no statutory authority to reject a state plan if the proposed standards or the enforcement scheme is more strict than the OSHA standards, but can reject the state plan if the standards are below the minimum limits set under OSHA standards.[17] These states are known as "state plan" states and territories.[18] As of 1995, there were 21 states and 2 territories with functional state plan programs.[19] Food Industry employers in state plan states and territories must comply with their states' regulations; federal OSHA plays virtually no role in regulation or enforcement.

The primary questions that food industry employers need to ask when determining jurisdiction under the OSH Act are:

1. Am I a covered employer under the OSH Act?
2. If I am a covered employer, what regulations must I follow to ensure compliance?

The answer to the first question is "yes" for every class of private sector employer. Any employer in the United States that employs one or more persons and is engaged in a business that in any way affects interstate commerce is within the scope of the OSH Act.[20] The phrase "interstate commerce" has been broadly construed by the U.S. Supreme Court, which found that interstate commerce "goes well beyond persons who are themselves engaged in interstate or foreign commerce."[21] In essence, anything that crosses state lines, whether a person or goods and services, places the employer in interstate commerce. Although there are exceptions to this general statement,[22] "interstate commerce" generally has been "liberally construed to effectuate the congressional purpose" of the OSH Act.[23]

Upon finding that it is covered by the OSH Act, an employer must distinguish between state plan jurisdiction and federal OSH Act jurisdiction. If its facilities or operations are located within a state plan state, an employer must comply with the regulations of that state. Safety and health professionals should contact their state department of labor to acquire the pertinent regulations and standards. If facilities or operations are located in a federal OSHA state, the applicable standards and regulations can be acquired from an area OSHA office or found in the Code of Federal Regulations at 29 C.F.R. Section 1910 et seq.

A common jurisdictional mistake occurs when an employer operates multiple facilities in different locations.[24] Safety and health professionals should ascertain which state or federal agency has jurisdiction over particular facilities or operations, and which regulations and standards apply.

The OSH Act requires that a covered food industry employer comply with specific occupational safety and health standards and all rules, regulations, and orders issued pursuant to the OSH Act that apply to the workplace.[25] The OSH Act also requires that all standards be based on research, demonstration, experimentation, or other appropriate information.[26] The Secretary of Labor is authorized under the Act to "promulgate, modify, or revoke any occupational safety and health standard,"[27] and the OSH Act describes the procedures that the Secretary must follow when establishing new occupational safety and health standards.[28]

The OSH Act authorizes three ways to promulgate new standards. From 1970 to 1973, the Secretary of Labor was authorized in Section 6(a)[29] of the Act to adopt national consensus standards, and was permitted to establish federal safety and health standards without following lengthy rulemaking procedures. Many of the early OSHA standards were adapted mainly from other areas of regulation, such as the National Electric Code and American National Standards Institute (ANSI) guidelines. But this promulgation method is no longer in effect.

The usual method of issuing, modifying, or revoking a new or existing OSHA standard, set out in Section 6(b) of the OSH Act, is known as informal rulemaking. It requires notice to interested parties, through subscription in the Federal Register of the proposed regulation and standard, and provides an opportunity for comment in a nonadversarial administrative hearing.[30] The proposed standard can also be advertised through magazine articles and other publications, thus letting interested parties know of the proposed standard and regulation. This method differs from the requirements of most other administrative agencies that follow the Administrative Procedure Act,[31] in that the OSH Act provides interested persons an opportunity to request a public hearing with oral testimony and requires the Secretary of Labor to publish in the Federal Register notice of the time and the place of such hearings. Although it is not required under the OSH Act, the

Secretary of Labor has directed by regulation that OSHA follow a more rigorous procedure for comment and hearing than other administrative agencies.[32] Upon notice and request for a hearing, OSHA must provide a hearing examiner to listen to oral testimony, and all testimony is preserved in a verbatim transcript. Interested persons are provided an opportunity to cross-examine OSHA representatives or others on critical issues. The Secretary must state the reasons for the action to be taken on the proposed standard, and the statement must be supported by substantial evidence in the record as a whole.

The Secretary of Labor has authority not to permit oral hearings and to call for written comment only. Within 60 days after the period for written comment or oral hearings, the Secretary must decide whether to adopt, modify, or revoke the standard in question. The Secretary can also decide not to adopt a new standard. The Secretary then must publish a statement of the reasons for any decision in the Federal Register, and OSHA regulations mandate that the Secretary provide a supplemental statement of significant issues in the decision. Safety and health professionals should be aware that the standard as adopted and published in the Federal Register may be different from the proposed standard. The Secretary is not required to reopen hearings when the adopted standard is a "logical outgrowth" of the proposed standard.[33]

The final method, and the one most infrequently used, is the emergency temporary standard permitted under Section 6(c).[34] The Secretary of Labor may establish a standard immediately if it is determined that employees are subject to grave danger from exposure to substances or agents known to be toxic or physically harmful, and an emergency standard would protect the employees from the danger. An emergency temporary standard becomes effective on publication in the Federal Register and may remain in effect for six months. During this six-month period, the Secretary must adopt a new permanent standard or abandon the emergency standard.

Only the Secretary of Labor can establish new OSHA standards. Recommendations or requests for an OSHA standard can come from any interested person or organization, including employees, employers, labor unions, environmental groups, and others.[35] When the Secretary receives a petition to adopt a new standard or to modify or revoke an existing standard, he or she usually forwards the request to NIOSH and the National Advisory Committee on Occupational Safety and Health (NACOSH),[36] or the Secretary may use a private organization such as ANSI for advice and review.

A food industry employer is required to maintain a place of employment free from recognized hazards that are causing or are likely to cause death or serious physical harm, even if there is no specific OSHA standard addressing the circumstances. Under Section 5(a)(1), the general duty clause, a food industry employer may be cited for a violation of the OSH Act if the condition causes harm or is likely to cause harm to employees, even if OSHA has not promulgated a standard specifically addressing the particular hazard. The general duty clause

Table 9.1. Violation and Penalty Schedule

Penalty	Old Penalty Schedule (in dollars)	New Penalty Schedule (1990) (in dollars)
De minimis notice	0	0
Nonserious	0–1,000	0–7,000
Serious	0–1,000	0–7,000
Repeat	0–1,000	0–70,000
Willful	0–10,000	*25,000 minimum 70,000 maximum
Failure to abate notice	0–1,000 per day	0–7,000 per day
New posting penalty		0–7,000

*The minimum monetary fine is calculated in accordance with the number of employees. The minimum monetary fine in this category is $5,000.00 for small employers and $25,000.00 for large employers.

is a "catch-all" standard encompassing potential hazards that have not been specifically addressed in the OSHA standards. For example, if a food industry company is cited for an ergonomic hazard, and there is not an ergonomic standard to apply, the hazard will be cited under the general duty clause.

Prudent food industry managers often take a proactive approach to maintain their competency in this expanding area of OSHA regulations. As noted previously, the first notice of any new OSHA standard, modification of an existing standard, revocation of a standard, or emergency standard must be published in the Federal Register. Safety and health professionals use the Federal Register, or professional publications that monitor it, to track the progress of proposed standards. With this information, they can provide testimony to OSHA when necessary, prepare their organizations for acquiring resources and personnel necessary to achieve compliance, and get a head start on developing compliance programs to meet requirements in a timely manner.

The OSH Act provides for a wide range of penalties, from a simple notice with no fine to criminal prosecution. The Omnibus Budget Reconciliation Act of 1990 multiplied maximum penalties sevenfold. Violations are categorized and penalties may be assessed as outlined in Table 9.1.

Each alleged violation is categorized and the appropriate fine issued by the OSHA area director. It should be noted that each citation is separate and may carry with it a monetary fine. The gravity of the violation is the primary factor in determining penalties.[37] In assessing the gravity of a violation, the compliance officer or the area director must consider (1) the severity of the injury or illness that could result and (2) the probability that an injury or illness could occur as a result of the violation.[38] Specific penalty assessment tables assist the area director or the compliance officer in determining the appropriate fine for the violation.[39]

After selecting the appropriate penalty table, the area director or the compliance officer determines the degree of probability that injury or illness will occur by considering:

1. The number of employees exposed.
2. The frequency and the duration of the exposure.
3. The proximity of employees to the point of danger.
4. Factors, such as the speed of the operation, that require work under stress.
5. Other factors that might significantly affect the degree of probability of an accident.[40]

OSHA has defined a serious violation as "an infraction in which there is a substantial probability that death or serious harm could result . . . unless the employer did not or could not with the exercise of reasonable diligence, know of the presence of the violation."[41] Section 17(b) of the OSH Act requires that a penalty of up to $7,000 be assessed for every serious violation cited by the compliance officer.[42] In assembly line operations in the food industry with duplicate machinery and processes, if one process is cited as possessing a serious violation, it is possible that each of the duplicate processes or machines may be cited for the same violation. Thus, if a serious violation is found in one machine, and there are many other identical machines in the enterprise, a very large monetary fine for a single serious violation is possible.[43]

Currently the greatest monetary liabilities are for repeat violations, willful violations, and failure to abate cited violations. A repeat violation is a second citation for a violation that was cited previously by a compliance officer. OSHA maintains records of all violations and must check for repeat violations after each inspection. A willful violation is the employer's purposeful or negligent failure to correct a known deficiency. This type of violation, in addition to carrying a large monetary fine, exposes the employer to a charge of an "egregious" violation and the potential for criminal sanctions under the OSH Act or state criminal statutes if an employee is injured or killed as a direct result of the willful violation. Failure to abate a cited violation has the greatest cumulative monetary liability of all. OSHA may assess a penalty of up to $1,000 per day per violation for each day in which a cited violation is not brought into compliance. In assessing monetary penalties, the area or regional director must consider the good faith of the employer, the gravity of the violation, the employer's past history of compliance, and the size of the employer. Joseph Dear, Assistant Secretary of Labor, noted recently that OSHA would start using its egregious case policy, which has seldom been invoked in recent years.[44] Under the egregious violation policy, when violations are determined to be conspicuous, penalties are cited for each violation, instead of the violations being combined to produce a single, smaller penalty.

Besides providing for potential civil or monetary penalties, OSHA regulations may be used as evidence in negligence, product liability, workers' compensation, and other actions involving employee safety and health issues.[45] OSHA standards and regulations are baseline requirements for safety and health that must be met, not only to achieve compliance with the OSHA provisions, but also to safeguard an organization against other potential civil actions.

The OSH Act provides for criminal penalties in four circumstances.[46] First, anyone inside or outside of the Department of Labor or OSHA who gives advance notice of an inspection without authority from the Secretary may be fined up to $1,000, imprisoned for up to six months, or both. Second, any employer or person who intentionally falsifies statements or OSHA records that must be prepared, maintained, or submitted under the OSH Act may, if found guilty, be fined up to $10,000, imprisoned for up to six months, or both. Third, any person responsible for a violation of an OSHA standard, rule, order, or regulation that causes the death of an employee may, upon conviction, be fined up to $10,000, imprisoned for up to six months, or both. If the person is convicted for a second violation, punishment may be a fine of up to $20,000, imprisonment for up to one year, or both.[47] Finally, if an individual is convicted of forcibly resisting or assaulting a compliance officer or other Department of Labor personnel, a fine of $5,000, three years in prison, or both can be imposed. Any person convicted of killing a compliance officer or other OSHA or Department of Labor personnel acting in an official capacity may be sentenced to prison for any term of years or life.

OSHA does not have authority to impose criminal penalties directly; instead, it refers cases for possible criminal prosecution to the U.S. Department of Justice. Criminal penalties must be based on violation of a specific OSHA standard, not on a violation of the general duty clause. These prosecutions are conducted like any other criminal trial, with the same rules of evidence, burden of proof, and rights of the accused. A corporation may be criminally liable for the acts of its agents or employees.[48] The statute of limitations for possible criminal violations of the OSH Act, as for other federal noncapital crimes, is five years.[49]

The OSHA Inspection

An OSHA inspection is not uncommon in the food industry. OSHA performs all enforcement functions under the OSH Act. Under Section 8(a) of the Act, OSHA compliance officers can enter any workplace of a covered employer without delay, inspect and investigate a workplace during regular hours and at other reasonable times, and obtain an inspection warrant if access to a facility or an operation is denied.[50] Upon arrival at an inspection site, the compliance officer must present his or her credentials to the owner or designated representative of the employer before starting the inspection. An employer representative and an employee and/or union representative may accompany the compliance officer on the inspection. Compliance officers can question the employer and employees and inspect required records, such as the OSHA 200 form, which records injuries and illnesses.[51] Most compliance officers cannot issue on-the-spot citations; they only have authority to document potential hazards and report or confer with the OSHA area director before issuing a citation.

A compliance officer or other employee of OSHA may not provide advance notice of inspection under penalty of law.[52] The OSHA area director is, however, permitted to provide notice under the following circumstances:

1. In cases of apparent imminent danger, to enable the employer to correct the danger as quickly as possible.
2. When the inspection can most effectively be conducted after regular business hours or where special preparations are necessary.
3. To ensure the presence of employee and employer representatives or appropriate personnel needed to aid in inspections.
4. When the area director determines that advance notice would enhance the probability of an effective and thorough inspection.[53]

Compliance officers (i.e., OSHA inspectors) can also take environmental samples and take or obtain photographs related to the inspection. Additionally, compliance officers can use other "reasonable investigative techniques," including personal sampling equipment, dosimeters, air sampling badges, and other equipment.[54] Compliance officers must, however, take reasonable precautions when using photographic or sampling equipment to avoid creating hazardous conditions (i.e., a spark-producing camera flash in a flammable area) or disclosing a trade secret.[55]

An OSHA inspection normally has four basic components: (1) the opening conference, (2) the walk-through inspection,[56] (3) the closing conference, and (4) the issuance of citations, if necessary. In the opening conference, the compliance officer may explain the purpose and the type of inspection to be conducted, request records to be evaluated, question the employer, ask for appropriate representatives to accompany him or her during the walk-through inspection, and ask additional questions or request more information. The compliance officer may provide the employer with copies of the applicable laws and regulations governing procedures and health and safety standards. The opening conference is usually brief and informal, its primary purpose being to establish the scope and the purpose of the walk-through inspection.

After the opening conference and review of appropriate records, the compliance officer, usually accompanied by a representative of the employer and a representative of the employees, conducts a physical inspection of the facility or worksite. The general purpose of this walk-through inspection is to determine whether the facility or worksite complies with OSHA standards. The compliance officer must identify potential safety and health hazards in the workplace, if any, and document them to support issuance of citations.[57]

The compliance officer uses various forms to document potential safety and health hazards observed during the inspection. The most commonly used form is the OSHA-1 Inspection Report, where the compliance officer records information gathered during the opening conference and walk-through inspection, including:

- The establishment's name.
- The inspection number.
- The type of legal entity.
- The type of business or plant.
- Additional citations.
- Names and addresses of all organized employee groups.
- The authorized representative of the employees.
- The employee representative contacted.
- Other persons contacted.
- Coverage information (state of incorporation, type of goods or services in interstate commerce, etc.).
- Date and time of entry.
- Date and time when the walk-through inspection began.
- Date and time when the closing conference began.
- Date and time of exit.
- Whether a follow-up inspection is recommended.
- The compliance officer's signature and date.
- The names of other compliance officers.
- Evaluation of safety and health programs (checklist).
- Closing conference checklist.
- Additional comments.

Two additional forms are usually attached to the OSHA Inspection Report. The OSHA-1A form, known as the "narrative," is used to record: information gathered during the walk-through inspection; names and addresses of employees, management officials, and employee representatives accompanying the compliance officer on the inspection; and other information. A separate worksheet, the OSHA-1B, is used by the compliance officer to document each condition that he or she believes could be an OSHA violation. One OSHA-1B worksheet is completed for each potential violation noted by the compliance officer.

When the walk-through inspection is completed, the compliance officer conducts an informal meeting with the employer or the employer's representative to "informally advise (the employer) of any apparent safety or health violations disclosed by the inspection."[58] The compliance officer informs the employer of the potential hazards observed and indicates the applicable section of the standards allegedly violated, advises that citations may be issued, and informs the employer or the representative of the appeals process and the employer's rights.[59] Additionally, the compliance officer advises the employer that the OSH Act prohibits discrimination against employees or others for exercising their rights.[60]

In unusual circumstances, the compliance officer may issue citations on the spot. When this occurs, the compliance officer informs the employer of the abatement period in addition to the other information provided at the closing conference. In most circumstances the compliance officer will leave the workplace and file a report with the area director, who has authority, through the Secretary of Labor, to decide whether a citation should be issued, compute any penalties to be assessed, and set the abatement date for each alleged violation. The area director, under authority from the Secretary, must issue the citation with "reasonable promptness."[61] Citations must be issued in writing and must describe with particularity the violation alleged, including the relevant standard and regulation. There is a six-month statute of limitations, and the citation must be issued or vacated within this time period. OSHA must serve notice of any citation and proposed penalty by certified mail, unless there is personal service to an agent or an officer of the employer.[62]

After issuance of the citation and notice of proposed penalty, but before the notice of contest by the employer is filed, the employer may request an informal conference with the OSHA area director. The general purpose of an informal conference is to clarify the basis for the citation, modify abatement dates or proposed penalties, seek withdrawal of a cited item, or otherwise attempt to settle the case. This conference, as its name implies, is an informal meeting between the employer and OSHA, and employee representatives must have an opportunity to participate. Safety and health professionals should note that the request for an informal conference does not stay the 15-working-day period to file a notice of contest to challenge the citation.[63]

Under the OSH Act, an employer, employee, or authorized employee representative (i.e., a labor organization) is given 15 working days from when the citation is issued to file a notice of contest. If a notice of contest is not filed within 15 working days, the citation and proposed penalty become a final order of the Occupational Safety and Health Review Commission (OSHRC), and are not subject to review by any court or agency. If a timely notice of contest is filed in good faith, the abatement requirement is tolled, and a hearing is scheduled. The employer also has the right to file a petition for modification of the abatement period (PMA) if unable to comply with the abatement period provided in the citation. If OSHA contests the PMA, a hearing is scheduled to determine whether the abatement requirements should be modified.

When the notice of contest by the employer is filed, the Secretary must immediately forward the notice to the OSHRC, which then schedules a hearing before its administrative law judge (ALJ). The Secretary of Labor is known as the "complainant," and the employer as the "respondent." The ALJ may affirm, modify, or vacate the citation, any penalties, or the abatement date. Either party can appeal the ALJ's decision by filing a petition for discretionary review (PDR). Additionally, any member of the OSHRC may direct review of any decision by an ALJ, in whole or in part, without a PDR. If a PDR is not filed and no member of the OSHRC directs a review, the decision of the ALJ becomes final in 30 days. Any party may appeal a final order of the OSHRC by filing a petition for review in the U.S. Court of Appeals for the circuit in which the violation is alleged to have occurred or in the U.S. Court of Appeals for the District of Columbia Circuit. This petition for review must be filed within 60 days from the date of the OSHRC's final order.

As the food industry has learned, there is no replacement for a well-managed proactive safety program that is in compliance with the OSHA standards. Food industry employers have realized that they cannot simply "get by" in the area of safety and health, and they often establish programs that far exceed the basic OSHA requirements. Safety and health is one of the most important priorities for most food industry employers—if not *the* most important one.

OVERVIEW OF WORKERS' COMPENSATION SYSTEMS

The rising cost of workers' compensation for most food industry employers has caused management to focus on this area. Food industry employers, always cognizant of the bottom line, often find that their workers' compensation costs have significantly increased for a variety of reasons, including, but not limited to, increased injuries and illnesses, increased medical and rehabilitation costs, increased time loss days and benefits, and other factors. Having to pay increased attention to these costs, food industry managers are often thrust into the administrative world of workers' compensation with little or no training and education about its rules, regulations, and requirements. As in the safety and health arena, many of the potential liabilities encountered in the area of workers' compensation are the result of acts of omission rather than commission. Food industry managers should understand the basic structure and mechanics of the workers' compensation system, and the specific rules, regulations, and requirements of their individual states' systems. Virtually all state workers' compensations systems are fundamentally no-fault mechanisms through which employees who incur work-related injuries and illnesses are compensated with monetary and medical benefits. In essence, workers' compensation is a compromise, in that employees are guaranteed a percentage of their wages and payment for their medical costs in a timely fashion when injured on the job, and employers are guaranteed a reduced monetary cost for these injuries or illnesses and are provided a bar to additional or future legal action by the employees for the injuries. Most workers' compensation systems were designed to be liberally construed in favor of the injured employee, thus making benefits relatively easy to acquire; but, for the employer, the potential monetary damages that the injury or illness may bring if taken before a court of law are substantially lower than they would be without such systems, and are uniformly set by statute.

Workers' compensation system possess a number of common features:

1. Every state in the Union has a workers' compensation system. There may be variations in amounts, rules, administration, and so on, from state to state; but in most states, workers' compensation is the exclusive remedy for on-the-job injuries and illnesses.
2. Coverage for workers' compensation is limited to employees injured on the job. The specific location—what constitutes the work premises and on the job—may vary from state to state.
3. Negligence or fault is largely inconsequential. Whether the employer is at fault or the employee is negligent, the injured employee will receive workers' compensation coverage for any injury or illness incurred on the job.
4. Workers' compensation coverage is automatic; employees are not required to sign up for workers' compensation coverage. Most workers' compensation systems require that workers' compensation coverage and benefits be liberally construed in favor of the employee.
5. Employees' injuries or illnesses that "arise out of or in the course of employment" are usually compensable. This definition can expand the worksite beyond the four corners of the workplace to include work-related injuries and illnesses incurred on the highways, at out-of-town sites, and at other remote locations.
6. Most workers' compensation systems include wage-loss benefits (sometimes called time loss benefits) that are usually between one-half and three-fourths of the employee's average weekly wage. These benefits are normally tax-free.
7. Most workers' compensation systems require payment of all medical costs, including such expenses as hospital, rehabilitation, and prothesis expenses.
8. If an employee is killed, workers' compensation benefits for burial expenses and wage-loss benefits are usually paid to the employee's dependent.
9. When an employee incurs an injury or an illness that will be permanent in nature, most workers' compensation systems provide a dollar value for the percentage of loss to the injured employee. This is normally known as "permanent partial disability" or "permanent total disability."
10. In accepting workers' compensation benefits, the injured employee is

normally required to waive any common law action to sue the employer for damages from the injury or illness.

11. If the employee is injured by a third party, the employer usually is required to provide workers' compensation coverage but is reimbursed for these costs from any settlement that the injured employee receives through legal action or other methods.

12. Administration of the workers' compensation system in each state normally is assigned to a commission, which usually has developed an administrative agency located within state government to oversee and manage the workers' compensation program within the state.

13. The workers' compensation act in each state is a statutory entity that can be amended by the state legislature. The budgetary requirements normally are authorized and approved by the state legislature. Also, the workers' compensation rules and regulations usually are statutory and thus approved by the legislature.

14. The workers' compensation commission in each state normally develops administrative rules and regulations (i.e., rules of procedure, evidence, etc.) for the administration of workers' compensation claims in the state.

15. Employers with one or more employees normally are required to possess workers' compensation coverage. Employers usually are provided several avenues through which to acquire this coverage. Employers normally can elect to acquire workers' compensation coverage from private insurance companies or state-funded insurance programs, or to become "self-insured" (i.e., after posting bond, the employer pays all costs directly from its coffers).

16. Most state workers' compensation systems allow a long-enough period of time prior to an on-the-job injury claim for it not to be barred under the statute of limitations. For injury claims, most states grant between 1 and 10 years in which to file the claim for benefits. For work-related illnesses, the statute of limitations may be as high as 20 to 30 years from the time when the employee first noticed the illness or it was diagnosed. An employee who incurred a work-related injury or illness normally is not required to be employed with the employer when the claim for benefits is filed.

17. Workers' compensation benefits do not depend on the employment status of the injured employee. An injured employee continues to maintain workers' compensation benefits even if the employment relationship is terminated, the employee is laid off, or other significant changes are made in the employment status.

18. Most state workers' compensation systems possess some type of administrative hearing procedures. Most workers' compensation acts have designed a system of administrative "judges" (normally known as administrative law judges or ALJs) to hear any disputes involving workers' compensation issues. An appeal from the decision of an administrative

law judge normally is directed to the workers' compensation commission. Some states permit appeals to the state court system after all administrative appeals have been exhausted.

Food industry managers should be very aware that the workers' compensation system in every state is administrative in nature, so a substantial amount of paperwork must be completed for benefits to be paid in a timely manner. In most states, specific generic forms have been developed for use in applying for workers' compensation coverage.

The most important form used to initiate workers' compensation coverage in most states is the first report of injury/illness form. This form may be called a "First Report" form or may be called by some other name or an acronym (e.g., the SF-1). Frequently divided into three parts so that information can be provided by the employer, the employee, and the attending physician, this form often is the catalyst that activates the workers' compensation system. If this form is absent or misplaced, no action is taken by the system, and no benefits are provided to the injured employee.

Under most workers' compensation systems, many forms must be completed in an accurate and timely manner. Normally specific forms must be completed if an employee is to be off work or is returning to work—forms for the transfer from one physician to another, forms for independent medical examinations, forms for the payment of medical benefits, and forms for the payment of permanent partial or permanent total disability benefits. Food industry managers responsible for workers' compensation are advised to acquire a working knowledge of the appropriate forms used under their state workers' compensation program. In most states, information regarding the rules, regulations, and forms can be acquired directly from the state workers' compensation commission. Other sources for this information include the insurance carrier, the self-insurance administrator, or the state-fund administrator.

Food industry managers should be aware that workers' compensation claims possess a "long tail" (i.e., stretch out over a long period of time). Under the OSHA recordkeeping system, with which most food industry managers are familiar, every year the injuries and the illnesses are totaled on the OSHA 200 log, and a new year begins. This is not the case with workers' compensation; once an employee sustains a work-related injury or illness, the employer is responsible for the management and costs until such time as the injury or the illness reaches a state of maximum medical recovery, or the time limitations are exhausted. When an injury reaches maximum medical recovery, the employer may be responsible for payment of permanent partial or permanent total disability benefits prior to closure of the claim. Additionally, in some states, the medical benefits can remain open indefinitely and cannot be settled or closed with the claim. In many circumstances, the workers' compensation claim for the work-related injury or illness may remain open for several years, and thus the claim will require proper management and administration throughout the duration of the claim process.

To summarize, food industry managers possessing responsibility for the management of a workers' compensation program should become knowledgeable about the rules, regulations, and procedures of their individual state's workers' compensation program. Food industry managers with facilities or operations in several states should be aware that although general concepts may be the same, the state workers' compensation programs possess specific rules, regulations, schedules, and procedures that may vary greatly between states. There is no substitute for knowing the rules and regulations of one's own state's workers' compensation system.

OVERVIEW OF EMPLOYMENT DISCRIMINATION LAWS

Federal Laws

- Equal Pay Act of 1963 (Section 6(d) of the Fair Labor Standard Act of 1938, 29 U.S.C. § 206(d)), which extends protection against sexual discrimination and requires equal pay for equal work by forbidding pay differentials predicated on gender.
- The Civil Rights Act of 1964 (Title VII) (42 U.S.C. § 2000 et seq.), which prohibits employment discrimination on the basis of race, color, religion, sex, age, or national origin by employers who employ 15 or more employees and are engaged in industry affecting commerce.
- The Age Discrimination in Employment Act of 1967 (29 U.S.C. §§ 621–634), which prohibits employment discrimination against persons over the age of 40.
- Rehabilitation Act of 1973 (§§ 501, 503, 504 29 U.S.C. §§ 791, 793, 794), which prohibits discrimination on the basis of disability by programs receiving federal funds or by federal agencies. This law is the precursor of the Americans with Disabilities Act and was created to assist individuals with disabilities in obtaining access to public buildings and enjoying equal employment opportunities.
- Americans with Disabilities Act of 1990 (also known as the ADA) (42 U.S.C. § 12,101), which prohibits discrimination against qualified individuals with disabilities. The primary purpose of this law was to provide an estimated 43 million individuals with disabilities equal access to employment opportunities, programs, services, and activities provided by public and private sector employers.
- Civil Rights Act of 1991 (42 U.S.C. § 1981 et seq.), which in essence reversed a series of cases decided by the U.S. Supreme Court in 1989. The Act, which reinstated the earlier interpretations of the Civil Rights Act of

1964, includes permitting full jury trials and, under certain circumstances, allowing for the recovery for emotional suffering and punitive damages.

- Family and Medical Leave Act of 1993 (29 U.S.C. § 2601 et seq.), which requires employers with 50 or more employees to provide eligible employees up to 12 weeks of unpaid, job-protected leave for family and medical reasons, including activities such as the birth of a child, adoption, and care of a spouse, child, or parent.
- The Pregnancy Discrimination Act (42 U.S.C. § 2000 (e) (k)), which prohibits sexual discrimination and amends the Civil Rights Act of 1964 to include pregnancy, childbirth-, and pregnancy-related medical conditions as protected against employment discrimination.
- Vietnam Era Veterans Readjustment Assistance Act (38 U.S.C. §2012), which requires federal contractors with contracts over $10,000 to hire qualified veterans of any war who have disabilities and specifically qualified Vietnam Veterans who may or may not have disabilities.

NOTES

1. 29 U.S.C. § 63 et seq.
2. Id. § 1975.3(d).
3. Id. § 652(7).
4. See Atomic Energy Act of 1954, 42 U.S.C. § 2021.
5. 29 U.S.C.A. § 652(5) (no coverage under OSH Act when U.S. government acts as employer).
6. Id.
7. See *Navajo Forest Prods. Indus.*, 8 O.S.H. Cases 2694 (OSH Rev. Comm'n 1980), affirmed, 692 F.2d 709, 10 O.S.H. Cases 2159.
8. 29 U.S.C.A. § 654(a)(1).
9. Id. § 659(c).
10. 29 U.S.C. § 671.
11. Id. § 669(b), (e).
12. Id. §651(b)(11).
13. Id.
14. Id. § 667(c). After an initial evaluation period of at least three years, during which OSHA retains concurrent authority, a state with an approved plan gains exclusive authority over standard setting, inspection procedures, and enforcement of health and safety issues covered under the state plan. See also *Noonan v. Texaco*, 713 P.2d 160 (Wyo. 1986); Plans for the Development and Enforcement of State Standards, 29 C.F.R. §§ 667(f) (1982) and 1902.42(c) (1986). Although the state plan is implemented by the individual state, OSHA continues to monitor the program and may revoke the state

authority if the state does not fulfill the conditions and assurances contained within the proposed plan.

15. Some states incorporate federal OSHA standards into their plans and add only a few of their own standards as a supplement. Other states, such as Michigan and California, have added a substantial number of separate and independently promulgated standards. See generally Employee Safety and Health Guide (CCH) §§ 5000–5840 (1987) (compiling all state plans). Some states also add their own penalty structures. For example, under Arizona's plan, employers may be fined up to $150,000 and sentenced to one and one-half years in prison for knowing violations of state standards that cause death to an employee, and may also have to pay $25,000 in compensation to the victim's family. If the employer is a corporation, the maximum fine is $1 million. See Ariz. Rev. Stat. Ann. §§ 13-701, 13-801, 23-4128, 23-418.01, 13-803 (Supp. 1986).

16. For example, under Kentucky's state plan regulations for controlling hazardous energy (i.e., lockout/tagout), locks would be required rather than locks or tags being optional as under the federal standard. Lockout/tagout is discussed in more detail in Chapter 7.

17. 29 U.S.C. § 667.

18. 29 U.S.C.A. § 667; 29 C.F.R. § 1902.

19. The states and territories operating their own OSHA programs are Alaska, Arizona, California, Hawaii, Indiana, Iowa, Kentucky, Maryland, Michigan, Minnesota, Nevada, New Mexico, North Carolina (partial federal OSHA enforcement), Oregon, Puerto Rico, South Carolina, Tennessee, Utah, Vermont, Virginia, Virgin Islands, Washington, and Wyoming.

20. M., Corn, *Policies, Objectives and Plans of OSHA*, 1976 ABA Nat'l Inst. on Occupational Safety & Health Law 229.

21. E.g., *NLRB v. Fainblatt*, 306 U.S. 601, 604–05 (1939). See also *U.S. v. Ricciardi*, 357 F.2d 91 (2d Cir.), cert. denied, 384 U.S. 942, 385 U.S. 814 (1966).

22. *Secretary v. Ray Morin*, 2 O.S.H. Cases 3285 (1975).

23. *Whirlpool Corp. v. Marshall*, 445 U.S. 1, 8 O.S.H. Cases 1001 (1980).

24. For example, consider a company with a corporate headquarters in Delaware and operations in Kentucky, Utah, California, and West Virginia. Facilities in Delaware and West Virginia are under federal OSHA jurisdiction, whereas the operations in Kentucky, Utah, and California are under state plan jurisdiction.

25. 29 U.S.C. § 655(b).

26. 29 U.S.C.A. § 655(b)(5).

27. 29 U.S.C. § 655.

28. 29 C.F.R. § 1911.15. (By regulation, the Secretary of Labor has prescribed more detailed procedures than the OSH Act specifies to ensure participation in the process of setting new standards, 29 C.F.R. § 1911.15.)

29. 29 U.S.C. § 655(a).
30. 29 U.S.C. § 655(b).
31. 5 U.S.C. § 553.
32. 29 C.F.R. § 1911.15.
33. *Taylor Diving & Salvage Co. v. Department of Labor*, 599 F.2d 622, 7 O.S.H. Cases 1507 (5th Cir. 1979).
34. 29 U.S.C. § 655(c).
35. Id. § 655(b)(1).
36. Id. § 656(a)(1). NACOSH was created by the OSH Act to "advise, consult with, and make recommendations . . . on matters relating to the administration of the Act." Id. Normally, for new standards, the Secretary has established continuing committees and ad hoc committees to provide advice regarding particular problems or proposed standards.
37. 41 *OSHA Compliance Field Operations Manual (OSHA Manual)* at XI-C3c (Apr. 1977).
38. Id.
39. Id. at XI-C3c(2).
40. Id. at (3)(a).
41. 29 U.S.C. § 666.
42. Id. § 666(b).
43. For example, if a company possesses 25 identical machines, and each of these machines is found to have the same serious violation, this would constitute 25 violations rather than one violation on 25 machines, and a possible monetary fine of $175,000 rather than a maximum fine of $7,000.
44. *Occupational Safety and Health Reporter*, 23, No. 32 (Jan. 12, 1994).
45. See infra § 1.140.
46. 29 U.S.C. § 666(e)–(g). See also, *OSHA Manual,* supra note 62, at VI-B.
47. A repeat criminal conviction for a willful violation causing an employee's death doubles the possible criminal penalties.
48. 29 C.F.R. § 5.01(6).
49. *U.S. v. Dye Const. Co.*, 510 F.2d 78, 2 O.S.H. Cases 1510 (10th Cir. 1975).
50. See infra §§ 1.10 and 1.12.
51. 29 C.F.R. § 1903.8.
52. 29 U.S.C. § 17(f). The penalty for providing advance notice, upon conviction, is a fine of not more than $1,000, imprisonment for not more than six months, or both.
53. *Occupational Safety and Health Law* (1988): 208–9.
54. 29 C.F.R. § 1903.7(b) [revised by 47 Fed. Reg. 5548 (1982)].
55. See 29 C.F.R. § 1903.9. Under § 15 of the OSH Act, all information gathered or revealed during an inspection or proceeding that may reveal a trade secret as specified under 18 U.S.C. § 1905 must be considered confidential, and breach of that confidentiality is punishable by a fine of not more than $1,000,

imprisonment for not more than one year, or both, and removal from office or employment with OSHA.

56. Some safety and health professionals use the term "walkaround" rather than "walk-through." Other terms include "wall-to-wall" and "site" inspections.

57. *OSHA Manual*, N. 62, at III-D8.

58. 29 C.F.R. § 1903.7(e).

59. *OSHA Manual* supra note 62, at III-D9.

60. 29 U.S.C. § 660(c)(1).

61. Id. § 658.

62. Fed. R. Civ. P. 4(d)(3).

63. 29 U.S.C. § 659(a).

Chapter 10

Selected Cases

Following are a few selected cases that identify, analyze, and decide some of the issues discussed in this text. Issues such as jurisdiction, negligence, evidence, and regulations relative to food safety are set forth in the cases. It is intended that the reader may gain some insight into how the courts review and decide these cases.

1.
The VONS COMPANIES, INC., Cross-Complainant and Appellant,
v.
SEABEST FOODS, INC. et al., Cross-Defendants and Respondents.
No. B094228.

Court of Appeal, Second District, Division 5.

Aug. 16, 1995.

As Modified Aug. 30, 1995.

Rehearing Denied Sept. 7, 1995.

Review Granted Nov. 16, 1995.

Action was brought against California meat processor in connection with serious illness and death attributed to presence of Escherichia coli (E. coli) bacteria in fast-food hamburgers. Processor filed cross-complaint against fast-food franchisees, alleging that franchisees failed to properly cook hamburger patties in Washington and thereby caused E. coli outbreak. The Superior Court, San Diego County, No. JCCP3101, Robert C. Baxley, J., granted franchisees' motion to quash service on ground that court lacked personal jurisdiction over them. Processor appealed. The Court of Appeal, Turner, P.J., held that causal link between franchisees' assignors' franchise relationship with franchisor in California, and alleged failure to properly cook hamburgers in Washington, was too attenuated to say that injury arose from franchisees' activities in California.

Affirmed.

1. Courts ⚖35

When defendant moves to quash service of process for lack of personal jurisdiction, plaintiff bears initial burden of proof that minimum contacts exist between defendant and California to justify imposition of personal jurisdiction; once that burden is met, burden shifts to defendants to demonstrate that assumption of jurisdiction would be unreasonable. West's Ann.Cal.C.C.P. § 410.10.

2. Courts ⚖39

Determination whether personal jurisdiction exists turns on facts of each individual case. West's Ann.Cal.C.C.P. § 410.10.

3. Corporations ⚖665(1)

Court lacked general jurisdiction over Washington fast-food franchisee for purposes of California meat processor's cross-claim against franchisee in consumers' action against processor arising from serious illness and death attributed to bacteria in hamburger that processor delivered to franchiser in California; notwithstanding that franchisee's assignors were California residents, that franchise agreements were in large part executed in California, and that assignors used California office address in connection with procurement of franchises, franchisee never had any place of business in California, was never authorized to do business in California, had no agent for service of process or employees there, and owned no real or personal property there. West's Ann.Cal.C.C.P. § 410.10.

4. Corporations ⚖665(1)

Washington fast-food franchisee's contacts with California were insufficient to warrant exercise of specific personal jurisdiction over them on meat processor's cross-claim against them in consumers' action against processor for serious illness and death attributed to bacteria in hamburgers that processor sold to franchisor, which in turn supplied them to franchisees; franchisees' act alleged to have caused damage to processor was undercooking of hamburgers in Washington, and causal link between franchisees' assignors' franchise relationship with California franchisor and alleged failure to properly cook hamburgers in Washington was too attenuated to say injury arose from activities of franchisees in California. West's Ann.Cal.C.C.P. § 410.10.

5. Courts ⚖12(2.10)

For court to assert specific jurisdiction over nonresident, particular cause of action must arise out of or be connected with defendant's forum-related activity. West's Ann.Cal. C.C.P. § 410.10.

Munger, Tolles & Olson, Gregory P. Stone, Joseph D. Lee, Susan R. Szabo, Kristin A. Linsley, and Kristin S. Escalante, Los Angeles, for cross-complainant and appellant.

Neil, Dymott, Perkins, Brown & Frank and Thomas M. Dymott; Laskero & Associates and Michael G. Roddy, San Diego, for cross-defendants and respondents.

I. INTRODUCTION

TURNER, Presiding Justice.

This litigation stems from an outbreak in January 1993 of serious illness and death attributed to the presence of Escherichia coli (E. coli) bacteria in Jack-in-the-Box hamburgers. The Vons Companies, Inc. (Vons) processed the hamburger patties involved in the outbreak at its facility in El Monte, California. The E. coli outbreak led to numerous personal injury lawsuits against Vons. In a cross-complaint, Vons sought damages and indemnification from numerous entities including certain Jack-in-the-Box franchisees, two of whom operated hamburger fast food establishments in the State of Washington. Vons alleged the franchisees failed to properly cook the hamburger patties in the State of Washington and thereby caused the E. coli outbreak. Two Washington franchisees, Seabest Foods, Inc. (Seabest) and Washington Restaurant Management, Inc. (WRMI) successfully moved to quash service on the ground the court lacked personal jurisdiction over them. Vons appealed.

In its cross-complaint, Vons asserted causes of action against Seabest and WRMI for: intentional interference with prospective economic advantage; negligent interference with prospective economic advantage; negligence; comparative indemnity; and equitable indemnity. Vons alleged: the defendants[1] "were aware that Vons had actual and prospective economic relationships with customers that shopped in its numerous stores"; despite that knowledge the employees of the two Washington entities "intentionally and/or recklessly violated the applicable governmental internal cooking standards for beef served to the general public"; and defendants breached a duty not to mishandle hamburgers processed by Vons by negligently failing to adequately cook them in the State of Washington. Vons alleged it suffered financial and commercial injury.

II. THE EVIDENCE

A. Vons and Foodmaker, Inc.

Foodmaker, Inc. (Foodmaker) was a Delaware corporation with its principal place of business in San Diego, California. Foodmaker was the franchiser of Jack-in-the-Box restaurants. Vons entered into a three-year agreement with Foodmaker in January 1990 to process beef into hamburger patties. The processing occurred at Vons' El Monte, California assembly plant. Vons agreed to deliver the hamburger patties to Foodmaker in California.

B. Seabest

Joseph Zacher, Terry Herrick, William O'Connor, and Sudesh Sood entered into 10 franchise agreements with Foodmaker in their individual capacities. Foodmaker did not permit corporations to be franchisees. The initial six franchise agreements involving Seabest and Foodmaker were executed in July 1988, in San Diego, California. Four subsequent franchise agreements were executed in California except that Mr. Zacher executed the agreements in Washington. The franchise agreements involving Foodmaker and Seabest were expressly deemed made and entered into in California. The agreements involving Seabest and Foodmaker were governed by California law, with exclusive venue in San Diego. In 1988, the four individuals formed Seabest, a Washington corporation. They assigned their franchise interests to it as an independent contractor. However, the four individuals remained obligated under the franchise agreements in addition to Seabest. They also served as the directors of Seabest and had equal interests in the venture.[2] Mr. Zacher was the only one of the four who received a salary. Mr. Zacher lived in California during negotiation of the franchise agreements. He moved to Washington in 1988 to oversee operation of the Jack-in-the-Box restaurants there. Seabest's board of directors held its annual directors meeting in California on approximately two occasions; meetings were also held in Washington and, once, in Hawaii. Prior to the incorporation of Seabest, Mr. Zacher, Mr. O'Connor, Mr. Herrick, and Mr. Sood used the address of Mr. O'Connor's office in Granada Hills, California.[3]

---

1. For ease of reference, we refer to the cross-defendants Seabest and WRMI as defendants.

2. Following Mr. O'Connor's death, his wife succeeded to his interest in Seabest and became a director thereof.

3. The Granada Hills address also appeared on a lease dated September 1989 between Seabest and Sunset Square Joint Ventures as a "business home office address." However, Mr. Zacher's Washington address was also listed as a "business home office address."

Mr. Zacher received accounting training from Foodmaker in San Diego in July 1988. The training occurred over a three-day period. Mr. Zacher received no other training in California. Mr. Zacher and his district manager, Debbie Lee, attended training sessions conducted by Foodmaker representatives from San Diego at Foodmaker restaurants *in Washington* three times a year.

Seabest corresponded with Foodmaker at its San Diego, California, and Tukwila, Washington offices. Seabest "telepaid" its day-to-day bills to Foodmaker by calling an 800 number in Denver, Colorado. Seabest's checking account in Washington would be debited for the amounts owed to Foodmaker. The Denver "exchange house" transmitted the payments to Foodmaker in San Diego. For approximately the first year of operations, however, Seabest mailed payments to Foodmaker in San Diego. Monthly profit and loss statements for each of Seabest's 10 franchises were prepared by accountants in San Diego. Mr. Zacher sent the necessary information to the accountants in San Diego. The accountants forwarded the profit and loss statements to Foodmaker. The accounting firm in question was chosen because it had experience with Jack-in-the-Box franchises.

Foodmaker quality specialists residing in Washington inspected Seabest's Jack-in-the-Box restaurants at least once a month. Foodmaker quality specialists from California rarely inspected Seabest locations; approximately five such visits were made between 1988 and 1994. Mr. Zacher attended approximately 10 meetings on behalf of Seabest in California between 1988 and 1994. These meetings included once or twice a year "franchise communications" meetings, attended by "all the franchisees in a geographic area." Mr. O'Connor, Mr. Herrick, and Mr. Sood also attended the franchise communications meetings.

Throughout the operation of the franchises, at least some of the food for each location was purchased from Foodmaker. The food items purchased from Foodmaker were delivered from its Tukwila, Washington distribution center. All hamburger patties were delivered to Seabest from Foodmaker's Tukwila distribution center. Foodmaker's Tukwila distribution center generated all invoices for food delivered to Seabest. Seabest "telepaid" the invoices through the Denver "exchange house." If any of the food purchased from Foodmaker came from California, Mr. Zacher was not aware of it. Foodmaker did not provide any training to any Seabest representatives in cooking hamburgers or any other food products in Califor-

nia. Further, Foodmaker did not send representatives to Washington for that purpose. On at least one occasion, Seabest paid Washington state tax on equipment purchased from Foodmaker. Vons had no contractual relationship with Seabest.

C. WRMI

Dennis Earls, Lisa Earls, Delmer Earls, and Roger Butler entered into franchise agreements with Foodmaker in their individual capacities. They thereafter assigned their interests to WRMI, which was incorporated in May 1987. Delmer Earls signed one of four franchise agreements while in Riverside, California, attending a family reunion. At that time he also signed an assignment of individual franchise interests. The franchise agreements were expressly deemed made and entered into in California. The franchise agreements were governed by California law with exclusive venue in San Diego.

Dennis Earls met with Foodmaker representatives in California on two occasions prior to being approved as a franchisee. Two of the WRMI restaurant managers attended training sessions in California. Ms. Earls received financial training in San Diego over a four day period in May 1987. Dennis Earls attended Franchise Advisory Council meetings in California six or eight times. Also, he acted as the representative of franchisees in Washington, Oregon, Hawaii, and Nevada. Dennis Earls stated he attended meetings with Foodmaker in California five or six times between 1987 and 1994. According to Foodmaker's director of franchise services, he met with Dennis Earls in California in excess of 10 times.

WRMI made monthly rent, marketing, and royalty payments to Foodmaker by "telepayment." Prior to introduction of the telepayment system, the payments were made by mail to San Diego. WRMI received updates on manuals or similar documents from Foodmaker from time to time. They were sent half of the time from Tukwila, Washington. On the remaining occasions, the material were sent from San Diego. WRMI: communicated with Foodmaker in San Diego concerning the sale of a restaurant; faxed financial information to Foodmaker's San Diego offices; and communicated by telephone with Foodmaker regarding financial information approximately three times a year.

WRMI purchased some equipment from Foodmaker. Approximately 90 percent of it came from Tukwila, Washington; the other 10 percent came by mail directly from the vendors. Foodmaker shipped cash registers, telemoniters, and computers that make up the "sales tracking equipment" to WRMI from California. The equipment was ordered through a franchise representative in Seattle, Washington. Once or twice Foodmaker was contacted in California to order new restaurant equipment.

WRMI received food for sale to customers from Foodmaker's Tukwila, Washington distribution center, including hamburger patties. There was never an occasion when WRMI served hamburger patties to customers that did not come from the Tukwila, Washington distribution center. In 1993, following the E. coli outbreak, WRMI learned Vons produced the hamburger patties for Foodmaker in California and delivered them to Seattle, Washington. Prior to the E. coli outbreak, WRMI did not know from where the Tukwila distribution center was getting the hamburger patties. Vons had no contractual relationship with WRMI.

III. DISCUSSION

A court of this state may exercise jurisdiction over the parties on any basis consistent with the federal and state Constitutions. (Code Civ.Proc., § 410.10; *Cornelison v. Chaney* (1976) 16 Cal.3d 143, 147, 127 Cal. Rptr. 352, 545 P.2d 264.) As the Supreme Court explained in *Cornelison v. Chaney, supra,* 16 Cal.3d at pages 147–148, 127 Cal. Rptr. 352, 545 P.2d 264: "In a significant line of cases beginning with *Internat. Shoe Co. v. Washington* (1945) 326 U.S. 310 [66 S.Ct. 154, 90 L.Ed. 95], the United States Supreme Court has defined the parameters of the power of the states to compel nonresidents to defend suits brought against them in the state's courts. [Citations.] The general rule is that the forum state may not exercise jurisdiction over a nonresident unless his relationship to the state is such as to make the exercise of such jurisdiction reasonable. [Citation.] [¶] If a nonresident defendant's activities may be described as 'extensive or wide-ranging' [citation] or 'substantial . . . continuous and systematic' [citation], there is a constitutionally sufficient relationship to warrant jurisdiction for all causes of action asserted against him. In such circumstances, it is not necessary that the specific cause of action alleged be connected with the defendant's business relationship to the forum. [¶] If, however, the defendant's activities in the forum are not so pervasive as to justify the exercise of general jurisdiction over him, then jurisdiction depends

upon the quality and nature of his activity in the forum in relation to the particular cause of action. In such a situation, the cause of action must arise out of an act done or transaction consummated in the forum, or defendant must perform some other act by which he purposefully avails himself of the privilege of conducting activities in the forum, thereby invoking the benefits and protections of its laws. Thus, as the relationship of the defendant with the state seeking to exercise jurisdiction over him grows more tenuous, the scope of jurisdiction also retracts, and fairness is assured by limiting the circumstances under which the plaintiff can compel him to appear and defend. The crucial inquiry concerns the character of defendant's activity in the forum, whether the cause of action arises out of or has a substantial connection with that activity, and upon the balancing of the convenience of the parties and the interests of the state in assuming jurisdiction. [Citations.]" (*Cornelison v. Chaney, supra,* 16 Cal.3d at pp. 147–148, 127 Cal.Rptr. 352, 545 P.2d 264; fn. omitted.)

[1, 2] When a defendant moves to quash service of process for lack of personal jurisdiction, the plaintiff bears the initial burden of proof that minimum contacts exist between the defendant and this state to justify imposition of personal jurisdiction. (*State of Oregon v. Superior Court* (1994) 24 Cal. App.4th 1550, 1557, 29 Cal.Rptr.2d 909.) Once that burden is met, the burden shifts to the defendant to demonstrate that assumption of jurisdiction would be unreasonable. *(Ibid.)* The applicable standard of review was set forth in *Great-West Life Assurance Co. v. Guarantee Co. of North America* (1988) 205 Cal.App.3d 199, 204, 252 Cal.Rptr. 363, as follows: "When the evidence of jurisdictional facts is not conflicting, 'the question of whether defendant is subject to personal jurisdiction is one of law.' [Citation.] In such a case, the lower court's determination is not binding on the reviewing court. [Citation.] While the parties at times contested each other's characterization of the facts, the evidence presented by each side was not in conflict. We therefore engage in an independent review of the record." (Accord, *Pennsylvania Health & Life Ins. Guaranty Assn. v. Superior Court* (1994) 22 Cal.App.4th 477, 481, 27 Cal.Rptr.2d 507.) Further, the determination whether personal jurisdiction exists turns on the facts of each individual case. (*Burger King Corp. v. Rudzewicz* (1985) 471 U.S. 462, 486, 105 S.Ct. 2174, 2189–2190, 85 L.Ed.2d 528; *Cornelison v. Chaney, supra,* 16 Cal.3d at p. 150, 127 Cal.Rptr. 352, 545 P.2d 264.)

A. There is No General Jurisdiction over Seabest

[3] Vons contends our courts have general jurisdiction over Seabest. We disagree. In *Cornelison v. Chaney, supra,* 16 Cal.3d at pp. 148–149, 127 Cal.Rptr. 352, 545 P.2d 264, the Supreme Court considered whether a defendant's activities in this state justified the exercise of general jurisdiction over him. The defendant hauled goods by truck in interstate commerce. He had made 20 trips into this state over a seven year period to deliver and obtain goods, had an independent contractor relationship with a California broker, and was licensed by the Public Utilities Commission to haul freight. The California Supreme Court held those contacts were insufficient to justify the exercise of general jurisdiction over the defendant. *(Ibid.)*

In *Helicopteros Nacionales de Colombia, S.A. v. Hall* (1984) 466 U.S. 408, 409–411, 104 S.Ct. 1868, 1869–1871, 80 L.Ed.2d 404, the defendant, a Colombian corporation with its principal place of business in Bogota, was sued in Texas for wrongful death arising out of a helicopter accident in Peru. The defendant had sent its chief executive officer to Houston, Texas to negotiate a contract to provide helicopters to a Peruvian consortium. The Peruvian consortium was the alter ego of a Houston, Texas joint venture. The contract was signed in Peru. Thereafter, the defendant purchased helicopters, spare parts, and accessories from a company in Fort Worth, Texas. It also sent prospective pilots to Forth Worth for training and to ferry helicopters to South America. Further, it sent management and maintenance personnel to Fort Worth "to receive 'plant familiarization' and for technical consultation." *(Id.* at p. 411, 104 S.Ct. at 1870.) The defendant received over $5 million dollars in payments from the Peruvian consortium drawn on a Houston bank into bank accounts in New York and Florida. The United States Supreme Court held the contacts between the defendant and the State of Texas were insufficient to impose general jurisdiction. The court noted: "Helicol never has been authorized to do business in Texas and never has had an agent for the service of process within the State. It never has performed helicopter operations in Texas or sold any product that reached Texas, never solicited business in Texas, never signed any contract in Texas, never had any employee based there, and never recruited an employee in Texas. In addition, Helicol never has owned real or personal property in Texas and never has maintained an office

or establishment there. Helicol has maintained no records in Texas and has no shareholders in that State." *(Id.* at pp. 411–412, 104 S.Ct. at 1870–1871.) The court held the chief executive officer's trip to Houston to negotiate the contract was not "a contact of a 'continuous or systematic' nature. . . ." *(Id.* at p. 416, 104 S.Ct. at 1873.) In addition, the unilateral act of a third person in drawing checks against a Houston bank was not an appropriate consideration.[4] *(Id.* at pp. 416–417, 104 S.Ct. at 1872–1874.) The court held further: "[W]e hold that mere purchases, even if occurring at regular intervals, are not enough to warrant a State's assertion of in personam jurisdiction over a nonresident corporation in a cause of action not related to those purchase transactions. Nor can we conclude that the fact that Helicol sent personnel into Texas for training in connection with the purchase of helicopters and equipment in that State in any way enhanced the nature of Helicol's contacts with Texas. The training was a part of the package of goods and services purchased by Helicol from Bell Helicopter. The brief presence of Helicol employees in Texas for the purpose of attending the training sessions [was not a significant contact]." *(Id.* at p. 418, 104 S.Ct. at 1874.)

Seabest's activities in this state likewise cannot be described as "'extensive or wideranging'" or "'substantial . . . continuous and systematic.'" *(Cornelison v. Chaney, supra,* 16 Cal.3d at p. 147, 127 Cal.Rptr. 352, 545 P.2d 264.) Seabest's *assignors* were California residents who entered into franchise agreements with Foodmaker to operate Jack-in-the-Box

---

4. The activity in question must be initiated *by the defendant. (Rocklin de Mexico, S.A. v. Superior Court* (1984) 157 Cal.App.3d 91, 97, 203 Cal.Rptr. 547.) Contact with the forum involving the defendant which is instituted by another person does not meet the constitutional requirements. *(Ibid.)* In other words, unilateral activity by Vons or Foodmaker cannot satisfy the requirement of the defendants' contact with this state. *(Burger King Corp. v. Rudzewicz, supra,* 471 U.S. at pp 474–475, 105 S.Ct. at pp. 2183–2184; *Hanson v. Denckla* (1958) 357 U.S. 235, 253, 78 S.Ct. 1228, 1239–1240, 2 L.Ed.2d 1283; *Cornelison v. Chaney, supra* 16 Cal.3d at p. 149, 127 Cal.Rptr. 352, 545 P.2d 264; *J.M. Sahlein Music Co. v. Nippon Gakki Co., Ltd.* (1987) 197 Cal.App.3d 539, 544–545, 243 Cal.Rptr. 4.)

restaurants in the State of Washington. The franchise agreements were in large part executed in California and were expressly deemed to have been made and entered into in this state. Prior to Seabest's incorporation, its *assignors,* Mr. Zacher, Mr. O'Connor, Mr. Herrick, and Mr. Sood, used Mr. O'Connor's office address in Granada Hills, California, in connection with the procurement of the franchises. However, Seabest never had any place of business in California. Following the successful negotiation of the agreements, Mr. Zacher, one of the *assignors,* moved to the state of Washington to oversee operation of the Jack-in-the-Box restaurants there. In July 1988, he returned to San Diego for three days of accounting training. Mr. Zacher, one of Seabest's assignors, also attended meetings on behalf of Seabest in California approximately 10 times between 1988 and 1994. These included "franchise communications" meetings. Seabest assignors, Mr. O'Connor, Mr. Herrick, and Mr. Sood also attended "franchise communications" meetings. Two annual board of directors meetings were held in California. Others were held in Washington, and once, in Hawaii. During the first year of operation, Seabest mailed royalty and other payments to Foodmaker in San Diego. Thereafter, such bills were "telepaid" through an "exchange house" in Denver, Colorado. Seabest used accountants in California who forwarded financial information to Foodmaker. In short, the contacts between Seabest and this state all related to their franchise arrangement with Foodmaker. Seabest has never been authorized to do business in California and nor ever had an agent for service of process in this state. It has never operated its business in this state nor ever solicited business here. Seabest has no employees based here. In addition, Seabest owns no real or personal property in California and has never maintained an office or establishment here. Trips to California by Seabest personnel have all been for the purpose of negotiation, training, or meetings in connection with its franchises in Washington. Under these circumstances, we find Seabest's contacts with California are insufficient to support the exercise of general jurisdiction over it.

B. There is no Specific Jurisdiction over Seabest or WRMI

[4] We next consider whether a court of this state can exercise specific jurisdiction over Seabest and WRMI. The United States Supreme Court has held: "The Due Process Clause protects an individual's liberty interest in not being subject to the binding judgments of a forum with which he has established no meaningful 'contacts, ties, or relations.' *International Shoe Co. v. Washington[, supra,]* 326 U.S. at [p.] 319 [66 S.Ct. at p. 160]. By requiring that individuals have 'fair warning that a particular activity may subject [them] to the jurisdiction of a foreign sovereign,' [citation], the Due Process Clause 'gives a degree of predictability to the legal system that allows potential defendants to structure their primary conduct with some minimum assurance as to where that conduct will and will not render them liable to suit,' [citation.] [¶] Where a forum seeks to assert specific jurisdiction over an out-of-state defendant who has not consented to suit there, this 'fair warning' requirement is satisfied if the defendant has 'purposefully directed' his activities at residents of the forum, [citation], and the litigation results from alleged injuries that 'arise out of or relate to' those activities [citation]. . . . And with respect to interstate contractual obligations, we have emphasized that parties who 'reach out beyond one state and create continuing relationships and obligations with citizens of another state' are subject to regulation and sanctions in the other State for the consequences of their activities. [Citations.]" (*Burger King Corp. v. Rudzewicz, supra,* 471 U.S. at pp. 471–472, 105 S.Ct. at pp. 2181–2182, fns. omitted.) A finding of specific jurisdiction requires three things: "'(1) The nonresident defendant must do some act or consummate some transaction within the forum or perform some act by which he purposefully avails himself of the privilege of conducting activities in the forum, therby invoking the benefits and protections of its laws[;] (2) [t]he claim must be one that arises out of or results from the defendant's forum-related activities[; and] (3) [the] [e]xercise of jurisdiction must be reasonable.'" (*Thiebaut v. Blue Cross of Indiana* (1986) 178 Cal.App.3d 1157, 1160, 224 Cal.Rptr. 277; *Cubbage v. Merchent* (9th Cir.1984) 744 F.2d 665, 668.) Courts have consistently focused on the requirement that a specific jurisdiction finding "'depends upon the quality and nature of [its] activity in the forum in relation to the particular cause of action.'" (*Pennsylvania Health & Life Ins. Guaranty Assn. v. Superior Court, supra,* 22 Cal. App.4th at p. 481, 27 Cal.Rptr.2d 507; *J.M. Sahlein Music Co. v. Nippon Gakki Co., Ltd., supra,* 197 Cal.App.3d at pp. 543–545, 243 Cal.Rptr. 4; accord, *Cornelison v. Chaney, supra,* 16 Cal.3d at p. 148, 127 Cal.Rptr. 352, 545 P.2d

264; *Fisher Governor Co. v. Superior Court* (1959) 53 Cal.2d 222, 226, 1 Cal.Rptr. 1, 347 P.2d 1; *Edmunds v. Superior Court* (1994) 24 Cal.App.4th 221, 233, 29 Cal.Rptr.2d 281.)

1. Purposeful availment

The California Supreme Court has held: "[A] defendant's activity must consist of 'an act done or transaction consummated in the forum State,' or 'some [other] act by which the defendant purposefully avails itself of the privilege of conducting activities within the forum State, thus invoking the benefits and protections of its laws.' [Citation.]" (*Buckeye Boiler Co. v. Superior Court* (1969) 71 Cal.2d 893, 898, 80 Cal.Rptr. 113, 458 P.2d 57.) We need not decide whether defendants' activities in this state meet these criteria. Even if defendants' purposefully availed themselves of the privilege of conducting activities in this state, the cause of action at issue here did not arise out of or relate to those activities.

Vons relies on *Burger King Corp. v. Rudzewicz, supra,* 471 U.S. at page 472, 105 S.Ct. at pages 2181–2182, a contract breach and trademark infringement case, for the proposition the defendants purposefully directed their activities into California. Specific jurisdiction in *Burger King Corp.,* a case based entirely on a contractual agreement, was premised on a Florida long-arm statute extending jurisdiction to any nonresident who breached a contract in that state. The long-arm statute applied to a nonresident who failed to perform acts required by the contract to be performed in Florida "so long as the cause of action arises from the alleged contractual breach." (*Id.* at pp. 463–464, 105 S.Ct. at p. 2177.) The cause of action in that case was for breach of a franchise agreement and trademark infringement brought by Burger King Corporation, a Florida corporation, against a Michigan franchisee. (*Ibid.*) Hence the cause of action "grew directly out of" the franchise contract, the defendant's only contact with Florida. (*Id.* at p. 479, 105 S.Ct. at pp. 2185–2186.) Notably, the United States Supreme Court stated that "an individual's contract with an out-of-state party alone [cannot] automatically establish sufficient minimum contacts in the other party's home forum. . . ." (*Id.* at p. 478, 105 S.Ct. at p. 2185.) Whether defendants in the present case, consistent with the Due Process Clause, could be required to litigate an action for breach of their franchise agreements with Foodmaker, the issue in *Burger King Corp. v. Rudzewicz, supra,* 471

U.S. at page 463, 105 S.Ct. at page 2177, is not the question before this court.

2. Arising out of

[5] In order for a court to assert specific jurisdiction over a nonresident, the particular cause of action must arise out of or be connected with the defendant's forum-related activity. The Court of Appeal discussed this aspect of the analysis in *Ratcliffe v. Pedersen* (1975) 51 Cal.App.3d 89, 95–96, 123 Cal.Rptr. 793. The court stated: "When seeking to invoke jurisdiction based upon minimum contacts, it is enough to show that the cause of action is 'sufficiently connected' with the forum-related activity so that it cannot be said that the cause of action is 'entirely distinct' from that activity. [Citations.] One test is to ascertain whether the economic activity put in motion the events which ultimately gave rise to [the plaintiff's] cause of action. Under this test, the cause of action is 'sufficiently connected' with the defendant's forum-related activity whenever there is a causal connection between the two in the sense that the cause of action would not have arisen except for the economic activity." (*Ibid.*) Our courts have adopted a "but for" test in determining whether a cause of action arises out of or is related to a defendant's contacts with the forum. (*Dialysis at Sea, Inc. v. Superior Court* (1989) 216 Cal.App.3d 788, 795, 265 Cal.Rptr. 71; *Sklar v. Princess Properties International, Ltd.* (1987) 194 Cal.App.3d 1202, 1208, 240 Cal.Rptr. 102; *Circus Circus Hotels, Inc. v. Superior Court* (1981) 120 Cal.App.3d 546, 569, 174 Cal.Rptr. 885.) In *Circus Circus Hotels, Inc.,* California residents brought an action here against a Nevada hotel. The hotel had advertised in California newspapers and supplied a toll-free number for reservations. The plaintiffs' hotel room in Nevada had been burglarized. The Court of Appeal held the "but for" test was not met. The court held: "The acts or omissions of defendant alleged to be the proximate cause of the loss were the failure to rekey the lock to room 1319 and failure to warn plaintiffs of the earlier burglary of that very room. It could not be seriously contended that the defendant's advertising was the proximate cause of the burglary, i.e., that the burglary would not have happened *but for* the advertising. (*Circus Circus Hotels, Inc. v. Superior Court, supra,* 120 Cal.App.3d at p. 569, 174 Cal.Rptr. 885; original italics.) Similarly, in *Sklar v. Princess Properties International, Ltd., supra,* 194 Cal.App.3d at page 1205, 240

Cal.Rptr. 102, the plaintiff filed an action in California against a Bermuda hotel for injuries sustained in a slip and fall at the hotel. The Court of Appeal, in an opinion authored by our colleague, Presiding Justice Mildred Lillie, held there was an insufficient connection for purposes of specific jurisdiction between the hotel's advertising activities in California and the plaintiff's accident. The court stated: "It cannot seriously be contended that sale to plaintiff in California of accommodations at defendant's hotel in Bermuda was the proximate cause of plaintiff's personal injuries . . .; in other words, it cannot be said that the accident would not have happened but for the sale of the hotel accommodations to plaintiff." (*Id.* at p. 1208, 240 Cal.Rptr. 102.)

In the present case, defendants' act or omission alleged to have caused damage to Vons and for which it seeks indemnification is the undercooking of hamburgers in the state of Washington. It cannot seriously be contended that *but for* defendants activities in California, as assignees of the franchisees, the hamburger patties would not have been undercooked in Washington. Stated differently, the franchiser-franchisee relationship in the present case between defendants' assignors and Foodmaker did not brings *Vons* into "tortious 'striking distance'" of Seabest and WRMI. (*Dialysis at Sea, Inc. v. Superior Court, supra,* 216 Cal.App.3d at p. 795, 265 Cal.Rptr. 71.) Defendants and their assignors had no relationship with Vons. Defendants and their assignors made no purchases from Vons. Indeed, prior to the E. coli outbreak, defendants and their assignors were unaware the hamburger patties they purchased from Foodmaker were processed by Vons. In short, the causal link between defendants' assignors' franchise relationship with Foodmaker and the alleged failure to properly cook hamburgers in Washington is too attenuated to say the injury arose from the activities of Seabest and WRMI in this state. (*Fisher Governor Co. v. Superior Court, supra,* 53 Cal.2d at pp. 223, 226, 1 Cal.Rptr. 1, 347 P.2d 1 [California sales activity insufficient to permit suit when accident occurred in Idaho]; *Watson's Quality Turkey Products, Inc. v. Superior Court* (1974) 37 Cal.App.3d 360, 368, 112 Cal.Rptr. 345 [cause of action unrelated to defendant's California activities]; accord, *Cornelison v. Chaney, supra,* 16 Cal.3d at p. 149, fn. 5, 127 Cal.Rptr. 352, 545 P.2d 264; cf. *Secrest Machine Corp. v. Superior Court* (1983) 33 Cal.3d 664, 671, 190 Cal.Rptr. 175, 660 P.2d 399 [*Fisher* distinguished because defective machine used in California].)

Vons cites *Shute v. Carnival Cruise Lines* (9th Cir.1990) 897 F.2d 377, 386, reversed in *Carnival Cruise Lines, Inc. v. Shute* (1991) 499 U.S. 585, 589–597, 111 S.Ct. 1522, 1525–1529, 113 L.Ed.2d 622 in arguing this court should adopt a less stringent standard of causation. In *Shute,* the Ninth Circuit Court of Appeals held a nonresident cruise line was subject to specific jurisdiction in a personal injury action arising from an injury on its ship. The court held that but for the cruise line's advertising and solicitation of business in the state of Washington, the plaintiff would not have boarded the ship and her injury would not have occurred. (*Id.* at p. 386; accord, *Alexander v. Circus Circus Enterprises, Inc.* (9th Cir.1991) 939 F.2d 847, 853, opn. vacated *Alexander v. Circus Circus Enterprises, Inc.* (9th Cir.1992) 972 F.2d 261, 262.) We decline to adopt this more expansive test. The Ninth Circuit itself has questioned the continuing vitality of the test applied in *Shute.* In *Omeluk v. Langsten Slip & Batbyggeri A/S* (9th Cir.1995) 52 F.3d 267, 271–272, the court stated: "The authority of our decision in *Shute* is questionable. The Supreme Court reversed our decision in *Carnival Cruise Lines, Inc. v. Shute,* 499 U.S. 585, 111 S.Ct. 1522, 113 L.Ed.2d 622 (1991). The Supreme Court did not reach the issue of whether the 'but for' test was appropriate in *Carnival Cruise Lines.* But neither did the Court expressly note that the jurisdiction issue was not before it, [citation], or limit its grant of certiorari to a separable issue. Because of the posture of the Court's reversal of *Shute,* it is not clear whether the 'but for' test survives."

Vons also cites *In re Oil Spill by Amoco Cadiz Off Coast of France* (7th Cir.1983) 699 F.2d 909, 915–917, for the proposition "that where the relevant contact with the forum state is a contractual relationship, claims by plaintiffs who are not parties to the contract can 'arise out of' such contacts." The Seventh Circuit has emphasized *Amoco Cadiz* involved a suit where the non-resident's contractual duties in the forum state were at issue. (*J. Walker & Sons v. DeMert & Dougherty, Inc.* (7th Cir.1987) 821 F.2d 399, 403–404.) We have no quarrel with that proposition in the abstract. We simply hold the causes of action in this case asserted by Vons did not arise out of defendants' assignors' contractual relationship with Foodmaker in this case.

3. Reasonableness

Because Seabest and WRMI's contacts with California are insufficient to justify the exercise of personal jurisdiction over them, we need not consider whether the exercise of such jurisdiction would be reasonable. (*Sibley v. Superior Court of Los Angeles County,* 16 Cal.3d 442, 448, 128 Cal.Rptr. 34, 546 P.2d 322.)

IV. DISPOSITION

The orders granting motions to quash service of summons brought by Seabest Foods, Inc. and Washington Restaurant Management, Inc. are affirmed. Seabest Foods, Inc. and Washington Restaurant Management, Inc. are to recover their costs on appeal from The Vons Companies, Inc.

ARMSTRONG and GODOY PEREZ, JJ., concur.

2.

239 Ill.App.3d 403
179 Ill.Dec. 1013

Gema LAVAZZI, Adm'x of the Estate of Cayetano Lavazzi, Deceased, Plaintiff-Appellant,

v.

McDONALD'S CORPORATION, Defendant-Appellee (Weiler and Company et al., Defendants and Third-Party Plaintiffs; Otto and Sons, Inc., Third-Party Defendant).

No. 2–92–0163.

Appellate Court of Illinois, Second District.

Dec. 31, 1992.

Administrator of estate of worker employed by meat processing plant brought wrongful death action against franchisor that plant supplied with meat products. The Circuit Court, Du Page County, Robert R. Thomas, J., granted defendant's motion for summary judgment, and plaintiff appealed. The Appellate Court, Unverzagt, J., held that: (1) by conducting periodic inspections of meat processing plant that supplied it with hamburger patties for its fast food restaurants, defendant did not assume any duty of care for safety of plant's employees, and (2) defendant did not exert sufficient control over meat processing plant to have any duty to provide for plant employees' safety.

Affirmed.

1. Judgment ⊙181(3)

Summary judgment is proper when court may determine issue as matter of law.

2. Judgment ⊙181(4)

While expeditious disposition of lawsuit by means of summary judgment is to be encouraged, summary judgment is drastic means of terminating litigation and should be used only when right of moving party is clear and free from doubt.

3. Judgment ⊙185(2)

On motion for summary judgment, court must construe evidence strictly against movant and liberally in favor of nonmoving party.

4. Judgment ⊙185(2)

To survive motion for summary judgment, nonmoving party must come forward with evidence establishing a genuine issue of fact.

5. Judgment ⊙181(1)

Summary judgment may be entered in favor of defendant, where plaintiff has not established essential element of cause of action.

6. Negligence ⊙2

Essential element of negligence claim is existence of duty owed by defendant to plaintiff.

7. Negligence ⊙1

Liability can arise from negligent performance of duty voluntarily undertaken.

8. Judgment ⊙181(33)

Whether defendant has voluntarily undertaken legal duty to plaintiff, such as might support negligence claim, is question of law for court, which is properly addressed on motion for summary judgment.

9. Negligence ⊙29

By conducting periodic inspections of meat processing plant that supplied it with hamburger patties for its fast-food restaurants, defendant did not assume any duty of care for safety of plant's employees, though audit reports prepared by defendant's inspector occasionally took note of limited worker safety considerations, where purpose of inspections was to ensure that plant complied with defendant's sanitation standards, and manager of plant testified that she was responsible for worker safety and never discussed safety matters with any of defendant's employees.

10. Negligence ∞29

Fast food franchisor that purchased all of meat processing plant's products for use in franchisor's restaurants did not exert sufficient control over plant's operation to have any duty of care as regards safety of plant's employees, though meat processing plant employed franchisor's name and logo on its outdoor sign and was required to meet strict sanitation standards established by franchisor, where franchisor had no control over plant's day-to-day operations, such as hiring and firing employees, plant had its own safety personnel and procedures, and all safety procedures followed by plant's employees came from plant's safety supervisors.

11. Master and Servant ∞318(2)

Mere fact that franchisee (independent contractor) uses its franchisor's (employer's) logo is not sufficient basis upon which to impose liability on franchisor for franchisee's negligent acts, where franchisee retains day-to-day control over its operations, such as hiring and firing employees, payroll, workers' compensation insurance and taxes.

12. Master and Servant ∞318(1)

Franchisor's (employer's) right to rescind its contract with franchisee (independent contractor) is generally insufficient to establish control and to impose liability on franchisor for safety of franchisee's workers.

Roy I. Peregrine, Peregrine, Stime, Newman, Ritzman & Bruckner, Ltd., Wheaton. Keith L. Davidson, Louis G. Davidson & Associates, Ltd., Chicago, for Gema Lavazzi, Administrator.

Michael J. Pavlisin, and John J. O'Connor, McKenna, Storer, Rowe, White & Farrug, Wheaton, for McDonald's Corp.

Horvath & Wigoda, Chicago, Foley & Lardner, Milwaukee, Wis., for Weiler & Co.

French Kezelis Kominiarek, Chicago, for Boldt Industries.

Sweeney & Riman, Ltd., Chicago, for Otto & Sons.

Justice UNVERZAGT delivered the opinion of the court:

Plaintiff, Gema Lavazzi, administratrix of the estate of her husband, Cayetano Lavazzi, brought an action against several defendants for the wrongful death of her husband. One of the defendants was McDonald's Corporation (McDonald's). In count IV of her amended complaint, the only count directed against McDonald's, plaintiff alleged that the negligence of McDonald's (hereinafter referred to as defendant) was one of the causes of the death of her husband. After determining as a matter of law that defendant did not owe a duty to plaintiff's deceased (decedent), the trial court granted summary judgment in favor of defendant and ordered that there was no just reason to delay enforcement or appeal. Plaintiff appeals the summary judgment. The issue on appeal is whether defendant owed a legal duty to decedent and whether the trail court properly decided that question as a matter of law by summary judgment.

The relevant facts are as follows. On April 23, 1988, decedent was cleaning and operating a meat mixing and grinding machine (mixer/grinder) in the course of his employment with Otto and Sons, Inc. (Otto). Somehow, decedent got inside the mixer/grinder and was found dead inside the mixer/grinder. When decedent was found, the mixer/grinder was running in the mixing mode. At the time of decedent's death, Otto was a meat products supplier to defendant, a corporation engaged in the management and franchising of restaurants in Illinois and elsewhere.

Defendant and Otto had a close business relationship. Peter Mazza, an employee of defendant, testified during his deposition that Otto had been "McDonaldized." Mazza explained that by this he meant that Otto understood "our culture, they know how to get around within the company, who to talk to, and how to get things done."

Defendant did not have a written contract with Otto. Otto was one of only five United States suppliers of ground beef patties and other meat products to defendant. Otto was the exclusive supplier of these meat products to defendant's franchisees within a designated area of the country. Defendant was Otto's only customer. Defendant purchased Otto's entire output.

Defendant required Otto to meet and maintain certain standards with respect to the quality of the meat products defendant purchased from Otto. Defendant required Otto to supply only wholesome, high-grade meat; to deliver the meat in a certain specific condition; to maintain certain standards of cleanliness; and to conduct its operation in a manner to maintain the quality and safety of the meat products.

Defendant monitored the quality of the meat products it purchased from Otto in several ways. Among the ways defendant monitored Otto was through periodic quality assurance reviews, sanitation audits, and supplier status reports. Defendant generally refers to these monitoring activities as audits. Some of the audits occurred at Otto's plant.

Pretrial discovery disclosed records of three audits in defendant's files. The earliest of these audit records was a quality assurance review report. Paul Simmons, employed by defendant as a quality assurance supervisor, drafted the report in 1985. The report consists of two, single-spaced typewritten pages containing about 23 separate items of information. Plaintiff cites two of the items in the report. The first item states "[t]he equipment is in good working order and maintenance staff are very knowledgeable of equipment." The second item states "[m]anagement could spend more time on the production floor to review product and equipment, as well as spending more time with the employees at their work stations. Field Service could also benefit by spending some time on the production floor."

The second audit report found in defendant's files was a sanitation audit report. Simmons also prepared this report. The sanitation audit report was a summary of a meeting at Otto's plant on September 24, 1987, which was attended by Simmons and eight other people including Otto's plant supervisor and other Otto employees. The information in the sanitation audit report could have come from either the defendant's employees or Otto's employees who attended the meeting. The report consists of three typewritten pages. The first item in the report is a statement showing that the purpose of the meeting was to "Review the sanitation program and determine the level of food safety at the facility." The specific evidence plaintiff points to in this sanitation audit report is a statement that the "Plant is equipped with electrical lockouts including lighted indicators for employee safety." Plaintiff also notes that the report lists one of the benefits of reducing high pressure and increasing nozzle size as "Safety."

The third audit report found in defendant's files was a plant visit and supplier status report dated December 13, 1988 (nearly eight months after the incident in question here). Plaintiff notes that the report, under the heading "Plant Requirements and Recommendations," contains the following statement:

> "General GMP's [Good Manufacturing Practices] and attention to detail were lacking. Examples—Production Supervisors were not wearing hair nets or beard nets, they were wearing watches and jewelry. Tools were laying [sic] on equipment with no holders or safety precautions. Broken Combo's in cooler, bloody floor. Large cage [sic] of alcohol in production cooler (Christmas gifts). In general, plant was not its usual quality condition."

In addition to the audit reports, plaintiff notes that the sign outside Otto's plant shows that Otto & Sons are "PROCESSORS OF MEAT PRODUCTS FOR McDONALDS." The sign also contains defendant's logo, the golden arches.

Plaintiff contends that the foregoing facts are sufficient to show that, or at least raise a question of fact whether, defendant had a legal duty to exercise due care in guarding against injury to decedent during the course of decedent's employment with Otto. Plaintiff argues that this duty arose from defendant's voluntary undertaking of the duty or from defendant's total control of Otto and Otto's plant.

Defendant denies that it had total control of Otto or Otto's plant. Defendant asserts that it had a business relationship with Otto in which it purchased goods from Otto but did not control Otto. Defendant specifically points to the fact that it never required or directed Otto to use a certain type of mixer/grinder at its plant. Defendant also notes that it is undisputed that defendant did not participate in the design, purchase, or installation of the mixer/grinder and that there is no evidence showing defendant ever inspected the mixer/grinder.

Defendant asserts that plaintiff has not shown a voluntary undertaking of a duty by defendant for the safety of Otto's employees. Defendant contends that the 1985 quality assurance review report drafted by Simmons was a compilation of information obtained from several sources. These sources included Simmons' visits to Otto's plant as well as observations from other employees of the defendant, restaurant licensees, and other suppliers. Defendant argues that the information was only used to monitor the quality of the meat product and plant sanitation.

Defendant further contends that the sanitation audit report also contained information from several sources. Defendant notes that the report was based on a combination of observations and information from all those in attendance at the September 24, 1987, meeting, including five of Otto's employees. Defendant maintains that the observation about the electric lockout was most likely made by the cleaning specialist in attendance at the meeting or one of Otto's employees. Defendant notes that Simmons' only responsibility during a sanitation audit was to check the quality of the meat product and that Simmons did not check to see if the equipment was in good working order. Finally, defendant notes that Joseph Zeisberger, Otto's plant engineer since 1973, is responsible for maintaining all the mechanical systems and equipment at Otto's plant.

Defendant asserts that whether it owed a duty to decedent is a question of law properly decided by a trial court. Defendant argues that the trial court properly ruled that it owed no duty to decedent and therefore properly granted its motion for summary judgment.

[1] A court should grant a motion for summary judgment when the pleadings, depositions, admissions and affidavits show that there is no genuine issue of material fact and the moving party is entitled to judgment as a matter of law. (See Ill.Rev.Stat.1989, ch. 110, par. 2–1005(c).) Thus, summary judgment is proper when a court may determine an issue as a question of law. *Wojdyla v. City of Park Ridge* (1992), 148 Ill.2d 417, 421, 170 Ill.Dec. 418, 592 N.E.2d 1098.

[2, 3] While the goal of expeditious disposition of a lawsuit by the use of summary judgment is encouraged, it is a drastic means to disposing of litigation and should only be allowed when the right of the moving party is clear and free from doubt. (*Loyola Academy v. S & S Roof Maintenance, Inc.* (1992), 146 Ill.2d 263, 271, 166 Ill.Dec. 882, 586 N.E.2d 1211.) Accordingly, a court ruling on a motion for summary judgment must strictly construe the evidence against the movant and liberally in favor of the nonmoving party. *Logan v. Old Enterprise Farms, Ltd.* (1990), 139 Ill.2d 229, 234, 151 Ill.Dec. 323, 564 N.E.2d 778.

[4–6] Nonetheless, in order to survive a motion for summary judgment, the nonmoving party must come forward with evidence establishing a genuine issue of fact. (*Hotze v. Daleiden* (1992), 229 Ill.App.3d 301, 305, 170 Ill.Dec. 675, 593 N.E.2d 564.) Summary judgment in favor of a defendant is proper where a plaintiff has not established an essential element of a cause of action. (*Gresham v. Kirby* (1992), 229 Ill.App.3d 952, 954–55, 172 Ill.-Dec. 138, 595 N.E.2d 201.) One of the essential elements of an action for negligence which the plaintiff must set out is the existence of a duty owed by the defendant to the plaintiff. *Vesey v. Chicago Housing Authority* (1991), 145 Ill.2d 404, 411, 164 Ill.Dec. 622, 583 N.E.2d 538.

Here, plaintiff concedes that there is no independent duty in Illinois or at common law for a buyer of goods such as defendant with respect to the safety of the employees of the supplier of the goods. However, plaintiff claims that defendant voluntarily undertook a duty of care for the safety of Otto's employees and that this duty extended to decedent. In addition, plaintiff claims that defendant exercised such total control of Otto that defendant's control of Otto gave rise to a duty for defendant to guard against injury to Otto's employees. We will first consider the voluntary undertaking claim.

[7, 8] Liability can arise from the negligent performance of a voluntarily undertaken duty. (*Pippin v. Chicago Housing Authority* (1979), 78 Ill.2d 204, 209, 35 Ill.Dec. 530, 399 N.E.2d 596.) Whether a defendant has voluntarily undertaken a legal duty to a plaintiff seeking to bring a negligence action must be determined by a court as a question of law and is properly addressed by the court on a motion for summary judgment. *Morgan v. 253 East Delaware Condominium Association* (1992), 231 Ill.App.3d 208, 211–12, 171 Ill. Dec. 908, 595 N.E.2d 36.

[9] Based upon the foregoing principles of law, we find that a review of the facts of this case supports the trial court's grant of summary judgment in favor of defendant. We agree with the circuit court that as a matter of law, defendant did not voluntarily undertake a legal duty of care for decedent's safety. Construing the evidence in the record liberally in plaintiff's favor clearly shows that defendant did not undertake a duty to care for the safety of Otto's employees. While it could be argued that strictly construing the references to safety in defendant's audit reports shows that the defendant had some concern for the safety of Otto's workers, the record as a whole does not support an inference that defendant undertook a duty of care for their safety. Defendant limited its

monitoring of Otto to audits intended to insure that the products it purchased from Otto met its sanitation standards and was safe for its consumers. Defendant's employees testified that defendant never conducted worker safety inspections at Otto's plant. The testimony of Otto's employees agreed. Otto's plant manager testified she was responsible for worker safety at the plant and she never discussed this with any of defendant's employees. Defendant certainly never inspected the mixer/grinder in question. The design, selection, installation, modification and maintenance of the mixer/grinder was done by or under the supervision of Otto's employees without input from defendant. Based on the record as a whole, we find that as a matter of law defendant did not voluntarily undertake a duty to care for the safety of Otto's employees including decedent.

Plaintiff's reliance on *Nelson v. Union Wire Rope Corp.* (1964), 31 Ill.2d 69, 199 N.E.2d 769, is misplaced. In *Nelson,* our supreme court, construing Florida law, held that the defendant insurance company's gratuitous safety inspections and safety engineering services with respect to a hoist on a construction site gave rise to a duty to plaintiff construction workers. (*Nelson,* 31 Ill.2d at 83, 199 N.E.2d 769.) The plaintiffs were employees of the insured general contractor and various subcontractors. Seven of the plaintiffs were killed and thirteen others severely injured when the hoist cable broke and the hoist carrying the plaintiffs plunged six floors to the ground. In reaching its conclusion, the *Nelson* court specifically noted: (1) that defendant had repeatedly advertised that it provided safety engineering services which could increase an insured's worker safety and lower an insured's costs; (2) that defendant's safety engineer, a qualified elevator inspector, made frequent safety inspections which included careful inspection of the hoist which he knew was used as an elevator by the construction workers; (3) that defendant's safety engineer filed reports of his safety inspections with defendant and the insured and the reports specifically mentioned the hoist and sometimes included recommendations for changes to improve safety; and (4) that the insured relied on defendant's safety inspections and did not employ a safety engineer or safety inspector of its own. *Nelson,* 31 Ill.2d at 79–83, 199 N.E.2d 769.

Here, plaintiff posits on appeal that defendant's conduct was similar to the defendant's conduct in *Nelson* and even went far beyond the conduct in *Nelson.* We disagree. In this case, defendant did not hold itself out to Otto as a provider of safety engineering services or safety inspections. While defendant established sanitation standards for the product it purchased from Otto and monitored the product to insure these standards were met, the record shows that defendant did not make safety inspections of Otto's plant to insure worker safety there. At most, the audit reports in the record indicate that defendant occasionally took note of limited worker safety considerations. In addition, the record clearly shows that defendant, unlike the *Nelson* defendant, did not specifically focus any attention during its audits on the piece of equipment involved in the injury. This case is also different than *Nelson* because Otto had its own safety personnel and procedures including a plant engineer whose duties included safety inspections of the machinery in the plant. In contrast, Simmons, defendant's employee who drafted two of the audit reports, was not a safety inspector or engineer of any kind. Finally, this case is different from *Nelson* in that the record shows that Otto did not rely on defendant for employee safety. Otto's plant supervisor testified during her deposition that she was in charge of employee safety throughout the plant, that she frequently met with defendant's employees, but that she had never discussed the safety of Otto's employees with any of defendant's employees.

Based on the foregoing, we conclude that defendant did not voluntarily undertake a duty to guard against injury to Otto's employees. We find that the circuit court properly decided this issue as a question of law.

[10] We next consider plaintiff's claim that defendant exercised total control of Otto or Otto's plant and that this control gave rise to a duty for defendant to care for the safety of Otto's employees. Plaintiff first repeats its contentions that defendant's audit reports show that defendant conducted safety inspections and expected Otto to conform its conduct to the standards and recommendations contained in the audit reports. As seen above, the evidence in the record does not support these contentions. There is no evidence that defendant made worker safety inspections. There is no evidence that defendant made recommendations concerning Otto's workers' safety. The 1985 quality assurance review report simply notes that the equipment was in good working order, the maintenance staff is knowledgeable about the equipment, and that management could spend more time on the production floor. When viewed in the context of the entire report, these statements do not show that defendant controlled Otto but are simply observations made in support of a product quality review. Similarly, the 1987 sanitation audit report merely

notes that the plant is equipped with electrical lockouts and lighted indicators for employee safety. This statement does not show that these devices were inspected and does not make any recommendation regarding them. In the context of the entire report, the statement is merely a detailed observation made in an overall general observation of the plant's equipment with respect to sanitation. The plant visit and supplier status report was dated December 13, 1988, nearly eight months after the incident in question here. The report merely listed several facts to support its conclusion that the plant was not in its usual quality condition. This statement was made in the context of product quality, not worker safety. Contrary to plaintiff's assertions, we find that none of the audit reports either individually or cumulatively supports an inference that defendant controlled Otto or the safety of Otto's employees.

Plaintiff next contends that defendant's "complete right to control" Otto is evidenced by the nature of Otto's business relationship with defendant. Plaintiff points to the fact that defendant was Otto's only customer, posits that defendant therefore had the power to determine Otto's very survival, and concludes that defendant "possessed complete economic control" of Otto.

We find plaintiff's reasoning unpersuasive. Except for the fact that defendant is Otto's only customer, plaintiff's analysis is purely speculative. Plaintiff does not provide any authority for her position that a customer who purchases the entire output of a supplier therefore necessarily controls the supplier. Nor does plaintiff provide any authority for her contention that if a customer has economic control of a supplier, than the customer is responsible for the supplier's workers' safety.

Plaintiff's reliance on *Martin v. McDonald's Corp.* (1991), 213 Ill.App.3d 487, 157 Ill.Dec. 609, 572 N.E.2d 1073, is inapposite. In *Martin,* the defendant licensor controlled one aspect of its licensee's operation-security. The *Martin* court concluded that by its control of the licensee's security procedures the defendant voluntarily undertook to provide for the security of its licensee's employees and that a duty to provide security thus arose. (*Martin,* 213 Ill.App.3d at 492, 157 Ill.Dec. 609, 572 N.E.2d 1073.) In reaching this conclusion, the court noted that defendant's regional security supervisor acted directly as the security supervisor of the licensee, that the licensee did not have an operations manager or security supervisor of its own, and that defendant provided detailed security procedures to be followed by the licensee's employees. (*Martin,* 213 Ill.App.3d at

491–92, 157 Ill.Dec. 609, 572 N.E.2d 1073.) In this case, none of defendant's employees acted as direct supervisors of Otto's employees, Otto had its own safety personnel and procedures, and all of the safety procedures to be followed by Otto's employees came from Otto's safety supervisors.

Based on the foregoing, we conclude that plaintiff's claim that defendant controlled Otto because of defendant's economic relationship with Otto is without merit. Furthermore, assuming, *arguendo,* that defendant did exercise economic control of Otto, plaintiff has failed to show that this gave rise to a duty for defendant to guard against injury to Otto's employees. Plaintiff has also failed to show that defendant specifically controlled Otto's safety procedures. The record clearly shows that Otto exercised independent control of its workers' safety. Finally, we are guided by a recent supreme court decision which took a narrow construction of an alleged voluntary undertaking of duty on public policy grounds. (*Frye v. Medicare-Glaser Corp.* (1992), 143 Ill.2d 637, 167 Ill.-Dec. 399, 587 N.E.2d 1014.) We believe there are public policy grounds for taking a narrow construction of any assumption of duty by control in this case. The public policy concern is that such a precedent could lead to a result where any buyer who purchased the entire output of a supplier would necessarily be held responsible for the safety of the supplier's workers.

Plaintiff's last contention with respect to defendant's alleged control giving rise to a duty concerns Otto's use of defendant's name and logo (the golden arches) on its outdoor sign. Plaintiff does not cite any authority to support its contention that Otto's use of defendant's name and logo is tantamount to control by defendant.

[11, 12] Defendant argues that the situation is analogous to franchisor-franchisee cases which hold that when a franchisee uses the franchisor's logo it does not necessarily mean that the franchisor controls the franchisee. These cases and the related independent contractor cases generally hold that when a franchisee which uses a franchisor's logo or an independent contractor which uses an employer's logo retains day-to-day control of operations such as hiring and firing employees, payroll, workers compensation insurance, and taxes, then the franchisee or independent contractor is deemed to control itself and therefore to be liable for its worker's safety and the franchisor or employer of the independent contractor is not liable. (*Coty v. U.S. Slicing Machine Co.*

(1978), 58 Ill.App.3d 237, 240–42, 15 Ill.Dec. 687, 373 N.E.2d 1371.) A right to rescind a contract or call off the work is generally insufficient to establish control and impose liability for workers' safety under either the franchisee or employer-independent contractor theories. *Coty,* 58 Ill.App.3d at 242, 15 Ill.Dec. 687, 373 N.E.2d 1371.

Here, the record does not specifically categorize the relationship between defendant and Otto. There is nothing to show that defendant is a franchisor of Otto. The relationship is more in the nature of an employer-independent contractor. The question then becomes whether defendant had control over Otto's day-to-day operations. The record shows that defendant did not have such control. Defendant's employees testified that the purpose of their audits was to insure that the quality of the product met defendant's standards. There is nothing in the record to show that defendant had any control over Otto's day-to-day operations such as hiring and firing employees, payroll, workers compensation, or taxes. This is supported by the testimony of Otto's plant manager. We therefore conclude that defendant did not have control of Otto despite the fact that Otto used defendant's name and logo on its outdoor plant sign. The fact that Otto may have been "McDonaldized" does not change our conclusion.

For all the above reasons, we conclude that defendant did not control Otto or Otto's employees' safety and therefore did not have a duty of care for the safety of Otto's workers, including decedent. This question was correctly decided by the circuit court as a matter of law.

The circuit court grant of summary judgment in favor of defendant is affirmed.

Affirmed.

WOODWARD and McLAREN, JJ., concur.

3.
93-2060, 93-2061 (La.App. 4 Cir. 8/17/94)
Vesta GRAY
v.
Dr. Marcos FeBORNSTEIN.
Norman N. GRAY, M.D.
v.
ANTOINE'S RESTAURANT, Tulane University Medical Center, Marcos FeBornstein, M.D. and Henri' Alciatore.
Nos. 93–CA–2060, 93–CA–2061.

Court of Appeal of Louisiana,
Fourth Circuit.
Aug. 17, 1994.

Survivor brought wrongful death action against restaurant and maitre d', medical school, and doctor rendering assistance after son died from choking on meat at medical school-sponsored banquet. Defendant's motions for summary judgment were granted by the Civil District Court, Parish of Orleans, Yada T. Magee, J., and survivor appealed. The Court of Appeal, Barry, J., held that: (1) good samaritan statute did not require that victim be stranger to doctor rendering care, and (2) restaurant and maitre d' did not breach duty owed to patron.

Affirmed.

Armstrong, J., concurs in result.

1. Appeal and Error ⊙893(1)

Appellate courts review summary judgments de novo and use same criteria as trial court.

2. Judgment ⊙185(6)

Summary judgment is proper if pleadings, admissions, depositions, and supporting affidavits show there is no issue of material fact and mover is entitled to judgment as matter of law. LSA-C.C.P. art. 966, subd. B.

3. Judgment ⊙185(2)

Burden is on mover for summary judgment to prove absence of any genuine issue of material fact; any doubt shall be resolved against mover and in favor of trial on merits. LSA-C.C.P. art. 966, subd. B.

4. Judgment ⊙185(2)

Affidavits submitted by mover for summary judgment must be closely scrutinized while those of opponent are treated indulgently. LSA-C.C.P. art. 966, subd. B.

5. Physicians and Surgeons ⊙16

Good samaritan statute does not require that victim be stranger to doctor rendering care. LSA-R.S. 37:1731.

6. Physicians and Surgeons ⊙16

Under good samaritan statute, doctor who in good faith gratuitously rendered emergency care and tried to save life could not be held liable in wrongful death action, notwithstanding fact that decedent was known to doctor. LSA-R.S. 37:1731.

7. Negligence ⚖32(2.8)

Restaurant and maitre d' did not breach duty to patron who choked on food by failing to control crowd or direct rescuers to move accessible exit where patron was apparently highly intoxicated when he tried to consume steak and was surrounded by many physicians who rendered immediate emergency medical services, obstruction in his throat was very large piece of meat, and within moments there were repeated attempts to clear his air passageway, to no avail.

Don M. Richard, Denechaud & Denechaud, New Orleans, for plaintiff/appellant, Norman N. Gray, M.D.

Gregory C. Weiss, Lastrapes & Weiss, New Orleans, for defendants/appellees, Tulane Education Fund and Marcos FeBornstein, M.D.

Scott G. Jones, Hulse, Nelson & Wanek, New Orleans, for defendant/appelle, Henri' Alciatore.

Before BARRY, LOBRANO and ARMSTRONG, JJ.

BARRY, Judge.

Dr. Norman Gray appeals summary judgments granted to several defendants in his wrongful death action.[1] According to Dr. Gray's petition his son, Dr. Martin Gray, was attending a Tulane University Medical Center School of Medicine function at Antoine's Restaurant on June 10, 1989. During the meal a large mass of meat lodged in his throat and he was asphyxiated. He sued Tulane University Medical Center School of Medicine [Tulane], Dr. Marcos FeBornstein, Antoine's Restaurant and its maitre d', Henri' Alciatore, and the City of New Orleans and the Health Department Emergency Medical Service.

---

1. Dr. Gray's petition for appeal of the August 20, 1993 summary judgment granted to Henri' Alciatore is not signed by the trial court. It was clocked in on September 2, 1993 at 3:46 p.m. just minutes after he filed his petition for appeal of the August 2, 1993 summary judgment (granted to Dr. FeBornstein and Tulane Medical Center). Henri' Alciatore did not contest the petition for appeal. Any opposition to the appeal of the August 20, 1993 judgment is considered waived.

Dr. Norman Gray alleged the negligence of Tulane doctors and residents when they attempted to assist his son. Dr. Gray alleged that Dr. FeBornstein was negligent because he was not able to remove the obstruction. He claimed Antoine's Restaurant and Alciatore were negligent because Alciatore did not control the spectators which made it difficult for emergency technicians to carry his ailing son from the restaurant and did not show them the more accessible way out. The deceased's mother, Vesta Gray, only sued Dr. FeBornstein. The cases are consolidated. (#93–CA–2060 c/w #93–CA–2061). Mrs. Gray did not appeal.

Dr. Norman Gray argues that: (1) Tulane Medical Center breached its duty to exercise reasonable care; (2) Dr. FeBornstein did not act with reasonable and due care; (3) Henri' Alciatore breached his duty of reasonable care; and (4) summary judgment is improper when material issues of fact remain.

THE LAW

[1, 2] Appellate courts review summary judgments **de novo** and use the same criteria as the trial court. *Schroeder v. Board of Supervisors of Louisiana State University,* 591 So.2d 342 (La.1991); *Kantack v. Progressive Insurance Company,* 618 So.2d 494 (La.App. 4th Cir.1993), *writ denied,* 620 So.2d 845 (La.1993). Summary judgment is proper if the pleadings, admissions, depositions and supporting affidavits show there is no issue of material fact and the mover is entitled to judgment as a matter of law. La.C.C.P. art. 966B; *Barham & Churchill v. Campbell,* 503 So.2d 576 (La.App. 4th Cir.1987), *writ denied,* 503 So.2d 1018 (La.1987).

[3, 4] The burden is on the mover to prove the absence of any genuine issue of material fact. Any doubt shall be resolved against the mover and in favor of a trial on the merits. *Sassone v. Elder,* 626 So.2d 345 (La.1993); *Raine v. CECO Corporation,* 627 So.2d 713 (La.App. 4th Cir.1993). Affidavits submitted by the mover must be closely scrutinized while those of the opponent are treated indulgently. *Urbeso v. Bryan,* 583 So.2d 114 (La.App. 4th Cir.1991).

DR. FEBORNSTEIN AND TULANE MEDICAL CENTER

Dr. FeBornstein and Tulane attached to the motion for summary judgment: (1) Dr. Daniel Winstead's affidavit; (2) New Orleans

Health Department Emergency Medical Service Ambulance run report; (3) Dr. FeBornstein's affidavit; (4) Dr. Martin Gray's autopsy protocol dated June 11, 1989; (5) the death summary progress notes at Charity Hospital dated June 10, 1989; (6) the coroner's laboratory report dated June 21, 1989; and (7) the medical review panel opinion.

Dr. Winstead declared that he attended the departmental graduation dinner in the Japanese Room of Antoine's Restaurant on June 10, 1989. At about 8:00 p.m. he observed Dr. Martin Gray stagger into the room. Dr. Nancy Chiarello accompanied him to a place at her table which she had reserved for him. Shortly afterward he observed Dr. Gray retching and in distress and Dr. Tomlinson went to assist. Dr. Tomlinson instructed a waiter to call an ambulance and suggested the Heimlich maneuver to remove the obstruction. Dr. Winstead and others pulled Dr. Gray to his feet and Dr. Tomlinson administered five or six forceful Heimlich maneuvers. Dr. Gray was not breathing, but a neurology resident determined his pulse was 60 and strong. Dr. FeBornstein arrived on the scene and began mouth-to-mouth resuscitation. Dr. Gray's pulse remained strong but he was not breathing. Dr. FeBornstein unsuccessfully attempted to clear Dr. Gray's airway with a spoon. Someone suggested a tracheostomy and asked a waiter to bring a knife. Within seconds the emergency medical technicians arrived and an ambu bag was used to try to move air. Dr. Bray's pulse failed, closed chest massage was initiated and again there was talk of a tracheostomy. However, the emergency technicians insisted that Dr. Gray be taken to a hospital and they could use equipment in the ambulance. As Dr. Gray was being taken to the ambulance, Dr. FeBornstein continued his attempts at mouth-to-mouth resuscitation. Dr. Tomlinson continued to administer closed chest massage. Dr. FeBornstein boarded the ambulance with Dr. Gray.

Dr. FeBornstein stated that he attended the graduation dinner. At about 8:00 p.m. he left to make a telephone call, stepped into the hallway and saw Dr. Gray on the floor in a cyanotic condition and not breathing. Dr. Gray's heart was beating and he had a pulse. Dr. FeBornstein was told that an ambulance had been called. He began mouth-to-mouth resuscitation and stuck his fingers into Dr. Gray's mouth, but he could not clear the obstruction. Dr. Gray's tongue had collapsed, Dr. FeBornstein attempted unsuccessfully to clear the airway with a spoon. Seconds later emergency technicians arrived with an ambu bag and a laryngoscope. He used the laryngoscope to look down Dr. Gray's throat; however, the laryngoscope was either straight or not lighted and he was unable to observe an obstruction. As the emergency technicians took Dr. Gray to the ambulance he continued mouth-to-mouth resuscitation while Dr. Tomlinson continued to administer closed chest massage. Dr. FeBornstein rode in the ambulance and told the emergency technicians to give Epinephrine, Atropine and sodium bicarbonate. Dr. Gray was still in asystole and no pulse was detected. When the ambulance arrived at Charity Hospital, the emergency staff took over.

According to the autopsy protocol, the final diagnosis was asphyxia secondary to aspiration of foreign matter (mass unchewed meat) and the death was classified as accidental. The laboratory report showed that Dr. Gray had a blood alcohol level of .29 percent. According to the medical review panel there was no evidence that Dr. FeBornstein obstructed the efforts of the emergency medical technicians. The EMT reports shows only a momentary deferral to Dr. FeBornstein. The opinion stated that Dr. FeBornstein tried his best with his fingers, a spoon and a laryngoscope to remove the obstruction, which was very deep and required a special instrument to remove it. The panel found no negligence on the part of Dr. FeBornstein and Tulane in providing gratuitous medical treatment to Dr. Gray.

In his opposition and appellate brief Dr. Norman Gray argued that La.R.S. 37:1731, the Good Samaritan Statute, applies to rendering medical care to a stranger. Because Dr. Gray was a guest at the party and was known to Dr. FeBornstein, he claimed that the statute did not apply. Dr. Gray claims that his son was an invitee and was owed a duty of care by Tulane and the doctors in attendance at the party who had a duty to protect Dr. Gray from foreseeable dangers. Because eating and drinking were involved in the Tulane function, the defendant hosts should have foreseen such a problem. Alternatively, Dr. Gray submits that the Good Samaritan Statute applies to doctors, not to Tulane Medical Center. He claims that whether or not Dr. FeBornstein was negligent by taking control of a medical situation remained at issue.

La.R.S. 37:1731 provides:

No physician or surgeon licensed under the provisions of Chapter 15 of this Title, or nurses licensed under the provisions of Chapter 11 of this Title who in good faith gratuitously renders emergency care or services at the scene of an emergency, except in a public or private hospital of this State, to a person or persons in need thereof shall be liable for any civil damages as a result of any act or omission by such person in rendering the care or services or as a result of any act or failure to act to provide or arrange for further medical treatment or care for the person involved in the said emergency.

[5, 6] The statute does not require that the victim be a stranger. Dr. FeBornstein, in good faith, gratuitously rendered emergency care and tried to save the life of Dr. Martin Gray. Under La.R.S. 37:1731 he cannot be liable. Although Dr. Norman Gray argues that material issues of fact remain as to Tulane's liability, he does not state what those facts are.

There is no basis to hold Tulane University Medical Center liable. Summary judgment was properly granted.

ALCIATORE AND ANTOINE'S RESTAURANT

Henri' Alciatore filed a motion for summary judgment and attached Dr. Norman Gray's deposition which admitted that he did not know whether Alciatore was at the restaurant on the night of the incident. Alciatore noted that in two years Dr. Norman Gray did not produce any evidence to connect him to the dinner or the aftermath. He disputed the claims that he required the ambulance attendants to climb steep stairs to reach Dr. Gray, and that he failed to control the crowd in order to allow the attendants to move Dr. Gray. Alciatore argued that the stairs from the Japanese Room are the only way to enter or exit. Alciatore said the crowd around Dr. Gray were doctors. He argued that if he had forced the doctors to move from Dr. Gray's side he could be negligent for obstructing their attempts to render assistance.

Dr. Norman Gray argued that there are factual disputes including whether or not Alciatore was in the restaurant that night. He stated that more depositions had to be taken, but he did not explain why they were not taken during the two years before the hearing, to oppose the summary judgment. Dr. Norman Gray claims that the narrow entrance and exit to the dining room is a contested issue because he believes it played a part in his son's death. Dr. Gray did not dispute the fact that the stairway was the only in or out to the Japanese Room. He argued

that Alciatore should have been trained to assist persons who choke on food and he failed in that duty to his son.

[7] Dr. Martin Gray was apparently highly intoxicated when he tried to consume a steak. He was surrounded by many physicians who rendered immediate emergency medical services. The obstruction in his throat was a very large piece of meat. Within moments there were repeated attempts to clear his air passageway, to no avail. There are no issues of material fact and the defendants are entitled to summary judgment as a matter of law.

The trial court properly granted summary judgments to Dr. FeBornstein, Tulane University Medical Center and Henri' Alciatore. The judgments are affirmed.

AFFIRMED.

ARMSTRONG, J., concurs in result.

4.

322 Ark. 751

R. Don CAPLENER and Kathy Caplener, Appellants,

v.

BLUEBONNET MILLING COMPANY; Fry's Reproductive Center; and English Lawn Garden & Feed, Appellees.

No. 95–221.

Supreme Court of Arkansas.

Dec. 18, 1995.

Ostrich owners brought action against manufacturer, wholesaler, and retailer of seed, alleging that seed caused death of ostriches. The Circuit Court, White County, Darrell Hickman, J., granted summary judgment for defendants, denied defendants' request for award of attorney fees, and both parties appealed. The Supreme Court, Newbern, J., held that: (1) affidavit of veterinarian who was expert witness for plaintiffs that directly contradicted his earlier deposition testimony was not usable to establish question of fact to ward off grant of summary judgment; (2) plaintiffs failed to present sufficient evidence to create fact issue as to whether seed caused death of ostriches; and (3) defendants were not entitled to award of attorney fees.

Affirmed.

Glaze, J., filed dissenting opinion in which Brown, J., joined.

Brown, J., filed dissenting opinion in which Glaze, J., joined.

1. Judgment ∞185(2)

Once movant for summary judgment makes prima facie showing of entitlement of summary judgment, respondent must meet proof with proof to demonstrate remaining genuine issue of material fact. Rules Civ.Proc., Rule 56(c).

2. Judgment ∞185(6)

When party cannot present proof on essential element of claim, party moving for summary judgment is entitled to judgment as matter of law. Rules Civ.Proc., Rule 56(c).

3. Judgment ∞185.3(21)

Affidavit in which veterinarian testified that ostriches died because there was something wrong with their feed which caused it to impact, directly contradicted his earlier deposition testimony that he did not know what had caused ostriches to die and did not plan to testify on subject, and so was not usable to establish question of fact to ward off granting of summary judgment for manufacturer, wholesaler, and retailer of seed used to feed ostriches in ostrich owners' products liability action alleging that feed caused death of ostriches. Rules Civ.Proc., Rule 56(c).

4. Products Liability ∞45

Evidence submitted by owners of ostriches that died, that feed manufacturer and its distributors had received complaints about feed having mold, being in clumps, and being discolored, was not sufficient to show that feed eaten by ostriches caused their deaths. Rules Civ.Proc., Rule 56(c).

5. Trial ∞139.1(9)

Generally, trial court looks for substantial evidence when determining whether to grant motion for directed verdict; "substantial evidence" is that which is sufficient to compel conclusion one way or other and which induces factfinder to go beyond mere suspicion or conjecture.

See publication Words and Phrases for other judicial constructions and definitions.

6. Appeal and Error ∞1073(1)

Although trial court should not have said that ostrich owners failed to present "substantial evidence," in order granting summary judgment, for which nonmoving party need only establish evidence sufficient to raise fact issue, in ostrich owners' products liability action against feed manufacturer and distributors for death of ostriches, error was not prejudicial, since owners were unable to present any evidence to show that defect in feed supplied by defendants was cause of deaths of ostriches. Rules. Civ.Proc., Rule 56(c).

7. Appeal and Error ∞1031(1)

Supreme Court does not presume that prejudice has resulted from trial court's error, and will not reverse for error unless prejudice is demonstrated.

8. Costs ∞194.36

Award of attorney fees is discretionary under statute allowing for award of fees in action arising from contract relating to purchase or sale of goods. A.C.A. § 16–22–308.

9. Appeal and Error ∞984(5)

Trial court has discretion in determining whether violation of rule prohibiting frivolous pleading warranting award of attorney fees has occurred, and only if that discretion is abused will Supreme Court reverse. Rules Civ.Proc., Rule 11.

10. Costs ∞194.44

Feed retailer failed to establish, in ostrich owners' products liability action that alleged that defect in feed caused death of ostriches, any bad faith or harassment or that claim was without any reasonable basis, as required to entitle retailer to award of attorney fees. A.C.A. § 16–22–309.

11. Statutes ∞190

When language of statute is plain and unambiguous, Supreme Court gives language its plain and ordinary meaning.

———————

Samuel A. Perroni, Little Rock, for appellants.

Margaret Meads, Searcy, Thomas F. Meeks, Little Rock, for appellees.

NEWBERN, Justice.

In the summer of 1993, 23 young ostriches belonging to the appellants, Don and Kathy Caplener, died. The Capleners sued Bluebonnet Milling Company (Bluebonnet) which manufactured the feed they had fed the ostriches. They also sued the feed wholesaler, Fry's Reproductive Center (Fry's), and the retailer, English Lawn, Garden & Feed (English). The Trial Court entered summary judgment in favor of the defendants. The Capleners contend summary judgment was inappropriate as a genuine issue of material fact remained whether defective feed caused the deaths of the Ostriches. We affirm due to the failure to produce evidence that the feed caused the ostriches to die. We also affirm on cross-appeal the Trial Court's refusal to award attorney's fees to the prevailing parties and his denial of English's request for indemnification for litigation expenses from Bluebonnet.

Mr. Caplener's deposition testimony was that his ostriches, which ranged in age from one month to four months, were being fed Bluebonnet Chick Starter. Between May 28, 1993, and June 9, 1993, four bags of the feed were purchased from English and used. On June 16, 1993, some of the ostriches began to show symptoms of illness.

Dr. James W. Mills, a veterinarian, executed an affidavit on September 9, 1993. He said he was called to treat the birds. He initially prescribed antibiotics and electrolytes and then flushing with water. The birds did not respond to the treatment. Dr. Mills then recommended changing to a different brand of feed. None of the treatments succeeded. From postmortem operations Dr. Mills discovered the feed had impacted in the birds' stomachs and that caused their deaths. He stated, "blood tests . . . showed normal cultures . . . and no bacteria or infection present which could have caused death."

The Capleners had a laboratory analysis performed on a sample of the feed which had been left in a feed pan after most of the Bluebonnet feed had been removed. The results from the first sample sent to the laboratory were negative, but a second sample contained four parts per billion of aflatoxin. It is undisputed that aflatoxin, in concentrated amounts, can be lethal to ostriches. According to Mr. Caplener's deposition, lettuce or boiled eggs had been sprinkled on the Bluebonnet feed occasionally to encourage the birds to eat.

The complaint alleged the feed was adulterated due to the presence of aflatoxin. It was amended to add the allegation of failure to warn and, after the motion for summary judgment was filed, it was amended to allege liability based on the feed being indigestible.

In a deposition, Dr. Mills contradicted his earlier affidavit. He admitted that both e. coli and klebsiella pathogens were found in the intestines of the ostriches, and that death by bacterial pathogen could not be ruled out. His deposition testimony was also internally contradictory. At one point, Dr. Mills opined that the birds died from feed impaction, but in another part of his deposition, he stated he could not give a definite opinion as to why the birds died. Finally, when questioned on the quality of the feed, the following colloquy occurred:

MR. MEETS [counsel for Bluebonnet]: What caused the impaction?

DR. MILLS: I don't know the answer to that.

* * * * * *

MR. MEEKS: Okay. Well, I guess what I'm asking: Are you going to testify at trial that there was something wrong with the food and that caused them to impact?

DR. MILLS: No, because I don't know that there was anything wrong with the food.

MR. MEEKS: Okay.

DR. MILLS: And I can't stand up and say that the food was bad. No, I can't do that.

On August 15, 1994, Fry's and English filed a joint motion for summary judgment. Bluebonnet moved for summary judgment on the same day. Both motions were based on the Capleners' failure to produce evidence that the feed proximately caused the deaths of the birds. Attached to Bluebonnet's motion were excerpts from the depositions of Dr. Mills and Richard Plant, a chemist who had examined some of the leftover feed and found low levels of aflatoxin. Mr. Plant said he was not an expert on the effects of aflatoxin on ratites and that he did not know how much aflatoxin it would take to kill an ostrich. He stated that his opinion was based simply on the fact that toxins are known to vary widely in their concentration within a batch of feed. He also stated that he was not going to testify that aflatoxin killed the birds. Also attached were affidavits from Dr. John Reagor, the head of the Texas Diagnostic Toxicology Department, and Dr. Karen Hicks-Alldredge, a veterinary expert on the care of ratites. Both concluded, based on the deposition testimony in the record, that the birds did not die from aflatoxin poisoning.

With their response to the motion for summary judgment the Capleners filed a second affidavit of Dr. Mills, dated August 17, 1994, in which he stated, in contrast to his deposition testimony, "I believe that there was something wrong with the commercial feed that prevented it from digesting properly. As I testified, I did not test the feed and could not say in what way the feed was defective."

The Trial Court granted a motion by Bluebonnet to strike Dr. Mill's second affidavit and granted the defendants' motions for summary judgment. The Capleners moved for reconsideration. Attached to the motion, in addition to Dr. Mills's two affidavits and excerpts from his deposition testimony, were several customer complaint forms which showed that other ostrich farmers had complained of molded feed. The Trial Court denied the motion for reconsideration.

The Trial Court also refused to award attorney's fees and refused to order Bluebonnet to indemnify English and Fry's for the cost of the litigation. The Capleners appeal from the summary judgment. Bluebonnet and English appeal from the denial of attorney's fees, and English appeals from the denial of indemnification.

1. Material fact issue

When summary judgment is sought, the Trial Court must decide if "the pleadings, depositions, answers to interrogatories and admissions on file, together with the affidavits, if any, show that there is no genuine issue as to any material fact and that the moving party is entitled to judgment as a matter of law." Ark.R.Civ.P. 56(c); *Oglesby v. Baptist Medical System,* 319 Ark. 280, 891 S.W.2d 48 (1995); *Forrest City Mach. Works v. Mosbacher,* 312 Ark. 578, 851 S.W.2d 443 (1993).

Among the attachments to Bluebonnet's summary judgment motion were excerpts from Dr. Mills's deposition testimony as well as testimony of the toxicology expert who said the postmortem evidence did not indicate the ostriches died from aflatoxins. Also included was testimony of the ratite expert who concluded there was insufficient information to identify the specific cause of death of the ostriches.

[1, 2] Once the movant makes a prima facie showing of entitlement to summary judg-

ment, the respondent must meet proof with proof to demonstrate a remaining genuine issue of material fact. *Sanders v. Banks,* 309 Ark. 375, 830 S.W.2d 861 (1992). When a party cannot present proof on an essential element of the claim, the moving party is entitled to judgment as a matter of law. *Id.*

[3] In response to the motion for summary judgment, the Capleners were required to produce some evidence which would raise a material question of fact as to whether the feed manufactured by Bluebonnet caused the impaction. They submit that the second affidavit of Dr. Mills, in which he stated the feed was "indigestible," was sufficient to create a fact issue as to whether the feed caused the birds to die. We hold that the Trial Court correctly excluded the second affidavit when considering the motions for summary judgment.

Our summary judgment rule, Ark.R.-Civ.P. 56, is virtually the same as F.R.C.P. 56. The General Assembly adopted the Federal Rule 56 initially by Act 123 of 1961, and we continued to follow the federal model upon adoption of the Arkansas Rules of Civil Procedure which became effective in 1979. As we do with others of our rules modeled on the federal rules, we refer to federal court decisions in our interpretation of Rule 56. *Irvin v. Jones,* 310 Ark. 114, 832 S.W.2d 827 (1992); *Short v. Little Rock Dodge,* 297 Ark. 104, 759 S.W.2d 553 (1988).

While we have not addressed the issue, federal courts have held that an affidavit which is inherently and blatantly inconsistent with prior deposition testimony may not be used to establish a question of fact to ward off the granting of a summary judgment motion. *Camfield Tires, Inc. v. Michelin Tire Corp.,* 719 F.2d 1361 (8th Cir.1983); *Radobenko v. Automated Equip. Corp.,* 520 F.2d 540 (9th Cir.1975); *Perma Research & Development Co. v. Singer Co.,* 410 F.2d 572 (2d Cir.1969); *Vanlandingham v. Ford Motor Co.,* 99 F.R.D. 1 (N.D.Ga.1993). *See also Jacobs v. Fire Ins. Exch.,* 36 Cal.App.4th 1258, 42 Cal.Rptr.2d 906 (3 Dist.1995). These cases indicate that a subsequent affidavit may perhaps be used to explain internally inconsistent deposition testimony, *see Kennett-Murray Corp. v. Bone,* 622 F.2d 887 (5th Cir.1980); however, as the Court said in the *Perma Research* case, "If a party who has been examined at length on deposition could raise an issue of fact simply by submitting an affidavit contradicting his own prior testimony, this would greatly diminish the utility of summary judgment as a procedure for screening out sham issues of fact."

Although Dr. Mills's deposition testimony was not a model of clarity, he stated definitely that he did not know what had caused the Capleners' ostriches to die and did not plan to testify on the subject. In his later affidavit he said the birds died because there was something wrong with their feed which caused it to impact. The contradiction is direct, and we hold it was not error for the Trial Court to disregard Dr. Mills's second affidavit.

[4] In addition to Dr. Mills's affidavits, the Capleners presented other evidence in their motion for reconsideration that Bluebonnet and its distributors had received other complaints about feed having mold, being in "clumps," and being discolored. Even if that evidence were to be appropriate for consideration at the late date it was presented, it was insufficient to raise an issue of fact whether the feed eaten by the Capleners' ostriches caused their deaths.

2. The evidence standard

The Capleners also argue that Trial Court used the wrong standard in determining whether to grant the motion for summary judgment. The contention is based on the Trial Court's letter ruling in which he wrote, "There is no substantial evidence why [the ostriches] died. There is no substantial evidence the feed was defective or that it caused the deaths." In responding to the Capleners' motion for reconsideration, the Trial Court did not use the term "substantial evidence," but it did appear in the order granting summary judgment.

[5] Generally, a trial court looks for substantial evidence when determining whether to grant a motion for a directed verdict. *See Mahan v. Hall,* 320 Ark. 473, 897 S.W.2d 571 (1995); *See also Jackson v. State,* 290 Ark. 375, 720 S.W.2d 282 (1986). We have, however, said that if the defendant conclusively shows that some fact essential to the plaintiff's cause of action is wanting and the plaintiff is unable to offer substantial evidence to the contrary, a summary judgment is proper. *See Tillotson v. Farmers Ins. Co.,* 276 Ark. 450, 637 S.W.2d 541 (1982); *Lee v. Doe,* 274 Ark. 467, 626 S.W.2d 353 (1981); *Akridge v. Park Bowling Ctr., Inc.,* 240 Ark. 538, 401 S.W.2d 204 (1966). Our use of the term "substantial evidence" in opinions describing the evidence which must be produced in response to a motion for summary judgment was ill advised. Substantial evidence is that which is sufficient to compel a conclu-

sion one way or the other and which induces the fact finder to go beyond mere suspicion or conjecture. *Aronson v. Harriman,* 321 Ark. 359, 901 S.W.2d 832 (1995); *Barnes, Quinn, Flake & Anderson, Inc. v. Rankins,* 312 Ark. 240, 848 S.W.2d 924 (1993).

[6, 7] As discussed above, the standard to be applied in summary judgment cases is whether there is evidence sufficient to raise a fact issue rather than evidence sufficient to compel a conclusion on the part of the fact finder. Although it was wrong for the Trial Court to have used the term "substantial evidence," some of our prior cases notwithstanding, the error was not prejudicial. As noted in the first segment of this opinion, the Capleners were unable to present evidence to show that a defect in the ostrich feed supplied by the defendants was the cause of the birds' deaths; thus no genuine issue of material fact remained to be decided. We do not presume that prejudice has resulted from a trial court's error, and we will not reverse for error unless prejudice is demonstrated. *People's Bank & Trust Co. v. Wallace,* 290 Ark. 589, 721 S.W.2d 659 (1986). *See also Mikel v. Hubbard,* 317 Ark. 125, 876 S.W.2d 558 (1994); *Carton v. Missouri Pac. R.R.,* 315 Ark. 5, 865 S.W.2d 635 (1993); *Webb v. Thomas,* 310 Ark. 553, 837 S.W.2d 875 (1992).

3. Attorney's fees

Bluebonnet and English argue that the Trial Court should have awarded attorney's fees based on Ark.Code Ann. § 16–22–308 and pursuant to Ark.R.Civ.P. 11. The statute provides:

In any civil action to recover on an open account, statement of account, account stated, promissory note, bill, negotiable instrument, or contract relating to the purchase or sale of goods, wares, or merchandise, or for labor or services, or breach of contract, unless otherwise provided by law or the contract which is the subject matter of the action, the prevailing party may be allowed a reasonable attorney fee to be assessed by the court and collected as costs.

[8] The award of attorney's fees is discretionary under the statute. *Little Rock Wastewater Util. v. Larry Moyer Trucking,* 321 Ark. 303, 902 S.W.2d 760 (1995). Neither party cites authority or presents argument indicating that the Trial Court abused his discretion. Absent such authority or argument, we find no abuse

of discretion in denying attorney's fees pursuant to the statute.

[9] Rule 11 requires an attorney to make a reasonable inquiry into the law prior to signing a pleading, motion, or other paper. The rule states, in part, "If a pleading, motion or other paper is signed in violation of this rule, the court . . . shall impose upon the person who signed it . . . an appropriate sanction, which may include an order to pay . . . the amount of the reasonable expenses incurred." Ark.R.-Civ.P. 11; *Whetstone v. Chadduck,* 316 Ark. 330, 871 S.W.2d 583 (1994). The Trial Court has discretion in determining whether a violation occurred. *Whetstone v. Chadduck, supra; See also Bratton v. Gunn,* 300 Ark. 140, 777 S.W.2d 219 (1989). Only if this discretion is abused will we reverse. *Whetstone v. Chadduck, supra; Ward v. Dapper Dan Cleaners and Laundry, Inc.,* 309 Ark. 192, 828 S.W.2d 833 (1992). The Trial Court did not find a violation of Rule 11, and there is simply no evidence that the determination was an abuse of discretion.

[10] English makes the separate contention that it was entitled to attorney's fees pursuant to Ark.Code Ann. § 16–22–309 (Repl.1994) which provides for award of an attorney's fee when a claim is brought absent a justiciable issue. The statute describes a claim lacking a justiciable issue as one commenced "in bad faith solely for purposes of harassing or maliciously injuring another or delaying adjudication without just cause or that the party or the party's attorney knew, or should have known, that the . . . claim . . . was without any reasonable basis in law or equity and could not be supported by a good faith argument of an extension, modification, or reversal of existing law."

Had discovery shown the feed which impacted the ostriches' stomachs to have been defective, perhaps by a greater presence of aflatoxin, an issue might have arisen as to how it appeared in the feed, and that could have raised questions about its handling and storage by English. There has been no showing of bad faith or harassment or that the claim was without "any reasonable basis."

4. Indemnity

English submits that it is entitled to indemnification under Ark.Code Ann. § 16–116–107 (1987). The statute provides that "a supplier of a *defective product* who was not the manufacturer shall have a cause of action for indemnity from the manufacturer of a *defective product* arising from the supplying of the *defective product.*" [Emphasis added.]

[11] When the language of a statute is plain and unambiguous, we give the language its plain and ordinary meaning. *Omega Tube & Conduit Corp. v. Maples,* 312 Ark. 489, 850 S.W.2d 317 (1993); *City of Fort Smith v. Tate,* 311 Ark. 405, 844 S.W.2d 356 (1992). In this instance, the defective product claim has failed.

Affirmed.

GLAZE and BROWN, JJ., dissent.

GLAZE, Justice, dissenting.

I join in Justice Brown's dissent, but I also believe this case must be reversed and remanded because the trial court utilized the wrong standard in granting the appellees summary judgment. The majority opinion recognizes this point, states the trial court's use of the "substantial evidence" was incorrect, but then affirms the trial court's ruling, saying the error was not prejudicial. From the record, we cannot be sure the trial court was not requiring plaintiffs to prove their case by substantial evidence. That fact, alone, is sufficient prejudice.

BROWN, J., joins this dissent.

BROWN, Justice, dissenting.

In the case at hand Dr. Mills, a veterinarian, was adamant throughout that impacted bird feed had caused the birds to die. He had performed the post-mortems on the birds and knew whereof he spoke.

On September 9, 1993, which was months before the first complaint was filed by the Capleners on January 31, 1994, Dr. Mills averred by way of affidavit:

> After the birds died, I posted them, *i.e.,* cut them open and examined them. They were all impacted with commercial bird feed. They did not have sufficient grass within them to cause a problem. There were no other foreign objects inside them. Their stomachs were swollen with food. They died from food impaction by commercial bird feed.
>
> . . . .
>
> I advised Don to change bird feed after a few of the ostriches died because I determined that the ostriches ate the food and the food impacted them, which caused their deaths.

On July 15, 1994, Dr. Mills's deposition was taken, and he testified that impaction killed the birds but that he did not know what caused the impaction.

Motions for summary judgment were filed by the appellees on August 15, 1994, and two days later on August 17, 1994, Dr. Mills averred again by way of affidavit:

After reviewing my deposition, I discovered that my answers left it unclear as to my belief regarding cause of death of Don Caplener's ostriches.

It is my belief that the primary cause of death of these birds was feed impaction resulting from indigestible feed. I believe a virus or bacteria contracted by any of these birds would have been a secondary infection that resulted from the feed impaction. I did not observe anything to indicate that these birds were suffering from shock or stress. On posting, these birds appeared generally healthy and I did not observe any other abnormalities.

For these reasons, I believe that there was something wrong with the commercial feed that prevented it from digesting properly. As I testified, I did not test the feed and could not say in what way the feed was defective.

On August 25, 1994, and August 26, 1994, the respective appellees moved to strike Dr. Mills's second affidavit. The trial court's letter opinion of September 6, 1994, struck the second affidavit and granted the appellees' motions for summary judgment.

The majority decision affirms the striking of the second Mills affidavit on the basis that it contradicts Dr. Mills's deposition. But there was a reason for the second affidavit. Dr. Mills is a veterinarian, not a chemist or toxicologist. He did not test the feed or know precisely how it was defective and why it impacted. Thus, he stated at deposition that he could not testify at trial what exactly was wrong with the feed. But he never wavered from his opinion that feed impaction caused the birds to die.

A reasonable explanation for a statement made in deposition seems perfectly permissible to me, and I would not decide this case by striking the second Mills affidavit. Moreover, there is still the first Mills affidavit where he unmistakably opined that the birds died of feed impaction and where he states that he advised the Capleners to change bird feed.

Admittedly, why the commercial feed impacted remains an open question. The affidavits supporting the appellees' motions for summary judgment discounted aflatoxin as a cause, as the majority opinion points out, but in appellants'

second amended complaint allegations of adulterated feed go beyond the assertions related to aflatoxin. The appellants should have the right to further develop their case.

I would reverse the order of summary judgment and remand.

GLAZE, J., joins.

5.

Victor C. TOMKA, Appellant,

v.

HOECHST CELANESE CORP. d/b/a Hoechst-Roussel Agri-Vet Co., Appellee.

No. 93–869.

Supreme Court of Iowa.

Feb. 22, 1995.

Operator of custom cattle feeding operation brought action against manufacturer of synthetic growth hormone with which cattle were treated at customer's request, asserting claims sounding in tort and express and implied warranty. After manufacturer filed motion for directed verdict, operator sought to amend pleading to add claims premised on manufacturer's alleged violation of federal regulation. The District Court for Carroll County, Gary L. McMinimee, J., denied motion to amend and granted directed verdict, and operator appealed. The Court of Appeals affirmed, and further review was sought. The Supreme Court, Ternus, J., held that: (1) operator could not recover under tort theories for economic damages resulting solely from fact that cattle gained weight at slower pace than would be expected; (2) operator was at best nonprivity buyer seeking to recover only consequential economic loss damages, and could not rely on express warranty theory; (3) operator could not recover for solely consequential economic loss damages under implied warranty theories; and (4) amendment was properly denied on ground that it would have substantially changed operator's claims midway through trial.

Affirmed.

1. Appeal and Error ⬤866(3)

Court's grant of motion for directed verdict is reviewed for correction of errors of law.

2. Appeal and Error ⬤866(3), 927(7)

In reviewing grant of motion for directed verdict, reviewing court must decide whether trial court correctly determined that there was insufficient evidence to submit case to jury; in making such decision, reviewing court views evidence in light most favorable to nonmoving party.

3. Drugs and Narcotics ⊶18

Even if operator of custom cattle feeding operation had property interest as bailee of customer's cattle, he could not recover under theories of strict liability or negligence from manufacturer of synthetic growth hormone with which cattle were treated; although operator contended that cattle were damaged, evidence showed that they merely gained weight at slower pace than would be expected and that cattle were otherwise in good clinical health, and failure of hormones to promote growth as intended was not type of damage tort theories were designed to protect against.

4. Sales ⊶255

Operator of custom cattle feeding operation could not recover under theory of express warranty from manufacturer of synthetic growth hormone with which cattle were treated at customer's request; operator was not in privity with manufacturer inasmuch as he purchased hormone from veterinarians, and damages he sought for lost profits and loss of good will were consequential economic loss damages that could not be recovered by nonprivity buyer.

5. Contracts ⊶186(1)

Whether party is in privity with another party depends on whether they are parties to contract; if parties have contracted with each other, they are in privity, while parties are not in privity if they have not contracted with each other.

6. Sales ⊶255

Operator of custom cattle feeding operation, as nonprivity buyer of synthetic growth hormone from veterinarians, could not recover consequential economic loss damages from hormone manufacturer under implied warranty theories of merchantability and fitness for particular purpose. I.C.A. §§ 554.2314, 554.2315.

7. Sales ⊶272

Under Iowa law, warranty that goods sold are merchantable is implied in contract for their sale. I.C.A. § 554.2314.

8. Sales ⊶273(3)

If seller has reason to know at time of contracting that buyer is purchasing goods for particular purpose and that buyer is relying on seller's skill and judgment to furnish suitable goods, there arises warranty that goods should be fit for that purpose. I.C.A. § 554.2315.

9. Sales ⊶255

Purchaser may not maintain suit for breach of implied warranties by remote manufacturer where only damages sought are for consequential economic loss. I.C.A. §§ 554.2314, 554.2315.

10. Pleading ⊶248(10, 17)

In action in which operator of custom cattle feeding operation initially asserted tort and warranty claims against manufacturer of synthetic growth hormone, trial court was justified in refusing to permit operator to amend his petition to add theories of intentional tort and gross negligence based on manufacturer's alleged violation of federal regulation; amendment would have substantially changed claims against manufacturer midway through trial, and admission of evidence of manufacturer's conduct that allegedly violated regulation without objection by manufacturer did not establish manufacturer's consent to new theories of recovery because evidence was relevant to warranty claims.

11. Appeal and Error ⊶959(1)

Trial court's refusal to allow amendment of petition will be reversed only upon showing of clear abuse of discretion.

12. Pleading ⊶237(1)

Although leave to amend pleading should be freely given, amendment to conform to proof should not be allowed if it will substantially change claim.

Robert Kohorst of the Kohorst Law Firm, Harlan, for appellant.

Roland D. Peddicord and Joseph M. Barron of Peddicord, Wharton, Thune & Spencer, Des Moines, for appellee.

Considered by HARRIS, P.J., and LAR-

SON, LAVORATO, ANDREASEN, and TER-
NUS, JJ.

TERNUS, Justice.

Plaintiff, Victor Tomka, sued defendant,
Hoechst Celanese Corporation d/b/a Hoechst-
Roussel Agri-Vet Co., a manufacturer of synthetic growth hormones. Tomka sought to recover damages he sustained when cattle he was
custom feeding were implanted with a hormone
manufactured by Hoechst.

The trial court granted Hoechst's motion
for directed verdict and the court of appeals
affirmed. Both the trial court and the court of
appeals held that Tomka could not recover economic losses in the absence of any damage to
his property. Because Tomka did not own the
cattle that were implanted, both courts concluded that Tomka did not suffer any property
damage and so could not maintain his case. We
affirm because we agree Hoechst was entitled to
a directed verdict for reasons we discuss below.

Tomka also appeals from the trial court's
denial of his motion for leave to amend. The
court of appeals affirmed this ruling and so
do we.

I. *Background Facts and Proceedings.*

Tomka had a custom cattle feeding operation. In 1988 and 1989, he contracted with Bob
Brummer to feed cattle owned by Brummer.
Pursuant to these contracts, Brummer delivered
heifers owned by Brummer to Tomka's facilities. Tomka agreed to feed the cattle until they
reached market weight. At that time Brummer
would presumably sell the cattle. Brummer
promised to pay Tomka forty cents per pound
for the first 300 pounds of weight gained and
fifty cents per pound of weight gained after that.

Brummer wanted the cattle implanted
with Synovex and Finaplix, two synthetic
growth hormones. Tomka arranged for the implants to be done by local veterinarians. These
veterinarians implanted the hormones and
billed Brummer for the cost of the hormones
and the charge for implanting them. Finaplix
is manufactured by Hoechst.

Tomka testified that the cattle became
restless several days after the implants and exhibited bullish behavior. He claims they did not
gain weight as they should have and consequently the cattle were sold later than he expected. As a result, he lost money on his contracts with Brummer.

Tomka sued several parties but only
Hoechst remained as a defendant at the time

of trial. Tomka relied on theories of breach of
express warranty, breach of the implied warranties of merchantability and fitness for a particular purpose, negligence and strict products liability.

Tomka's expert witness testified that implanting both Synovex and Finaplix overdosed
the cattle on male hormones, causing aggres-
sive behavior. He said that animals receiving
the dual implants would be in good clinical
health but would not gain much weight. In his
opinion, Hoechst should have warned against
the usage of Finaplix in combination with other
male hormones.

At the close of Tomka's case, the trial court
sustained Hoechst's motion for a directed verdict. Simultaneously, Tomka sought leave to
amend his petition to add claims of intentional
tort and gross negligence. These new claims
were based on Hoechst's alleged violation of a
federal regulation by indirectly promoting the
use of Finaplix in combination with other implants. The trial court denied this motion, concluding in part that Hoechst had no notice of
these theories and they were not tried by consent.

II. *Scope of Review of Directed Verdict.*

[1, 2] We review the court's grant of a
motion for directed verdict for correction of errors of law. *Spaur v. Owens-Corning Fiberglas
Corp.,* 510 N.W.2d 854, 858 (Iowa 1994). We
must decide whether the trial court correctly determined that there was insufficient evidence to
submit the case to the jury. *Smith v. Smithway
Motor Xpress, Inc.,* 464 N.W.2d 682, 684 (Iowa
1990). In making this decision, we view the evidence in the light most favorable to the nonmoving party. *Spaur,* 510 N.W.2d at 858.

III. *Motion for Directed Verdict on Tort
Theories.*

[3] The trial court granted Hoechst's
motion for directed verdict on the strict liability
and negligence theories on the basis that Tomka
sought to recover solely economic losses. The
court relied on the principle of law that a plaintiff
may not recover economic losses under strict
liability or negligence theories if the plaintiff's property or person has not sustained damage. *See Nelson v. Todd's Ltd.,* 426 N.W.2d 120,
123 (Iowa 1988) ("purely economic injuries
without accompanying physical injury to the
user or consumer or to the user or consumer's
property are not recoverable under strict liability"); *Nebraska Innkeepers, Inc. v. Pittsburgh-*

Des Moines Corp., 345 N.W.2d 124, 126 (Iowa 1984) ("a plaintiff who has suffered only economic loss due to another's negligence has not been injured in a manner which is legally cognizable or compensable"). Tomka argues for the first time on appeal that he had a property interest in the cattle as a bailee. Therefore, he concludes, he suffered physical injury to his property, the cattle, in addition to the economic losses he sustained.

We need not address the bailment issue because we believe that the directed verdict was properly granted even if Tomka had a property interest in the cattle. Although Tomka argues that the cattle were damaged, the evidence showed that the cattle merely gained weight at a slower pace than one would expect of cattle injected with a growth hormone. In fact, Tomka's own expert testified that cattle given dual implants were in good clinical health.[1]

We think Tomka's damages fall squarely within the holding of our *Nelson* case. In *Nelson* a curing agent for meat purchased by the plaintiffs failed to work. *Nelson,* 426 N.W.2d at 121. Consequently, substantial quantities of meat sold by the plaintiffs spoiled and were returned by their customers. *Id.* The plaintiffs sought recovery from the manufacturer of the curing agent under theories of strict liability and breach of express warranty. *Id.* The trial court submitted both theories to the jury which returned a verdict in plaintiff's favor. *Id.*

On appeal, we held that the trial court erred in submitting both theories to the jury. *Id.* at 125. In analyzing whether contract law or tort law applied, we focused not on the presence or absence of physical harm but on whether the defect in the product was dangerous to the user. *Id.* at 122–25. We quoted with approval from an Illinois case:

> "We see no reason to make the presence or absence of physical harm the determining factor; the distinguishing central feature of economic loss is not its purely physical characteristic, but its relation to what the product was supposed to accomplish. For example, if a fire alarm

fails to work and a building burns down, that is 'economic loss' even though the building was physically harmed; but if the fire is caused by a short circuit in the fire alarm itself, that is not economic loss."

Id. at 124 (quoting *Fireman's Fund Am. Ins. Cos. v. Burns Elec. Security Serv.,* 93 Ill.App.3d 298, 48 Ill.Dec. 729, 731, 417 N.E.2d 131, 133 (1981)). In other words, contract law protects a purchaser's expectation interest that the product received will be fit for its intended use. *Moorman Mfg. Co. v. National Tank Co.,* 91 Ill.2d 69, 61 Ill.Dec. 746, 751, 435 N.E.2d 443, 448 (1982); *Northridge Co. v. W.R. Grace & Co.,* 162 Wis.2d 918, 471 N.W.2d 179, 185 (1991). The essence of products liability law is that the plaintiff has been exposed, through a dangerous product, to a risk of injury to his person or property. *Moorman Mfg. Co.,* 435 N.E.2d at 448; *Northridge Co.,* 471 N.W.2d at 185. As the Wisconsin Supreme Court summarized, "defects of suitability and quality are redressed through contract actions and safety hazards through tort actions." *Northridge Co.,* 471 N.W.2d at 185.

We think the damage sustained by Tomka here clearly falls within contract-warranty theories, not tort theories. As Tomka's own attorney said, "[T]his product is designed here to promote growth in cattle and yet we are alleging that the product failed to do that." Tort law does not encompass this type of damage and therefore, the trial court properly directed a verdict on Tomka's strict liability and negligence theories.[2] *G & M Farms v. Funk Irrigation Co.,* 119 Idaho 514, 808 P.2d 851, 864 (1991) (court affirmed dismissal of negligent misrepresentation claim alleging that manufacturer failed to disclose that irrigation system could not meet plaintiff's needs, holding that remedy for purely economic damages falls within implied warranty, not tort).

---

[1]. Tomka testified that some of the cattle died. His expert testified that autopsies on the cattle showed they died from heat stress. Neither the expert nor any other witness testified that Hoechst's hormone was the cause of the cattle's death.

---

[2]. After the trial court had ruled on Hoechst's motion for directed verdict, Tomka argued for the first time that he had suffered damage to his good will. He claimed that this harm constituted property damage and therefore, he did not seek recovery solely for economic losses. We disagree. For purposes of warranty and tort analysis, loss of good will is an economic loss. *Beyond the Garden Gate, Inc. v. Northstar Freeze-Dry Mfg., Inc.,* 526 N.W.2d 305 (Iowa 1995). *See generally* 1 James J. White & Robert S. Summers, *Uniform Commercial Code* § 11–6, at 539 (3d ed.1988).

IV. *Motion for Directed Verdict on Warranty Theories.*

Hoechst challenged Tomka's ability to recover under warranty theories on several bases. Among Hoechst's arguments were (1) Tomka was not the "buyer" of the implant, and (2) Tomka could not recover because he sustained only economic losses and no physical damage to his property. Tomka took the position that he was the "functioning purchaser" and therefore entitled to rely on warranty theories of recovery. We conclude that even if Tomka can be considered the buyer of the hormones, he is still not entitled to recover from Hoechst—a remote seller—because he sustained only economic loss damages.

[4] A. *Breach of express warranty.* We have recently held that non-privity buyers cannot recover consequential economic loss damages under a theory of express warranty. *Beyond the Garden Gate, Inc. v. Northstar Freeze-Dry Mfg., Inc.,* 526 N.W.2d 305, 309–10 (Iowa 1995). This rule bars any recovery by Tomka under his express warranty theory.

[5] Whether a party is "in privity" with another party depends on whether they are parties to a contract. If the parties have contracted with each other, they are in privity. 1 James J. White & Robert S. Summers, *Uniform Commercial Code* § 11–2, at 528 (3d ed. 1988) (hereinafter "White and Summers"). If they have not, they are not in privity. *Id.* White and Summers gives an example of a non-privity plaintiff as one who purchases a product but does not buy it directly from the defendant. *Id.*

That is the situation we have here. Even if Tomka can be considered a buyer, he did not buy the product from the defendant manufacturer. He purchased Finaplix from the veterinarians. Therefore, Tomka was not in privity with Hoechst.

Additionally, the damages that Tomka seeks to recover are consequential economic loss damages. As we explained in *Beyond the Garden Gate,* "direct economic loss" damage is " 'the difference between the actual value of the goods accepted and the value they would have had if they had been as warranted.' " *Beyond the Garden Gate, Inc.,* 526 N.W.2d at 309 (quoting White and Summers at 536). "Consequential economic loss" includes " 'loss of profits resulting from the failure of the goods to function as warranted, loss of goodwill, and loss of business reputation.' " *Id.* Tomka seeks damages for lost profits and loss of good will. Therefore, his damages are consequential economic loss.

Because Tomka is at best a non-privity buyer and because he seeks to recover only consequential economic loss damages, he may not rely on a theory of breach of express warranty. *Id.* at 310. The trial court correctly directed a verdict for the defendant on this theory of liability.

[6–8] B. *Implied warranties of merchantability and fitness for a particular purpose.* Under Iowa law a warranty that goods sold are merchantable is implied in a contract for their sale. Iowa Code § 554.2314 (1993). Additionally, if the seller has reason to know at the time of contracting that the buyer is purchasing the goods for a particular purpose and that the buyer is relying on the seller's skill and judgment to furnish suitable goods, there arises a warranty that the goods shall be fit for that purpose. *Id.* § 554.2315. We have never allowed recovery for solely consequential economic losses under these implied warranty theories by one not in privity with the defendant. We decline to do so now.

The same reasons we found persuasive in *Beyond the Garden Gate* to disallow recovery under an express warranty theory apply here. In addition, an extension of implied warranty theories to non-privity buyers would seriously hamper the ability of remote sellers to disclaim warranties as allowed by the Uniform Commercial Code. *See Professional Lens Plan, Inc. v. Polaris Leasing Corp.,* 234 Kan. 742, 675 P.2d 887, 898 (1984) (extension of implied warranties to remote manufacturers would spawn numerous problems in the operation of the Uniform Commercial Code). We should not lightly undermine the legislative schemes for governance of commercial transactions. *See Szajna v. General Motors Co.,* 115 Ill.2d 294, 104 Ill.Dec. 898, 905, 503 N.E.2d 760, 767 (1986) (refusing to extend implied warranties to remote buyer seeking economic loss damages as such would be judicial legislation).

[9] In summary, we hold that a purchaser may not maintain a suit for breach of implied warranties by a remote manufacturer where the only damages sought are for consequential economic loss. *Rhodes v. General Motors Corp.,* 621 So.2d 945, 947 (Ala.1993); *Prairie Prod., Inc. v. Agchem Division-Pennwalt Corp.,* 514 N.E.2d 1299, 1301–02 (Ind.Ct.App.1987); *Professional Lens Plan, Inc.,* 675 P.2d at 898–99; *Arell's Fine Jewelers, Inc. v. Honeywell, Inc.,* 170 A.D.2d 1013, 566 N.Y.S.2d 505, 507 (1991). We note that a purchaser such as Tomka is not left without a remedy. He bought the hormones from local veteri-

narians and he may look to them for recovery under warranty theories.

V. *Motion for Leave to Amend.*

[10] After Hoechst made its motion for a directed verdict, Tomka sought leave to amend his petition to add theories of intentional tort and gross negligence based on Hoechst's alleged indirect promotion of dual implants in violation of a federal regulation. The trial court denied Tomka's motion.

[11, 12] We will reverse the trial court's refusal to allow an amendment of the petition only upon a showing of a clear abuse of discretion. *Porter v. Good Eavespouting,* 505 N.W.2d 178, 180 (Iowa 1993). Leave to amend pleadings should be freely given. *Id.* However, an amendment to conform to the proof should not be allowed if it will substantially change the claim. *W & W Livestock Enters. Inc. v. Dennler,* 179 N.W.2d 484, 488 (Iowa 1970).

We agree with the trial court that the amendment Tomka sought to make would have substantially changed the plaintiff's claims against the defendant midway through the trial. We also agree that the admission of evidence of indirect promotion of dual implants without objection by Hoechst does not show Hoechst's consent to these new theories of recovery because this evidence was arguably relevant to Tomka's warranty claims. We conclude the trial court did not abuse its discretion in refusing to allow Tomka to amend his petition to conform to the proof.

DECISION OF COURT OF APPEALS AND JUDGMENT OF DISTRICT COURT AFFIRMED.

6.

Charles W. and Joann BROOKS, Petitioners,

v.

COMMONWEALTH of Pennsylvania, DEPARTMENT OF AGRICULTURE, Respondent.

Commonwealth Court of Pennsylvania.

Argued Dec. 11, 1989.

Decided Feb. 14, 1990.

Reargument Denied April 19, 1990.

Poultry farmers brought suit to recover additional compensation for losses they incurred in selling chickens infected with avian influenza. Following remand, 105 Pa.Cmwlth.

196, 523 A.2d 845, additional compensation was denied by order of the Department of Agriculture, Case No. 1988–4, and farmers petitioned for review. The Commonwealth Court, No. 1051 C.D. 1989, Barbieri, Senior Judge, held that the case was moot because state fund from which farmers sought additional compensation was exhausted and there was no indication that legislature intended to appropriate any further monies.

Dismissed.

Doyle, J., dissented.

Action ⊶6

Case in which owners and operators of poultry farm sought additional compensation for losses they incurred in selling chickens infected with avian influenza was moot where state fund from which additional compensation was sought was exhausted and there was no indication that the legislature intended to appropriate any further monies.

G. David Pauline, Harrisburg, for petitioners.

Stephen R. Pelcher, York, for respondent.

Before DOYLE and PALLADINO, JJ., and BARBIERI, Senior Judge.

BARBIERI, Senior Judge.

Charles W. and Joann Brooks (Petitioners) petition for review of the order entered by the Secretary of the Department of Agriculture (Department) denying them additional compensation for losses they incurred in selling chickens infected with avian influenza.[1]

---

1. Petitioners commenced suit against the Commonwealth on February 20, 1986 by complaint addressed to our original jurisdiction. In a previous decision, we addressed the issue of our jurisdiction and concluded that this case should have been brought in our appellate jurisdiction. We then remanded to the Department for a hearing and adjudication since there was neither a record nor a statement of agreed upon facts to enable us to perform our appellate review function. *Brooks v. Department of Agriculture,* 105 Pa.Commonwealth Ct. 196, 523 A.2d 845 (1987).

Petitioners are owners and operators of a poultry farm. In late October of 1983, they discovered that their chickens were infected with avian influenza. In order to avoid further losses due to the deaths of their chickens from avian influenza, Petitioners requested and were granted permits to ship their remaining infected chickens to a New Jersey poultry processor. While en route, 5,000 chickens died.

Upon delivery of the chickens, the New Jersey poultry processor paid Petitioners .58 cents per chicken for the chickens that reached New Jersey alive. Petitioners thereafter also received reimbursement from a fund created by the state legislature[2] at a rate of $1.80 per chicken for the chickens that died on their farm and en route to New Jersey.

Petitioners subsequently sought, but were denied, additional compensation for the difference between the Commonwealth's reimbursement rate of $1.80 per chicken and the .58 cents per chicken they received from the New Jersey poultry processor. This denial is now before us for review.

Because the state fund from which Petitioners seek additional compensation is exhausted and there is no indication that the legislature intends to appropriate any further monies, we are presented with the issue of whether Petitioner's action is moot. Mootness exists when the circumstances surrounding a controversy make the legal issue therein an academic one. *See Consolidated Coal Co. v. District 5, United Mine Workers of America,* 336 Pa. Superior Ct. 354, 485 A.2d 1118 (1984). "Intervening changes in the factual matrix of a pending case, which eliminate an actual controversy and make it impossible for the requested relief to be granted, render a legal question moot." *Zemprelli v. Thornburgh,* 78 Pa.Commonwealth Ct. 45, 48, 466 A.2d 1123, 1124 (1983).

---

2. This fund was created by the Second Supplemental General Appropriation Act of 1983 (Act 1–A of 1984), § 212, 1984 Pa.Laws 1311, 1315–16, which provided in relevant part:

For payments to indemnify owners of poultry which died or were destroyed on or after September 1, 1983 for the market value of such animals and for any extraordinary or incidental expenses incurred which are associated with the Avian Influenza Epidemic of 1983 . . .

Inasmuch as the fund from which Petitioners seek additional compensation is exhausted, Petitioners cannot now be provided the relief requested. Accordingly, we must dismiss this case as moot. *Zemprelli.*

DOYLE, J., dissents.

ORDER

AND NOW, this 14th day of February, 1990, the above-captioned matter is dismissed as moot.

7.

NATIONAL PORK PRODUCERS COUNCIL, an Iowa Corporation; Charles Grassley; Tom Hagedorn; and Steven Symms; and National Independent Meat Packers Association, Appellees,

v.

Bob BERGLAND, Secretary of Agriculture; Carol Tucker Foreman, Assistant Secretary of Agriculture for Food and Consumer Services; and Donald Houston, Acting Administrator, Food Safety and Quality Service, United States Department of Agriculture, Appellants.

No. 80–1229.

United States Court of Appeals, Eighth Circuit.

Submitted June 13, 1980.

Decided Sept. 23, 1980.

The Secretary of Agriculture and others appealed from a decision of the United States District Court for the Southern District of Iowa, William C. Stuart, Chief Judge, 484 F.Supp. 540, which declared invalid regulations that permitted nitrate-free and nitrite-free meat products to be sold under product names traditionally reserved for foods containing those preservatives. The Court of Appeals, Heaney, Circuit Judge, held that: (1) the regulation, which provided that meat and meat products not preserved by nitrates, nitrites or other preservatives could be sold under their traditional names so long as the word "Uncured" appeared on the label as part of the product name and the label stated, "No Nitrate or Nitrite Added" and "Not Preserved-Keep Refrigerated Below 40° F. At All Times," did not exceed the authority of the Secretary or otherwise manifest an arbitrary and capricious decision; (2) the record did not support the allegation that the Secretary promulgated the regulation for the unlawful purpose of promoting a market for uncured products; (3) the requirement that uncured products be similar in size, flavor, consistency and general appearance to their cured counterparts bore a national relationship to the purposes of identity standards as intended by Congress in enacting the Meat Inspection Act; and (4) there was no need to file an environmental impact statement in connection with the regulation.

Reversed.

1. Food ⊃1.10

The Department of Agriculture properly exercised its authority when it issued regulations permitting nitrite-free and nitrate-free meat products to be sold under product names traditionally reserved for foods containing those compounds so long as the word "Uncured" appeared on the label as part of the product name and so long as the label stated "No Nitrate or Nitrite Added" and "Not Preserved-Keep Refrigerated Below 40° F. At All Times."

2. Administrative Law and Procedure ⊃754, 763

Standard for reviewing regulations promulgated pursuant to the notice and comment provision of the Administrative Procedure Act is the standard which authorizes reviewing court to set aside agency actions found to be arbitrary, capricious, an abuse of discretion or otherwise not in accordance with law. 5 U.S.C.A. § 553(c).

3. Administrative Law and Procedure ⊃797

Unless an inadequate evidentiary development before the administrative agency can be shown and supplemental information submitted by the agency does not provide an adequate basis for judicial review, in reviewing regulations promulgated pursuant to the notice and comment provision of the Administrative Procedure Act, court should limit its inquiry to the administrative record already in existence supplemented, if necessary, by affidavits, depositions or other proof of an explanatory nature. 5 U.S.C.A. § 553(c).

4. Food ⊃1.10

Promulgation by the Department of Agriculture of regulations permitting nitrate-free

and nitrite-free meat products to be sold under product names traditionally reserved for foods containing those compounds did not reflect the unlawful purpose to promote a market for uncured products where the USDA stated, both in its rule-making notice and in explanation accompanying the final rule, that the regulations were proposed in response to requests by individual consumers, consumer interest groups and manufacturers and where the regulation bore a rational relationship to the claimed purpose of availability. Federal Meat Inspection Act, § 2, 21 U.S.C.A. § 602.

5. Food ⊃1.10

The section of the Federal Meat Inspection Act which expressly charges the Department of Agriculture with assuring that meat and meat food products distributed to consumers are wholesome, not adulterated and properly marked, labelled and packaged authorizes the Department to insure that products desired by consumers are made available to them in a form and manner consistent with the public health and welfare. Federal Meat Inspection Act, § 2, 21 U.S.C.A. § 602.

6. Food ⊃1.7

The Department of Agriculture should not promote a particular company or a particular product of a particular company; however, merely fulfilling consumer desires while insuring consumer health and safety does not constitute such unlawful promotion. Federal Meat Inspection Act, § 2, 21 U.S.C.A. § 602.

7. Food ⊃1.10

Producers of meat products preserved with nitrates and nitrites have no right to be free from competition.

8. Food ⊃1.10

In view of finding of the Secretary of Agriculture that it was in the public interest to permit marketing of nitrate-free and nitrite-free meat products under names traditionally reserved for foods containing nitrates and nitrites, the competitive effect of this decision on producers of nitrate-preserved and nitrite-preserved products was of no consequence. Federal Meat Inspection Act, § 1 et seq., 21 U.S.C.A. § 601 et seq.

9. Food ⊕1.10

Requirement, found in Department of Agriculture regulation permitting nitrate-free and nitrite-free meat products to be sold under product names traditionally reserved for foods containing nitrates and nitrites, that the uncured products be similar in size, flavor, consistency and general appearance to products commonly prepared with nitrates and nitrites had a rational relationship to the purposes of the identity standard provisions of the Meat Inspection Act in that the regulation was designed to prevent sale, under traditional names, of products bearing no resemblance to items commonly sold under those names and, therefore, the regulation was not contrary to law. Federal Meat Inspection Act, § 7(c), 21 U.S.C.A. § 607(c).

10. Food ⊕1.10

Promulgation of regulation designed to prevent sale of products under traditional names when those products bear no resemblance to items commonly sold under those names is well within the powers granted to the Secretary of Agriculture by the Meat Inspection Act provision which, in relevant part, authorizes the Secretary to prescribe labelling requirements to avoid false or misleading labelling as well as definitions and standards of identity or composition whenever he determines such action is necessary to protect the public. Federal Meat Inspection Act, § 7(c), 21 U.S.C.A. § 607(c).

11. Health and Environment ⊕25.10(2)

The Department of Agriculture regulations permitting nitrate-free and nitrite-free meat products to be sold under product names traditionally reserved for foods containing those compounds did not require an environmental impact statement where there was no basis for finding that consequences significantly affecting the quality of the human environment might result from implementation of the regulations and where it was clear that the Department of Agriculture considered the potential for such effects and determined no significant health dangers were presented. National Environmental Policy Act of 1969, § 102, 42 U.S.C.A. § 4332.

Alice Daniel, Asst. Atty. Gen., Eloise E. Davies, Susan M. Chalker, Attys., Civ. Div., Dept. of Justice, Washington, D.C., for Bob Bergland et al.

Edwin H. Pewett, James M. Kefauver, James B. Davis, Glassie, Pewett, Beebe & Shanks, Washington, D.C., for National Meat Ass'n.

James L. Fox, Donald P. Colleton, Abramson & Fox, Chicago, Ill., for National Pork Producers.

Before HEANEY and BRIGHT, Circuit Judges, and HUNGATE, District Judge.*

HEANEY, Circuit Judge.

[1] This appeal presents the question of whether the United States Department of Agriculture (USDA) properly exercised its authority when it issued regulations permitting nitrate and nitrite-free meat products to be sold under product names traditionally reserved for foods containing these compounds. The district court held that it did not. We reverse.

I.

The history of nitrate and nitrite use in curing meat and poultry products is a long one. As early as Homer's time (900 B.C.), curing meat with salt was an established practice. Although it surely was not known at the time, the desert salts used in the curing process contained nitrate impurities, which caused cured meat to develop a characteristic spicy flavor and pink color. In addition, the curing process helped preserve the meat from bacterial spoilage. The cure was particularly effective, it is now known, in inhibiting the growth of *Clostridium botulinum,* the bacteria that produce the deadly toxin responsible for the food poisoning known as botulism.

Although curing is a centuries-old practice, it was not until the first part of the twentieth century that scientists identified the active agent responsible for the cure. The color, flavor and preservative effects were caused by the meat's reaction with nitric oxide, which was formed from nitrite, which was, in turn, formed from the nitrate used in the curing process. Because these reactions are difficult to control when meat products are cured with nitrate, the USDA formally authorized the direct addition of nitrite in 1925. In some products, such as bacon, some form of nitrite is required by USDA regulations. *See* 9 C.F.R. § 318.7(b) (1980). Because nitrite was recognized as potentially toxic, however, a maximum residual amount of 200 parts per million

---

was established. Nitrate was not directly regulated.

In the late 1960's, concern developed over nitrite use as studies suggested that nitrites combined with other compounds in the food or in the body to form nitrosamines, which were known to be potent carcinogens in animals. As one report presented to a Senate Committee indicates, the possibility that nitrites could cause cancer touched off a flurry of activity:

> In October 1969, meat industry scientists met with the Assistant Secretary of Agriculture to discuss the possibility of a nitrosamine problem existing in U.S. cured meat products. In December of 1969, a group of USDA, FDA, and industry scientists met to discuss the problem, resulting in the scheduling of a cooperative research program to be funded by industry and actively participated in by industry, FDA, and the Department. The Food and Drug Administration (FDA) and the U.S. Department of Agriculture organized a scientific study group to review appropriate information and data. In 1971, the House Intergovernmental Relations Subcommittee conducted hearings on the issue of nitrosamine formation and the possible involvement of nitrate in cured foods. The matter was widely discussed by the public and the media, and further studies were carried out by the scientific community. Numerous conferences were held during 1972, to discuss available information on the role of nitrite in curing and preserving, and to determine what new information was needed.

* * * * * *

Because of the widespread interest in the subject, the Secretary appointed an Expert Panel in 1973 to assess the data concerning the presence of nitrosamines in foods, to evaluate the public health significance and specific problems identified with the use of nitrites in foods, and to determine if alternate methods of processing were available.

Agriculture, Rural Development, and Related Agencies Appropriations for Fiscal Year 1979: Hearings before a Subcomm. of the Senate Comm. on Appropriations, 95th Cong., 2d Sess. 2936, 2937 (1978) (Final Report on Nitrites and Nitrosamines to the Secretary of Agriculture by the Expert Panel on Nitrites and Nitrosamines).

One conclusion of the new round of studies was that nitrosamines are formed in nitrite-cured bacon when it is fried at high temperatures, particularly if it is cooked until crisp.

As a result, in 1978, the USDA promulgated revised regulations that reduced the permissible levels of nitrite in bacon, required that other additives be used to lessen the likelihood that nitrosamines would form, and established procedures for testing bacon to ensure that it contains no confirmable levels of nitrosamines after cooking. 9 C.F.R. § 318.7(b) (1980); *see American Meat Inst. v. Bergland,* 459 F.Supp. 1308 (D.D.C.1978).

Another, more tentative, conclusion of the scientific studies on nitrate and nitrite use was stated in 1978 by Paul Newberne of the Massachusetts Institute of Technology. The Newberne Report determined that nitrites themselves caused cancer in laboratory animals, even if nitrosamines had not formed prior to ingestion. This report prompted a wave of criticism from the meat industry on the one hand, and resulted in increased pressure on the USDA to completely ban the use of nitrites on the other. The Department resisted these pressures, however, finding that greater scientific study was required.[1] *See Schuck v. Butz,* 500 F.2d 810 (D.C.Cir.1974).

---

1. Following the release of the 1978 Newberne Report, the FDA and the USDA established an Interagency Working Group on Nitrite Research to evaluate the MIT study. The interagency group, composed of scientists from the FDA, the USDA, the National Cancer Institute and the National Institute of Environmental Health Sciences, evaluated the design and conduct of the study and ordered an intensive pathology review of Dr. Newberne's diagnoses. In a report dated August 15, 1980, the group announced their findings, concluding that "insufficient evidence exists to support the conclusion that sodium nitrite *per se* fed to rats causes cancer, based on the MIT study." The FDA and USDA announced in a news release accompanying the report that they have decided to contract with the National Academy of Sciences to review all relevant data on nitrite before additional action is taken. The agencies stated that the National Academy of Sciences "will conduct an independent assessment of all available scientific information about nitrite and will analyze scientific data and develop a research agenda on potential alternatives to nitrite as a preservative in meats and poultry." The release concluded: "Because of its widespread usage, we believe that our agencies must continue to be concerned about the effects, if any, that nitrite consumption might have on the public's health."

As the USDA and FDA studies continued, public awareness of the problem resulted in increased consumer demand for nitrate and nitrite-free products. USDA regulations, however, prohibited the production, sale or distribution of nitrate and nitrite-free products under their traditional names such as frankfurters, bacon, etc. As a result, consumers complained of some difficulty in identifying or finding the products they desired.

The Food Safety and Quality Service of the USDA responded to these complaints on April 28, 1978, by publishing a notice of proposed rulemaking in the *Federal Register.* 43 Fed.Reg. 18,193 (1978). In this notice, the USDA proposed to amend the federal meat inspection regulations to permit the sale of nitrate and nitrite-free products under their traditional names, provided that certain labeling and quality requirements were met.

In the sixty-day comment period following notice of the proposed rule, the USDA received 365 comments from individual consumers, consumer organizations, and industry and trade associations. In addition, the USDA consulted the National Advisory Committee on Meat and Poultry Inspection about the proposal and the comments. On June 14, 1979, the USDA issued a Final Impact Statement on the proposed rule, detailing the need for the rule, the options considered, and the expected impact of its implementation. On August 21, 1979, the USDA promulgated the final regulation, to be effective September 20, 1979. *See* 9 C.F.R. §§ 317.17(b) & (c), 318.7, 319.2.[2] The final rule provides that meat and meat products that are not cured with nitrates, nitrites or other preservatives may be sold under their traditional names, so long as the word "Uncured" appears on the label as part of the product name and the label states. "No Nitrate or Nitrite Added" and "Not Preserved-Keep Refrigerated Below 40° F. At All Times." In addition, the regulation requires that the uncured products be similar in size, flavor, consistency and general appearance to the products commonly prepared with nitrate or nitrite.[3]

---

2. 9 C.F.R. § 318.7, which prohibits the use of nitrates or nitrites in baby, junior or toddler foods, is not being challenged in this action.

3. The final regulations in question read as follows:

§ 317.17 *Interpretation and statement of labeling policy for cured products; special labeling requirements concerning nitrate and nitrite.*

II

On September 20, 1979, the National Pork Producers Council, a trade organization representing approximately 92,500 United States pork producers, together with three members of the United States House of Representatives, filed this lawsuit challenging the regulations. The National Independent Meat Packers Association, a trade association representing approximately 300 meat packers, was subsequently granted leave to intervene as a party plaintiff. The plaintiffs sought declaratory and injunctive relief.

---

*   *   *   *   *   *

(b) Any products, such as bacon and pepperoni, which is required to be labeled by a common or usual name or descriptive name in accordance with § 317.2(c)(1) and to which nitrate or nitrite is permitted or required to be added may be prepared without nitrate or nitrite and labeled with such common or usual name or descriptive name when immediately preceded with the term "Uncured" as part of the product name in the same size and style of lettering as the product name, provided that the product is found by the Administrator to be similar in size, flavor, consistency, and general appearance to such product as commonly prepared with nitrate or nitrite, or both.

(c)(1) Products described in paragraph (b) of this section or § 319.2 of this subchapter, which contain no nitrate or nitrite shall bear the statement "No Nitrate or Nitrite Added." This statement shall be adjacent to the product name in lettering of easily readable style and at least one-half the size of the product name.

(2) Products described in paragraph (b) of this section and § 319.2 of this subchapter shall bear, adjacent to the product name in lettering of easily readable style and at least one-half the size of the product name, the statement "Not Preserved-Keep Refrigerated Below 40° F. At All Times" unless they have been thermally processed to F° 3 or more; they have been fermented or pickled to pH of 4.6 or less; or they have been dried to a water activity of 0.92 or less.

(3) Products described in paragraph (b) of this section and § 319.2 of this subchapter shall not be subject to the labeling requirements of paragraphs (b) and

On February 12, 1980, the district court entered a final order permanently enjoining the government from enforcing or applying the challenged regulations.[4] The court rested its decision on four grounds:

(1) The Secretary of Agriculture acted arbitrarily and capriciously because he failed to consider whether consumers would be subjected to botulism poisoning if they were to handle uncured products in the fashion in which they now handle cured products, and because there was no rational basis in the record for assuming that the required labels would effectively prevent confusion between the two types of products.

(2) The Secretary exceeded his authority under the Federal Meat Inspection Act, 21 U.S.C. § 601 *et seq.*, because the regulation was promulgated for the unlawful purpose of promoting or encouraging a market for nitrate and nitrite-free products.

(3) The Secretary exceeded his authority because the similarity requirement bore no rational relationship to the purposes of the Federal Meat Inspection Act and because it constituted a subjective standard of identity rather than an objective recipe or formula.

(c) of this section if they contain an amount of salt sufficient to achieve a brine concentration of 10 percent or more.

* * * * * *

§ 319.2   *Products and nitrates and nitrites.*

Any product, such as frankfurters and corned beef, for which there is a standard in this part and to which nitrate or nitrite is permitted or required to be added, may be prepared without nitrate or nitrite and labeled with such standard name when immediately preceded with the term "Uncured" in the same size and style of lettering as the rest of such standard name: *Provided,* That the product is found by the Administrator to be similar in size, flavor, consistency, and general appearance to such product as commonly prepared with nitrate and nitrite: *And provided further,* That labeling for such product complies with the provisions of § 317.17(c) of this subchapter.

9 C.F.R. §§ 317.17, 319.2 (1980).

4. The district court had earlier denied a motion for a temporary restraining order, but had granted a motion for a preliminary injunction.

(4) The Secretary failed to comply with the requirements of the National Environmental Policy Act, 42 U.S.C. § 4321 *et seq.*, because he neither filed nor considered the need for an Environmental Impact Statement (EIS).[5]

III

[2, 3]   Before discussing in detail the reasoning of the district court, we briefly consider the appropriate standard for reviewing regulations, such as these, promulgated pursuant to the "notice and comment" provision of the Administrative Procedure Act, 5 U.S.C. § 553(c). The standard "is that specified by 5 U.S.C. § 706(2)(A), which authorizes a reviewing court to set aside agency action found to be 'arbitrary, capricious, an abuse of discretion, or otherwise not in accordance with law.' " *Independent Meat Packers Ass'n v. Butz,* 526 F.2d 228, 238 (8th Cir. 1975), *cert. denied,* 424 U.S. 966, 96 S.Ct. 1461, 47 L.Ed.2d 733 (1976). Furthermore, "unless an inadequate evidentiary development before the agency can be shown and supplemental information submitted by the agency does not provide an adequate basis for judicial review, the court *   *   * should limit its inquiry to the administrative record already in existence supplemented, if necessary, by affidavits, depositions, or other proof of an explanatory nature." *Id.* at 239. The district court explicitly recognized this standard in its opinion, but it nevertheless held a hearing that included the presentation of some evidence beyond "proof of an explanatory nature." We turn now to an independent examination of the record to determine whether the USDA acted arbitrarily, capriciously, or otherwise not in accordance with law.

IV

A. Arbitrary and capricious action.

The district court's reasons for holding that the Secretary's action was arbitrary and capricious were that the USDA failed to consider whether consumers would be subjected to botulism poisoning if they were to handle uncured products in the same manner they now

---

5. In addition, the court rejected the plaintiffs' contention that the nitrate and nitrite-free products must be labeled "imitation" in accordance with 21 U.S.C. § 601(n)(3) finding that the uncured products were not imitations of their cured counterparts.

handle cured products and whether the labeling requirements would eliminate the risk. We find these rationales unconvincing.

First, it is clear from the record that the USDA was very concerned with the possible problem of botulism poisoning. The dangers of botulism and the handling practices necessary to ensure safety were carefully considered by the Secretary. As noted earlier, the USDA and other governmental agencies have been studying the health effects of nitrates and nitrites at least since the 1960's. These agencies have been looking for alternative preservatives and have sought ways to make nitrates and nitrites less dangerous without destroying their ability to control the growth of *Clostridium botulinum*. When the agency promulgated regulations to reduce the levels of nitrites in bacon, it reduced them only to the lowest level thought necessary to control these bacteria. More importantly, the agency expressly recognized the potential botulism danger in the official documents in this administrative proceeding. The notice of proposed rulemaking stated:

> The Administrator recognizes that meat products prepared without nitrate and/or nitrite or with reduced levels of nitrate and/or nitrite may better support the growth and toxin production of *Clostridium botulinum* that [sic] meat products prepared with the traditional levels of nitrate and/or nitrite currently permitted by regulation * * *. *Clostridium botulinum* intoxication (botulism) is a type of food poisoning which often causes death.

43 Fed.Reg. 18,193 (1978).

Similarly, the explanation accompanying the final rule reflected the agency's awareness of the dangers of botulism and the value of nitrites in reducing that danger. *See* 44 Fed.Reg. 48,959 (1979). Indeed, it was this awareness that prompted the strict labeling requirements in the regulations.

The agency was not only fully aware of the botulism risk, it considered evidence of the effect of the proposed regulation, particularly the labeling requirements, on that risk. It noted that some of the 365 comments submitted to it "expressed concern whether such labeling provisions would be adequate to protect against botulism with respect to * * * unpreserved products. In this connection, some commentators questioned whether products would always be handled in accordance with the warnings on the labeling and be kept below 40° F." 44 Fe-

d.Reg. 48,959 (1979). Nevertheless, the agency found persuasive evidence that the benefits of the regulation would outweigh any potential safety problem. Many of the comments demonstrated consumer awareness of the potential dangerous consequences of marketing and consuming meat products that do not contain nitrates or nitrites.[6] Many commentators referred to the positive safe experiences they had had with purchasing uncured products in the past. Others stated that their knowledge of food products came from a careful reading of product labels. Still others indicated an understanding of the term "uncured" and expressed a willingness to adhere to the instructions on the label in exchange for an opportunity to buy meat products without nitrates or nitrites. Indeed, even the comment of the plaintiff-congresspersons in this action recognized the efficacy of warning labels; the congresspersons suggested, *inter alia,* that a revised regulation require strict warning labels.

Moreover, not only was the agency aware of the botulism danger at the outset, and not only did it consider further evidence of the danger, once it reviewed the evidence, it took positive steps to eliminate the chance of any danger resulting from the regulations. The final rule differed from the proposed rule in two significant respects. First, the labels on nitrate or nitrite-free products were required to contain the word "Uncured" as part of the product name. The agency described its reasons for the change as follows:

> [T]he Administrator has determined, based on the comments, that the use of nitrates and nitrites is of such importance in products preserved by these substances, that products prepared without such substances should have different names from those prepared with nitrates or nitrites in order to more clearly distinguish such products. Under these circumstances, it has been determined that such products prepared without nitrates or nitrites may bear the traditional name, but that the traditional name must be preceded by the term "Uncured."

44 Fed.Reg. 48,959 (1979).

Second, the proposed rule had permitted the sale,

---

6. The public record also supports the proposition that consumers have become increasingly aware of the role of nitrates and nitrites in preserving meat products.

under traditional names, of products with low nitrate levels if they were labeled "Not Fully Preserved, Must Be Refrigerated Below 40° F. At All Times." This provision was deleted, partly in response to concern about whether "consumers might misuse such products not otherwise preserved, based on a false assurance that the listing of nitrates or nitrites in the ingredients statement would be understood to represent that products could be handled under the same circumstances acceptable for products fully preserved by nitrates or nitrites." *Id.* at 48,960. These changes in the regulation are further proof that the agency carefully considered the evidence of botulism risk and made a reasoned determination in response to that evidence.[7]

After considering the submitted comments, consulting the Advisory Commission, and reviewing the relevant evidence before it, the agency made the following statement:

> The Administrator * * * is aware that products requiring such special handling such as pork sausage, bratwurst and bockwurst have presented no apparent health hazards even though prepared without nitrates or nitrites and marketed unfrozen. He concludes that consumers have demonstrated a knowledge of the handling practices necessary for any of such products prepared without nitrates or nitrites and that the prescribed labeling for such products, i.e., "Not Preserved-Keep Refrigerated Below 40° F. At All Times," will adequately inform the consumer of how to maintain such products in a wholesome condition until consumed.

Id.

Although the record contains some evidence that would suggest a different conclusion, we cannot say that the Secretary's determination is without basis in the record. Accordingly, the district court erred in holding that the Secretary acted arbitrarily and capriciously in promulgating these regulations.

B. *Unlawful purpose.*

[4] The district court determined that the Secretary was without authority to promulgate the regulations in question because they were issued for the unlawful purpose of promoting a market for uncured products. In support of this position, the district court quotes the Final Impact Statement released by the USDA on June 14, 1979, which states that one of the purposes of the regulations is "to allow the use of familiar names for the traditional, but nitrite-free processed meat products. Allowing these products to be marketed by traditional names will increase consumer awareness of their availability as well as consumption by those wishing to forego consumption of nitrite cured products." In addition, the court noted that the agency considered continuing the prohibition on the use of traditional product names on meat products without nitrates or nitrites, but rejected this option because "it does not facilitate the development of markets for nitrate and/or nitrite-free products." This, the court concluded, proves that the agency acted with an improper purpose.

[5, 6] We disagree. Congress expressly charged the USDA with "assuring that meat and meat food products distributed to [consumers] are wholesome, not adulterated, and properly marked, labeled, and packaged." 21 U.S.C. § 602. In our view, this directive authorizes the Department to ensure that the products desired by consumers be made available to them in a form and manner consistent with the public health and welfare. Every time the Secretary approves a product's ingredients or label, he, in one sense, is promoting that product. To be sure, the agency should not be promoting a particular company or a particular product of a particular company, but merely fulfilling consumer desires, while ensuring consumer health and safety, does not constitute such unlawful promotion.

The district court overlooked the agency's statement, both in the rulemaking notice and the explanation accompanying the final rule, that the regulations were proposed in response to requests by individual consumers, consumer interest groups and manufacturers. The comments support the agency's determination that nitrate and nitrite-free products were difficult to locate or not available to consumers. The regulation bears a rational relationship to this claimed purpose of availability.

[7, 8] Moreover, contrary to what the appellees would have us think, the producers of nitrate and nitrite-preserved products have

---

7. To further guard against any botulism risk, the USDA printed, primarily for distribution to consumers in supermarkets, educational pamphlets warning of the handling requirements of uncured products.

no right to be free from competition. *See Hiatt Grain & Feed, Inc. v. Bergland,* 602 F.2d 929, 933 (10th Cir. 1979), *cert. denied,* 444 U.S. 1073, 100 S.Ct. 1019, 62 L.Ed.2d 755 (1980). *See also Westport Taxi Serv., Inc. v. Adams,* 571 F.2d 697, 700 n.3 (2d Cir.), *cert. denied,* 439 U.S. 829, 99 S.Ct. 103, 58 L.Ed.2d 122 (1978). The challenged regulation is actually an exception to USDA regulations that formerly prohibited selling nitrate and nitrite-free products under their traditional names. The producers of nitrited products enjoyed a benefit from the old rule, but they have no vested right in the continuation of it. Upon the Secretary's finding that it was in the public interest to permit marketing under traditional names, the competitive effect on the producers of nitrate and nitrite-preserved products is of no consequence.

Finally, we emphasize the modest nature of the USDA proposal. Despite sustained pressure to ban the use of all nitrites,[8] the agency determined that regulations permitting the sale of nitrate and nitrite-free products under traditional names would be sufficient to serve the public interest at this time. Under the new rules, no meat packer is required to manufacture nitrate and nitrite-free products, no wholesaler is required to supply them, and no retailer is required to stock them. Furthermore, the production and sale of nitrate and nitrite-preserved products are unaffected. In short, we conclude that the regulations are a rational response to the legitimate requests of concerned consumers and were not promulgated for an unlawful purpose.

---

8. The district court stated that the public health threat from nitrite-induced cancer could not be considered as a valid purpose for the rule, because the USDA did not indicate in the final rules that the regulations' purpose was cancer prevention. We note that the failure to mention the alleged carcinogenic effects of nitrites was probably no accident. While the agency was studying the proposed rule, the United States Attorney General, in response to a USDA request, issued an opinion stating that if nitrites were found to be carcinogenic in animals, current law would require the USDA to ban their use in food products. *See* 43 Op. Att'y Gen. 1 (1979). Because scientific studies were not complete, the Secretary wisely decided to promulgate regulations not based on the asserted cancer dangers.

C. *Similarity requirement.*

[9]   The district court's third rationale for invalidating the USDA regulations was that the requirement that uncured products be similar in size, flavor, consistency and general appearance to their cured counterparts was contrary to law. The court gave three reasons for this holding.

First, the court determined that "the similarity requirement is a standard of identity that bears no rational relationship to the purpose of such standards." In support of this assertion, the district court cited several cases purporting to define the purpose of the identity standards provisions of the Meat Inspection Act, 21 U.S.C. § 607(c). The court read these cases as holding that the purpose of such standards is to prevent the "economic adulteration" or to promote the "integrity" of meat food products. The similarity requirement in the challenged regulation does not serve this purpose, the court concluded, because it "will confuse, if not deceive, consumers as to the identity of the products they are receiving and the handling requirements of those products."

[10]   We cannot agree that the similarity requirement bears no rational relationship to the purposes of identity standards as intended by Congress. Initially, we note that none of the cases cited by the court involved successful challenges to USDA standards of identity. More importantly, we think it clear that Congress intended the USDA to have the authority to issue the type of regulation here in question. Section 21 of the Act, 21 U.S.C. § 621, gives the agency broad authority to implement the statute: "[The] Secretary shall * * * make such rules and regulations as are necessary for the efficient execution of the provisions of this Act." Section 7(c) of the Act, 21 U.S.C. § 607(c), specifically provides that the Secretary may prescribe labeling requirements "to avoid false or misleading labeling" as well as definitions and standards of identity or composition "whenever he determines such action is necessary for the protection of the public." In our view, the similarity requirement is well within these powers granted the Secretary by Congress. It is designed to prevent the sale of products under traditional names when those products bear no resemblance to items commonly sold under those names. When a consumer buys a product labeled "Uncured Hot Dog," he will receive a product similar to any other "Hot Dog." Thus, the requirement fur-

thers the goals of the Act by promoting truthful labeling.

The second reason given by the district court for holding the similarity requirement unlawful is that it "is a subjective standard of identity that is beyond the [USDA's] authority to promulgate or enforce." The court offers no authority for this proposition, however, other than to say that a standard of identity "normally sets forth a 'recipe' for a food." (quoting *American Frozen Food Inst. v. Mathews,* 413 F.Supp. 548, 554 (D.D.C.1976), *aff'd on other grounds,* 555 F.2d 1059 (D.C.Cir.1977)).

We find this reasoning unpersuasive. As noted earlier, the statutory grant of authority to the Secretary is broad, and no restrictions on the permissible types of standards are contained in the statute. The Secretary's implementation of the Act shows that subjective standards were contemplated; a number of current USDA regulations specify standards of identity that are not based on objective criteria. *See, e.g.,* 9 C.F.R. § 319.15(c) (*"Beef Patties"*—"Binders [and other ingredients may be added] only in amounts such that the product characteristics are essentially that of a meat pattie."); §§ 319.15(e) & 319.29 (*"Partially defatted beef fatty tissue"* & *"Partially defatted pork fatty tissue"*—"Such product shall have a pinkish color and a fresh odor and appearance"); § 319.80 (*"Barbecued Meats"*—must have "the usual characteristics of a barbecued article"); § 319.181 (*"Cheesefurters and similar products"*—"resemble frankfurters except that they contain sufficient cheese to give definite characteristics to the finished article."); § 319.700(a)(3)(iv) (*"Oleomargarine or margarine"*—may contain "[a]ny safe and suitable artificial flavoring substance that imparts to the food a flavor in semblance of butter."). The district court disregarded these regulations, noting that the Administrator of the USDA's Food Safety and Quality Service told the Advisory Committee that the Department did not regulate flavor and taste. This reliance on the comment of the Administrator is misplaced; the regulations speak for themselves. The court apparently was persuaded by the difficulty in enforcing subjective standards, and it may well be that the Administrator would wish to avoid such standards for that reason. Nevertheless, if the Secretary decides he is willing to assume the burden of enforcing this subjective standard of identity, it is not for us to say it would be too difficult.

The district court's final reason for invalidating the similarity requirement is that it "is so unorthodox and contrary to previous USDA policy and practice that it was incumbent upon defendants to give a reasoned explanation for their decision to impose the requirement." The soundness of this reasoning, obviously, is dependent upon the validity of the district court's finding that the USDA had not previously established subjective standards of identity for food products. For the reasons stated above, we are satisfied that the Secretary has set such standards in the past. Accordingly, the district court's third rationale for holding the similarity requirement invalid must fall.

D. *EIS requirement.*

[11] Section 102(2)(C) of the National Environmental Policy Act, 42 U.S.C. § 4332(2)(C), provides in part that a federal agency must prepare a "detailed statement," commonly known as an EIS, whenever it proposes "major Federal actions significantly affecting the quality of the human environment." The district court held that the USDA did not fulfill the requirements of the Act when it promulgated the regulations involved in this case because it failed "to make a determination as to whether an EIS should have been prepared and [it failed] to develop a reviewable administrative record supporting a negative decision * * *."

We are not willing to find the regulations infirm on this basis. The EIS requirement of 42 U.S.C. § 4332(2)(C) is triggered when an agency proposes major federal action "significantly affecting the quality of the human environment." In this case, the record does not support a finding that such environmental effects may result from implementation of the regulations; moreover, it is clear that the agency considered the potential for such effects. The only "environmental" effects mentioned by the district court were the "significant public health concerns * * * implicated by the regulation." As detailed earlier in this opinion, however, the record shows that the USDA gave full consideration to the question of the regulations' health effects and determined that no significant health dangers were presented. Consequently, the sole ground for finding the existence of a major federal action "significantly affecting the quality of the human environment" is unsupported, and no EIS need be filed.

The decision of the district court is reversed.

8.

WILSON FOODS CORPORATION,
Successor in Interest to Wilson
and Company, Petitioner,

v.

**Carel V. PORTER and The State
Industrial Court of Oklahoma,
Respondents.**

No. 52472.

Supreme Court of Oklahoma.

May 6, 1980.

Rehearing Denied June 30, 1980.

Action was brought to recover workmen's compensation benefits for claimant's contraction of disease of brucellosis. The Industrial Court awarded $4,500 to claimant as compensation for permanent partial disability. The Court of Appeals affirmed award, and employer petitioned for certiorari. The Supreme Court, Hargrave, J., held that: (1) a malady normally considered a disease may be categorized as an accidental injury for purposes of workmen's compensation only where usual ingredients of accidental injury arising out of covered employment are proved; (2) under proper factual situations, contraction of brucellosis can be characterized as accidental injury; and (3) evidence was sufficient to support finding that claimant had sustained compensable accidental injury as result of his contraction of brucellosis.

Opinion of Court of Appeals vacated and trial court affirmed.

1. Workers' Compensation ⇔549

Since brucellosis is not a compensable occupational disease, to be compensable the disease may be recognized as an accidental injury. 85 O.S.1971, § 3(7, 16).

2. Workers' Compensation ⇔532

In spite of being recognized as a disease, brucellosis can still be categorized as accidental injury for workmen's compensation purposes. 85 O.S.1971, § 3(7, 16).

3. Workers' Compensation ⇔532

Although brucellosis occurs among people in contact with infected cattle, hogs or goats, it does not occur with regularity or to extent that it is a usual and expected result of working with such animals, and thus low number of

cases of brucellosis among many people working with cattle, hogs or goats qualified brucellosis as an accidental injury for workmen's compensation purposes. 85 O.S.1971, § 11.

4. Workers' Compensation ⇔516, 609

A causal connection must exist between employment and injury and some proof of accidental injury must exist before there can be workmen's compensation award. 85 O.S.1971, § 11.

5. Workers' Compensation ⇔1362

Claimant, who sought workmen's compensation benefits because of his contraction of brucellosis, had burden of establishing accidental injury and consequent resulting disability. 85 O.S.1971, § 11.

6. Workers' Compensation ⇔1361

When a claimant attempts to bring an illness within ambit of accidental injury, he is bound to prove that infirmity conforms to criteria laid down in an accidental injury situation. 85 O.S.1971, § 11.

7. Workers' Compensation ⇔1502

Lack of proof of specific date of infection was not fatal to claimant's recovery of workmen's compensation for his contraction of brucellosis where, within rather indefinite incubation period for disease, claimant testified to several contaminating incidents that occurred with frequency, consisting of handling hides with cracked skin, smoking while on duty, and having hide-contaminated salt splash in his eyes. 85 O.S.1971, § 11.

8. Workers' Compensation ⇔1502

Record, which contained no evidence that disease could have been contracted at place other than plaintiff's place of employment, was sufficient to support finding that claimant's contraction of brucellosis was an accidental injury resulting from employment. 85 O.S. 1971, § 11.

———————

Certiorari to the Court of Appeals, Division 2.

Certiorari to the Court of Appeals, Division 2, in an action to recover workmen's compensation benefits resulting from accidental injury occurring during covered employment by reason of infection of claimant with the disease of brucellosis. It is determined that a malady nominally considered a disease may be categorized as an accidental injury for purposes of workmen's compensation only where the usual ingredients of accidental injury arising out of covered employment are proved.

OPINION OF COURT OF APPEALS, DIVISION 2, VACATED; TRIAL COURT AFFIRMED.

Mort G. Welch, Abowitz & Welch, Oklahoma City, for petitioner.

George J. McCaffrey, Oklahoma City, for respondent, Carel V. Porter.

Jan Eric Cartwright, Atty. Gen., Oklahoma City, for respondent, State Industrial Court.

HARGRAVE, Justice.

In June, 1974, the respondent, Carel Porter, began working for Wilson & Company. In September, he was assigned to work in the hide cellar where his duties included removing cow hides from salt packs, processing the hides through a machine to remove salt and moisture, and folding, tying, and bundling the hides for shipment. Since September, 1974, the time the respondent was assigned to work in the hide cellar, his body, particularly his face and hands, has been in constant contact with the salt, the moisture, and the animal hair present in the work area. This constant exposure to the salt solution has caused the respondent's skin on his hands to crack, especially around his fingernails.

In October, 1975, the respondent began experiencing fever and chills, and after consulting several doctors was diagnosed as having brucellosis, a disease endemic in cattle, hogs, and goats. Claiming that the contraction of brucellosis was a compensable accidental injury sustained in the course of his employment, the respondent sought relief through the Industrial Court. On January 16, 1978, an award of $4500 was made to the respondent as compensation for eighteen per cent permanent partial disability. The award was affirmed by the Industrial Court en banc on June 9, 1978, and by the Oklahoma Court of Appeals on July 10, 1979.

The Court of Appeals ruled not only that the contraction of brucellosis could be an accidental injury within the statute, 85 O.S. 1971 § 11 (amended 85 O.S. Supp. 1980 § 11), but also that the evidence presented by the respon-

dent warranted such a finding in this case. Wilson & Company, through their successor in interest, Wilson Foods Corporation, petitioned for a writ of certiorari in this Court, which was granted September 24, 1979. The petitioner alleged that the Court of Appeals erred in finding that the contraction of brucellosis could be classified as an accidental injury within the statute and in finding that the evidence supported such a classification in this case.

We agree with the appellate court's decision that indeed under the proper factual situations the contraction of brucellosis can be characterized as an accidental injury and with the appellate court's decision that the evidence presented was sufficient to find that the respondent in this case had sustained a compensable accidental injury. Certiorari has been granted to establish the necessary items of proof when a claimant seeks to categorize what nominally is considered a disease as an accidental injury.

[1] Since brucellosis is not a compensable occupational disease within the statute,[1] *Ridley Packing Co. v. Holliday,* Okl., 467 P.2d 480 (1970), to be compensable under the statute the disease must be recognized as an accidental personal injury. Title 85, Section 3(7) of the Oklahoma Statutes provides that an " '[I]njury or personal injury' means only accidental injuries arising out of and in the course of employment and such *disease or infection* as many naturally result therefrom. . . .." 85 O.S. 1971 § 3(7) (Emphasis added). As stated in *Vaughn & Rush v. Stump,* 156 Okl. 125, 127, 9 P.2d 764, 765 (1932), (citing *In re Sullivan,* 265 Mass. 497, 499, 164 N.E. 457, 458 (1929)), "[t]he physical condition resulting, and not the nomenclature, is the decisive factor in determining whether a so-called disease is a compensable personal injury. A personal injury may be the direct and consequential result of employment, although a condition may arise, termed in some connections, a disease."

[2] Therefore, in spite of being recognized as a disease, brucellosis can still be categorized as a accidental personal injury. This categorization depends upon an examination of the essential characteristics of an accidental injury and a determination that such characteristics did attend the contraction of the disease here, brucellosis.

---

1. 85 O.S.1971 § 3(16) (amended by 85 O.S. Supp. 1980 § 10.)

An accident has been defined as "an event happening without any human agency, or if happening through human agency, an event which, under the circumstances, is *unusual* and *not expected to the person to whom it happens."* *Andrews Mining & Milling Co. v. Atkinson,* 192 Okl. 322, 323, 135 P.2d 960, 961–62 (1943). (Emphasis added.) The Court of Appeals cited in their opinion a medical report that stated brucellosis is "common in people working with these three animals [cattle, hogs, and goats] and is therefore for the most part seen in farmers, veterinarians and slaughterhouse workers," and a statistic, cited in Beeson & MacDermott, *Textbook of Medicine* at 389 (14th Ed. 1975), that fewer than 200 cases of brucellosis are diagnosed each year in the United States.

[3] Using the statistic to interpret the medical report, although brucellosis occurs among people in contact with infected cattle, hogs, or goats, it does *not* occur with regularity or to the extent that it is a *usual* and *expected* result of working with cattle, hogs or goats. Since "the basis of a claim for compensation must be a casualty occurring without expectation or foresight . . . ," *St. Louis Mining & Smelting Co. v. State Industrial Comm'n,* 113 Okl. 179, 182, 241 P. 170, 172 (1925), the low number of cases of brucellosis among the many people working with cattle, hogs or goats qualifies brucellosis as just such a casualty in this case.

The definition of an accidental injury has been clarified further by its comparison to the definition of an occupational disease in that an accident "arises by some definite event, the date of which can be fixed with certainty, but which cannot be so fixed in the case of occupational disease." *Black, Sivalls & Bryson, Inc. v. Silvey,* 184 Okl. 176, 178, 86 P.2d 327, 328 (1938) (quoting *Indian Territory Illuminating Oil Co. v. Sharver,* 157 Okl. 117, 119, 11 P.2d 187, 188 (1932)). Although this somewhat strict requirement of a "definite event" has been mitigated by later decisions stating that the injury "may be inflicted progressively and over a more or less lengthy period rather than being confined to infliction on one definite date and as the result of an isolated or particular event," *Macklanburg-Duncan Co. v. Edwards,* Okl., 311 P.2d 250, 255 (1957), and that "[i]t is no longer necessary . . . that in order to make an injury compensable there must be a slip, fall, or impact," *Nelson v. City of Oklahoma City,* Okl., 573 P.2d 696, 698 (1977), it is important to remember that the Court was dealing with injuries sustained from repetitive trauma

(*Macklanburg-Duncan*) and from aggravation of a pre-existing condition (*Nelson*).

[4] Although the time frame for the occurrence of some types of injuries may have been expanded and the physical impact requirement abandoned, no decisions have refused to recognize the requirement that a causal connection must exist between the employment and the injury or have refused to recognize that some proof of an accidental injury must exist before there can be an award. *Loggins v. Wetumka General Hosp.,* Okl., 587 P.2d 455 (1978); *Bareco Oil Co. v. Green,* 194 Okl. 580, 154 P.2d 72 (1944). Even in *Macklanburg-Duncan* and *Nelson,* the claimants were able to determine the event or noticeable occurrence which resulted in the injuries.

[5] Therefore, a claimant has the burden of establishing an accidental injury and the consequent resulting disability. *St. Louis Mining and Smelting Co. v. State Ind. Commission,* 113 Okl. 179, 181, 241 P. 170, 172 (1925). Claimant has demonstrated the fact that he has a disability incurred from brucellosis, and the query narrows to review of the respondent's proof of accidental injury arising from employment.

The case of *City of Nichols Hills v. Hill,* 534 P.2d 931 (Okl.1975), presented a similar situation both factually and in legal principle. There the claimant contracted histoplasmosis and attempted successfully to bring that disease within the ambit of an accidental injury. Therein the period of infection of the body with the microorganism causing the disease was determined by expert testimony simply to be "compatible with" the single instance of exposure. We held the evidence presented was sufficient to support the award. We find the circumstantial evidence there held sufficient was less persuasive than that before us here. In *Hill, supra,* the opinion reflects that claimant mowed grass for the city and that the microorganism causing the illness was widespread. "Histoplasmosis is a widely occurring common infection . . ." Additionally, we stated "causative organisms are located in soil contaminated by droppings of various animals, and particularly fowl and birds." We do not find the circumstantial evidence any less persuasive in the case at bar simply because the injured party proved the disease was endemic where he worked and contaminating events happened frequently during the period the infirmity was contracted. Indeed, the respondent's circumstantial evidence was less compelling in *Hill, supra,* than in the instant proceeding because the respondent here produced evidence that the exposure was limited to the work site, where in *Hill*, one must draw the conclusion that the infection could have easily been acquired from breathing spore-ladden dust from any place birds frequent, not simply while engaged in the employer's task of mowing.

The respondent presented evidence in the form of a doctor's opinion. That opinion states, "Brucellosis is a disease endemic in cattle . . ." Webster's New International Dictionary (Third Ed. 1966) defines endemic as: "3: peculiar to a locality or region—used of a disease that is constantly present to a greater or less extent in a particular place; distinguished from epidemic, sporadic." Evidence as presented by the doctor's report is sufficient to establish that the respondent was exposed to this disease "constantly to a greater or lesser extent," and the Industrial Court was entitled to conclude the respondent was exposed to the disease at his place of employment. The transcript of proceedings before the trial authority discloses direct testimony from the respondent to the effect he had not come into contact with cattle or cow hides at places other than his work at Wilson and that during the time respondent contracted the disease his hands were cracked from the salt solution used in the hide room. Additionally, respondent testified that salt and associated fluids found their way into his eyes regularly.

The law applicable to this set of factors is set forth in *Terry Motor Co. v. Mixon*, 361 P.2d 180 (Okl.1961). There it was contended that the injury incurred did not arise out of the employment as a result of inability to prove the injury arose from a physical altercation which was not instigated by the claimant. No direct evidence was available to determine the instigator or the extent of claimant's participation. The court noted various circumstantial facts, such as the opponent's propensity to scuffle, and the fact that he was of more robust build and younger age than decedent. The Court then stated the record did not compel a finding that decedent's aggression caused the altercation but rather presented a chain of facts and circumstances from which reasonable men could draw opposite inferences. The Court upheld the award, making the following observations on circumstantial evidence in a workmen's compensation proceeding:

> In determining the question of whether an injury arose out of the employment the State Industrial Court is not restricted or confined to the proof adduced by the claimant but can properly consider the record in its entirety and may resolve such issue of fact from circumstantial evidence which does not rise to that degree of certainty as to preclude reasonable men from drawing opposite inferences. *Burch v. Slick* [167 Okl. 639, 31 P.2d 110], supra; *Tulsa Frozen Foods Co. v. Pendergraft*, Okl., 317 P.2d 1115; *Young v. Neely*, Okl., 353 P.2d 111. See also *Special Indemnity Fund v. Horne*, 208 Okl. 218, 254 P.2d 988. Any reasonable doubt as to whether an injury did in fact arise out of employment should be resolved in favor of the workman. *Town of Granite v. Kidwell*, [Okl., 263 P.2d 184] supra.

Terry Mtr. Co. v. Mixon, 361 P.2d 180 (Okl.1961).

This Court has stated repeatedly that circumstantial evidence may be utilized to establish a claim for compensation without evidence that excludes every reasonable conclusion other than that reached by the trial authority. *Matter of Death of May*, 586 P.2d 738 (Okl.1978); *Farmers Co-Op Exchange of Weatherford v. Krewall*, 450 P.2d 506 (1969); *Flint Construction v. Downum*, 444 P.2d 200 (Okl.1968); *Gulf Oil v. Harris*, 425 P.2d 957 (Okl.1967).

[6, 7] When a claimant attempts to bring an illness within the ambit of an accidental injury he is bound to prove the infirmity conforms to the criteria laid down in an accidental injury situation. Petitioner's objection that no proof of specific date of infection is fatal to recovery would obtain except for the fact that within the rather indeterminate incubation period for this disease the claimant testified several contaminating incidents occurred with frequency, and as previously mentioned they are, handling hides with cracked skin, smoking while on duty and having hide-contaminated salt splash in the eyes.

[8] The record presents no evidence that the disease could have been contracted at a place other than the place of employment. The circumstantial evidence presented will support a finding that the contamination was an event which was an accidental injury resulting from employment, notwithstanding the fact that the circumstantial evidence does not exclude every other reasonable conclusion but that found by the trial authority.

OPINION OF COURT OF APPEALS,

DIVISION 2, VACATED; TRIAL COURT AFFIRMED.

LAVENDER, C.J., IRWIN, V.C.J., and WILLIAMS, HODGES, BARNES, SIMMS and DOOLIN, JJ., concur.

OPALA, J., disqualified.

9.

Theresa M. SIMEON, et al.

v.

John DOE, d/b/a The Sweet Pepper Grill, et al.

No. 92–C–2353.

Supreme Court of Louisiana.

May 24, 1993.

Rehearings Denied, June 24, 1993.

Family members of restaurant patron brought action against restaurant and oyster supplier arising from patron's death. Supplier filed third-party demand against Department of Health and Human Resources (DHHR). The Civil District Court, Orleans Parish, Revius O. Ortique, Jr., J., held that neither supplier nor restaurant were liable, but that DHHR was liable for failure to warn, and appeal was taken. The Court of Appeal, 602 So.2d 77, held that none of the defendants were liable, and appeal was taken. The Supreme Court, Marcus, J., held that: (1) neither restaurant nor supplier could be held strictly liable for sale of raw oysters containing naturally-occurring vibrio vulnificus bacteria, absent showing that oysters containing bacteria were unreasonably dangerous to ordinary customer, and (2) DHHR's decision to warn physicians, rather than general public, of health hazards associated with eating raw oysters came within policymaking or discretionary acts doctrine.

Affirmed in part, vacated in part and remanded.

Watson, J., dissented and assigned reasons.

Lemmon, J., dissented and will assign reasons.

1. Negligence ⊕19

Injured person asserting strict liability must prove vice in person or thing whose act causes damage, and that damage resulted from vice; once this is proved, owner or guardian responsible for person or thing can escape lia- bility only if he shows harm was caused by fault of victim, by fault of third person, or by irresistible force. LSA-C.C. art. 2317-2322.

2. Food ⊕25

Neither restaurant nor supplier could be held strictly liable for sale of raw oysters containing naturally-occurring vibrio vulnificus bacteria, absent showing that oysters containing bacteria were unreasonably dangerous to ordinary consumer; bacteria was only harmful to those persons with specific underlying disorders such as liver or kidney disease. LSA-C.C. art. 2317-2322.

3. Products Liability ⊕14

Duty to warn applies to any danger inherent in normal use of product which is not within knowledge or ordinary user; however, for such duty to apply, plaintiff must prove that seller knew or should have known of defect.

4. Food ⊕25

If retailer or wholesaler of raw oysters knows or should know of health hazard to certain people from eating raw oysters, they have duty to warn of such danger.

5. Municipal Corporations ⊕728
Officers and Public Employees ⊕114, 116

In determining whether policymaking or discretionary acts doctrine applies, exempting public agency from liability, court must first determine whether statute governing regulation or policy specifically prescribes course of action for employee or agency to follow, in which case there is no discretion and thus no immunity; if discretion is involved, however, court must then decide whether such discretion is grounded in social, economic or political policy, in which case employer or agency is insulated from liability, or not, in which case employee or agency is liable for any negligence. LSA-R.S. 9:2798.1.

6. States ⊕112.2(2)

Department of Health and Human Resources' decision to warn physicians, rather than general public, of health hazards associated with eating raw oysters, was discretionary decision grounded in social, economic or political policy, and thus came within policymaking or discretionary acts doctrine, exempting Department from liability to estate of decreased oyster eater. LSA-R.S. 9:2798.1.

Thomas P. Breslin, Jr., Chehardy, Sherman, Ellis & Breslin, Charles S. LaBarre, Wendell H. Gauthier, Gauthier & Murphy, Metairie, for applicant.

Gustave A. Fritchie, III, Montgomery, Barnett, Brown, Reed & Hammond, H.F. Foster, III, Bienvenu, Foster, Ryan & O'Bannon, Craig R. Nelson, Christina Papastavros, Sarah Ann Lowman, Hulse, Nelson & Wanek, New Orleans, for respondent.

Lawrence S. Kullman, New Orleans, Daniel C. Palmintier, Lafayette, Michael C. Palmintier, Baton Rouge, for Louisiana Trial Lawyers Ass'n, amicus curiae.

MARCUS, Justice.*

On September 6, 1986, Floyd Simeon, Sr., age 63, and his son, Edward Simeon, age 38, went to the Sweet Pepper Grill, a restaurant at the River Walk shopping center in New Orleans. They ordered a dozen and a half raw oysters. The oysters were taken from a refrigerated area, shucked in front of them, and were placed on a single tray. Mr. Simeon ate approximately six oysters; his son ate nine or ten. His son testified the oysters smelled and looked "okay" and tasted "good." He testified he and his father had eaten raw oysters together for many years, and his father had never gotten sick from eating them.

Two days later, Mr. Simeon began running a fever and complained of pain in his ankle. The next day, his wife brought him to the hospital. His family doctor, Dr. Charles Magee, called in Dr. James D. Conway, a specialist in infectious diseases. Dr. Conway diagnosed Mr. Simeon as suffering from vibrio vulnificus septicemia, an infection resulting from ingestion of raw oysters containing the vibrio vulnificus bacteria. As the disease progressed, Mr. Simeon developed severe blisters on his legs and began to lose subcutaneous tissue. Dr. John Church, a plastic surgeon, was called in. Dr. Church applied antibiotic dressings and began debridement of the skin in an effort to stop the spread

of the infection. When this was unsuccessful, he was forced to amputate both of Mr. Simeon's legs. However, the doctors were unable to stop the spread of the infection and Mr. Simeon died on September 23, 1986.

On March 23, 1987, plaintiffs filed a petition for damages for the wrongful death of Mr. Simeon. Named as defendants were John Doe, d/b/a The Sweet Pepper Grill (Sweet Pepper)[1] and United States Fidelity and Guaranty Co. (USF & G), as insurer of Sweet Pepper. On September 15, 1987, plaintiffs filed a second supplemental and amended petition naming as an additional defendant M.J. Bilich Oyster Co. (Bilich), the supplier of oysters to Sweet Pepper. On November 17, 1987, plaintiffs filed a third supplemental and amended petition naming as defendant the Louisiana Department of Health and Human Resources (DHHR).

Evidence at trial indicated that vibrio vulnificus bacteria is not a pollutant and occurs naturally in the Gulf of Mexico. The oyster, because it feeds by filtering hundreds of gallons of seawater per day, concentrates the bacteria inside of itself. Studies suggested that under the appropriate conditions 55–60% of all oysters may contain the vibrio vulnificus bacteria in different doses. Proper cooking will kill the bacteria. Vibrio vulnificus bacteria is microscopic and in order to test for it, the oyster must be destroyed. Currently, there is no feasible way to prevent oysters containing vibrio vulnificus bacteria from reaching the consuming public.

The evidence indicated that vibrio vulnificus bacteria is not toxic to all people and can be killed by stomach acids or by the liver or kidneys. Those persons with gastric disorders, liver diseases (such as cirrhosis or hepatitis) and hemochromatosis (high iron content in the blood) are at risk; diabetics, people with suppressed immune systems (such as people on cancer chemotherapy), and people with renal disorders may possibly be at risk. Statistics indicated that between 1977–1982, the incidence of vibrio vulnificus infection in southern Louisiana was .6 to 1.9 cases per 100,000 population. Between 1977–1985, there were fourteen cases of primary septicemia related to the

----

----

1. On May 4, 1987, plaintiffs filed a first supplemental and amended petition substituting "Big Easy, Inc. d/b/a The Sweet Pepper Grill" for "John Doe d/b/a The Sweet Pepper Grill."

eating of raw oysters;[2] of those fourteen people, ten died. Once the bacteria gets into a person's bloodstream and septicemia develops, the mortality rate is 50–70%. In August 1982, the DHHR issued to physicians and hospitals a "Monthly Morbidity Report" dealing with vibrio vulnificus infections. The report stated, "[b]ecause of the severity and high case fatality rate for the septicemia cases, physicians should warn patients with chronic underlying liver and kidney diseases and other conditions causing, or capable of causing, impaired immune responses, to avoid eating raw oysters."

Dr. Magee, Mr. Simeon's family doctor since 1970, testified that he diagnosed Mr. Simeon as having cirrhosis of the liver in 1983 and also operated on him that year for a malignancy in his lower colon. He also treated him in July 1986 for a duodenum ulcer. After he found the liver cirrhosis, he advised Mr. Simeon not to consume alcoholic beverages and to watch the amount of sodium he consumed, but did not remember telling him not to eat raw shellfish. He testified that his office received the monthly morbidity reports from DHHR, but could not recall seeing the August 1982 report.

At the conclusion of the plaintiffs' case, the trial judge granted a motion for involuntary dismissal in favor of Sweet Pepper and Bilich finding neither party strictly liable. The judge denied DHHR's motion for involuntary dismissal based on La.R.S. 9:2798.1 (the policy-making or discretionary acts doctrine). At the conclusion of the trial, the judge rendered judgment in favor of plaintiffs and against DHHR, finding DHHR had a non-discretionary duty to warn the general public of the dangers of eating raw oysters. Plaintiffs appealed that portion of the judgment which held neither Sweet Pepper nor Bilich liable. DHHR appealed that portion of the judgment holding it liable. A five judge panel of the court of appeal affirmed the portion of the judgment finding no liability on the part of Sweet Pepper and Bilich and reversed that portion of the judgment holding DHHR liable.[3]

---

2. Vibrio vulnificus infections can also be acquired through wounds.

3. 602 So.2d 77 (La.App. 4th Cir.1992). Two judges concurred in the part of the majority opinion exonerating Sweet Pepper and Bilich from liability, but dissented from the part of the opinion exonerating DHHR from liability.

We granted certiorari to review the correctness of that decision.[4]

The issue before us is whether Sweet Pepper, Bilich and/or DHHR are liable to plaintiffs.

Liability of Sweet Pepper and Bilich

Plaintiffs argue that the principles of strict liability should apply to Sweet Pepper and Bilich for the sale of the oysters containing the vibrio vulnificus bacteria.

[1] The principle of legal fault or strict liability underlies articles 2317–22 of the civil code.[5] When harm results from the conduct of a person or defect of a thing which creates an unreasonable risk of harm to others, a person legally responsible under these code articles for the supervision, care, or guardianship of the person or thing may be held liable for the damage thus caused, despite the fact that no personal negligent act or inattention on the former's part is proved. The injured person must prove the vice (i.e, unreasonable risk of injury to another) in the person of thing whose act causes the damage, and the damage resulted from this vice. Once this is proved the owner or guardian responsible for the person or thing can escape liability only if he shows the harm was caused by the fault of the victim, by the fault of a third person, or by an irresistible force. *Halphen v. Johns-Manville Sales Corp.*, 484 So.2d 110, 116 (La.1986); *Loescher v. Parr,* 324 So.2d 441 (La.1975).

The concept of unreasonable risk of harm is analogous to the concept of "unreasonably dangerous" developed in products liability. "Unreasonably dangerous" has been defined as meaning "the article which injured the plaintiff was dangerous to an extent beyond that which would be contemplated by an ordinary con-

---

4. 608 So.2d 155 (La.1992).

5. Strict liability under the civil code closely resembles the principle of strict products liability developed in *Weber v. Fidelity & Casualty Ins. Co.,* 259 La. 599, 250 So.2d 754 (1971). La.R.S. 9:2800.52(6) of the 1988 Louisiana Products Liability Act specifically exempts "harvesters and other producers of . . . oysters . . . in their natural state" from the scope of the act; however, that act has been held to be non-retroactive and would not apply to the present case. *See Gilboy v. American Tobacco Co.,* 582 So.2d 1263 (La.1991).

sumer." *DeBattista v. Argonaut–Southwest Ins. Co.,* 403 So.2d 26, 30 (La.1981). *DeBattista* points out that the "unreasonably dangerous" requirement came into our jurisprudence as a result of section 402A of the Restatement (Second) of Torts, which itself developed from common law statutes applying to persons supplying food and drink. Comment i of that section makes it clear that a product is not unreasonably dangerous simply because it cannot be made "entirely safe for all consumption." Examples given in the comment show that while ordinary sugar is a "deadly poison" for diabetics and whiskey is "especially dangerous" to alcoholics, neither product is considered unreasonably dangerous.

[2]   Based on the record, we are unable to say that raw oysters containing the vibrio vulnificus bacteria are unreasonably dangerous to the ordinary consumer. The evidence is uncontroverted that vibrio vulnificus bacteria in raw oysters poses little, if any, threat to a healthy person. The bacteria is only harmful to those persons with specific underlying disorders such as liver or kidney disease. Seen in this light, the "defect" is really found in the person rather than the product, much in the same way that sugar is harmful only when used by someone with diabetes. Therefore, we find no error in the trial judge's conclusion that Sweet Pepper and Bilich are not strictly liable.[6]

---

6. Both the trial judge and court of appeal applied the so-called "foreign-natural" test. *See Title v. Pontchartrain Hotel,* 449 So.2d 677 (La.App. 4th Cir.1984), *writ denied,* 450 So.2d 967 (La.1984); *Loyocano v. Continental Ins. Co.,* 283 So.2d 302 (La.App. 4th Cir.1973); *Musso v. Picadilly Cafeterias, Inc.,* 178 So.2d 421 (La.App. 1st Cir.1965), *writ denied,* 248 La. 468, 179 So.2d 641 (1965); *see also Mexicali Rose v. Superior Court,* 1 Cal.4th 617, 4 Cal.Rptr.2d 145, 822 P.2d 1292 (1992) (citing *Title, Loyocano* and *Musso*). We recognized that this test has long been applied by our courts and the courts of other states in cases dealing with food, and has recently been applied by the California court of appeal to a case involving raw oysters containing vibrio cholera bacteria in *Kilpatrick v. Superior Court,* 8 Cal.App.4th 1717, 11 Cal.Rptr.2d 323 (1st Dist.1992). Nonetheless, we do not believe the foreign-natural test is the correct test to apply in present case. The foreign-natural test has traditionally been applied to cases where the

[3]   However, a finding that Sweet Pepper and Bilich are not strictly liable does not necessarily mean they are entitled to be dismissed from the suit. As we stated in *Halphen,* 484 So.2d at 117:

> An injured person cannot recover under the codal theory of strict liability if he fails to prove there was an unreasonable risk of injury inherent in the thing which caused his damage. Failing in his attempt to provide a vice in the thing, the injured person cannot rely on strict liability but must pursue a theory of recovery instead which requires him to impugn the conduct of the defendant. Analogy to the product liability field indicates, therefore, that an injured consumer who fails to prove that the product is unreasonably dangerous per se or has a construction defect must pursue a less strict theory of recovery which impugns the conduct of the manufacturer, such as *an action for failure to warn* or for failure to adopt an alternative design. [emphasis added].

The duty to warn applies to "any danger inherent in the normal use of the product which is not within the knowledge of an ordinary user." *Winterrowd v. Travelers Indem. Co.,* 462 So.2d 639, 642 (La.1985); *Hebert v. Brazzel,* 403 So.2d 1242 (La.1981). However, for such a duty to apply, the plaintiff must prove that the seller knew or should have known of the defect. *Chappuis v. Sears, Roebuck & Co.,* 358 So.2d 926, 930 (La.1978). In the context of products liability cases, we have held that "[i]n performing this duty a manufacturer is held to the knowledge and skill of an expert. It must keep abreast of scientific knowledge, discoveries, and advances and is presumed to know what is imparted thereby." *Halphen,* 484 So.2d at 115. Under this failure to warn theory, "evidence as to the knowledge and skill of an expert may be admissible in determining whether the manufacturer breached its duty." *Id.*

[4]   Turning to the facts of the present case, it is clear that there was a danger inherent

---

substance (such as bone in ground meat) presented a potential danger to all persons. By contrast, vibrio vulnificus bacteria affects only a very small number of persons—those persons in a specific risk group. Because of this difference, the foreign-natural distinction is not useful in the present context.

in the normal use of the product not within the knowledge of an ordinary user, i.e., that people with certain specific underlying conditions may become seriously ill or die as a result of eating raw oysters. Given the magnitude of the possible harm, we believe a warning is particularly necessary.[7] However, we find it unclear from the record whether a reasonable retailer or wholesaler of oysters on September 6, 1986 would have known or should have known, when held to the standard of an expert, of the potential danger to certain people from eating raw oysters. Since we now apply a different theory of recovery than the presented by plaintiffs at trial, we find it is appropriate to remand the case to the trial court to take further evidence on this issue.

Liability of DHHR

[5] DHHR argues that it should be exempt from liability, on the basis of the policy-making or discretionary acts doctrine, La.R.S. 9:2798.1, which provides in pertinent part:

> B. Liability shall not be imposed on public entities or their officers or employees based upon the exercise or performance or the failure to exercise or perform their policy-making or discretionary acts when such acts are within the course and scope of their lawful powers and duties.
> C. The provisions of Subsection B of this Section are not applicable:
> (1) To acts or omissions which are not

reasonably related to the legitimate governmental objective for which the policymaking or discretionary power exists; or
> (2) To acts or omissions which constitute criminal, fraudulent, malicious, intentional, willful, outrageous, reckless, or flagrant misconduct.

In *Fowler v. Roberts,* 556 So.2d 1 (La.1989) (on rehearing), we set out a two step inquiry, derived from *Berkovitz v. United States,* 486 U.S. 531, 108 S.Ct. 1954, 100 L.Ed.2d 531 (1988), to determine whether the policy-making or discretionary acts doctrine applied in a specific fact situation. First, a court must determine whether a statute, regulation or policy specifically prescribes the course of action for the employee or agency to follow. If so, there is no discretion on the part of the employee or agency and therefore no immunity. If a court determines discretion is involved, the court must then determine whether that discretion "is the kind which is shielded by the exception, that is, one grounded in social, economic or political policy." *Fowler,* 556 So.2d at 15. If it is, then the doctrine applies and the employee or agency is insulated from liability; if it is not, the employee or agency is liable for any negligence.

[6] Applying this test to the facts of the present case, we find no statute, regulation or policy *mandating* DHHR to issue warnings on potentially dangerous diseases.[8] Since there is no statute, regulation or policy, we must decide whether DHHR's decision to warn physicians rather than the general public was a discretionary decision grounded in social, economic or political policy. We find that it is. The record

---

7. Although not applicable to the present case, we note that in 1991, DHHR amended Chapter IX, § 9:045 of the State Sanitary Code to read:
All establishments that sell or serve raw oysters must display signs, menu warnings, table tents, or other clearly visible warnings at point of sale with the following words:
"WARNING: CONSUMPTION OF *RAW* OYSTERS CAN CAUSE SERIOUS ILLNESS IN PERSONS WITH LIVER, STOMACH, BLOOD, OR IMMUNE SYSTEM DISORDERS. FOR MORE INFORMATION, READ THE INFORMATIONAL BROCHURE OR CONSULT YOUR PHYSICIAN."
The warning must also be placed on containers of pre-packaged raw oysters and sacks or other containers of unshucked raw oysters.

---

8. La.R.S. 40:4(A)(13) empowers and authorizes the DHHR to issue "emergency rules and orders," but does not specifically mandate that it do so:
The state health officer, through the office of health services and environmental quality, shall be expressly empowered and authorized to issue emergency rules and orders when necessary and for the purpose of controlling nuisances dangerous to the public health and communicable, contagious, and infectious diseases, and any other danger to the public life and health and health-safety.
618 So.2d–21

clearly shows that DHHR made a discretionary policy decision that it was preferable to warn physicians (through the August 1982 Monthly Morbidity Report) rather than issue a warning to the general public. Dr. Henry Bradford, Director of Division Laboratories for the Department of Public Health, testified:

> I think we tried to notice those people that if they were at risk that they had a particular problem and we had to do that through the normal channels of going through the medical community. It is those people that is the physicians of this state that can best understand and appreciate those that are at risk and how to best handle those individuals and how to communicate that information to them so that they understand.

Likewise, the testimony of Dr. Louise McFarland, Chief Epidemiologist for the Office of Public Health, reveals that a policy decision to warn physicians was made:

> When we gathered a certain amount of information and we're finished with some studies back in 1982, we wrote an article that you have already used this morning, the morbidity report from the State, sent out to probably 7 thousand doctors cross the State, and said to the doctors, in doing this we sent out these morbidity notices, used to be every month but now it's every two months, Sir, put this in your file because this is something you will need to talk with your patients about. So always prefer to work with physicians for them to say to their patients[s] that have these underlying diseases that I know we have already talked about, we can talk about them again if we need to, so that a doctor would say to a patient you should not be eating raw oysters, raw beef, raw pork, raw vegetables, whatever, if you have this underlying condition.

Therefore, we find DHHR's decision to issue warnings only to physicians is a discretionary act under La.R.S. 9:2798.1(B) and DHHR is immune from liability arising out of this act. Further, we find DHHR's action was reasonable under the circumstances, and does not constitute criminal, fraudulent, malicious, intentional, willful, outrageous, reckless, or flagrant misconduct under La.R.S. 9:2798.1(C)(2). The court of appeal correctly found that DHHR was not liable to plaintiffs.[9]

DECREE

For the reasons assigned, the judgment of the court of appeal is affirmed insofar as it dismisses plaintiffs' suit against the Louisiana Department of Health and Human Resources. The judgment is vacated and set aside insofar as it dismisses plaintiffs' suit against the Sweet Pepper Grill and M.J. Bilich Oyster Co. The case is remanded to the district court to take evidence and render a decision on the issue of whether a reasonable retailer or wholesaler of oysters on September 6, 1986 would have known or should have known of the potential danger to certain people from eating raw oysters, and thereafter to render a judgment as to the liability of the Sweet Pepper Grill and/or M.J. Bilich Oyster Co. In the event liability is imposed, the previous damage awards should be reinstated. The rights of all parties to appeal the issues of liability and damages to the court of appeal are reserved. All costs will await the final outcome of the case.

WATSON, J., dissents and assigns reasons.

LEMMON, J., dissents and will assign reasons.

WATSON, Justice, dissenting.

The trial court correctly concluded that the Louisiana Department of Health and Human Resources (DHHR) was liable for its failure to give adequate warnings of the danger involved in eating raw oysters. There was abundant evi-

---

9. In addition to its holding that DHHR was immune under the policy-making or discretionary acts doctrine, the court of appeal also found that plaintiff's action against DHHR was prescribed, as it was not brought within one year of the occurrence and there was no timely filed suit against a solidary obligor to interrupt prescription. Since we are remanding the case to the trial court to determine the liability of Sweet Pepper and Bilich, there is a possibility that they could be held liable, and the suit against DHHR (as a solidary obligor) would therefore be timely. However, as we find DHHR is immune from liability under La.R.S. 9:2798.1, it is unnecessary to consider the question of prescription, and DHHR is entitled to be dismissed from the suit at this time.

dence that the DHHR was aware of the Vibrio vulnificus risk.

In April of 1982, Dr. Floyd G. Wickboldt presented a paper on Vibrio vulnificus (Plaintiffs' Exhibit 124), which was circulated at the Department of Health and Human Resources in an interoffice memo. The paper states:

> Patients with advanced liver disease, diabetes mellitus, lymphoproliferative malignancy and congestive heart failure at an increased risk of dieing [sic] from infection with *Vibrio vulnificus*. Those with advanced liver disease may also be more susceptible to developing septicemia.
>
> *   *   *   *   *   *
>
> *Vibrio vulnificus* is unique among Vibrio species in its ability to produce systemic, rapidly progressive, and frequently lethal disease. Insight into the virulence of this organism has been provided by several groups of laboratory investigators.
>
> *   *   *   *   *   *
>
> *Vibrio vulnificus* infection is being reported with increasing frequency particularly in coastal regions of the United States. Raw seafood consumption and/or wounds acquired in a marine environment predispose to infection. *Vibrio vulnificus* is a virulent pathogen producing significant morbidity and mortality.

Dr. Henry B. Bradford, an employee of the Louisiana Department of Public Health and an associate editor of *Vibrios in the Environment,* directs the division of laboratories. In 1982, the Department of Public Health decided that people at risk should be warned and a decision was made to warn those people through their physicians.

Louisiana's Vibrio vulnificus statistics (Plaintiffs' Exhibit 5) show to deaths in 1980; six in 1981; two in 1982; one in 1983; two in 1984; two in 1985; and five in 1986. Of the twenty deaths, ten had eaten raw oysters; one had eaten raw crabs; one had shucked oysters; and the other eight had unknown seafood contacts. In Dr. Bradford's opinion, those statistics are probably not accurate. Only the most severe cases are recognized.

An August, 1982, morbidity report regarding Vibrio vulnificus, circulated to approximately 7,000 Louisiana physicians, (Plaintiffs' Exhibit 6) stated:

> All 14 cases presented with a variety of

underlying illnesses that included seven with liver disease (cirrhosis or chronic active hepatitis), five with hematopoietic disorders, three with renal failure requiring dialysis, three with history of peptic ulcer disease, four with diabetes mellitus and four with heart disease.

> Ten of the 14 cases died, nine of which died within two days of onset. . . .

> Ten of the 14 patients were known to have consumed raw oysters within two weeks prior to onset. Also, the other four were known frequent or occasional consumers of raw oysters; . . .

The report recommended:

> Because of the severity and high case fatality rate for the septicemia cases, physicians should warn patients with chronic underlying liver and kidney diseases and other conditions causing, or capable of causing, impaired immune responses, to avoid eating raw oysters.

In 1982, Louisiana had a Vibrio cholera problem and there was public notification. Everyone is at risk for Vibrio cholera, but it can be successfully treated. Vibrio vulnificus affects fewer people but has a high mortality rate.

Dr. James D. Conway, an internist with a subspecialty in infectious diseases, had seen 10 to 12 people with Vibrio vulnificus infections. He was consulted in Floyd Simeon's case. In Dr. Conway's opinion, the bacterium is foreign to the oyster but natural to seawater. It is commonly found in oysters but is not part of the oyster. Dr. Conway did not recall seeing the August, 1982 morbidity report. Because his office location had changed, he may not have received it. Dr. Conway testified that many doctors are unfamiliar with Vibrio vulnificus infections.

An April, 1984 article in the *Journal of Infectious Diseases,* using data from the Centers for Disease Control (CDC) in Atlanta, Georgia, (Plaintiffs' Exhibit 13h) concluded:

> [i]nfections with *V vulnificus* are often life threatening, and many may be prevented; therefore, we recommend that patients with liver disease avoid raw or undercooked seafood.

Dr. Louise McFarland, chief of the epidemiology section, Office of Public Health, Department of Health and Hospitals, testified that she gathers information which is the basis for state health warnings. She occasionally recommends a warning, and higher officials suggest additional study. Health notices and warnings are a duty of the Department of Health, which decided that the best way to inform about Vibrio vulnificus was through notice to physicians. Dr. McFarland believed in a general warning about Vibrio vulnificus. In 1982, prior to the morbidity report, she publicly declared that Vibrio vulnificus infections may be more common than typhoid. Prior to 1986, Dr. McFarland knew of 50 Vibrio vulnificus cases.

Dr. McFarland co-authored an article on Vibrio vulnificus in the *Journal of the American Medical Association* on May 17, 1985. (Plaintiffs' Exhibit 13n). She gave an interview to Diane Mack on Channel 6 television and also fielded calls from several newspapers and radio stations. No follow-up to the August, 1982 morbidity report was ever made.

The oyster industry is regulated by the Louisiana Department of Public Health. Prior to the end of 1986, no effort was made to warn lay people about the risk of Vibrio vulnificus. The state health department checks the bacteria in all oyster-producing waters by legislative mandate. Each sack of oysters is tagged to identify: the bay; the lease number, if any; the date; the name of the vessel; and the operator. The oysters consumed by Floyd J. Simeon came from oyster grounds owned by the State of Louisiana.

DHHR'S DUTY TO WARN

The Louisiana Constitution provides in article 12, section 10(A):

> Neither the state, a state agency, nor a political subdivision shall be immune from suit and liability in contract or for injury to person or property.

LSA–R.S. 40:4(A)(13) states:

> The state health officer, through the office of health services and environmental quality, shall be expressly empowered and authorized to issue emergency rules and orders when necessary and for the purposes of controlling nuisances dangerous to the public health and communicable, contagious, and infections diseases, and any other danger to the public life and health and health-safety.

The authority granted by the statute is discretionary.

LSA–R.S. 9:2798.1 immunizes public entities for policy making or discretionary acts within the scope of their lawful powers. See Professor David W. Robertson's article on *Tort Liability of Governmental Units in Louisiana* at 64 Tulane Law Review 857. The discretionary function exception to liability, codified in LSA–R.S. 9:2798.1, is modeled on the federal discretionary function exception to liability in 28 U.S.C.A. § 2680(a). Since the exception is in derogation of the Louisiana Constitution's waiver of sovereign immunity, the government has the burden of proving that the exception applies. See *Prescott v. United States,* 973 F.2d 696 (9th Cir.1992), and *Erickson v. United States,* 976 F.2d 1299 (9th Cir.1992).

There is a two-step test to determine whether the exception applies. *Berkovitz v. United States,* 486 U.S. 531, 108 S.Ct. 1954, 100 L.Ed.2d 531 (1988). If there is a statute, regulation or policy which prescribes a course of action, there is no choice or discretion involved and the exception does not apply. No statute, regulation or policy mandates a public warning of infectious diseases by the DHHR: the pertinent statute, *supra,* gives discretionary authority. When acts of government employees involve an element of choice, they are protected by the exception if the choices are based on public policy considerations. *United States v. Gaubert,* — U.S. —, 111 S.Ct. 1267, 113 L.Ed.2d 335 (1991). Although decisions at an operational level can be discretionary, a choice must be grounded in social, economic or political policy to be shielded by the exception. *Berkovitz; Gaubert.* See *Lundstrum v. Lyng,* 954 F.2d 1142 (6th Cir.1991).

There is no evidence that the DHHR's decision not to warn the general public about the dangers of Vibrio vulnificus was based on public policy considerations. This was clearly not a policy decision because Dr. McFarland talked to the news media about the problem on a random basis. The DHHR decided to warn the public through a one-time 1982 notice to physicians. The decision to warn physicians instead of the general public was not based on public policy. The DHHR merely concluded, erroneously, that warning physicians once in August of 1982 was the best way to communicate the danger to those at risk.

When a failure to warn is a negligent omission not involving policy considerations, it is not protected by the exception. See *Andrulonis v. United States,* 924 F.2d 1210 (2d Cir.1991), vacated and remanded, — U.S. —, 112 S.Ct. 39, 116 L.Ed.2d 18; reinstated, 952 F.2d 652 (2d Cir.1991); cert. den. — U.S. —, 112 S.Ct. 2992, 120 L.Ed.2d 869 (1992). *An-*

drulonis involved a rare form of infection from aerosol exposure to a potent virus. The fact that the type of infection was rare, statistically insignificant, did not prevent government liability for failing to warn Andrulonis of the disastrous consequences from aerosol exposure. See also *Mandel v. United States,* 793 F.2d 964 (8th Cir.1986).

The DHHR had a policy of warning the public when consumption of raw oysters created a hazard. There was public warning of the 1978 Vibrio cholera problem. The DHHR undertook a duty to warn by warning physicians about Vibrio vulnificus. By failing to make an effective warning about Vibrio vulnificus, a much more serious hazard than Vibrio cholera because of its fatal consequences, the DHHR breached its own safety policy. See *Summers v. United States,* 905 F.2d 1212 (9th Cir.1990); *Boyd v. United States,* 881 F.2d 895 (10th Cir.1989); and *Smith v. United States,* 546 F.2d 872 (10th Cir.1976). Oyster vendors relied on the DHHR for information about raw oysters, but the DHHR warned in an ineffective and careless manner. Although the danger of Vibrio vulnificus was not reduced between 1982 and 1986, no warning was issued after 1982.

Where the government undertakes a duty to warn and there is detrimental reliance on that public duty, the government is liable for negligent performance. *Indian Towing v. United States,* 350 U.S. 61, 76 S.Ct. 122, 100 L.Ed. 48 (1955). A government entity can be liable to an individual for breach of a duty owed to the general public. *Stewart v. Schmieder,* 386 So.2d 1351 (La.1980); *Fowler v. Roberts,* 556 So.2d 1 (La.1989).

The DHHR could have reasonably anticipated further deaths in 1986 because of the abundant available data about the deadly Vibrio vulnificus bacteria. Thus, the risk of death from Vibrio vulnificus was within the scope of the DHHR's duty. See *Hill v. Lundin & Associates, Inc.,* 260 La. 542, 256 So.2d 620 (La.1972), and *Socorro v. City of New Orleans,* 579 So.2d 931 (La.1991).

It is unnecessary to reach the trial court's conclusion that the DHHR's omissions constitute intentional and reckless misconduct under LSA–R.S. 9:2798.1.C(2) because the state produced no evidence that the DHHR's decisions in regard to the Vibrio vulnificus bactera were grounded in public policy. Thus, the statutory discretionary function exception to the state's liability does not apply. There was detrimental reliance by the oyster industry on warnings by the state DHHR, and the DHHR undertook a duty to warn, which was negligently performed.

The DHHR recognized a need to warn in 1982, but negligently performed that duty by a one-time notice issued only to physicians. In subsequent years, it was apparent that the fatal danger of Vibrio vulnificus remained, but no further warning was made. The duty to warn was increased by the magnitude of the risk. That risk was disproportionate to the expense of a warning. See *Socorro v. City of New Orleans,* 579 So.2d 931 (La.1991). The DHHR must have anticipated further deaths from Vibrio vulnificus: Simeon's death was a foreseeable result of the DHHR's failure to warn. See *Pitre v. Opelousas General Hosp.,* 530 So.2d 1151 (La.1988).

Balancing the grave danger to those at risk against the minimal cost of a public warning, it is clear that a warning was required. Conceding, arguendo, that the 1982 warning was sufficient at the time, it did not suffice for all time in the face of a continuing danger. The law imposes liability for failure to protect against remote risks if the cost of the protection is relatively low. *Levi v. S.W. La. Elec. Membership Co-op.,* 542 So.2d 1081 (La.1989).

The trial court's conclusion that the DHHR breached its duty to warn the public of Vibrio vulnificus' fatal impact was not manifestly erroneous. If Floyd Simeon had been warned that eating raw oysters could kill him, there is a presumption that he would have heeded that warning. Compare *Bloxom v. Bloxom,* 512 So.2d 839 (La.1987), where the presumption was rebutted by evidence that a warning would not have been heeded. In *Winstead v. Ed's Live Catfish & Seafood, Inc.,* 554 So.2d 1237 (La.App. 1st Cir.1989), writ denied, 558 So.2d 570 (La.1990), a similar oyster case, plaintiff was unaware he had a preexisting liver disfunction and would not have realized he was at risk if there had been a warning. Here, the DHHR's failure to warn was a cause in fact of Floyd Simeon's death.

Simeon was predisposed to injury from Vibrio vulnificus, a susceptible victim. However, neither he nor his doctor were aware of the danger. The DHHR, which had superior knowledge, had a duty to warn Simeon and those similarly situated of the hazard posed by raw oysters. The fact that there was no danger to most people did not eliminate a duty to those under a disability.

LIABILITY OF SWEET PEPPER

The Sweet Pepper Grill was a professional vendor in the business of selling food. "The responsibility of a professional vendor or distributor is the same as that of a manufacturer." *Shortess v. Touro Infirmary,* 520 So.2d 389 at 391 (La.1988).

Strict liability was applied to food vendors before its extension into other areas of the law.

> Since very early times the common law has applied more stringent rules to sales of food than to sales of other merchandise. It has long been a well-established rule that in sales of food for domestic use there is an implied warranty that it is wholesome and fit for human consumption. *Race v. Krum,* 222 N.Y. 410, 118 N.E. 853, L.R.A. 1918F, 1172; *Wiedeman v. Keller,* 171 Ill. 93, 49 N.E. 210; *Houston Cotton Oil Co. v. Trammell,* Tex.Civ.App., 72 S.W. 244; 55 C.J. 764; 24 R.C.L. 195; 37 Tex.Jur. 299. A majority of the American courts that have followed this holding have not based such warranty upon an implied term in the contract between buyer and seller, nor upon any reliance by the buyer on the representation of the seller, but have imposed it as a matter of public policy in order to discourage the sale of unwholesome food. *Jacob E. Decker & Sons, Inc. v. Capps,* 164 S.W.2d 828 at 829 (Texas 1942).

See *Prosser & Keeton, The Law of Torts,* (5th ed. 1984), § 97, p. 690.

Selling food which has a fatal impact is an act causing damage under LSA–C.C. art. 2315. Strict liability results from a defect in a thing which creates an unreasonable risk of harm to others. *Loescher v. Parr,* 324 So.2d 441 (La.1975); *DeBattista v. Argonaut-Southwest Ins. Co.,* 403 So.2d 26 (La.1981). A food vendor is conclusively presumed to know the condition of the food sold and to represent that it is wholesome. *Doyle v. Fuerst & Kraemer,* 129 La. 838, 56 So. 906 (1911). Although the *Doyle* vender also prepared the food, those selling food to the public, either raw or cooked, warrant its wholesomeness. A warranty of wholesomeness extends between food vendors and consumers. *LeBlanc v. Louisiana Coca Cola Bottling Co.,* 221 La. 919, 60 So.2d 873 (1952).

Judge, now Justice, Lemmon correctly noted in a concurring opinion that strict liability is the law of Louisiana in cases involving food consumption injury. *Loyacano v. Continental Insurance Company,* 283 So.2d 302 at 306 (La.App. 4th Cir.1973).

Louisiana follows the rule in *Restatement, Second Torts,* § 402A, which states:

> Special Liability of Seller of Product for Physical Harm to User or Consumer

> (1) One who sells any product in a defective condition unreasonably dangerous to the user or consumer or to his property is subject to liability for physical harm thereby caused to the ultimate user or consumer, or to his property, if

> > (a) the seller is engaged in the business of selling such a product, and

> > (b) It is expected to and does reach the user or consumer without substantial change in the condition in which it is sold.

> (2) The rule stated in Subsection (1) applies although

> > (a) the seller has exercised all possible care in the preparation and sale of his product, and

> > (b) the user or consumer has not bought the product from or entered into any contractual relation with the seller.

Louisiana's jurisprudence has some intermediate appellate support for the foreign/natural test, under which sellers of food are liable for foreign adulteration but not natural bones, pearls or toxins. See *Title v. Pontchartrain Hotel,* 449 So.2d 677 (La.App. 4th Cir.1984), writ denied, 450 So.2d 967 (La.1984). For criticism of the test, see *Jackson v. Nestle-Beich, Inc.,* 147 Ill.2d 408, 168 Ill.Dec. 147, 589 N.E.2d 547 (1992), and the dissent in *Mexicali Rose v. Superior Court (Clark),* 1 Cal.4th 617, 4 Cal.Rptr.2d 145, 822 P.2d 1292 (1992). The trial court concluded that Vibrio vulnificus bacteria are foreign to oysters. That factual finding has ample support in the record and the court of appeal erred in deciding that the bacteria are natural. Vibrio vulnificus bacteria are natural to seawater but foreign to raw oysters. However, the foreign/natural test is a jurisprudential anachronism unsupported by Louisiana's codal law. *Title* and other intermediate appellate cases applying the foreign/natural test should be disapproved.

Raw oysters contaminated with Vibrio vulnificus are unreasonably dangerous, frequently fatal to persons with underlying physical problems. Since raw oysters cannot be made safe for those who are vulnerable, a warning of the danger should have been given.

As a matter of public policy, a medically handicapped consumer, who does not reasonably anticipate a deadly food defect, may recover against a seller who has failed to warn of that defect. See *Halphen v. Johns-Manville Sales Corp.*, 484 So.2d 110 (La.1986). The inability of the seller to know or prevent the risk is not a defense to strict liability but may reduce the seller's fault. See *Hunt v. City Stores, Inc.*, 387 So.2d 585 (La.1980), and *Halphen*.

LIABILITY OF BILICH

M.J. Bilich Oyster Co., a broker of oysters, bought unopened oysters from harvesters and sold them to restaurants. There is no evidence of negligence or improper handling. Strict liability applies to those selling food to the public. It does not extend to nonmanufacturers that sell to retailers without altering or opening the product. Bilich was ignorant of any vice in the oysters. LSA–C.C. art 2545. Since Bilich did not sell oysters to the public, the company was not in a position to warn those at risk. Bilich should not be liable for Floyd Simeon's death.

PRESCRIPTION

The alternative ground for the court of appeal's opinion was that any cause of action against the DHHR had prescribed. However, both the trial court and the court of appeal erred in finding no liability on the part of The Sweet Pepper Grill. The Sweet Pepper Grill should be strictly liable for selling lethal food with its liability diminished by the DHHR's failure to give adequate warnings to restaurants selling oysters or the general public. The obligation of The Sweet Pepper Grill and the DHHR should be solidary. LSA–C.C. art. 1793.

APPORTIONMENT OF FAULT

The principle of comparative fault may apply in strict liability cases. *Bell v. Jet Wheel Blast, Div. of Ervin Ind.*, 462 So.2d 166 (La.1985). The Sweet Pepper Grill should be strictly liable as a vendor of lethal food. Its fault should be diminished by its ignorance that the fatal bacteria existed. The DHHR was aware of the deadly danger. Because of the DHHR's failure to warn, not only the general public, but even those selling raw oysters, the overwhelming share of fault should attach to the DHHR. *Watson v. State Farm Fire and Cas. Ins. Co.*, 469 So.2d 967 (La.1985). The fault of The Sweet Pepper Grill should be fixed at 25 per-

cent, and the fault of the DHHR should be fixed at 75 percent. Because Floyd Simeon was ignorant of the risk he encountered in eating raw oysters, no blame or fault should attach to him. The majority errs in dismissing plaintiffs' suit against the Louisiana Department of Health and Human Resources and remanding the case as to The Sweet Pepper Grill and M.J. Bilich Oyster Co.

I respectfully dissent.

10.

Dorothy M. VEDROS, Earline Vedros Schmidt, and Earlis J. Vedros

v.

PUBLIC GRAIN ELEVATOR OF NEW ORLEANS, INC., St. Charles Grain Elevator, Dockside Elevators, Bunge Corporation, Cargill, Inc., Continental Grain Company, Continental Reserve Elevator Corporation, Farmer's Export Co-op, ADM Growmark River System, Inc, Peavy Company, Delta Bulk Terminal, Inc., Mississippi River Grain Elevator, Inc., n/k/a Ferruzzi USA, Inc., Sears, Roebuck and Company, American Optical Corporation, Minnesota Mining and Manufacturing Company and National Union Fire Insurance Company.

No. 92–CA–1078.

Court of Appeal of Louisiana, Fourth Circuit.

June 30, 1993.

Widow and children of longshoreman brought maritime negligence suit against operator of grain elevator in connection with longshoreman's death from grain asthma. The Civil District Court, Parish of Orleans, Frank V. Zaccaria, Sr., J., ad hoc, dismissed claims for loss of consortium, and plaintiffs appealed. The Court of Appeal, Landrieu, J., held that federal maritime law did not permit plaintiffs to recover for nonpecuniary losses.

Affirmed.

Waltzer, J., dissented with reasons.

Death ⊕88
Husband and Wife ⊕209(4)
Parent and Child ⊕7.5

Claim of longshoreman's widow and children under federal maritime law against operators of grain elevator, for loss of consortium in connection with grain asthma sustained by longshoreman as a result of inhalation of grain dust while loading grain on vessels, was barred as prohibited claim for nonpecuniary loss.

Harry E. Forst, New Orleans, for plaintiffs/appellants.

Gary M. Zwain and Joseph B. Morton, III, Duplass, Witman, Zwain, & Williams, Metairie, for defendants/appellees.

Before SCHOTT, C.J., and CIACCIO, WARD, WALTZER and LANDRIEU, JJ.

LANDRIEU, Judge.

In this maritime action, plaintiffs, Dorothy M. Vedros, Earline Vedros Schmidt, and Earlis J. Vedros, appeal the dismissal of their loss of consortium claims on a motion for summary judgment granted in favor of defendants, Public Grain Elevator of New Orleans, Inc. and Peavy Company. Finding no error in the judgment of the trial court, we affirm.

FACTS

On August 1, 1979, Percy J. Vedros, Sr., a longshoreman employed by Louisiana Stevedores Inc., collapsed during the course and scope of his employment as a grain trimmer aboard a vessel moored at the Public Grain Elevator Dock in the Mississippi River at the Port of New Orleans.[1] Diagnosed with grain asthma, a lung disease which results from excessive grain dust inhalation, Mr. Vedros was placed on disability. Thereafter, he continued to reside at his lifelong home at 5333 Laurel Street, New Orleans, seven to eight blocks from the Public Grain Elevator. Due to excessive air pollution from leaking grain dust, Mr. Vedros was advised by his physician to move from his home, according to his allegations.

On November 24, 1986, Mr. Vedros died from the lung disease, grain asthma. His widow and children filed the instant suit against numerous defendants, none of whom was Mr. Vedros' employer. Plaintiffs' petition alleged two distinct causes of action: a maritime negligence suit

---

1. From 1952 to 1979, Mr. Vedros worked for various stevedoring companies loading grain onto vessels from defendants' grain elevators along the Mississippi River.

and a products liability suit against the manufacturers of protective respiratory equipment.

Following a hearing, the trial court granted summary judgment in favor of defendants, Public Grain Elevator of New Orleans, Inc. and Peavy Company, and dismissed plaintiffs' claim for damages other than loss of support. In its reasons for judgment, the trial court stated the following:

"This matter came up in a motion for summary judgment filed Public Grain of New Orleans, Inc. (hereafter referred to as "Public Grain") and Peavy Company, and on an exception of prescription filed by Board of Commissioners, Port of New Orleans (hereinafter referred to as "Board" (sic), all defendants herein.

The motion for summary judgment is based on the failure to claim a pecuniary loss in plaintiffs' petition by the wife and surviving children of decedent, Perez J. Vedros, Sr. They have each claimed damages for:

1. Loss of love, affection and society

2. Grief, mental anguish and distress

3. Damages for physical pain and suffering of the decedent Perez J.Vedros, Sr.

In *Ludwick Adam Torregano v. Apex Marine Corporation*, No. 89–1158, U.S. Supreme Justice O'Connor, as organ of the court, reaffirmed the holding in *Moragne v. States Marine Lines, Inc.*, 398 U.S. 375, [90 S.Ct. 1772, 26 L.Ed.2d 339 (1970)], followed in *Miles v. Apex Marine Corp.*, [498 U.S. 19], 111 S.Ct. 317 [112 L.Ed.2d 275 (1990)], wherein the wrongful death action allowed by the Death On High Seas Act (DOHSA) applied to seamen in territorial waters and is inclusive of longshoremen.

Torregano v. Apex, supra, also limited the recovery to loss of income of the seaman, or the support lost by dependents, during the decedent's lifetime.

In *Antill v. Public Grains [Grain]*, *Et Al*, 507 [577] So.2d 1039, (La. [App.] 4th Cir.1991) (sic) a very similar case as the instant one, recognized a grain elevator longshoreman as a seaman and governed by federal substantive law rather than by tort law of Louisiana.

Therefore, this court must maintain the motion for summary judgment relative to the claims for loss of love, etc., as recited hereinabove.[2]

DISCUSSION

Plaintiffs contend they are entitled to recover under Louisiana law because of a land based tort and that general maritime law does not preclude their claim for nonpecuniary losses.

The first claim is based on the theory that the decedent lived in the vicinity of defendants' facilities for many years and died from the inhalation of dust emitted from these facilities. However, plaintiffs failed to plead this cause of action. At a hearing on February 5, 1992, the trial court allowed plaintiffs until March 3rd to amend their pleadings to make this claim. Although they amended their petition on March 2nd, they still failed to include a claim for damages which was not work related, i.e., a pure Louisiana tort claim. Consequently, their theory has no merit in this Court because it was never properly pleaded and presented to the trial court. Since plaintiffs failed to plead a land based tort, they are left with the theory that decedent inhaled grain dust in his capacity as a longshoreman loading grain onto vessels. In this respect their case is indistinguishable from *Antill v. Public Grain Elevator, et al,* 577 So.2d 1039 (La.App. 4th Cir.1991), *writ denied,* 581 So.2d 684 (1991), and their claim is governed by federal substantive law and not by Louisiana tort law. Thus, the issue becomes whether federal maritime law permits recovery by plaintiffs for nonpecuniary losses.

We begin with the premise that there is "no recovery for loss of society for a wrongful death of a Jones Act seaman whether the claim is brought under DOHSA, the Jones Act, or general maritime law." *Miles v. Apex Marine Corp.,* 498 U.S. 19, 33, 111 S.Ct. 317, 326, 112 L.Ed.2d 275 (1990).

With respect to the survivors of a longshoreman, Congress amended the LHWCA, 33 U.S.C. § 905(b) in 1972 to bar recovery from shipowners for the death or injury of a longshoreman resulting from breach of the duty of seaworthiness. *Miles,* 498 U.S. at 27, 111 S.Ct. at 323. This amendment rendered *Gaudet v. Sea-Land Services, Inc.,* 463 F.2d 1331 (5th Cir.1972)[3] inapplicable on its facts.[4] *Miles,* 498 U.S. at 31, 111 S.Ct. at 325.

Gaudet was a longshoreman who was severely injured aboard a vessel in state territorial waters. He sued the vessel owner for unseaworthiness. Shortly thereafter, he died and his widow brought a wrongful death action. The widow was allowed to recover nonpecuniary losses based upon the recent trend in permitting such recovery. *Gaudet,* 414 U.S. at 591, 94 S.Ct. at 818.

Gaudet applies only in territorial waters, and it applies only to longshoremen. *Miles,* 498 U.S. at 31, 111 S.Ct. at 325. Although the *Miles* court did not reverse *Gaudet* or specifically limit it to its facts, it seems appropriate because it creates an anomaly in the law.

The need for uniformity in maritime law is recognized and was the overriding concern of the *Miles* court. Since *Gaudet,* the 1972 amendments to the LHWCA and the decision of the U.S. Supreme Court in *Miles* evidences the trend in federal jurisprudential and statutory law to bar claims for nonpecuniary loss.

For the foregoing reasons, the judgment of the trial court is affirmed.

AFFIRMED.

WALTZER, J., dissents with written reasons.

WALTZER, Judge, dissenting.

This is an appeal from a February 5, 1992 judgment of the Civil District Court for the Parish of Orleans, the Honorable Frank V. Zaccaria, Sr., Judge Ad Hoc, presiding. The judgment provides as follows:

> "The motion for Summary Judgment urged by Public Grain Elevator of New Orleans, Inc. and Peavey Company denying the claim for damages other than the loss of support by dependents during decedent's lifetime is maintained as a matter of general maritime law.
>
> The motion for partial summary judgment based upon failure to allege a claim for dependency and loss of support during decedent's lifetime is held in abeyance until March 3, 1992. During said pe-

---

2. The remainder of the document discussed the homeowners' action which is moot due to plaintiff's amendment and the exception of prescription was not appealed.

---

3. *Gaudet* was affirmed by *Sea-Land Services, Inc. v. Gaudet,* 414 U.S. 573, 94 S.Ct. 806, 39 L.Ed.2d 9 (1974).

4. If *Gaudet* were limited to its facts, then it would no longer have any applicability at all.

riod plaintiffs will be permitted to amend pleadings to show dependency and loss of support during decedent's lifetime and any claim for damages arising out of any damages sustained by grain inhalation by decedent which is not work related.

The exception of prescription is denied herein."

From that judgment plaintiff appeals.

On August 1, 1979, Percy Vedros, an employee of Louisiana Stevedoring, Inc., while unloading grain at his job as a longshoreman, collapsed with acute respiratory failure. He was diagnosed as having grain asthma, a lung disease similar to silicosis and asbestosis and which results from excessive grain dust inhalation. Mr. Vedros was placed on disability. He continued to reside at his lifelong home at 5333 Laurel Street, seven to eight blocks from the Public Grain Elevator. Plaintiff alleges that upon advice of his physician, he was forced to move from his home due to excessive air pollution from leaking grain dust. Mr. Vedros moved. On November 24, 1986, Mr. Vedros died from the lung disease grain asthma. His widow and children filed the instant suit against numerous defendants, *none of whom were Mr. Vedros' employer.*

Plaintiffs' petition alleges numerous distinct causes of action. It alleges a wrongful death suit under general maritime law, a Longshoremen's and Harborworker's Compensation action under 33 U.S.C. § 901 et seq., an unseaworthiness action against a non-employer third-party vessel owner, an executive officer suit, an intentional tort fraudulent concealment suit, an absolute liability ultrahazardous activity suit, a strict liability suit, a failure to warn suit, a products liability suit, a breach of warranty action to a purchaser, a breach of contract action to a purchaser, and a design defect suit. In addition, plaintiff included a "savings clause" for any additional acts provable at trial.

The original petition filed November 24, 1987 provided in part as follows:

18.

The deceased, Percy J. Vedros, Sr. was employed by Louisiana Stevedores, Inc. and other stevedoring companies during the period 1952–1979 as a longshore laborer. In the course of his employment, Mr. Vedros was required to come into contact with grain and other harmful dusts which were being loaded onto vessels. The grain and other harmful dusts were being unloaded from the defendant grain elevators and placed onboard vessels. Mr. Vedros would shovel the grain as it came into the hull of a vessel. Mr. Vedros inhaled the grain dust and chemicals used to control pests both on land and over the Mississippi River.

19.

That Public Grain Elevator of New Orleans, Inc., St. Charles Grain Elevator, Dockside Elevators, Inc., Bunge Corporation, Cargill, Inc., Continental Grain Company, Continental Reserve Elevator Corporation, Farmer's Export Co-Op, Mississippi River Grain Inc., Peavy Company, Delta Bulk Terminal, Inc., and their executive officers knew the danger of exposure to grain dusts and other harmful dusts and that exposure to these harmful dusts was hazardous to decedent's health, and yet they failed and refused to warn or inform the decedent of that danger, thereby exposing him to continued harm and an aggravation of his condition. The decedent, Percy J. Vedros, Sr. did contract grain asthma relative to this exposure to grain dust and other harmful dusts, and died because of that lung condition on November 24, 1986.

20.

In addition to the above described acts, these defendants are guilty of the following:

a. in failing to use proper dust control methods to reduce the risks of inhalation to the deceased;

b. in failing to reveal and knowingly concealing the dangers of the inhalation of grain dust and chemicals that are used to control pests in the grain;

c. in failing to provide necessary protection to decedent;

d. *all other acts which may be revealed at the time of trial.* (emphasis supplied).

21.

That defendant, American Optical Corporation, manufactured and distributed masks which were ultimately used by the decedent while he engaged in his employment in the vicinity of grain and other harmful dusts. Due to the defective nature

of the equipment, decedent was caused to
suffer serious injuries and death.

22.

That the defendant, Sears, Roebuck
and Company, distributed and placed their
name on an American Optical Corporation
mask and other masks which were ultimately used by decedent while he engaged
in his employment in the vicinity of grain
and other harmful dusts. Due to the defective nature of the equipment, decedent was
caused to suffer serious injuries and death.

23.

That the defendant, Minnesota Mining and Manufacturing Company, manufactured and distributed masks which were
ultimately used by the decedent while he
engaged in his employment in the vicinity
of grain and other harmful dusts. Due to
the defective nature of the equipment, decedent was caused to suffer serious injuries
and death.

24.

That the defendant, National Union
Fire Insurance Company was and is the insurer of the defendant, Farmer's Export
Co-Op, insuring it and its executive officers for the liability and damages claimed
herein.

25.

Among other reasons, the defendants, American Optical Corporation,
Sears, Roebuck and Company and Minnesota Mining and Manufacturing Company,
were negligent in failing to produce a product reasonably fit for the purposes intended:

a. in failing to adequately and safely design its product to prevent workers from
contracting grain asthma;

b. in failing to warn of the hazards which
would result from the use of their products;

c. in failing to instruct, recommend or prescribe safety precautions;

d. in failing to avail themselves of the expert and specialized knowledge which existed as to proper and reasonably safe design of their particular product;

e. in failing to inspect or prevent the hazards which resulted in the injury and death
to decedent.

26.

That the defendants, American Optical Corporation, Sears, Roebuck and Company and Minnesota Mining and Manufacturing Company manufactured and
distributed a mask which was unreasonably dangerous in normal use and therefore, they are strictly liable to the widow
and children of Percy J. Vedros, Sr. for the
injuries he received while using their product and his death.

27.

The defendants, Public Grain Eleva-
tor of New Orleans, Inc., St. Charles Grain
Elevator, Dockside Elevators, Bunge Corporation, Cargill, Inc., Continental Grain
Company, Continental Reserve Elevator
Corporation, Farmer's Export Co-Op,
ADM Growmark River System, Inc.,
Peavy Company, Delta Bulk Terminal,
Inc., Mississippi River Grain Elevator,
Inc., n/k/a Ferruzzi USA, Inc., are strictly
liable to petitioners for the following reasons: the grain is a product that is unreasonably dangerous in normal use, and, therefore, since the above named defendants
had custody and control of that defective
product, they are therefore strictly liable to
petitioners.

All defendants are jointly, severally
and in solido liable to petitioners for the
damages asserted herein.

29.

That the activity of loading grain
from an elevator onto a vessel, is an ultrahazardous activity, i.e. that no matter what
precautions are taken, there is still a risk of
harm to an individual working in that grain
dust. Accordingly, all of the defendants,
since they were engaged together in this
activity, are absolutely liable to the widow
and children of the decedent, Percy J.
Vedros, Sr. for his injuries and death.

30.

Solely by reason of the defendants'
negligence and acts of strict liability, the
petitioner was caused to contract grain
asthma. He suffered from that condition
and it later caused his death. His widow
and children have been denied his love,
consortium and companionship. They
have been denied his inheritance which

would have been considerably larger had he been able to work.

31.

That the defendants, American Optical Corporation, Sears, Roebuck and Company and Minnesota Mining and Manufacturing Company are also liable to petitioner under the theory of breach of warranty and breach of contract. Decedent, Percy J. Vedros, Sr. purchased the Sears, Roebuck and Company dust mask that was manufactured by American Optical Corporation and other companies and it was warranted to him at the time that the product was good for its intended use, that is, for protection against grain dust and other harmful dusts. However, in fact, the product was defective and did not provide the warranted and contracted protection. Therefore, these defendants breached their warranty and contract to decedent.

Plaintiff's Supplemental and Amending Petition filed March 26, 1990 added the Board of Commissioners of the Port of New Orleans a defendant and the owner of the Public Grain Elevator, which it also operated until 1964 when it leased the elevator to Public Grain Elevator of New Orleans, Inc.

Defendants Public Grain Elevator of New Orleans and Peavey Company filed motions for partial summary judgment on the grounds that in order for Mr. Vedros's children to recover under 33 U.S.C. § 901 et seq. they must allege that they were financially dependent upon him and that they failed to allege dependency. Defendants also argued that loss of consortium is not recoverable and moved for partial summary judgment on the grounds of prescription.

After a hearing, the trial court rendered judgment providing that the partial motion for summary judgment urging denial of the claim for damages other than the loss of support by dependents during decedent's lifetime was maintained as a matter of general maritime law, that the failure to allege a claim for dependence was held in abeyance until March 3, 1992 during which period plaintiffs would be allowed to amend their petition, that plaintiffs during such period also amend their petition to include any claim for damages arising out of any damages sustained by grain inhalation by decedent which was not work related, and denied the exception of prescription.

On March 2, 1992, plaintiffs filed an amended petition adding two new paragraphs:

19.(a)

Prior to Percy Vedros' injuries decedent was a strong, able-bodied man capable of earning and actually earning $40,000.00 a year. At the time of his death he was sixty-seven years of age. Decedent's dependents who are his widow and two major children have also suffered great pecuniary loss and damage as a result of his death. Those pecuniary losses include a loss of support, loss of inheritance, and funeral expenses.

20.(a)

Plaintiffs are also entitled to recover punitive damages under the general maritime law from the defendant grain elevators. The grain elevators' actions and inactions as outlined in Paragraphs 19 and 20 of the petition constitute a willful and wanton misconduct reflecting a reckless disregard for the safety of the decedent and others situated like him.

The majority opinion states:

"Since plaintiffs failed to plead a land based tort . . ."

Plaintiffs did plead land based torts, specifically product liability, design defect, and intentional fraudulent concealment. Additionally plaintiff pled a land-based contract action, namely the breach of warranty to a purchaser of goods purchased by him at Sears, Roebuck, i.e. on hand.

Turning to the issue of plaintiffs' claim for damages other than loss of support, the trial court rendered the following written reasons for judgment:

"This matter came up in a motion for summary judgment filed by Public Grain of New Orleans, Inc. (hereinafter referred to as "Public Grain") and Peavey Company, and on an exception of prescription filed by Board of Commissioners, Port of New Orleans (hereinafter referred to as "Board" (sic), all defendants herein.

The motion for summary judgment is based on the failure to claim a pecuniary loss in plaintiffs' petition by the wife and surviving children of decedent, Perez J. Vedros, Sr. They have each claimed damages for:

1. Loss of love, affection and society.
2. Grief, mental anguish and distress.

3. Damages for physical pain and suffering of the decedent Perez J. Vedros, Sr.

In *Ludwick Adam Torregano v. Apex Marine Corporation,* No. 89–1158, U.S. Supreme Justice O'Connor, as organ of the Court, reaffirmed the holding in *Moragne v. States Marine Lines, Inc.,* 398 U.S. 375 [90 S.Ct. 1772], followed in *Miles v. Apex Marine Corp.,* [498 U.S. 19], 111 S.Ct. 317, wherein the wrongful death action allowed by the Death On High Seas Act (DOHSA) applied to seamen in territorial waters and is inclusive of longshoremen.

Torregan v. Apex, supra, also limited the recovery to loss of income of the seaman, or the support lost by dependents, during the decedent's lifetime.

In *Antill v. Public Grain, Et Al,* 507 [577] So.2d 1039, (La. [App.] 4th Circuit 1991) a very similar case as the instant one, recognized a grain elevator longshoreman as a seaman and governed by federal substantive law rather than by tort law of Louisiana.

Therefore, this court must maintain the motion for summary judgment relative to the claims for loss of love, etc., as recited hereinabove . . ."[1]

The trial court is correct in citing *Antill,* above, for the proposition that "virtually all of the cases . . . in which the injury occurred during the loading or unloading of cargo have found *admiralty* jurisdiction (as opposed to state tort law) appropriate" (at 1042) (Emphasis supplied). The trial court is wrong, however, when it states that *Antill* found that a harborworker is a seaman. Although it failed to use the word anywhere with it, *Antill* was a federal preemption case, namely did federal admiralty law preempt state law. Admiralty law includes many different types of recovery including the Jones Act, the Longshoremen and Harbor Workers Act, the Death on the High Seas Act (DOHSA), and the general maritime law which includes unseaworthiness actions and actions for maintenance and cure among others.

---

1. The remainder of the document discusses the homeowner's action which is moot due to plaintiff's amendment and the exception of prescription was not appealed.

Generally, the Jones Act provides tort remedies for seamen. In 1926, in *International Stevedoring Co. v. Haverty,* 272 U.S. 50, 47 S.Ct. 19, 71 L.Ed. 157 (1926), longshoremen were declared to be "seamen" and within the purview of the Jones Act when injured on a navigable waterway. However, after its passage the Longshoremen's and Harbor Workers' Compensation Act became the exclusive remedy *against their employer* by the injured *longshoremen* and effectively withdrew them from the benefits of the Jones Act. Thus after the passage of this act, a longshoreman or harborworker is *never* a seaman under the Jones Act. The Jones Act became available only to "true seamen", who are defined as those who aid in the navigation of the ship.

The Longshoremen's and Harbor Workers' Compensation Act was intended to provide compensation for a class of employees, harbor workers, at work on a vessel in navigable waters, who although they might be classed as "seamen" were nonetheless regarded as distinct from the members of a "crew" because they were not performing the traditional work of seamen in aiding navigation. They served on vessels as laborers, at the type of work performed by longshoremen and harbor workers, and thus are distinguished from those employees on the vessel who are naturally and primarily on board to aid in navigation. Thus a harborworker inside the hold of a ship shoveling grain into the hold is never a seaman, but is always a longshoreman, even though he is physically located on a ship. *Southern Pacific Co. v. Jensen,* 244 U.S. 205, 37 S.Ct. 524, 61 L.Ed. 1086 (1917) resulted in the doctrine that state law could not constitutionally afford compensation to maritime employees. The gap created by *Jensen* was filled by the passage of the Longshoremen's and Harbor Workers' Compensation Act. It is roughly the maritime equivalent of state workers' compensation laws.

Formerly under general maritime law there was no liability for wrongful death. *The Harrisburg,* 119 U.S. 199, 213, 7 S.Ct. 140, 146, 30 L.Ed. 358 (1886). In the absence of statute, it was held there could be no recovery in the admiralty courts for death on the high seas. *Western Fuel Co. v. Garcia,* 257 U.S. 233, 42 S.Ct. 89, 66 L.Ed. 210 (1921). In 1920, Congress passed the Death on the High Seas Act. The Death on the High Seas Act gives a right of action for *pecuniary losses* to the personal representative of the deceased for the exclusive benefit of the wife, husband, parent, child or dependent relative of the deceased against the vessel, person, or corporation liable for the death, when the death is caused by a wrongful act on the high seas *beyond a marine league (approximately 3 miles) from the shore of any state,* the District of Columbia, or the territories or dependencies of the United States. The act does not apply to injuries resulting in death occurring on water within the territorial waters of any state, i.e. within 3 miles of the coastline of the state.

The Death on the High Seas Act is not applicable to injuries involving wrongful deaths on artificial island drilling rigs located more than a marine league off the Louisiana coast. The islands were not erected primarily as navigational aids. In enacting the Outer Continental Shelf Lands Act, 43 U.S.C. § 1331 et seq., Congress decided that these artificial islands, although surrounded by the high seas, were not themselves to be considered within maritime jurisdiction. The Outer Continental Shelf Lands Act and the law of the adjacent State furnish the appropriate remedy.

The Death on the High Seas Act, however, resulted in a gap such that longshoremen and harbor workers who died on vessels a marine league out from the state had a wrongful death action, whereas longshoremen and harbor workers doing the same jobs and killed in the same way who died on land, on the dock, on a docked vessel, or on a vessel within 3 miles of the state shore, i.e. the state's territorial waters, had no wrongful death action.

Accordingly, in 1970 in *Moragne v. States Marine Lines, Inc.,* 398 U.S. 375, 408, 90 S.Ct. 1772, 1792, 26 L.Ed.2d 339 (1970), the United States Supreme Court found that an action does lie under the general maritime law for wrongful death, expressly overruling *The Harrisburg,* above. In *Sea-Land Services, Inc. v. Gaudet,* 414 U.S. 573, 94 S.Ct. 806, 39 L.Ed.2d 9 (1974), the Supreme Court distinguished the recovery allowed under general maritime law wrongful death actions from the recovery allowed under Death on the High Seas Act wrongful death actions. Because the Death on the High Seas Act only allows for "pecuniary losses" courts have interpreted the statutory language to mean that loss of society is not recoverable under DOHSA. In contrast to DOHSA wrongful death actions, *the Court stated* that while only recovery for "pecuniary loss" is allowed under the express language of the Death on the High Seas Act, *a wrongful death action under general maritime law allows for loss of society* and funeral expenses:

"*Moragne,* on the other hand, requires that the shape of the new maritime wrongful-death remedy (not a statutory creation but judge-made, see *The Tungus v. Skovgaard,* 358 U.S. 588, 611, 70 [79] S.Ct. 503 [516], 3 L.Ed.2d 524 (1959) (opinion by Brennan, J.)) be guided by the principle of maritime law that "*certainly it better becomes the humane and liberal character of proceedings in admiralty to give than to withhold the remedy, when not required to withhold it by established and inflexible rules,*" *The Sea Gull,* 21 F.Cas. 909 (No. 12,578) (C.C.Md.1865), quoted in *Moragne,* 398 U.S. at 387, 90 S.Ct., at 1781. Since the policy underlying the remedy is to insure compensation of the dependents for *their* losses resulting from the decedent's death, the remedy should not be precluded merely because the decedent, during his lifetime, is able to obtain a judgment for his own personal injuries. No statutory language or 'established and inflexible rules' of maritime law require a contrary conclusion. (emphasis supplied).

* * * * * *

... under the maritime wrongful-death remedy, the decedent's dependents may recover damages for their loss of support, services, and society, as well as funeral expenses.

Recovery for loss of support has been universally recognized, and includes all the financial contributions that the decedent would have made to his dependents had he lived. Similarly the overwhelming majority of state wrongful-death acts and courts interpreting the Death on the High Seas Act have permitted recovery for the monetary value of services the decedent provided and would have continued to provide but for his wrongful death. Such services include, for example, the nurture, training, education, and guidance that a child would have received had not the parent been wrongfully killed. Services the decedent performed at home or for his spouse are also compensable.

Compensation for loss of society, however, presents a closer question. The term 'society' embraces a broad range of mutual benefits each family member receives from the others' continued existence, including love, affection, care, attention, companionship, comfort, and protection. Unquestionably, the deprivation of these benefits by wrongful death is a grave loss to the decedent's dependents. Despite this fact, a number of early wrongful-death statutes were interpreted by courts to preclude recovery for these losses on the ground that the statutes were intended to provide compensation only for 'pecuniary losses' and that the loss of society is not such an economic loss. Other wrongful-death statutes contain express language limiting recovery to pecuniary losses; for example, the Death on the High Seas Act limits recovery to 'a fair and just compensation for the *pecuniary* loss sustained by the person for whose benefit the suit is brought . . .' 46 U.S.C. § 762 (emphasis added), and consequently has been construed to exclude recovery for the loss of society.

A clear majority of States, on the other hand, have rejected such a narrow view of damages, and, either by express statutory provision or by judicial construction, permit recovery for loss of society. This expansion of damages recoverable under wrongful-death statutes to include loss of society has led one commentator to observe that '[w]hether such damages are classified as "pecuniary", or recognized and allowed as nonpecuniary, the recent trend is unmistakably in favor of permitting such recovery.' Speiser Wrongful Death 218. Thus, our decision to permit recovery for loss of society aligns the maritime wrongful-death remedy with a majority of state wrongful-death statutes. But if we are to shape the remedy to comport with the humanitarian policy of the maritime law to show 'special solicitude' for those who are injured within its jurisdiction. (at 814–816).

* * * * * *

Finally, in addition to recovery for loss of support, services, and society, damages for funeral expenses may be awarded under the maritime wrongful-death remedy in circumstances where the decedent's dependents have either paid for the funeral or are liable for its payment. A majority of States provided for such recovery under their wrongful-death statutes. Furthermore, although there is a conflict over whether funeral expenses are compensable under the Death on the High Seas Act, compare *The Culberson,*

61 F.2d 194 (CA3 1932), with *Moore v. the OS Fram,* 226 F.Supp. 816 (SD Tex.1963) aff'd sub nom. *Wilhelm Seafoods, Inc. v. Moore,* 328 F.2d 868 (CA5 1964), it is clear that funeral expenses were permitted under the general maritime law prior to *The Harrisburg,* see *e.g., Hollyday v. The David Reeves,* 12 F.Cas. 386 (No. 6,625) (Md.1879). We therefore find no persuasive reason for not following the earlier admiralty rule and thus hold that funeral expenses are compensable." (at 818).

The *Gaudet* case, above, involved the widow of a *seaman* in territorial waters, i.e. State territorial waters within a marine league, bringing a wrongful death action based upon unseaworthiness. *Gaudet* returned to the lower court for further proceedings. See: 463 F.2d 1331 (CA5 1972). Sea-Land filed motions to dismiss on the grounds of res judicata and failure to state a claim upon which relief could be granted. The Fifth Circuit found:

"... we hold that Mrs. Gaudet retained a compensable cause of action for Mr. Gaudet's death wholly apart from and not extinguished by the latter's recovery for his personal injuries ..." (at 1332).

The court further stated:

"[t]he personal injury and wrongful death suits assert two distinct causes of action designed to compensate for two separate losses—the first for the loss and suffering of the injured while he lived, and the second for the losses to his beneficiaries on account of his death ... Quite obviously the jury verdict recovered by Mr. Gaudet during his lifetime did not include damages done to others by his death which had not yet occurred ... the wrongful death action Mrs. Gaudet now attempts to bring never belonged to Mr. Gaudet and in fact did not even accrue until his death." (at 1332–1334).

Gaudet was filed prior to 1972 and was based upon a claim of unseaworthiness. In 1972 Congress amended 33 U.S.C. § 905(b) to add:

"The liability of the vessel under this subsection shall not be based upon the warranty of seaworthiness or a breach thereof at the time the injury occurred."

In the instant case, the trial court in its

reasons for judgment somewhat erroneously stated:

"In *Ludwick Adam Torregano v. Apex Marine Corporation,* No. 89–1158, U.S. Supreme Justice O'Connor, as organ of the Court, reaffirmed the holding in *Moragne v. States Marine Lines, Inc.,* 398 U.S. 375 [90 S.Ct. 1772], followed in *Miles v. Apex Marine Corp.,* [498 U.S. 19], 111 S.Ct. 317, wherein the wrongful death action allowed by the Death On High Seas Act (DOHSA) applied to seamen in territorial waters and is inclusive of longshoremen.

Torregan v. Apex, supra, also limited the recovery to loss of income of the seaman, or the support lost by dependents, during the decedent's lifetime."

Case Number 89–1158 is entitled *Mercedel W. Miles, Individually and as Administratrix of the Succession of Ludwick Adam Torregano, Petitioner v. Apex Marine Corporation et al.;* its citation is 498 U.S. 19, 111 S.Ct. 317, 112 L.Ed.2d 275 (1990) and West Publishing Company indicates that it should be cited as *Miles v. Apex Marine Corp.*

In *Miles,* above, the Court found that there was no recovery for loss of society in a general maritime action based on *unseaworthiness* for the wrongful death of a *Jones Act seaman* against his *employer.*

As so well stated by the court in *Mussa v. Cleveland Tankers,* 802 F.Supp. 84 (U.S.D.C., E.D.Mich., 1992):

"*Miles* was decided in the context of a Jones Act seaman (via his parent) suing his employer under the Jones Act for negligence and under general maritime law for unseaworthiness ... simply put, under the *Miles* Court's view, there should be no reason why a Jones Act seaman, unable to sue his employer for nonpecuniary damages directly under a Jones Act negligence claim, could sue his employer for such damages under a related general maritime law claim for unseaworthiness.

Total's argument that *Miles* compels a similar result in the present case goes too far. Such argument seeks to extend *Miles'* policy of uniformity to situations, such as the one presented in the cases at bar, where Jones Act seamen *are not suing their employer* under related Jones Act and general maritime law claims, *but in-stead, are suing a third-party,* here Total, under a single general maritime claim of negligence ... A Louisiana district court case, decided after *Miles,* supports this conclusion. In *Rebstock v. Sonat Offshore Drilling,* 764 F.Supp. 75 (E.D.La.1991), a Jones Act seaman, and his spouse, asserted negligence claims against a defendant ... third party who was not the plaintiff-seaman's employer, in relation to the plaintiff-seaman's injury. The defendant moved to dismiss the loss of consortium claim asserted against it by the plaintiff spouse. The district court denied such motion. In denying the motion, the court noted that *Miles did not compel a different result,* as in *Miles* the seaman had sued his employer under the Jones Act and under general maritime law for unseaworthiness and *that the Court's opinion did not concern negligence actions under general maritime law against third parties. Id.* at 76. The Court further noted that the facts in the case before it were highly similar to a pre-*Miles* decision of the Fifth Circuit, *Tullos v. Resource Drilling, Inc.,* 750 F.2d 380, 386 (5th Cir.1985), wherein a spouse of a seaman was allowed to recover loss of consortium damages against a third party under a general maritime law negligence claim. *Id.*" (at 86–87).

In *Rebstock,* above, the court further notes that:

"Under section 5(b) of the Long-shore and Harbor Workers' Act, 33 U.S.C. section 901–950, which *permits a long-shoreman to sue a nonemployer vessel owner for negligence,* the spouse of the longshoreman is permitted to recover loss of consortium damages. See T. Schoenbaum, *Admiralty and Maritime Law,* section 6–10, at 221." (at 76).

In *Dryden v. Calk,* 771 F.Supp. 181 (S.D.-Tex.1991) the court noted that:

" 'The holding of *Gaudet applies only in territorial waters,* and it applies only to longshoremen. *Gaudet* did not consider the preclusive effect of the Jones Act for death of true seamen.' *Miles,* 498 U.S. at 31, 111 S.Ct. at 325. *Gaudet* applies only to longshoremen. The case now before this court involves a seaman." (at 181).

Murray v. Anthony J. Bertucci Const. Co., Inc., 958 F.2d 127, 131 (5th Cir.1992) finds that *Miles,* above, holds "that only survivors of longshoremen killed in territorial waters may recover nonpecuniary damages under *Gaudet*".

We note that this court has examined *Miles,* above, before in *Dickey v. Ocean Drilling and Exploration,* 598 So.2d 1259 (La.App. 4th Cir.1992), but *Dickey* does not apply to the instant case, because *Dickey* was a Jones Act seaman.

In the instant case, the trial court erred in dismissing the nonpecuniary losses because:

    1. Mr. Vedros was injured within state territorial waters, i.e. within 3 miles of the Louisiana coastline or within a marine league.

    1. Mr. Vedros was a longshoreman, not a seaman;

    2. His dependents are suing in general maritime negligence, not in unseaworthiness;

    3. The defendants are third-parties, *not his employers.*

Thus the instant case fits the very limited factual context to which *Gaudet, above,* still applies. I note that although the trial court ruled that plaintiffs would not be able to recover for loss of society under their maritime claims, of course, they are able to recover for loss of society and other damages under their products liability, warranty, and other actions.

For the reasons discussed, the judgment of the district court should be reversed and the matter remanded for further proceedings.

11.

311 Ark. 1

RICH MOUNTAIN ELECTRIC COOPERATIVE, INC., Appellant,

v.

Jerry REVELS, Richard Leach, and Mary High, Appellees.

No. 92–422.

Supreme Court of Arkansas.

Nov. 9, 1992.

Poultry growers sued electrical utility for its failure to correct power outage which resulted in deaths of over 9,000 chickens. The Howard County Circuit Court, Ted C. Capeheart, J., found utility negligent. Utility appealed. The Supreme Court, Holt, C.J., held that: (1) utility was negligent, and (2) admission of irrelevant photos was harmless error.

Affirmed.

1. Appeal and Error ⇔1008.1(5), 1010.-1(6)

When case is tried by circuit court sitting without jury, Supreme Court's inquiry is not whether there is substantial evidence to support factual findings of court, but whether findings are clearly erroneous.

2. Appeal and Error ⇔931(1)

In reviewing findings of fact by trial court, Supreme Court considers evidence and all reasonable inferences in light most favorable to appellee.

3. Electricity ⇔11.1(2)

Finding that electrical utility was negligent in not correcting power outage caused by sagging line, which resulted in death of over 9,000 chickens, was supported by evidence that utility was aware of downed line on day prior to power outage and that utility was not actively diligent in discovering cause of outage and making repair on day of outage.

4. Electricity ⇔14(1)

Electric utility has duty to inspect and maintain its power lines in safe and working order.

5. Electricity ⇔14(1)

Electric utilities must exercise ordinary care in construction of their service lines, make inspections at reasonable times to see that equipment is kept in reasonably safe condition and diligently discover and repair defects.

6. Electricity ⇔14(1)

Electric utilities must use commensurate care to keep all electrical apparatus in proper state of repair.

7. Electricity ⇔14(1)

Obligation of repairing does not mean merely that electric utility is required to remedy defective conditions as are brought to its actual knowledge; utility is required to use active diligence to discover defects in its system.

8. Appeal and Error ⚬970(2)

Supreme Court must defer to trial judge's discretion in weighing witnesses' credibility.

9. Appeal and Error ⚬970(2)
Evidence ⚬99

Relevancy of evidence is within trial court's discretion, subject to reversal only if abuse of discretion is demonstrated.

10. Evidence ⚬359(1)

Test for determining whether photographs are admissible into evidence depends upon fairness and correctness of portrayal of subject.

11. Evidence ⚬99

Although definition of relevant evidence is broad, in order to be relevant, evidence must be probative of proposition towards which it is directed. Rules of Evid., Rule 401.

12. Evidence ⚬359(1)

Photographs depicting trees growing near power lines were not admissible as they were irrelevant to issue of electrical utility's negligence in failing to correct power outage caused by sagging lines; photographs were taken a year after incident in question at different site and did not depict trees which were blown into power lines after storm, as was case in power outage at issue. Rules of Evid., Rule 401.

13. Appeal and Error ⚬1054(1)

Erroneous admission of irrelevant photographs was harmless in action against electrical utility for negligent failure to correct power outage; trial court's finding of negligence was based upon utility's failure to diligently pursue cause of outage, rather than on photographs.

14. Appeal and Error ⚬1054(1)

Nonjury case should not be reversed because of admission of incompetent evidence, unless all of competent evidence is insufficient to support judgment or unless it appears that incompetent evidence induced court to make essential finding which would not otherwise have been made.

Barry E. Coplin, Little Rock, for appellant.

Greg Giles, Texarkana, for appellees.

HOLT, Chief Justice.

The appellees, Jerry Revels, Richard Leach and Mary High, are poultry growers in Howard County, Arkansas. After a nonjury trial the judge found the appellant, Rich Mountain Cooperative, Inc., fifty-one percent negligent in not correcting a power outage that resulted in the deaths of over 9,000 chickens owned by the appellees. The appellees were found forty-nine percent negligent because they failed to have adequate back-up generators. On appeal, Rich Mountain Electric argues that the trial court erred in considering certain photographs and that there was not substantial evidence to support the judgment. We agree that the court should not have admitted the photos into evidence as they are irrelevant. However, we find that the trial court's finding of substantial evidence to support a judgment was not clearly erroneous.

This situation arose out of the following scenario. Because of a severe storm the previous afternoon, there were power outages on the electric distribution line servicing the appellees' chicken houses. Apparently, the storm caused a tree to blow down into a phase wire causing it to sag within inches of the neutral wire (normally they are four feet apart). The following day's one hundred degree temperatures and high electricity usage made the line sag even more and become heavily loaded. Once the line sagged into the neutral stage, the circuit breaker would go out at the substation, and outages would occur.

Due to the power outages and appellees' lack of adequate back-up generators, the appellees did not have electricity to run the cooling equipment in their chicken houses. As a result of the ensuing heat, Mr. Revels lost approximately 6,300 chickens; Mr. Leach lost about 900 chickens; and Ms. High lost about 2,100 chickens.

There was testimony at trial that the power line problem had been discovered on the day before the outage and that the outage occurred when a pine tree fell into the power line. In support of this argument, the plaintiffs tendered several photographs of trees grown up in close proximity to power lines. The photos were taken over a year after the power outage and did not depict the same site as the power outage at issue. Over Rich Mountain Electric's objection, the trial judge admitted the photographs into evidence.

SUFFICIENCY OF THE EVIDENCE

In finding that there was substantial evidence, the court stated:

> [T]here is evidence that Defendant was negligent in that they could have more diligently pursued the cause of the outage. And, also, I believe these photographs are representative of the area and show that there's a general lack of maintenance on the easement right of way. Primarily I think they should have been more diligent. Maybe they were short-handed and had to run to other jobs is the reason they couldn't track down the tree across the line. And the plaintiffs also are somewhat negligent. I think anybody that's dependent upon electricity knows there are outages, especially if your livelihood depends on chickens. I think—even though Tyson's may not require you to have backup generators, I think it's a general rule everybody knows you ought to. The court finds that the defendant is 51 percent negligent and the plaintiffs are 49 percent negligent. They're entitled to their damages less 49 percent of their own negligence, which, I think, it was undisputed what those damages were.

[1, 2] When a case is tried by a circuit court sitting without a jury, our inquiry on appeal is:

> [N]ot whether there is substantial evidence to support the factual findings of the court, but whether the findings are clearly erroneous (clearly against the preponderance of the evidence). In reviewing a finding of fact by a trial court, we consider the evidence and all reasonable inferences in a light most favorable to the appellee.

City of Pocahontas v. Huddleston, 309 Ark. 353, 831 S.W.2d 138 (1992) (citations omitted).

[3] The court's findings that defendant should have been more diligent were not clearly erroneous. Evidence presented at trial indicated that Rich Mountain Electric was aware of the downed line on the day prior to the power outage and that the company was not actively diligent in discovering the cause of the outage on the day of the incident and making repair.

[4] An electric utility company has a duty to inspect and maintain its power lines in safe and working order. *Stacks v. Arkansas Power & Light Co.,* 299 Ark. 136, 771 S.W.2d 754 (1989). However:

> Negligence of the company can not be inferred merely from the occurrence of the accident. That must be proved, and the burden of establishing it is on the party who alleges it.
>
> It is recognized generally as well as by the courts that electric utility companies, such as appellant, must meet the public demand for a ready and adequate supply of power. In doing so they are not insurers against accident or injury, and are not held liable for such as can not be reasonably foreseen.

Arkansas Power & Light Co. v. Lum, 222 Ark. 678, 262 S.W.2d 290 (1953).

[5–7] Electric companies must exercise ordinary care in the construction of their services lines, to make inspections at reasonable times to see that equipment is kept in a reasonably safe condition and to diligently discover and repair defects. *Arkansas Power & Light Co. v. Johnson,* 260 Ark. 237, 538 S.W.2d 541 (1976). They must use commensurate care to keep all electrical apparatus in a power state of repair. *Arkansas Power & Light Co. v. Cates,* 180 Ark. 1003, 24 S.W.2d 846 (1930). "The obligation of repairing does not mean merely that the company is required to remedy defective conditions as are brought to its actual knowledge. The company is required to use active diligence to discover defects in its system." *Stacks v. Arkansas Power & Light Co.,* 299 Ark. 136, 771 S.W.2d 754 (1989), (citing *Arkansas Gen. Utils. Co. v. Shipman,* 188 Ark. 580, 67 S.W.2d 178 (1934)).

The evidence indicated that the electric company did not use active diligence to discover and correct the problem. Mr. Revels testified that Johnny Braswell, foreman for Rich Mountain Electric, told him that the power line problem was discovered on Monday. When Mr. Braswell testified, he denied having told the appellee that the sagging line had been discovered on Monday. However, Mr. Braswell admitted that a power company crew has a responsibility to resag a power line once this situation is discovered.

[8] Although the evidence of the power company's negligence in failing to resag the line the day prior to the outage rests in part on Mr. Revel's testimony, as opposed to Mr. Braswell's testimony, we must defer to the trial judge's discretion in weighing the witnesses' credibility. *State v. Massery,* 302 Ark. 447, 790 S.W.2d 175 (1990).

Mr. Braswell testified as to the steps taken to correct the outage on the day it occurred. According to his testimony, he received a call shortly before noon that the power on the appellees' line was out. He sent the lineman to the substation and Mr. Braswell patrolled the line between the substation and the first breaker. (The whole line is approximately eight to ten miles long from the substation to the end.) When the lineman got inside the substation, he reset the breaker. Once reset, the line held and the power stayed.

Approximately thirty minutes later, the line went off again. Mr. Braswell stated that he and the lineman repeated the same routine: the lineman reset the breaker, and Mr. Braswell patrolled another portion of the line. Once again, resetting the breaker brought the power back on.

At about 2:30 p.m., Braswell learned that the power on this same line was down again. Following the same procedure, he got power returned to the appellees without discovering the actual problem. Mr. Braswell testified that he then inspected the full line. In a wooded area just before the end of the line, he discovered the problem—the wires were out of sag. He found the wires, normally four feet apart, merely inches apart. He resagged the line and had the lineman reset the breaker. The electricity returned to the line and remained on.

Braswell indicated that he did not discover the actual cause of the sagging lines until after Mr. Revels made his inquiry. Mr. Braswell then returned to the site and discovered that a tree had blown over, probably causing the problem.

In sum, Mr. Braswell patrolled various sections of the line on three separate occasions; yet, he did not find the problem until he inspected the entire line, after the power had repeatedly failed. As stated in *Stacks, supra,* "The company is required to use active diligence to discover defects in its system." The evidence of record corresponds with the court's finding that Rich Mountain Electric had not been actively diligent in pursuing the outage. After reviewing this evidence in the light most favorable to the appellees, Mr. Revels, Ms. High and Mr. Leach, we find that the evidence is not clearly against the preponderance.

RELEVANCY OF PHOTOGRAPHS

[9, 10] The relevancy of evidence is within the trial court's discretion, subject to reversal only if an abuse of discretion is demonstrated. *Bradford v. State,* 306 Ark. 590, 815 S.W.2d 947 (1991); *Turner v. Lamitina,* 297 Ark. 361, 761 S.W.2d 929 (1988); *Ryker v. Fisher,* 291 Ark. 177, 722 S.W.2d 864 (1987). The test for determining whether photographs are admissible into evidence depends upon the fairness and correctness of the portrayal of the subject. *Ryker,* supra.

[11] A.R.E. Rule 401 defines relevant evidence as evidence having any tendency to make the existence of the fact that is of consequence to the determination of the action more probable or less probable than it would be without that evidence. Although the definition of relevant evidence is broad, in order to be relevant, the evidence must be probative of the proposition toward which it is directed.

[12] The photos depicted trees growing near power lines a year after the incident in question and in a different site. Further, they did not depict trees that were blown into power lines after a storm, as was the case in the power outage at issue.

The photos admitted into evidence did not fairly and correctly depict the situation at issue. They were not probative of the issue of whether the power company failed to clean up a situation after a storm, and for this reason, the trial court erred in accepting the pictures into evidence.

[13, 14] Although we find error on the part of the trial court, this error does not justify reversal. "[A] nonjury case should not be reversed because of admission of incompetent evidence, unless all of the competent evidence is insufficient to support the judgment or unless it appears that the incompetent evidence induced the court to make an essential finding which would not otherwise have been made." *Butler v. Dowdy,* 304 Ark. 481, 830 S.W.2d 534 (1991).

Even though the photographs were inadmissible, the trial court based its ruling on Rich Mountain Electric's failure to diligently pursue the cause of the outage, rather than on the photographs; for as the court stated, "[T]here is evidence that Defendant was negligent in that they could have more diligently pursued the cause of the outage."

Accordingly, we find that the admission

of the photographs was harmless error and that the trial court should be affirmed.

Affirmed.

12.

109 N.C.App. 314

Barbara SIMPSON, Executrix of the Estate of William Simpson, M.D.

v.

HATTERAS ISLAND GALLERY RESTAURANT, INC.

v.

WILLIE R. ETHERIDGE SEAFOOD CO., INC.

No. 9227SC51.

Court of Appeals of North Carolina.

March 16, 1993.

Wrongful death action was brought against restaurant operator and tuna supplier arising from death of patron after eating tuna at restaurant. The Superior Court, Cleveland County, John Mull Gardner, J., entered judgment on jury verdict against operator and supplier for $400,000 and entered judgment against supplier and in favor of restaurant for $400,000. Supplier appealed. The Court of Appeals, Wynn, J., held that: (1) jury determination that supplier breached implied warranty of merchantability when it sold tuna to restaurant was supported by evidence, and (2) motion to amend complaint to include tuna supplier as defendant commenced action against supplier, rather than ruling on motion, and thus, action against supplier was not barred by two-year statute of limitations.

Affirmed.

Greene, J., filed concurring opinion.

1. Sales ☞274

Sale of food or drink is a "sale of goods" subject to implied warranty of merchantability. G.S. § 25–2–314(1).

2. Sales ☞284(1)

In order for jury to find breach of implied warranty of merchantability, buyer must prove: that goods in question were subject to warranty; that goods were defective at time of sale, and as such did not comply with warranty; that resulting injury was caused by defective nature

of goods; and that damages were suffered. G.S. § 25–2–314(1).

3. Sales ☞284(1)

Important issue in determining defective nature of food product, for purposes of implied warranty of merchantability, is whether ordinary consumer would expect defect to be present and, thus, take precautions to avoid injury from that defect. G.S. § 25–2–314(1).

4. Sales ☞445(4)

Whether defect should reasonably be expected by ordinary consumer, for purposes of implied warranty of merchantability, is usually question for jury. G.S. § 25–2–314 (1).

5. Sales ☞441(3)

Jury determination that supplier of tuna breached implied warranty of merchantability when it sold tuna to restaurant was supported by evidence, in wrongful death suit arising from death of restaurant patron as a result of scombroid fish poisoning; patron had exhibited no signs of illness prior to dinner, but upon returning from dinner, he was very flushed and began experiencing shortness of breath and vomiting, remaining tuna loins in restaurant after patron's death had levels of histamine, which is an indicator of whether fish has been mishandled, ranging from 4.16 milligrams to 13.73 milligrams per 100 grams of fish, and expert testimony indicated that level of 10 milligrams is evidence of temperature abuse. G.S. § 25–2–314(1).

6. Indemnity ☞15(9)

Trial court's failure to submit issue on restaurant's claim against tuna supplier for indemnification, in wrongful death action arising from death of restaurant patron after eating tuna, was error, in light of negligence issues; if both parties were negligent, jury would have to determine whether restaurant's negligence was passive merely deriving from active negligence of supplier.

7. Indemnity ☞13.2(2)

Generally, joint tort-feasors are not entitled to indemnity from one another, but party secondarily liable is entitled to indemnity from party primarily liable even where both parties are denominated joint tort-feasors.

8. Appeal and Error ⊕1068(5)

Trial court's failure to charge jury on issue of indemnification of restaurant operator by tuna supplier, in wrongful death action arising from death of restaurant patron after he had eaten tuna, was harmless, where jury found no negligence and rendered judgment against supplier only on breach of implied warranty claim. G.S. § 25–2–314(1).

9. Sales ⊕442(13)

When goods are sold to dealer with warranty, it is assumed that dealer can resell them to his customers with similar warranty, and if such sale occurs and customer recovers damages from dealer, dealer has prima facie right to recover those damages from original supplier of goods.

10. Sales ⊕284(1), 442(13)

If supplier has breached warranty of merchantability, retailer who sells goods to customer without removing them from sealed container necessarily also breaches warranty of merchantability; retailer, however, has done nothing except act as middleman and any liability it incurs for customer's damages is merely derived from supplier's original breach of warranty. G.S. § 25–2–314(1).

11. Indemnity ⊕13.2(4.1)

Although restaurant's breach of warranty of merchantability with regard to tuna was separate and distinct from supplier's breach of warranty of merchantability, only one such breach was necessary to cause restaurant patron's death, and thus, restaurant, having committed secondary breach, was entitled to indemnification from supplier, as primary obligor, as a matter of law; jury found that neither party was negligent, but that both parties breached implied warranty of merchantability. G.S. § 25–2–314(1).

12. Limitation of Actions ⊕124

Plaintiff's motion to amend complaint in wrongful death action against restaurant which served patron tuna just before he died, to include tuna supplier as defendant, commenced action against supplier, rather than ruling on motion, and thus, action against supplier was not barred by two-year statute of limitations. G.S. § 25–2–314(1).

13. Limitation of Actions ⊕124, 127(1)

Relevant date for measuring statute of limitations, where amendment to pleading is concerned, is date of filing of motion, not date when court rules on that motion.

Hedrick, Eatman, Gardner & Kincheloe by Gregory C. York and G. Lee Martin, Charlotte, for third-party plaintiff.

Waggoner, Hamrick, Hasty, Monteith, Kratt & McDonnell by S. Dean Hamrick and Michael J. Rousseaux, Charlotte, for third-party defendant.

WYNN, Judge.

This appeal arises from a personal injury and wrongful death action brought by the plaintiff, Barbara Simpson, originally against the defendant and third-party plaintiff, Hatteras Island Gallery Restaurant, Inc. [hereinafter Restaurant], for the death of her husband, Dr. William Simpson. Dr. Simpson's death was determined to be the result of scombroid fish poisoning, which results from elevated levels of histamine in the scombroid fish family, allegedly incurred from his eating tuna at the Restaurant.

Mrs. Simpson filed her complaint against the Restaurant on 29 September 1989, claiming causes of action in negligence and breach of warranty of merchantability. The Restaurant subsequently filed a third-party complaint for indemnity against the Willie R. Etheridge Seafood Co., Inc. [hereinafter Etheridge] as the supplier of the tuna served to Dr. Simpson, and Mrs. Simpson was permitted to amend her complaint to file a direct action against Etheridge.

At trial, after the close of all the evidence, Etheridge moved for a directed verdict, which motion was denied. The jury then returned a verdict indicating that neither Etheridge nor the Restaurant was negligent in its handling of the tuna, and that both Etheridge and the Restaurant had breached an implied warranty of merchantability in their respective sales of the tuna. Because of the breach of warranty, the jury found that Mrs. Simpson was entitled to recover damages in the amount of $400,000.

On 24 May 1991 Etheridge filed a motion for a judgment notwithstanding the verdict. That motion was denied and on 12 July 1991, the trial court entered a written judgment on the verdict against Etheridge and the Restaurant in the total amount of $400,000 and entered a judgment against Etheridge in favor of the Restaurant in the amount of $400,000. Following the judgment, the Restaurant paid $400,000 to Mrs. Simpson, and thus neither Mrs. Simpson nor the Restaurant appealed the judgment. However, Etheridge gave notice of appeal on 31 July 1991.

I.

The third-party defendant, Etheridge, first assigns error to the trial court's denial of its motion for a directed verdict and subsequent motion for a judgment notwithstanding the verdict. Etheridge argues that the evidence is too remote and speculative to support a finding by the jury that Etheridge breached its implied warranty of merchantability. We disagree.

The issue presented by a motion for a directed verdict is whether the evidence is sufficient to go to the jury. The trial court, in ruling on such a motion, must examine the evidence in a light most favorable to the non-moving party, drawing all reasonable inferences from that evidence and resolving all discrepancies in favor of the non-movant. *Goodman v. Wenco Foods, Inc.*, 333 N.C. 1, 9, 423 S.E.2d 444, 447 (1992). A motion for a judgment notwithstanding the verdict essentially requests that judgment be entered in accordance with an earlier requested motion for a directed verdict, despite a contrary verdict entered by the jury. Testing the sufficiency of the evidence in such a motion involves a process identical to that for a directed verdict. *Taylor v. Walker*, 320 N.C. 729, 733–34, 360 S.E.2d 796, 799 (1987).

[1, 2] The sale of food or drink constitutes a sale of goods, and a warranty of merchantability is implied in all contracts for the sale of goods. *See* N.C.Gen.Stat. § 25–2–314(1) (1986). In order for a jury to find a breach of this implied warranty of merchantability the purchaser must prove (1) that the goods in question were subject to the implied warranty of merchantability, (2) that the goods were defective at the time of the sale, and as such did not comply with the warranty, (3) that the resulting injury was caused by the defective nature of the goods, and (4) that damages were suffered. *Goodman*, 333 N.C. at 10, 423 S.E.2d at 447–48.

[3, 4] The important issue in determining the defective nature of a food product is whether an ordinary consumer would expect the defect to be present and, thus, take precautions to avoid injury from that defect. *Id.* at 15,

423 S.E.2d at 450–51 (*Goodman* represents a clarification of the standard for determining whether a food product is defective at the time of sale such that it breaches the implied warranty of merchantability, and the Court steered away from an analysis based on whether the defect is natural or foreign to the product in question). Whether the defect should reasonably be expected by the ordinary consumer is usually a question for the jury. *Id.* at 16, 423 S.E.2d at 451.

[5] The evidence presented at trial, viewed in a light most favorable to the non-movants, tended to show the following: Dr. Simpson was an active individual with no physical health problems that would prevent him from engaging in physical activity. Both Dr. Simpson and Mr. James Havens ate tuna at the Restaurant on the night of Dr. Simpson's death. Prior to dinner, Dr. Simpson had exhibited no signs of illness or stomach problems. Upon returning from dinner, Dr. Simpson was very flushed and began experiencing shortness of breath, a rapid pulse, vomiting and diarrhea. Mr. Havens also became ill, his face, neck and ears were extremely flushed, his pulse was rapid, he became nauseated, and his ileostomy bag began to fill rapidly, and indication of diarrhea. Medical testimony indicated that Dr. Simpson died as a result of scombroid fish poisoning, the most striking characteristic of such poisoning being red or flushed coloring. The report of the autopsy on Dr. Simpson's body concluded that signs of other causes of death, such as a heart attack, blood clots, or acute bleeding into the brain were nonexistent and no explanation other than scombroid fish poisoning could be found for Dr. Simpson's death. There was also testimony that the histamine level in tuna immediately after it is caught is not above one milligram per 100 grams of fish tissue, and a level of ten milligrams or more of histamine per 100 grams of fish is an indication that the fish has been temperature abused and mishandled. The Restaurant purchased the tuna in question from Etheridge, receiving it in sealed plastic cryovak bags, and placed it in the freezer without breaking the seals. In preparing the tuna to be served, the employees of the Restaurant followed proper procedures, washing their hands and cleaning their knives in bleach before and after cutting the tuna into steaks. All refrigeration units in the Restaurant were in proper working condition. The tuna had been received by the Restaurant from Etheridge in the form of four loins. After Dr. Simpson's death, there were three

loins remaining in the refrigeration units at the Restaurant, and tests indicated the histamine levels to be 4.16 milligrams, 7.96 milligrams, and 13.73 milligrams per 100 grams of fish.

Etheridge contends in its brief that "[i]n order to establish liability on . . . [its part], there must be a showing by more than mere conjecture and speculation that at the time the tuna left . . . [its] possession eleven days prior to Dr. Simpson's death, the fresh tuna sold by it contained more than 50 milligrams of histamine per 100 grams of fish." This contention is based on testimony by Dr. Stephen Taylor that, in his opinion, if Dr. Simpson died of scombroid fish poisoning he would have had to have ingested more than 50 milligrams of histamine per 100 grams of fish. Dr. Taylor's testimony does not, however, clearly establish the level of histamine necessary to render tuna unmerchantable. In fact, Dr. Taylor's indication that a histamine level of ten milligrams per 100 grams of fish is evidence of temperature abuse and mishandling supports the conclusion that food products with this level of histamine exceed the standard of merchantability. This evidence was properly presented to the jury so that it could evaluate the testimony of Dr. Taylor and the other witnesses, weigh the evidence regarding the circumstances surrounding Dr. Simpson's death, consider the evidence of the histamine levels in the other tuna received by the Restaurant, and come to a conclusion regarding the merchantability of the tuna sold by Etheridge to the Restaurant and ultimately served to Dr. Simpson, based on the expectations of a reasonable consumer. We therefore find that the evidence viewed in a light most favorable to the non-moving parties warranted its submission to the jury, and further that the evidence was sufficient to uphold the jury verdict that Etheridge breached an implied warranty of merchantability when it sold the tuna to the Restaurant.

II.

Etheridge next assigns error to: (1) the trial court's failure to submit an issue on the Restaurant's claim for indemnification against Etheridge and (2) the trial court's failure to instruct the jury that a finding that both Etheridge and the Restaurant breached a warranty of merchantability would result in the court entering judgment for the entire amount of Mrs. Simpson's damages against Etheridge.

The trial judge refused Etheridge's request to submit an issue regarding indemnification to the jury. Instead, the jury was presented

with four questions: (1) Was the death of William Simpson caused by the negligence of the defendant, Gallery Restaurant? (2) Was the death of William Simpson caused by the negligence of the defendant, Etheridge Seafood? (3) Did the Gallery Restaurant breach an implied warranty of merchantability to William Simpson that the tuna was not injurious to human health, resulting in the death of William Simpson? and (4) Did Etheridge Seafood breach an implied warranty of merchantability to William Simpson that the tuna was not injurious to human health, resulting in the death of William Simpson? The jury answered "No" to the first two questions, finding neither Etheridge nor the Restaurant liable to Mrs. Simpson in negligence, and "Yes" to the third and fourth questions, finding both liable for breach of an implied warranty of merchantability. With regard to the third and fourth issues, the jury had been instructed as follows:

> The third issue, did the Gallery Restaurant breach an implied warranty of merchantability to William Simpson that the tuna was not injurious to human health, resulting in the death of William Simpson?
>
> Issue four, did Etheridge Seafood breach the implied warranty of merchantability to William Simpson that the tuna was not injurious to human health, resulting in the death of William Simpson?
>
> The burden of proof on each of these two issues is on the plaintiff. This means that as to each issue, for you to find in favor of the plaintiff, she must prove by the greater weight of the evidence the following three things:
>
> First, that there was an implied warranty of merchantability that the food would not be injurious to human health.
>
> Second, that the implied warranty was breached.
>
> And third, that *William Simpson died as a proximate result of the breach.*
>
> *   *   *   *   *
>
> Finally, as to the third issue, I instruct you that if the plaintiff has proved by the greater weight of the evidence that there was an implied warranty of merchantability that the food would not be injurious to human health, that the warranty was breached and that the breach was the proximate cause of William Simpson's death, then you would answer the issue "yes" in favor of the plaintiff.

On the other hand, if you fail to so find, then you would answer this issue "no" in favor of the defendant, Gallery Restaurant.

As to the fourth issue, I instruct you that if the plaintiff has proved by the greater weight of the evidence that there was an implied warranty of merchantability and that the food—that the food would not be injurious to human health, that the warranty was breached, *that the breach was the proximate cause of William Simpson's death,* then you would answer this issue "yes" in favor of the plaintiff.

On the other hand, if you fail to so find, then you would answer this issue "no" in favor of the defendant, Etheridge Seafood.

(Emphasis added).

The jury further assessed a total of $400,000 in damages against Etheridge and the Restaurant. The trial judge then ordered Etheridge to pay $400,000 to the Restaurant, effectively granting a directed verdict in favor of the Restaurant on the issue of indemnification. The issue we must decide, then, is whether the Restaurant was entitled to indemnification as a matter of law.

[6–8] Etheridge contends that the trial court should have presented the jury with the issue of indemnification and that the jury should have been instructed regarding that issue. We agree that it was error for the trial judge not to instruct on indemnity, but only in light of the *negligence* issues. Generally joint tort-feasors are not entitled to indemnity from one another. *Nationwide Mutual Ins. Co. v. Chantos,* 293 N.C. 431, 442, 238 S.E.2d 597, 604 (1977), *appeal after remand,* 298 N.C. 246, 258 S.E.2d 334 (1979). An exception to that rule provides, however, that "a party secondarily liable is entitled to indemnity from the party primarily liable even where both parties are denominated joint tort-feasors." *Id.* This concept of primary-secondary liability is illustrated where "the active negligence of one tortfeasor and the passive negligence of another combine to proximately cause injury to a third party, the passively negligent tort-feasor who is compelled to pay damages to the injured party is entitled to indemnity from the actively negligent tort-feasor." *Id.* Thus, in the present case, if the jury had returned a verdict finding both the Restaurant and Etheridge negligent in

proximately causing Dr. Simpson's death, then the jury would have to have determined further whether the Restaurant's negligence constituted "passive negligence" which merely derived from the active negligence of Etheridge, or if the Restaurant had also been actively negligent such that it was not entitled to indemnity for paying its share of the joint and several judgment. However, the jury in this case returned a verdict of no negligence on the part of either party. Because the jury found no negligence, it would not have reached the issue of indemnification. We, therefore, find that the failure to instruct on indemnity with regard to the issue of negligence was harmless error.

[9] Etheridge further argues that the trial court erred in failing to instruct on indemnity with regard to the breach of warranty issues. We disagree. When goods are sold to a dealer with a warranty, it is assumed that the dealer can resell them to his customers with a similar warranty. *Davis v. Radford,* 233 N.C. 283, 286, 63 S.E.2d 822, 825 (1951); *Aldridge Motors, Inc. v. Alexander,* 217 N.C. 750, 755, 9 S.E.2d 469, 472–73 (1940) (citing Williston on Contracts). Accordingly, if such sales occur and the customer recovers damages from the dealer, the latter has a *prima facie* right to recover those damages against the original supplier of the goods. *Davis,* 233 N.C. at 286, 63 S.E.2d at 825; *Alexander,* 217 N.C. at 755, 9 S.E.2d at 473. The *Davis* Court articulated that rule in the context of food sold for human consumption as follows:

[W]here the distributor or wholesale dealer sells to the retail dealer articles in original packages for human consumption with warranty of wholesomeness and the retail dealer sells under the same warranty to a customer, for the injury resulting the retail dealer may properly charge the wholesaler with *primary liability* for the loss sustained.

Davis, 233 N.C. at 287, 63 S.E.2d at 826 (emphasis added).

[10] The concept of primary-secondary liability, as discussed *supra* with regard to negligence, is illustrated in breach of warranty cases such as *Davis,* where the product at issue was in a sealed container. In instances where the product comes from a supplier in a sealed container, and the seller has not removed the product from its sealed package, it necessarily passes to the customer in exactly the same form in which it originally came from the supplier.

Therefore, if the supplier has breached a warranty of merchantability, the retailer necessarily also breaches a warranty of merchantability. The retailer, however, has done nothing except act as a middleman and any liability it incurs for a customer's damages is merely derived from the supplier's original breach of warranty.

[11] In situations such as the case at bar, however, where the retailer removes the product from its sealed package to prepare it for sale to a customer, the retailer may be subject to liability independent of the supplier's liability. That is, if the supplier had breached no warranty in its sale to the retailer but the retailer had, for instance, been negligent in its handling of the product and in some way contaminated it, the retailer would have breached a warranty of merchantability to the customer independent of any action by the supplier. In the case at bar, Etheridge impliedly warranted that the tuna was fit for human consumption. The Restaurant relied on that warranty and prepared the tuna for sale to Dr. Simpson. The jury found that the Restaurant was not negligent in preparing the tuna, effectively finding that the Restaurant had not tampered with or contaminated the tuna in any way. Therefore, the liability of the Restaurant is analogous to the liability of a retailer selling a product in a sealed container.

The jury in this case was afforded an opportunity to find that either the Restaurant or Etheridge had breached the warranty of merchantability, *or* that both of those entities had breached the warranty. Had the jury chosen to find that only one of the parties breached the warranty, then no issue of primary and secondary liability, and thus no issue of indemnity, would exist. The jury found, however, that *both* the Restaurant and Etheridge had breached their respective warranties. The instructions indicate that each such breach was the proximate cause of Dr. Simpson's death. It follows that, based on the jury determination that Etheridge breached a warranty of merchantability which breach was the proximate cause of Dr. Simpson's death, any breach by the Restaurant necessarily derives from Etheridge's original breach.

We conclude that, while the Restaurant's breach of warranty of merchantability is separate and distinct from Etheridge's breach of the warranty of merchantability, in accordance with the jury instructions only one such breach was necessary to cause Dr. Simpson's death. Accordingly, the Restaurant, having committed the secondary breach, is entitled to indemnification from the primary obligor, Etheridge, as a matter of law.

We note in passing that the concurring opinion, in essence, concludes that the record reflects no evidence of negligence on the part of the Restaurant. In light of the jury's unchallenged resolution of the negligence issue, however, we find it unnecessary, and in fact impermissible, to examine the record for evidence of the Restaurant's lack of reasonable care in its handling of the tuna.

III.

[12] Etheridge next assigns error to the trial court's failure to dismiss Mrs. Simpson's claim against it and its failure to enter a judgment notwithstanding the verdict on the grounds that the claim was barred by the two-year statute of limitations. In support of this contention, Etheridge argues that Mrs. Simpson's amendment to her complaint against the Restaurant to include Etheridge Seafood as a defendant was allowed after the two year period had expired and did not act to relate back to the original claim. We find no merit to this contention.

Etheridge argues that the requirements for an amendment to relate back to the original complaint are not met in the present case. The relation back principle, however, only applies where the complaint is amended outside the relevant statute of limitations. It need not be considered where a pleading is amended before the statute of limitations expires.

[13] In the present case, because a responsive pleading had already been entered, Mrs. Simpson could only amend her complaint by leave of the court. She filed a motion to amend, and an amended complaint, on 6 April 1990, which date was within the two year statute of limitations. The motion was scheduled to be heard first on 23 April 1990 and again on 11 June 1990, but was continued from both dates at the request of Etheridge's counsel. Consequently, the motion was not heard and the Order allowing the amendment to the complaint was not entered until 12 November 1990, which date was after the two-year statute of limitations had expired. The relevant date for measuring the statute of limitations where an amendment to a pleading is concerned, however, is the date of the *filing of the motion,* not the date the court rules on that motion. *Mauney v. Morris,* 316 N.C. 67, 71, 340 S.E.2d 397, 400 (1986). "The timely filing of the motion to amend, if later

allowed, is sufficient to start the action within the period of limitations." *Id.*

Thus, we find no merit to Etheridge's claim that the cause of action against it was barred by the statute of limitations.

IV.

We have examined the third-party defendant's final assignment of error and find it to be without merit.

For the foregoing reasons the decision of the trial court is,

Affirmed.

COZORT, J., concurs.

GREENE, J., concurs with separate concurring opinion.

GREENE, Judge, concurring.

I agree with the majority that, under the facts of this case, the trial court did not err in refusing to submit a separate issue to the jury on indemnification with regard to the defendants' breach of warranty. I reach this result, however, for somewhat different reasons.

In order to recover indemnity from Etheridge Seafood, the supplier of the fish, Hatteras Restaurant, the retailer of the fish, must allege and prove (1) that the supplier is liable to the plaintiff, and (2) that the retailer's liability to the plaintiff is derivative, that is, based solely upon the breach of the supplier. *See Kim v. Professional Business Brokers Ltd.,* 74 N.C.App. 48, 51, 328 S.E.2d 296, 299 (1985). A retailer's liability for breach of the implied warranty of merchantability is derivative if the retailer (1) acquires and sells a product in a sealed container, provided that the retailer does not damage or mishandle the product while it is in his possession, or (2) acquires and sells a product under circumstances in which he was afforded no reasonable opportunity to inspect the product in such a manner that would have or should have, in the exercise of reasonable care, revealed the existence of the condition

complained of, again provided that the retailer does not damage or mishandle the product while in his possession. N.C.G.S. § 99B–2(a) (1989); *see also Morrison v. Sears, Roebuck & Co.,* 319 N.C. 298, 303, 354 S.E.2d 495, 498–99 (1987). The retailer's liability is not derivative, and therefore is independent, if the retailer (1) acquires a product in a sealed container, but damages or mishandles the product before selling it, or (2) because of a failure to use reasonable care, fails to discover a defective condition in a product acquired from a supplier which a reasonable inspection would have revealed, or damages or mishandles the product while it is in his possession. *Id.*

In the instant case, the "sealed container" defense to breach of the implied warranty of merchantability, *see Morrison,* 319 N.C. at 303, 354 S.E.2d at 498–99, has no application. The restaurant after acquiring the fish from Etheridge froze it, thawed it, marinated it, put it on ice, then cooked and served it to Dr. Simpson. Rather, the restaurant's independent liability for breach of implied warranty depends on whether the restaurant was afforded a reasonable opportunity to inspect the fish in a manner that would have or should have, in the exercise of reasonable care, revealed the toxicity level of the fish, or, if not, whether the restaurant mishandled or damaged the fish while it was in its possession. Based upon my reading of the record, there is no evidence that the restaurant damaged or mishandled the fish such that it contributed to or increased its defective condition. In addition, the evidence indicates that no reasonable inspection would have revealed the deadly defect. There is no evidence that the elevated histamine level produced any unusual odor, color, or texture. Accordingly, there was no substantial evidence requiring submission to the jury of a separate issue of indemnity on the breach of warranty issues, as all of the evidence supports a conclusion that the restaurant's liability was derivative. Because its liability is derivative, the restaurant is entitled to full indemnification from the supplier and the trial court correctly ordered Etheridge to pay the full amount of the $400,000.00 judgment.

APPENDIXES

Humane Slaughter of Livestock

The following represents approved methods for the humane handling and slaughter of livestock according to the Department of Agriculture.

PART 313 – HUMANE SLAUGHTER OF LIVESTOCK

Sec.

313.1 Livestock pens, driveways, and ramps.
313.2 Handling of livestock.
313.5 Chemical; carbon dioxide
313.15 Mechanical; captive bolt.
313.16 Mechanical; gunshot.
313.30 Electrical; stunning or slaughtering with electric current.
313.50 Tagging of equipment, alleyways, pens or compartments to prevent inhumane slaughter or handling in connection with slaughter.
313.90 [Reserved]

AUTHORITY: 7 U.S.C. 1901 – 1906; 21 U.S.C. 601 – 695; 7 CFR 2.17, 2.55.

SOURCE: 44 FR 68813, Nov. 30, 1979, unless otherwise noted.

§313.1 Livestock pens, driveways and ramps.

(a) Livestock pens, driveways and ramps shall be maintained in good repair. They shall be free from sharp or protruding objects which may, in the opinion of the inspector, cause injury or pain to the animals. Loose boards, splintered or broken planking, and unnecessary openings where the head, feet, or legs of an animal may be injured shall be repaired.

(b) Floors of livestock pens, ramps, and driveways shall be constructed and maintained so as to provide good footing for livestock. Slip resistant or waffled floor surfaces, cleated ramps and the use of sand, as appropriate, during winter months are examples of acceptable conctruction and maintenance.

(c) U.S. Suspects (as defined in §301.2(xxx)) and dying, diseased, and disabled livestock (as defined in §301.2(y)) shall be provided with a covered pen sufficient, in the opinion of the inspector, to protect them from the adverse climatic conditions of the locale while awaiting disposition by the inspector.

(d) Livestock pens and driveways shall be so arranged that sharp corners and direction reversal of driven animals are minimized.

[44 FR 68813, Nov. 30, 1979, as amended at 53 FR 49848, Dec. 12, 1988]

§313.2 Handling of livestock.

(a) Driving of livestock from the unloading ramps to the holding pens and from the holding pens to the stunning area shall be done with a minimum of excitement and discomfort to the animals. Livestock shall not be forced to move faster than a normal walking speed.

(b) Electric prods, canvas slappers, or other implements employed to drive animals shall be used as little as possible in order to minimize excitement and injury. Any use of such implements which, in the opinion of the inspector, is excessive, is prohibited. Electrical prods attached to AC house current shall be reduced by a transformer to the lowest effective voltage not to exceed 50 volts AC.

(c) Pipes, sharp or pointed objects, and other items which, in the opinion of the inspector, would cause injury or unnecessary pain to the animal shall not be used to drive livestock.

(d) Disabled livestock and other animals unable to move.

(1) Disabled animals and other animals unable to move shall be separated from normal ambulatory animals and placed in the covered pen provided for in §313.1(c).

(2) The dragging of disabled animals and other animals unable to move, while conscious, is prohibited. Stunned animals may, however, be dragged.

(3) Disabled animals and other animals unable to move may be moved, while conscious, on equipment suitable for such purposes; e.g., stone boats.

(e) Animals shall have access to water in all holding pens and, if held longer than 24 hours, access to feed. There shall be sufficient room in the holding pen for animals held overnight to lie down.

(f) Stunning methods approved in §313.30 shall be effectively applied to animals prior to their being shackled, hoisted, thrown, cast, or cut.

§313.5 Chemical; carbon dioxide.

The slaughtering of sheep, calves and swine with the use of carbon dioxide gas and the handling in connection therewith, in compliance with the provisions contained in this section, are hereby designated and approved as humane methods of slaughtering and handling of such animals under the Act.

(a) *Administration of gas, required effect; handling.* (1) The carbon dioxide gas shall be administered in a chamber in accordance with this section so as to produce surgical anesthesia in the animals before they are shackled, hoisted, thrown, cast, or cut. The animals shall be exposed to the carbon dioxide gas in a way that will accomplish the anesthesia quickly and calmly, with a minimum of excitement and discomfort to the animals.

(2) The driving or conveying of the animals to the carbon dioxide chamber shall be done with a minimum of excitement and discomfort to the animals. Delivery of calm animals to the anesthesia chamber is essential since the induction, or early phase, of anesthesia is less violent with docile animals. Among other things this requires that, in driving animals to the anesthesia chamber, electrical equipment be used as little as possible and with the lowest effective voltage.

(3) On emergence from the carbon dioxide chamber the animals shall be in a state of surgical anesthesia and shall remain in this condition throughout shackling, sticking and bleeding. Asphyxia or death from any cause shall not be produced in the animals before bleeding.

(b) *Facilities and procedures*—(1) *General requirements for gas chambers and auxiliary equipment; operator.* (i) The carbon dioxide gas shall be administered in a chamber which accomplishes effective exposure of the animal. Two types of chambers involving the same principle are in common use for carbon dioxide anesthesia. They are the "U" type chamber and the "Straight Line" type chamber. Both are based on the principle that carbon dioxide gas has a higher specific gravity than air. The chambers open at both ends for entry and exit of animals and have a depressed central section. Anesthetizing carbon dioxide concentrations are maintained in the central section of the chamber. Effective anesthetization is produced in this section. Animals are driven from holding pens through a pathway constructed of pipe or other smooth metal onto a continuous conveyor device which moves the animals through the chamber. The animals are compartmentalized on the conveyor by impellers synchronized with the conveyor or are otherwise prevented from crowding. While impellers are used to compartmentalize the animal, a mechanically or manually operated gate will be used to move the animal onto the conveyor. Surgically anesthetized animals are moved from the chamber by the same continuous conveyor that carried them into and through the carbon dioxide gas.

(ii) Flow of animals into and through the carbon dioxide chamber is dependent on one operator. The operation or stoppage of the conveyor is entirely dependent upon this operator. It is necessary that he be skilled, attentive, and aware of his responsibility. Overdosages and death of animals can be brought about by carelessness of this individual.

(2) *Special requirements for gas chamber and auxiliary equipment.* The ability of anesthetizing equipment to perform with maximum efficiency is dependent on its proper design and efficient mechanical operation. Pathways, compartments, gas chambers, and all other equipment used must be designed to accommodate properly the species of animals being anesthetized. They shall be free from pain-producing restraining devices. Injury of animals must be prevented by the elimination of sharp projections or exposed wheels or gears. There shall be no unnecessary holes, spaces or openings where feet or legs of animals may be injured. Impellers or other devices designed to mechanically move or drive animals or otherwise keep them in motion or compartmentalized shall be constructed of flexible or well padded rigid material. Power activated gates designed for constant flow of animals to anesthetizing equipment shall be so fabricated that they will not cause injury. All equipment involved in anesthetizing animals shall be maintained in good repair.

(3) *Gas.* Maintenance of a uniform carbon dioxide concentration and distribution in the anesthesia chamber is a vital aspect of producing surgical anesthesia. This may be assured by reasonably accurate instruments which sample and analyze carbon dioxide gas concentration within the chamber throughout anesthetizing operations. Gas concentration shall be maintained uniform so that the degree of anesthesia in exposed animals will be constant. Carbon dioxide gas supplied to anesthesia chambers may be from controlled reduction of solid carbon dioxide or from a controlled liquid source. In either case the carbon dioxide shall be supplied at a rate sufficient to anesthetize adequately and uniformly the number of animals passing through the chamber. Sampling of gas for analysis shall be made from a representative place or places within the chamber and on a continuing basis. Gas concentrations and exposure time shall be graphically recorded throughout each day's operation. Neither carbon dioxide nor atmospheric air used in the anesthesia chambers shall contain noxious or irritating gases. Each day before equipment is used for anesthetizing animals, proper care shall be taken to mix adequately the gas and air within the chamber. All gas producing and control equipment shall be maintained in good repair and all indicators, instruments, and measuring devices must be available for inspection by

Program inspectors during anesthetizing operations and at other times. A suitable exhaust system must be provided to eliminate possible overdosages due to mechanical or other failure of equipment.

§313.15 Mechanical; captive bolt.

The slaughtering of sheep, swine, goats, calves, cattle, horses, mules, and other equines by using captive bolt stunners and the handling in connection therewith, in compliance with the provisions contained in this section, are hereby designated and approved as humane methods of slaughtering and handling of such animals under the Act.

(a) *Application of stunners, required effect; handling.* (1) The captive bolt stunners shall be applied to the livestock in accordance with this section so as to produce immediate unconsciousness in the animals before they are shackled, hoisted, thrown, cast, or cut. The animals shall be stunned in such a manner that they will be rendered unconscious with a minimum of excitement and discomfort.

(2) The driving of the animals to the stunning area shall be done with a minimum of excitement and discomfort to the animals. Delivery of calm animals to the stunning areas is essential since accurate placement of stunning equipment is difficult on nervous or injured animals. Among other things, this requires that, in driving animals to the stunning areas, electrical equipment be used as little as possible and with the lowest effective voltage.

(3) Immediately after the stunning blow is delivered the animals shall be in a state of complete unconsciousness and remain in this condition throughout shackling, sticking and bleeding.

(b) *Facilities and procedures—*(1) *General requirements for stunning facilities; operator.* (i) Acceptable captive bolt stunning instruments may be either skull penetrating or nonpenetrating. The latter type is also described as a concussion or mushroom type stunner. Penetrating instruments on detonation deliver bolts of varying diameters and lengths through the skull and into the brain. Unconsciousness is produced immediately by physical brain destruction and a combination of changes in intracranial pressure and acceleration concussion. Nonpenetrating or mushroom stunners on detonation deliver a bolt with a flattened circular head against the external surface of the animal's head over the brain. Diameter of the striking surface of the stunner may vary as conditions

require. Unconsciousness is produced immediately by a combination of acceleration concussion and changes in intracranial pressures. A combination instrument utilizing both penetrating and nonpenetrating principles is acceptable. Energizing of instruments may be accomplished by detonation of measured charges of gunpowder or accurately controlled compressed air. Captive bolts shall be of such size and design that, when properly positioned and activated, immediate unconsciousness is produced.

(ii) To assure uniform unconsciousness with every blow, compressed air devices must be equipped to deliver the necessary constant air pressure and must have accurate, constantly operating air pressure gauges. Gauges must be easily read and conveniently located for use by the stunning operator and the inspector. For purposes of protecting employees, inspectors, and others, it is desirable that any stunning device be equipped with safety features to prevent injuries from accidental discharge. Stunning instruments must be maintained in good repair.

(iii) The stunning area shall be so designed and constructed as to limit the free movements of animals sufficiently to allow the operator to locate the stunning blow with a high degree of accuracy. All chutes, alleys, gates and restraining mechanisms between and including holding pens and stunning areas shall be free from pain-producing features such as exposed bolt ends, loose boards, splintered or broken planking, and protruding sharp metal of any kind. There shall be no unnecessary holes or other openings where feet or legs of animals may be injured. Overhead drop gates shall be suitably covered on the bottom edge to prevent injury on contact with animals. Roughened or cleated cement shall be used as flooring in chutes leading to stunning areas to reduce falls of animals. Chutes, alleys, and stunning areas shall be so designed that they will comfortably accommodate the kinds of animals to be stunned.

(iv) The stunning operation is an exacting procedure and requires a well-trained and experienced operator. He must be able to accurately place the stunning instrument to produce immediate unconsciousness. He must use the correct detonating charge with regard to kind, breed, size, age, and sex of the animal to produce the desired results.

(2) *Special requirements.* Choice of instrument and force required to produce immediate unconsciousness varies, depending on kind,

breed, size, age, and sex of the animal. Young swine, lambs, and calves usually require less stunning force than mature animals of the same kind. Bulls, rams, and boars usually require skull penetration to produce immediate unconsciousness. Charges suitable for smaller kinds of livestock such as swine or for young animals are not acceptably interchanged for use on larger kinds or older livestock, respectively.

§313.16 Mechanical; gunshot.

The slaughtering of cattle, calves, sheep, swine, goats, horses, mules, and other equines by shooting with firearms and the handling in connection therewith, in compliance with the provisions contained in this section, are hereby designated and approved as humane methods of slaughtering and handling of such animals under the Act.

(a) *Utilization of firearms, required effect; handling.* (1) The firearms shall be employed in the delivery of a bullet or projectile into the animal in accordance with this section so as to produce immediate unconsciousness in the animal by a single shot before it is shackled, hoisted, thrown, cast, or cut. The animal shall be shot in such a manner that they will be rendered unconscious with a minimum of excitement and discomfort.

(2) The driving of the animals to the shooting areas shall be done with a minimum of excitement and discomfort to the animals. Delivery of calm animals to the shooting area is essential since accurate placement of the bullet is difficult in case of nervous or injured animals. Among other things, this requires that, in driving animals to the shooting areas, electrical equipment be used as little as possible and with the lowest effective voltage.

(3) Immediately after the firearm is discharged and the projectile is delivered, the animal shall be in a state of complete unconsciousness and remain in this condition throughout shackling, sticking and bleeding.

(b) *Facilities and procedure*—(1) *General requirements for shooting facilities; operator.* (i) On discharge, acceptable firearms dispatch free projectiles or bullets of varying sizes and diameters through the skull and into the brain. Unconsciousness is produced immediately by a combination of physical brain destruction and changes in intracranial pressure. Caliber of firearms shall be such that when properly aimed and discharged, the projectile produces immediate unconsciousness.

(ii) To assure uniform unconsciousness of the animal with every discharge where small-bore firearms are employed, it is necessary to use one of the following type projectiles: Hollow pointed bullets; frangible iron plastic composition bullets; or powdered iron missiles. When powdered iron missiles are used, the firearms shall be in close proximity with the skull of the animal when fired. Firearms must be maintained in good repair. For purposes of protecting employees, inspectors and others, it is desirable that all firearms be equipped with safety devices to prevent injuries from accidental discharge. Aiming and discharging of firearms should be directed away from operating areas.

(iii) The provisions contained in §315.15(b)(1)(iii) with respect to the stunning area also apply to the shooting area.

(iv) The shooting operation is an exacting procedure and requires a well-trained and experienced operator. He must be able to accurately direct the projectile to produce immediate unconsciousness. He must use the correct caliber firearm, powder charge and type of ammunition to produce the desired results.

(2) *Special requirements.* Choice of firearms and ammunition with respect to caliber and choice of powder charge required to produce immediate unconsciousness of the animal may vary depending on age and sex of the animal. In the case of bulls, rams, and boars, small bore firearms may be used provided they are able to produce immediate unconsciousness of the animals. Small bore firearms are usually effective for stunning other cattle, sheep, swine, and goats, and calves, horses, and mules.

§313.30 Electrical; stunning or slaughtering with electric current.

The slaughtering of swine, sheep, calves, cattle, and goats with the use of electric current and the handling in connection therewith, in compliance with the provisions contained in this section, are hereby designated and approved as humane methods of slaughtering and handling of such animals under the Act.

(a) *Administration of electric current, required effect; handling.* (1) The electric current shall be administered so as to produce, at a minimum, surgical anesthesia, i.e., a state where the animal feels no painful sensation. The animals shall be either stunned or killed before they are shackled, hoisted, thrown, cast, or cut. They shall be exposed to the electric current in a way that will accomplish the desired result quickly and effectively, with a minimum of excitement and discomfort.

(2) The driving or conveying of the animals to the place of application of electric current shall be done with a minimum of excitement and discomfort to the animals. Delivery of calm animals to the place of application is essential to ensure rapid and effective insensibility. Among other things, this requires that, in driving animals to the place of application, electrical equipment be used as little as possible and with the lowest effective voltage.

(3) The quality and location of the electrical shock shall be such as to produce immediate insensibility to pain in the exposed animal.

(4) The stunned animal shall remain in a state of surgical anesthesia through shackling, sticking, and bleeding.

(b) *Facilities and procedures; operator—* (1) *General requirements for operator.* It is necessary that the operator of electric current application equipment be skilled, attentive, and aware of his or her responsibility.

(2) *Special requirements for electric current application equipment.* The ability of electric current equipment to perform with maximum efficiency is dependent on its proper design and efficient mechanical operation. Pathways, compartments, current applicators, and all other equipment used must be designed to properly accommodate the species of animals being anesthetized. Animals shall be free from pain-producing restraining devices. Injury of animals must be prevented by the elimination of sharp projections or exposed wheels or gears. There shall be no unnecessary holes, spaces or openings where feet or legs of animals may be injured. Impellers or other devices designed to mechanically move or drive animals or otherwise keep them in motion or compartmentalized shall be constructed of flexible or padded material. Power activated gates designed for constant flow of animals shall be so fabricated that they will not cause injury. All equipment used to apply and control the electrical current shall be maintained in good repair, and all indicators, instruments, and measuring devices shall be available for inspection by Program inspectors during the operation and at other times.

(3) *Electric current.* Each animal shall be given a sufficient application of electric current to ensure surgical anesthesia throughout the bleeding operation. Suitable timing, voltage and current control devices shall be used to ensure that each animal receives the necessary electrical charge to produce immediate unconsciousness. The current shall be applied so as to avoid the production of hemorrhages or other tissue changes which could interfere with inspection procedures.

[44 FR 68813, Nov. 30, 1979, as amended at 50 FR 25202, June 18, 1985]

§313.50 **Tagging of equipment, alleyways, pens, or compartments to prevent inhumane slaughter or handling in connection with slaughter.**

When an inspector observes an incident of inhumane slaughter or handling in connection with slaughter, he/she shall inform the establishment operator of the incident and request that the operator take the necessary steps to prevent a recurrence. If the establishment operator fails to take such action or fails to promptly provide the inspector with satisfactory assurances that such action will be taken, the inspector shall follow the procedures specified in paragraph (a), (b), or (c) of this section, as appropriate.

(a) If the cause of inhumane treatment is the result of facility deficiencies, disrepair, or equipment breakdown, the inspector shall attach a "U.S. Rejected" tag thereto. No equipment, alleyway, pen or compartment so tagged shall be used until made acceptable to the inspector. The tag shall not be removed by anyone other than an inspector. All livestock slaughtered prior to such tagging may be dressed, processed, or prepared under inspection.

(b) If the cause of inhumane treatment is the result of establishment employee actions in the handling or moving of livestock, the inspector shall attach a "U.S. Rejected" tag to the alleyways leading to the stunning area. After the tagging of the alleyway, no more livestock shall be moved to the stunning area until the inspector receives satisfactory assurances from the establishment operator that there will not be a recurrence. The tag shall not be removed by anyone other than an inspector. All livestock slaughtered prior to the tagging may be dressed, processed, or prepared under inspection.

(c) If the cause of inhumane treatment is the result of improper stunning, the inspector shall attach a "U.S. Rejected" tag to the stunning area. Stunning procedures shall not be resumed until the inspector receives satisfactory assurances from the establishment operator that there will not be a recurrence. The tag shall not be removed by anyone other than an inspector. All livestock slaughtered prior to such tagging may be dressed, processed, or prepared under inspection.

Appendix *B*

Safety Audit Assessment

The following safety audit can be used by most facilities. The authors would highly recommend that the reader tailor the audit to their own specific facilities. This audit represents a fairly extensive review of a typical facility, but is not intended to cover all situations and circumstances. While every effort has been made to ensure a comprehensive audit, the laws in this area are constantly evolving. The authors provide no warranty, either expressed or implied as to the completeness of this audit or that compliance with the listed items will protect the user from exposure or liability.

SAFETY AUDIT ASSESSMENT

Quarterly Report for _____ **Quarter of** _____ **Year**

Facility Name _____

Total Points Available: <u>XXXXX</u>   Audit Performed by:_____

Total Points Scored: <u>XXXXX</u>   Signature:_____

Percentage Score: _____   Date:_____
(Total points scored divided by
 total points available)

Management Safety Responsibilities	Answer		Total Points	Score
1. Are the safety responsibilities of each management team member in writing?	YES	NO	10	
2. Are the safety responsibilities explained completely to each team member?	YES	NO	10	
3. Does each team member receive a copy of his/her safety responsibilities?	YES	NO	5	
4. Has each team member been provided the opportunity to discuss their safety responsibilities and add input into the methods of performing these responsible acts?	YES	NO	10	
SECTION TOTAL			35	
Safety Goals	**Answer**		**Total Points**	**Score**
1. Has each member of the management team been able to provide input into the development of the operations safety goals?	YES	NO	5	
2. Has each member of the management team been able to provide input into their department's goals?	YES	NO	10	
3. Are goals developed in more than one safety area?	YES	NO	10	
4. Are the goals reasonable and attainable?	YES	NO	10	
5. Is there follow-up with feedback on a regular basis?	YES	NO	15	
6. Is there a method for tracking the departments progress toward their goal?	YES	NO	15	
7. Is the entire program audited on a regular basis?	YES	NO	10	
8. Does your management team fully understand purpose of the Safety Goals Program?	YES	NO	10	
9. Does your management team understand the OSHA recordable rate, loss time rate, and days lost rate (per 200,000 manhours)?	YES	NO	10	
10. Does your management team fully understand the provisions and requirements when the safety goals are not achieved on a monthly basis?	YES	NO	10	
11. Is your management team provided with daily/weekly feedback regarding the attainment of their safety goals?	YES	NO	10	
Section Total			115	

Accident Investigations	Answer		Total Points	Score
1. Is your medical staff thoroughly trained in the completion of the Accident Investigation Report?	YES	NO	5	
2. Are all supervisory personnel thoroughly trained in the completion of the Accident Investigation Report?	YES	NO	10	
3. Are all management team members completing the Accident Investigation Report accurately?	YES	NO	5	
4. Are the Accident Investigation Reports accurate, complete and readable?	YES	NO	10	
5. Are the Accident Investigation Reports being monitored for timeliness and quality?	YES	NO	10	
6. Are management team members receiving feedback on the quality of the Accident Investigation Report?	YES	NO	10	
7. Are management team members receiving feedback on safety recommendations identified on the Accident Investigation Report?	YES	NO	10	
8. Is your Accident Investigation Report system computerized?	YES	NO	15	
9. Is there follow-up on any items identified on the Accident Investigation Report to insure correction on the deficiency before there is a reoccurrence?	YES	NO	15	
10. Are Accident Investigation Reports being discussed in staff meetings, line meetings, or safety committee meetings?	YES	NO	10	
Section Total			100	

Supervisory Training	Answer		Total Points	Score
1. Have all supervisors been orientated to the safety system, policies, and procedures?	YES	NO	10	
2. Have all supervisors completed the job safety observations?	YES	NO	10	
3. Have all supervisors been educated in the accident investigation procedure?	YES	NO	10	
4. Have all supervisors been given a list of the personal protection equipment which his/her employees are required to wear?	YES	NO	10	
5. Have all supervisors been instructed on how to properly conduct a safety meeting?	YES	NO	10	
6. Have all supervisors been instructed on how to properly conduct a line meeting?	YES	NO	10	
7. Have all supervisors been educated in proper lifting techniques?	YES	NO	15	
8. Have all supervisors been orientated in hazard recognition?	YES	NO	15	
9. Are the supervisors conducting the near miss investigations?	YES	NO	20	
10. Do all supervisors stop employees performing unsafe acts?	YES	NO	10	
11. Are all supervisors First Aid trained?	YES	NO	15	
12. Are all supervisors CPR trained?	YES	NO	5	

Supervisory Training	Answer		Total Points	Score
13. Are all supervisors educated in the evacuation procedure?	YES	NO	10	
14. Do all supervisors know their responsibilities in evacuation?	YES	NO	10	
15. Are all supervisors aware of the safety goals?	YES	NO	10	
16. Have all supervisors developed department and line safety goals?	YES	NO	10	
17. Are all supervisors forklift qualified?	YES	NO	10	
18. Do all supervisors check his/her employees personal protective equipment daily?	YES	NO	15	
19. Do all supervisors, superintendents, and/or other management team members talk with employees regarding cumulative trauma illnesses?	YES	NO	10	

		Answer		Total Points	Score
20.	Are all employees educated and trained in the respiratory protection program?	YES	NO	15	
21.	Have all supervisors been educated in and are completely familiar with the safety policies?	YES	NO	10	
22.	Have all supervisors completed the Hazard Communication program?	YES	NO	10	
23.	Are all supervisors aware of their responsibilities under the non-routine training section of the Hazard Communication program?	YES	NO	10	
	Section Total			260	

Hourly Employee Training		Answer		Total Points	Score
1.	Do you have a written safety orientation for new employees?	YES	NO	5	
2.	Do you use audiovisual aids to help employees understand safety precautions?	YES	NO	5	
3.	Do you discuss the reporting of all injuries and hazards with all employees?	YES	NO	10	
4.	Have all new employees read, understand, and signed the documentation sheet for all safety policies?	YES	NO	5	
5.	Does the trainer or supervisor discuss the proper use and method of wearing the required personal protective equipment?	YES	NO	10	
6.	Are all safety rules and regulations discussed with all employees?	YES	NO	10	
7.	Does the trainer/supervisor discuss muscle soreness and cumulative trauma illnesses with new employees?	YES	NO	10	
8.	Does the trainer/supervisor recommend exercises or other techniques to assist the employee through the "breaking-in" period?	YES	NO	10	
9.	Are specific job skill techniques taught?	YES	NO	15	
10.	Are proper cleaning procedures taught to all new employees?	YES	NO	10	
11.	Are the proper safety procedures taught to all new employees?	YES	NO	10	
12.	Is the new employee receiving follow-up instruction on specific skills techniques?	YES	NO	15	

Hourly Employee Training		Answer		Total Points	Score
13.	Does the supervisor/trainer discuss proper lifting techniques with each employee?	YES	NO	10	
14.	Is the proper method of performing the job thoroughly explained to the new employee?	YES	NO	10	
15.	Is the new employee receiving daily positive feedback from the supervisor?	YES	NO	15	
16.	Is the new employee encouraged to report all "pain" to the supervisor?	YES	NO	5	
	Section Total			155	

Fire Control		Answer		Total Points	Score
1.	Are weekly documented inspections being conducted on the fire extinguisher?	YES	NO	10	
2.	Are weekly/monthly documented inspections being conducted on all phases of the fire system?	YES	NO	10	
3.	Are all fire inspection records being kept updated?	YES	NO	10	
4.	Do you have a written fire plan?	YES	NO	15	
5.	Do you have a notification list of telephone numbers to call in case of a fire?	YES	NO	10	
6.	Do you have a fire investigation procedure?	YES	NO	5	
7.	Does the maintenance department utilize the call-in procedure whenever the fire system is shut down?	YES	NO	10	

8.	Do you have a designated individual thoroughly trained in the use of the fire system to conduct tours with the fire inspector, loss control personnel, etc.?	YES	NO	5	
9.	Is the Safety Department being notified on all fires?	YES	NO	10	
10.	Are you maintaining the required inspection documentation properly?	YES	NO	10	
	Section Total			95	

Disaster Preparedness	Answer		Total Points	Score
1. Do you have a written disaster preparedness plan for your plant?	YES	NO	20	
2. Do you have a written disaster preparedness responsibility list?	YES	NO	10	
3. Do you have a written evacuation plan?	YES	NO	15	
4. Are the evacuation routes posted?	YES	NO	10	
5. Do you have emergency lighting?	YES	NO	10	
6. Is the emergency lighting inspected on a weekly basis?	YES	NO	10	
7. Do you have a written natural disaster plan? (AKA tornado, hurricane)	YES	NO	10	
8. Is there a notification list for local fire department, ambulance, police, and hospital?	YES	NO	10	
9. Are all supervisory personnel aware of their responsibilities in an evacuation?	YES	NO	10	
10. Have triage and identification areas been designated?	YES	NO	5	
11. Has an employee identification/notification procedure been developed for the evacuation procedure?	YES	NO	5	
12. Have command posts been designated?	YES	NO	5	
13. Do you have quarterly meetings to review with your disaster preparedness staff?	YES	NO	10	
14. Do you have mock evacuation drills?	YES	NO	10	
15. Do you possess a Code Alpha procedure?	YES	NO	10	
16. Is your management team in full understanding of the Code Alpha procedure?	YES	NO	10	
SECTION TOTAL			160	

Medical	Answer		Total Points	Score
1. Is your medical staff fully qualified?	YES	NO	10	
2. Do you have all necessary equipment on hand?	YES	NO	10	
3. Are you inventorying and purchasing necessary medical supplies in bulk in order to achieve the best price?	YES	NO	5	
4. Are you equipped for a trauma situation? (i.e., air splints, oxygen, etc.)	YES	NO	15	
5. Is your medical staff fully trained in the plant system?	YES	NO	10	
6. Is your medical staff fully trained in the individual state requirements?	YES	NO	10	
7. Does your dispensary have an emergency notification with the telephone numbers of the ambulance, hospital, etc?	YES	NO	10	
8. Is your staff fully trained in the screening and physical examination procedures?	YES	NO	10	
9. Does you medical staff have daily communication with the insurance administrators?	YES	NO	10	
10. Does your medical staff contact local physicians and hospitals on time loss claims?	YES	NO	10	
11. Does you medical staff track all injuries and lost time cases?	YES	NO	15	
12. Does your medical staff conduct the home and hospital visitation program?	YES	NO	5	
13. Are your trauma kits inspected, cleaned, and restocked on a weekly basis?	YES	NO	10	
14. Is your medical staff involved in local medical community activities?	YES	NO	5	

15.	Does your medical staff tour the plant and know each area of the plant?	YES	NO	5	
16.	Is your medical staff conducting yearly evaluations on employees using the respiratory equipment?	YES	NO	10	
17.	Are the first aid boxes and stretchers inspected on a weekly basis?	YES	NO	10	
18.	Is your medical staff fully trained in the proper use of the alcohol/controlled substance testing equipment?	YES	NO	20	
19.	Is your medical staff conducting the alcohol/controlled substance testing properly?	YES	NO	20	
	Section Total			195	

Personal Protective Equipment		**Answer**		**Total Points**	**Score**
1.	Do you have a list of the required personal protective equipment for each job posted?	YES	NO	10	
2.	Are all supervisors checking his/her employees personal protective equipment on a daily basis?	YES	NO	15	
3.	Have all employees read and signed the Company's Personal Protective Equipment Policy?	YES	NO	10	
4.	Are all supervisors insuring any employee switching jobs is wearing the proper equipment before he/she is allowed to start the job?	YES	NO	15	
5.	Is the Company's Personal Protective Equipment Policy posted?	YES	NO	10	
6.	Is worn or broken equipment replaced immediately?	YES	NO	15	
7.	Do all supervisory personnel council/discipline employees for not wearing the proper personal protective equipment in accordance with the policy?	YES	NO	15	
8.	Do you have the necessary respiratory equipment in the plant?	YES	NO	15	
9.	Do you have a written respiratory protection program?	YES	NO	20	
10.	Is the respiratory protection equipment inspected on a weekly basis? (Documented inspection)	YES	NO	10	
11.	Is there annual training on the use and care of the respiratory equipment?	YES	NO	20	
12.	Are all supervisors properly completing the daily supervisor's inspection?	YES	NO	10	
	Section Total				

Safety Committee		**Answer**		**Total Points**	**Score**
1.	Do you have a safety committee?	YES	NO	10	
2.	Does the safety committee meet on a monthly basis?	YES	NO	10	
3.	Are minutes taken at each safety committee meeting?	YES	NO	10	
4.	Do you offer any educational, promotional, or informational information at these meetings? (i.e., safety meetings, statistics, literature, etc.)	YES	NO	5	
5.	Are safety committee members given a chance to discuss safety in the line meetings?	YES	NO	5	
6.	Are the items cited by the safety committee corrected and/or given an explanation why not corrected in a timely manner?	YES	NO	10	
7.	Do you have a safety circle committee?	YES	NO	10	
8.	Does your safety circle committee meet on a periodic basis?	YES	NO	10	
9.	Does your management team meet on a weekly basis to review your "STOP" observation cards?	YES	NO	10	
	Section Total			80	

Safety Promotion	Answer		Total Points	Score
1. Is safety being promoted on the bulletin boards?	YES	NO	5	
2. Are safety videos being played for the hourly personnel at lunch time?	YES	NO	5	
3. Do you use other safety promotional ideas?	YES	NO	5	
4. Are you utilizing an incentive program of any type?	YES	NO	5	
5. Are you using safety videotapes in your training program?	YES	NO	10	
Section Total			195	

Job Safety Analysis	Answer		Total Points	Score
1. Have you identified your high injury areas?	YES	NO	5	
2. Have you identified your high sprain/strain areas?	YES	NO	5	
3. Have you identified your back injury areas?	YES	NO	5	
4. Have you identified your potential occupational illness areas?	YES	NO	5	
5. Have you analyzed each job for required safety equipment?	YES	NO	10	
6. Have you analyzed each for proper safety techniques?	YES	NO	10	
7. Have you written a job hazard/safety analysis for each job?	YES	NO	10	
8. Have you identified the day of the week the alleged injuries most frequently occur?	YES	NO	5	
Section Total			55	

Lost Time/Restricted Duty Tracking	Answer		Total Points	Score
1. Do you have a system to track all lost time injuries?	YES	NO	10	
2. Do you follow-up and know the status of all lost time cases daily?	YES	NO	15	
3. Do you track and follow-up on all employees returning to restricted duty?	YES	NO	15	
4. Do you communicate with the attending physician and insurance administration on a daily basis on the Time Loss Claims?	YES	NO	15	
5. Are you insuring the restricted duty individuals are performing jobs meeting the limitations of the attending physician?	YES	NO	10	
6. Do you have a restricted duty log?	YES	NO	5	
7. Are you following up with the attending physician on restricted duty returns?	YES	NO	10	
8. Have you computerized your accident investigation system to identify trends?	YES	NO	10	
9. Is the data from the computerized system being provided to your management team?	YES	NO	10	
10. Are you analyzing the trends on your computerized system on at least a monthly basis?	YES	NO	10	
SECTION TOTAL			110	

Hearing Conservation	Answer		Total Points	Score
1. Are your nurses, employment personnel, safety manager or other appropriate personnel audiometric certified?	YES	NO	10	
2. Have you analyzed your plant and taken the appropriate measures to reduce noise levels?	YES	NO	10	
3. Is your audiometric calibrated? (Note: Annual test)	YES	NO	5	
4. Have you conducted annual documented noise level surveys?	YES	NO	5	
5. Are you conducting baseline hearing tests on all new employees?	YES	NO	10	
6. Are you conducting follow-up audiometric testing?	YES	NO	5	
7. Are employees required in required areas being issued hearing protection?	YES	NO	10	
8. Are employees utilizing this hearing protection?	YES	NO	10	
9. Are supervisory personnel enforcing the hearing protection policy?	YES	NO	15	
10. Are you conducting annual audiometric testing on all employees?	YES	NO	10	
11. Are all employees trained in the proper method of wearing and caring for hearing protection?	YES	NO	10	

12.	Is your program in compliance with OSHA guidelines?	YES	NO	10	
13.	Is your medical staff thoroughly trained in the Impact system?	YES	NO	10	
14.	Is your medical staff maintaining the hearing conservation records properly?	YES	NO	10	
15.	Is your medical staff providing the Impact reports to all personnel tested?	YES	NO	10	
16.	Is your medical staff working with employees and contractors to answer questions and insure compliance?	YES	NO	10	
17.	Do you have a written Hearing Conservation program?	YES	NO	10	
18.	Have all appropriate personnel completed the required training?	YES	NO	10	
19.	Are all management team members in full understanding of the personal protective equipment policy and the appropriate disciplinary action for failure to wear hearing protection?	YES	NO	10	
20.	Do you possess a copy of the OSHA Occupational Noise Exposure and Hearing Conservation Amendment?	YES	NO	10	
21.	Is a copy of the OSHA Occupational Noise Exposure and Hearing Conservation Amendment posted in your plant?	YES	NO	10	
22.	Is your plant management team reviewing the records and reports on a quarterly basis?	YES	NO	10	
23.	Is retesting and retraining being conducted for the personnel identified by the reports?	YES	NO	10	
24.	Does your management team have a good working relationship with outside contractors performing the testing (if applicable)?	YES	NO	10	
25.	Do you possess a hearing conservation written program?	YES	NO	10	
26.	Is your recordkeeping system and overall program in compliance?	YES	NO	10	
	Section Total			200	

	OSHA	Answer		Total Points	Score
1.	Do you possess the Company's procedure guide for OSHA?	YES	NO	5	
2.	Is your OSHA 200 being kept properly?	YES	NO	10	
3.	Are citations posted when required?	YES	NO	10	
4.	Are all required postings on bulletin boards? (i.e., General OSHA, noise, reporting or injuries, etc.)	YES	NO	10	
5.	Are cameras, tape players, etc., available if needed during an OSHA visit?	YES	NO	5	
6.	Has one individual been designated to act as a spokesman with OSHA?	YES	NO	5	
7.	Is the spokesman aware of the proper notification procedure when OSHA arrives?	YES	NO	10	
8.	Do you conduct a weekly safety inspection of your facility?	YES	NO	10	
9.	Does your management team conduct a periodic planned inspection of your facility?	YES	NO	10	
10.	Is your management team knowledgeable in the recordkeeping requirements for occupational injuries and illnesses?	YES	NO	25	
	Section Total			100	

	General Safety	Answer		Total Points	Score
1.	Is the "Lock Out and Tagout" procedure being utilized?	YES	NO	20	
2.	Have all appropriate personnel been trained in and signed the document regarding the lockout/tagout policy?	YES	NO	10	
3.	Are first aid stations and stretchers inspected weekly?	YES	NO	10	
4.	Is the "Welding Tag" procedure being utilized?	YES	NO	5	

5.	Is your piping color-coded?	YES	NO	5	
6.	Are safety glassed required in your shops?	YES	NO	10	
7.	Are company electrical standards being followed?	YES	NO	10	
8.	Are all employee's hand tools inspected on a regular basis?	YES	NO	5	
9.	Are all company standards for ladder and scaffolding being followed?	YES	NO	10	
10.	Are all company standards for stairways, floors, and wall coverings being followed?	YES	NO	10	
11.	Are safety items being repaired/replaced in a timely manner?	YES	NO	15	
12.	Do you have a confined entry program in writing? Does this program comply with the OSHA standard ? Are all elements of the entry and rescue procedures established ?	YES	NO	20	
13.	Have all appropriate personnel been trained in and signed the document regarding the confined space entry procedure? Do you possess all required PPE and monitoring equipment ? Is this equipment in working condition and calibrated (if necessary) ?	YES	NO	10	
14.	Is your confined space entry procedure being utilized?	YES	NO	20	
15.	Is your confined space entry procedure training documented?	YES	NO	15	
16.	Are the bottle gas procedures being followed?	YES	NO	10	
17.	Are all subcontractors following the Company safety policies and standards? Does your written contracts with subcontractors address safety and health requirements ? Do you have a procedure for notifying contractors for if violations of safety policies are identified ? If this notification in writing ?	YES	NO	15	
18.	Do you possess a copy of all appropriate training aids & videotapes on location?	YES	NO	10	
	Section Total			210	

Material Hazard Identification	Answer		Total Points	Score
. Does your plant have a written Material Hazard Communication Program?	YES	NO	15	
. Does your plant have safety data sheets for all chemicals?	YES	NO	15	
. Is there a list of chemicals used in the plant?	YES	NO	10	
. Does the medical personnel have the information regarding treatment for these chemicals?	YES	NO	15	
. Are the chemicals properly stored?	YES	NO	15	
. Are the chemicals properly ventilated?	YES	NO	10	
. Is fire protection available? (where needed?)	YES	NO	10	
. Do you have emergency eyewash properly located?	YES	NO	10	
. Do you have a chemical spill procedure? Do you have hazmat procedures in place ? Is you SARA regulated chemicals (i.e. ammonia, etc.) registered and in compliance with EPA standards ?	YES	NO	10	
0. Are you conducting periodic inspections of your facility to insure your chemical list is up to date? Do you require MSDS for all new chemicals entering the plant ?	YES	NO	10	
1. Are all chemicals, barrels, tanks, lines, etc., properly marked and labeled?	YES	NO	10	
Section Total			130	

Legal	Answer		Total Points	Score
. Is your staff knowledgeable in the areas of OSHA?	YES	NO	5	
. Does the medical/safety staff know the proper procedure for denying a workman's compensation claim?	YES	NO	10	
. Is the safety department knowledgeable in the worker's compensation laws of your state?	YES	NO	10	
. Do you utilize "outside" legal guidance personnel for worker's compensation claims?	YES	NO	5	
. Does the plant personnel have a good working relationship with outside attorneys and WC administrators?	YES	NO	5	
. Do you receive periodic updates on claims being handled by outside legal personnel?	YES	NO	5	
. Does the safety manager or designee attend all workman's compensation hearings?	YES	NO	10	
. Are all denial of workman's compensation benefits being approved after legal review ?	YES	NO	10	
SECTION TOTAL			60	

Reference Materials	Answer		Total Points	Score
1. Do you have a Company Safety Manual ?	YES	NO	5	
2. Do you have an OSHA General Standards Manual on location?	YES	NO	5	
3. Do you have a copy of the individual state's Worker's Compensation laws?	YES	NO	5	
4. Do you have a copy of your state's safety/health codes?	YES	NO	5	
5. Do you have a copy of the individual state's "fee schedule" or Workman's Compensation Rates?	YES	NO	5	
6. Do you receive the monthly safety report from the Company's safety department?	YES	NO	5	
7. Do you possess the other safety books, texts, and materials?	YES	NO	5	
8. Do you possess the training manual ?	YES	NO	5	
9. Do you possess the all required written compliance programs? Are your complaince programs updated on an annual basis ? Are all new standards provided a written program ? Are all modifications to current standards addressed in your written compliance programs ?	YES	NO	5	
Section Total			45	

Machine Guarding	Answer		Total Points	Score
1. Are all V-belt drivers guarded?	YES	NO	10	
2. Are all pinch points guarded?	YES	NO	10	
3. Are all sprockets guarded?	YES	NO	10	
4. Are all handrails in place where needed?	YES	NO	5	
5. Are all toeguards in place where needed?	YES	NO	5	
6. Do you have all necessary emergency stop bottons, cables, etc?	YES	NO	15	
7. Are emergency stops on all machinery, etc.?	YES	NO	15	
8. Are guards being replaced after cleaning maintenance, etc.?	YES	NO	15	
9. Have moving parts on all machinery been analyzed for guarding purposes?	YES	NO	10	
10. Are all augers guarded?	YES	NO	10	
11. Are all open pits, manholes, etc. guarded?	YES	NO	10	
12. Are all trailers jacked and chocked?	YES	NO	10	
13. Are all extended shafts cut off to specification or properly guarded?	YES	NO	10	
Section Total				

Medical Community	Answer		Total Points	Score
1. Has a designated representative of the Company met with the physicians in the community?	YES	NO	15	
2. Are you meeting with the attending physician in individual cases?	YES	NO	10	
3. Have you opened a line of communication with area hospitals, physicians, and medical community?	YES	NO	10	
4. Are you providing the attending physician with a letter completely describing the Restricted Duty position available on work related injuries?	YES	NO	20	
5. Have you invited the medical community to tour your facility?	YES	NO	10	
6. Are you following up on a regular basis with the attending physician on time loss cases?	YES	NO	15	
7. Are you visiting employees in the hospital?	YES	NO	15	

8.	Are you visiting employees on time loss at their home?	YES	NO	10	
9.	Are you explaining Workman's Compensation benefits to injured employees?	YES	NO	5	
10.	Are you explaining the Workman's Compensation billing procedures to the physician's office, hospital, etc.?	YES	NO	10	
	Section Total			125	

Testing	**Answer**		**Total Points**	**Score**
1. Do you have all necessary monitoring equipment? (i.e confined space entry, air monitoring, etc.)	YES	NO	5	
2. Do you have written programs and procedure?	YES	NO	5	
3. Do you have specific chemical monitoring procedures?	YES	NO	5	
4. Do you have a radiation monitor and procedure?	YES	NO	5	
5. Are you in compliance with the confined space standard?	YES	NO	5	
6. Are confined spaces tested prior to entry?	YES	NO	5	
7. Do you have a H_2S monitor and procedure?	YES	NO	5	
Section Total			35	

Evaluation of Program Efficiency	**Answer**		**Total Points**	**Score**
1. Are you performing this audit at least quarterly?	YES	NO	10	
2. Are you communicating the information generated by this audit to your management team?	YES	NO	10	
3. Are you progressing on the items identified by this audit as being deficient?	YES	NO	10	
Section Total			30	

Reporting	**Answer**		**Total Points**	**Score**
1. Are you notifying the safety department immediately on all serious injuries and fatalities? Who is responsible for contracting OSHA within 8 hours of a fatality ? Is your legal department notified on fatalities ?	YES	NO	10	
2. Are you notifying the President on all serious injuries and fatalities?	YES	NO	10	
3. Are you notifying Worker's Compensation department or administrator on all petitions for denial of claim? Notifying on all claims ? Are claims tracked or followed ?	YES	NO	10	
4. Are you notifying Risk Management or Insurance Company on all property losses?	YES	NO	10	
5. Are you notifying Corporate Safety on all fires?	YES	NO	10	
6. Are you notifying Corporate Legal whenever any governmental agency arrives at your plant?	YES	NO	10	
7. Are you notifying Risk Management whenever the fire system is shut down?	YES	NO	10	
Section Total			70	

Recordkeeping	**Answer**		**Total Points**	**Score**
1. Is your plant logging all injuries/illnesses on the OSHA 200 log?	YES	NO	10	
2. Is your nursing staff thoroughly trained in the completion of the OSHA 200 form?	YES	NO	10	
3. Are all OSHA 200 forms being kept permanently on file in your plant?	YES	NO	10	

4.	Does your management team know the OSHA criteria for recordability?	YES	NO	10	
5.	Does your management team understand the recordkeeping requirements for occupational injuries and illnesses?	YES	NO	10	
6.	Does your plant nurse, safety coordinator, personnel manager, and other members of the management team review each case before judging the case to be/not to be recordable?	YES	NO	10	
7.	Do you possess the guide to recordkeeping requirements for occupational injuries and illnesses (April 1986)?	YES	NO	10	
8.	Is your nursing staff thoroughly trained in the accurate completion of the month-end injury/illness summary report?	YES	NO	10	
9.	Is the month-end injury/illness summary report being reviewed by the management team before forwarding to corporate safety?	YES	NO	10	
10.	Are the nurses completing the worksheet attached to the month-end injury/illness summary report properly?	YES	NO	10	
11.	Are the nurses knowledgeable in the procedure for properly calculating the loss time days?	YES	NO	10	
12.	Do you have a system for tracking your lost time cases and lost time days?	YES	NO	10	
13.	Does your medical staff know the criteria for a lost time case?	YES	NO	10	
14.	Is your medical staff knowledgeable in the proper placement and procedure for recording petitions for denial of claims on the month-end injury/illness summary report?	YES	NO	10	
15.	Is your medical staff in full knowledge of the report deadlines?	YES	NO	10	
16.	Are you ensuring all claims for each month are recorded on the month-end injury/illness summary?	YES	NO	10	
17.	Are all first reports and Accident Investigation reports (or photocopies) for all claims being attached to the month-end injury/illness summary?	YES	NO	10	
18.	Are you checking each Accident Investigation report for completion in a timely manner?	YES	NO	10	
19.	Are you attaching computer analysis of all injury/illness to your month-end report?	YES	NO	10	
20.	Do you have a light duty/restricted duty log and/or tracking system?	YES	NO	10	
21.	Are you insuring all first reports forms necessary are being completed?	YES	NO	10	
22.	Are you insuring all necessary first reports are being completed for all necessary cases which have been evaluated by the in-plant physician?	YES	NO	10	
23.	Are you insuring that the Annual (year-end) Summary Report is being completed properly and posted during the month of February?	YES	NO	10	
24.	Is your medical staff knowledgeable in the procedure for handling the medical files for terminated employees? Requests by current employees ?	YES	NO	10	
25.	Do you have a system for documenting your in-plant physicians evaluation?	YES	NO	10	
26.	Are you sending a light duty/restricted duty letter to the treating physician on all time loss cases?	YES	NO	10	
27.	Is your medical staff knowledgeable in the procedure when an employee requests access to his/her medical file?	YES	NO	10	
28.	Are you utilizing outside investigators for potential fraud cases?	YES	NO	10	
29.	Are your providing your management team with a weekly lost time and restricted duty list?	YES	NO	10	
30.	Are all first reports and Accident Investigation reports being properly maintained and secured?	YES	NO	10	
31.	Is the safety manager's developing a monthly progress report for the management team ?	YES	NO	10	

	Answer		Total Points	Score
Section Total			310	
Safety Incentive Program	**Answer**		**Total Points**	**Score**
1. Do you possess a Safety Incentive Program ?	YES	NO	10	
2. Does your management team fully understand the program?	YES	NO	10	
3. Is your safety incentive program (if applicable) in compliance with this guideline?	YES	NO	10	
Section Total			30	

Supervisor's Daily Inspection Program	Answer		Total Points	Score
1. Have all supervisors been educated and thoroughly trained in this program?	YES	NO	10	
2. Are all supervisors in compliance with this program?	YES	NO	10	
3. Is the documentation for this program being properly maintained and stored?	YES	NO	10	
4. Are supervisors identifying and disciplining employees not wearing the required personal protective equipment?	YES	NO	10	
5. Are the supervisor's daily inspection forms being turned into the safety representative on a daily basis?	YES	NO	10	
6. Is the safety representative reviewing and evaluating all daily safety inspection reports?	YES	NO	10	
7. Is the plant manager reviewing and evaluating any questionable daily safety reports?	YES	NO	10	
Section Total			70	

Fall Protection Program	Answer		Total Points	Score
1. Do you have a written fall protection program?	YES	NO	10	
2. Do you have all of the necessary OSHA/ANSI approved fall protection equipment necessary for your plant?	YES	NO	10	
3. Do you have the fall protection program videotape?	YES	NO	5	
4. Are all appropriate employees properly trained in the use of fall protection equipment?	YES	NO	10	
5. Are all employees required to utilize the fall protection equipment using this equipment properly?	YES	NO	10	
6. Do you have a documented inspection procedure for your fall protection equipment?	YES	NO	10	
7. Do you have a signed document in each employee's personnel file showing he/she has read and understands the fall protection program?	YES	NO	10	
8. Do you have the fall protection program on file?	YES	NO	10	
9. Is your fall protection program in compliance?	YES	NO	10	
10. Do you have all of the necessary tie-off points?	YES	NO	10	
SECTION TOTAL			95	

Confined Space Entry Procedure	Answer		Total Points	Score
1. Do you have a written confined space program ?	YES	NO	10	
2. Do you have the necessary self contained breathing apparatus(s)?	YES	NO	10	
3. Are the self contained breathing apparatus inspected (documented) on a weekly basis?	YES	NO	10	
4. Are all appropriate employees properly trained in the use of the self contained breathing apparatus?	YES	NO	10	
5. Are all employees aware of and fully understand the safety procedures for blood tankers? boilers ? other vessels ?	YES	NO	25	
6. Have all appropriate employees signed documentation stating they have read and fully understand this policy/procedure?	YES	NO	10	
7. Do you have an oxygen monitor?	YES	NO	10	
8. Do you have other required monitoring devices?	YES	NO	10	
9. Are the above instruments calibrated?	YES	NO	10	
10. Is the calibration documented?	YES	NO	10	

				Total Points	Score
11.	Are all appropriate employees properly trained in the use of the oxygen monitor and other detectors?	YES	NO	10	
12.	Do you have the lifeline system in your plant?	YES	NO	10	
13.	Is the lifeline system being utilized?	YES	NO	10	
14.	Do you utilize spark proof flashlights, tools, etc., when working in the silos?	YES	NO	10	
15.	Is your confined space entry policy/procedure being utilized and enforced?	YES	NO	25	
16.	Is your confined space entry policy/procedure on file?	YES	NO	10	
17.	Are all appropriate employees and your management team properly trained in confined space entry procedures?	YES	NO	25	
	Section Total			215	

Subcontractor's Policy		Answer		Total Points	Score
1.	Do you have a subcontractor's safety policy?	YES	NO	10	
2.	Are your management team members aware of and fully understand this policy?	YES	NO	10	
3.	Is a copy of this policy included in your Hazard Communication program?	YES	NO	10	
4.	Are all appropriate subcontractors provided a copy of this policy and the attached questionnaire?	YES	NO	10	
5.	Are all subcontractors following the company's safety policies/procedures?	YES	NO	25	
6.	Does the safety manager inspect all subcontractor's working on premises on at least a weekly basis?	YES	NO	10	
7.	Are items cited during this inspection documented and provided to the subcontractor and appropriate company departments?	YES	NO	25	

		Answer		Total Points	Score
8.	Are the questionnaires being completed by the subcontractors?	YES	NO	10	
9.	Are the deficient items identified being corrected in a timely manner?	YES	NO	20	
	Section Total			120	

Radiation Procedures		Answer		Total Points	Score
1.	Do you have a written radiation safety program?	YES	NO	10	
2.	Do you have a written safety procedures?	YES	NO	25	
3.	Is your program in compliance?	YES	NO	25	
4.	Do you have a radiation monitor?	YES	NO	10	
5.	Is your radiation monitor properly calibrated?	YES	NO	10	
6.	Are documented inspections conducted on at least a weekly basis?	YES	NO	25	
7.	Are all employees properly trained?	YES	NO	10	
8.	Is your unit being sent back to the manufacturer for repairs and calibration?	YES	NO	25	
9.	Are annual inspections conducted by the manufacturer?	YES	NO	10	
10.	Is your unit registered with your appropriate state agency?	YES	NO	10	
11.	Do you have the appropriate posting placed in your bulletin board?	YES	NO	10	
12.	Are the operator instructions included in your written program?	YES	NO	10	
13.	Are all employees performing the inspection and use the radiation monitor properly trained?	YES	NO	10	
14.	Is your safety program in compliance with your state regulations?				
	Section Total			215	

Hazard Communication Program		Answer		Total Points	Score
1.	Do you have a written Hazard Communication program?	YES	NO	25	
2.	Is a complete list of chemicals for your plant included in your written program?	YES	NO	10	
3.	Is your routine and non-routine training outlined in your written program?	YES	NO	10	
4.	Do you have the MSDS reports for all chemicals noted in your list of chemicals?	YES	NO	10	
5.	Do you have a letter requesting the MSDS for any chemicals which you do not possess an MSDS report?	YES	NO	10	
6.	Do you possess the hazard communication training video tapes?	YES	NO	5	
7.	Have all appropriate employees been properly trained in the procedures outlined in your hazard communication program?	YES	NO	25	
8.	Is your hazard communication notice posted?	YES	NO	10	
9.	Are all necessary management team members provided a copy of the hazard communication program?	YES	NO	10	
10.	Are emergency procedures included in your hazard communication program?	YES	NO	10	
11.	Do you have a chemical spill procedure?	YES	NO	10	
12.	Do you have a chemical spill cart or station?	YES	NO	10	
13.	Have all appropriate employees signed the documentation sheet stating that they have read and understand this policy/procedure?	YES	NO	10	
14.	Does your state require a copy of your hazard communication program be kept on file with the local fire department, disaster preparedness agency, etc.?	YES	NO	10	
15.	If yes in #14, have these agencies been provided a copy of your program to be kept on file with the local fire department, disaster preparedness agency, etc.?	YES	NO	10	

		Answer		Total Points	Score
16.	Do the subcontractors working on premises have a hazard communication program?	YES	NO	10	
17.	Have all subcontractors submitted a list of all chemicals plus MSDS reports for each chemical to the safety manager before beginning a project?	YES	NO	10	
18.	Does the purchasing department, storeroom, maintenance, and other applicable departments require MSDS reports for all new chemicals before allowing their use in the plant?	YES	NO	10	
19.	Are subcontractor's chemicals inspected to insure compliance?	YES	NO	10	
20.	Is your hazard communication program in compliance with OSHA regulations?	YES	NO	25	
	Section Total			240	

Safety Equipment Procedure		Answer		Total Points	Score
1.	Have all employees read, understand, and signed your PPE policies? Do you possess a written PPE program complying with all elements of the April 5, 1994 Final Ruling ?	YES	NO	10	
2.	Do all new employees read, understand, and sign this policy? Has someone evaluated and "certified" the PPE for each job ? Is your initial and on-goinig training documented ? Are employees instructed on how to wear and care for PPE ? Instructed on how to replace worn or broken PPE ?	YES	NO	10	
3.	Is this documentation kept in the employee's personnel file? Are training records maintained in the written program ?	YES	NO	10	
4.	Is this policy posted? Is the written program readily accessible ?	YES	NO	10	
5.	Are all employees disciplined in accordance with this policy? Is this disciplinary action documented ?	YES	NO	10	
6.	Are daily safety inspections being performed and documented by all supervisors?	YES	NO	10	
	Section Total			60	

Unsafe Acts Procedures	Answer		Total Points	Score
1. Have all employees read, understand and signed this procedure?	YES	NO	10	
2. Is this policy posted?	YES	NO	10	
3. Are all employees disciplined in accordance with this policy?	YES	NO	10	
Section Total			30	

Seat Belt Policy	Answer		Total Points	Score
1. Do you have a copy of this policy?	YES	NO	10	
2. Have all management team members read and understand this policy?	YES	NO	10	
3. Are the seat belt stickers in all company vehicles on location?	YES	NO	10	
4. Are the seat belt signs posted at the exits from your plant?	YES	NO	10	
Section Total				40

Light Duty Policy	Answer		Total Points	Score
1. Do you have a copy of this policy?	YES	NO	10	
2. Have all management team members read and understand this policy?	YES	NO	10	
3. Is your plant in compliance with this policy?	YES	NO	10	
4. Is the safety manager developing and distributing a weekly restricted duty report?	YES	NO	10	
Section Total			40	

Reporting of Accident Policy	Answer		Total Points	Score
1. Do you have a copy of this policy?	YES	NO	10	
2. Is a copy of this policy posted?	YES	NO	10	
3. Are all employees in full understanding of this policy?	YES	NO	10	
4. Is your plant in compliance with this policy?	YES	NO	10	
Section Total			40	

Forklift Operator's Certification Program	Answer		Total Points	Score
1. Do you possess a written forklift operator's program	YES	NO	10	
2. Are all appropriate employee's properly trained in this program?	YES	NO	10	
3. Is classroom instruction and hands-on instruction included in your training program?	YES	NO	10	
4. Is written testing and hands-on testing conducted in your training program?	YES	NO	10	
5. Is your program in compliance with OSHA standards?	YES	NO	10	
6. Is your program in compliance with the Company's standards?	YES	NO	10	
7. Are certification cards and helmet stickers awarded to certified operators?	YES	NO	10	
8. Are safety videotapes used on the training program?	YES	NO	10	
9. Are vehicle inspection techniques taught in the training program?	YES	NO	10	
Section Total			90	

Safety Glass Policy	Answer		Total Points	Score
1. Do you possess a copy of the company's safety glass policy?	YES	NO	10	

		Answer		Total Points	Score
2.	Are you utilizing Norton 180 safety glasses?	YES	NO	10	
3.	Do you have a plant prescription safety glass policy?	YES	NO	10	
4.	Have your identified the areas in which safety glasses are required in your plant?	YES	NO	10	
5.	Have all employees been educated and trained in the safety glasses requirements in your plant?	YES	NO	10	
6.	Is your plant safety glass requirement posted?	YES	NO	10	
	Section Total			60	

Head Protection Program		Answer		Total Points	Score
1.	Do you possess a copy of the company head protection program?	YES	NO	10	
2.	Is your plant utilizing approved hard hats?	YES	NO	10	
3.	Are all personnel wearing the hard hats properly?	YES	NO	10	
4.	Have all personnel been trained in the proper use and card of hard hats?	YES	NO	10	
5.	Are periodic inspections being conducted on the hard hats?	YES	NO	10	
6.	Is your head protection program in compliance with OSHA and the company's requirements?	YES	NO	10	
	Section Total			60	

Cumulative Trauma Prevention Program (Ergonomics)		Answer		Total Points	Score
1.	Have you analyzed each job for possible ergonomic improvements?	YES	NO	20	
2.	Do you possess a copy of the company's cumulative trauma prevention program?	YES	NO	10	
3.	Have you applied any of the ergonomic study recommendations in your plant?	YES	NO	20	
4.	Do you possess the alcohol and controlled substance program in your plant?	YES	NO	20	
5.	Is the alcohol and controlled substance testing equipment calibrated and functioning properly?	YES	NO	10	
6.	Are all appropriate personnel properly trained in the use of alcohol and controlled substance testing equipment?	YES	NO	10	
7.	Do you possess the OSHA heat/cold stress film and program?	YES	NO	10	
8.	Have you developed a heat/cold stress film and program?	YES	NO	10	
9.	Have you evaluated/analyzed all hot and cold areas in your plant for safety purposes?	YES	NO	10	
10.	Have the appropriate preventative measures been taken to protect employees working in hot or cold environments?	YES	NO	10	
11.	Do you possess a copy of Dr. Ayoub's ergonomic study results?	YES	NO	10	
12.	Have you tested the B-6 vitamin programs at your plant?	YES	NO	10	
13.	Are you utilizing conservative treatment such as wrist splinting at your plant?	YES	NO	10	
14.	Are you utilizing the ethicon hand exercise program?	YES	NO	10	
15.	Have you tested the pre-work exercise program?	YES	NO	10	
16.	Have you developed a cumulative trauma prevention education program for your management team?	YES	NO	10	
17.	Have you developed a cumulative trauma prevention education program for your hourly workforce?	YES	NO	10	
18.	Have you analyzed your plant for possible job rotation and/or job combination positions?	YES	NO	10	

19.	Have you reviewed your alternate duty, restricted duty, and job change program?	YES	NO	10	
20.	Have you tested the Kaikut soft handle knives?	YES	NO	10	
21.	Have you reviewed the Ohio State study for Honda Motors on the wrist dimension theory?	YES	NO	10	
22.	Have you developed a "hardening" exercise program?	YES	NO	10	
23.	Have you reviewed the Bettcher Industry Ergonomic study on the Whizzard knives?	YES	NO	10	
24.	Do you possess appropriate ergonomic literature and reference books on location?	YES	NO	5	
25.	Do you possess a copy of the "Care" program?	YES	NO	10	
26.	Does your management team fully understand the "Care" program?	YES	NO	10	
27.	Has your plant implemented the "Care" program?	YES	NO	10	
28.	Has your management team provided input into the development of the cumulative trauma questionnaire?	YES	NO	5	
29.	Have all safety committees and communication committees completed the "STOP" non-supervisory training program?	YES	NO	10	
30.	Are all appropriate hourly personnel utilizing the orange "STOP" observation cards?	YES	NO	10	
	Section Total			320	

Safe Lifting Program	Answer		Total Points	Score
1. Do you possess a written safe lifting program?	YES	NO	20	
2. Have you reviewed your selection, physical examination, orientation, and placement procedures to insure compliance with the company standards?	YES	NO	20	
3. Have you conducted a Job Safety Analysis (JSA) on all jobs addressing ergonomics and safe lifting considerations?	YES	NO	10	
4. Do you have a pre-employment safe lifting program?	YES	NO	10	
5. Do you have a follow-up safe lifting program for all appropriate employees during the probationary period?	YES	NO	10	
6. Do you have annual safe lifting training for all appropriate personnel?	YES	NO	10	
7. Are all safe lifting training sessions documented?	YES	NO	10	
8. Does your safe lifting program meet all company requirements?	YES	NO	10	
9. Are you utilizing safe lifting promotional posters, etc.?	YES	NO	10	
10. Are you utilizing "weight lifter" belts, compvests, or other types of back supports for appropriate personnel?	YES	NO	10	
11. Are you conducting a thorough investigation on all alleged back injuries?	YES	NO	10	
12. Are you utilizing the Worker's Compensation Investigation department to assist in the investigation of alleged back injuries or other questionable type of alleged injuries?	YES	NO	10	
Section Total			140	

Bloodborne Pathogen Program	Answer		Total Points	Score
1. Have all employees read, understand and signed this procedure? Do you possess a written bloodborne pathogen program in compliance with the OSHA standard ?	YES	NO	10	
2. Is this procedure posted? Are all employees trained ? Is this training documented ? Are appropriate employees provided Hepatitis B injections ? Do you possess all of the appropriate PPE ? Sharps containers ?	YES	NO	10	
3. Are all employees disciplined in accordance with this policy/procedure? Do you [possess the appropriate clean-up and disposal procedures for biohazardous materials ?	YES	NO	10	
Section Total			30	
Control of Hazardous Energy	Answer		Total Points	Score
1. Do you have written lockout/tagout program ? Is this program in compliance with the OSHA standard ?	YES	NO	10	
2. Have all management team members read and understand this program? Have all employees been trained in this program ? Is this training documented ?	YES	NO	10	
3. Do you possess all of the required equipment for this program ? Has all electrical, pneumatic, hydraulic, steam , and other energy sources been analyzed and appropriate control mechanisms been installed ? Has stored energy issues been addressed ?	YES	NO	10	
4. Are employees disciplined for not complying with this program ? Is the disciplinary action documented ?	YES	NO	10	
Section Total				40
Indoor Air Quality	Answer		Total Points	Score
1. Do you have a copy of the proposed OSHA standard? Have you addressed air quality issues ? Have you conducted air quality sampling ?	YES	NO	10	
2. Have you discussed this proposed standard with your management team ?	YES	NO	10	
3. Are you taking a proactive approach to this proposed standard?	YES	NO	10	
4. Do you have any special air quality issues or areas in your facility?	YES	NO	10	
Section Total			40	
Workplace Violence	Answer		Total Points	Score
1. Do you possess any "at risk" positions ? Personnel ? Medical ? President's office ? (Note: OSHA cites this area under the general duty clause - 5(A)(1)).	YES	NO	10	
2. Have you addressed potential security risk areas ? Parking lots ?	YES	NO	10	
3. Have you addressed in house security issues?	YES	NO	10	
4. Are employees "at risk" for workplace violence ?	YES	NO	10	
Section Total			40	
TOTAL POINTS SCORED DIVIDED BY THE TOTAL POIINTS POSSIBLE WILL PROVIDE A PERCENTAGE EFFICIENCY WITH YOUR SAFETY AND HEALTH PROGRAM. YOU MAY ADD ADDITIONAL SAFETY AND HEALTH CONCERNS OR NEW STANDARDS AS NECESSARY.				

Appendix *C*

Food Service Sanitation Manual

The following Sanitation Manual can be used by most foodservice organizations to train and update their workers on proper sanitation and hygiene practices.

What is Food Service Sanitation?

Generally speaking, food service sanitation means keeping foods free from harmful bacteria and other microorganisms that can cause disease.

Your actions shall determine if the food you serve to the public will be:

- healthy and appealing
                or
- a source of serious illness

By using proper food sanitation procedures such as:

- maintaining a clean and healthy food service worker staff
- storing foods properly
- properly cleaning and sanitizing all dishware, utensils, pots, and pans
- taking extra care as you prepare, serve, and display foods
- keeping foods at proper temperatures throughout the process
- controlling pests, and
- staying alert for hazardous conditions

You will have made great strides in keeping foods safe and of good quality for your customer.

If Food Service Sanitation procedures are not utilized, the results can be devastating. Not only is there a chance that a customer may become ill, but also business will tend to decline.

However, the main concern of public health and hopefully of the food service establishment is preventing illness.

Food Sanitation - **Wholesome food handled in a clean environment by healthy food handlers in such a way that food is not contaminated with disease causing agents**

Foodborne Illness

Foodborne Illness can be described as illness caused by eating contaminated or improperly handled food. A more appropriate term than "food poisoning", foodborne illness includes those microbial contaminants than can infect the body. Clearly food infection and food poisoning are two completely different types of illness.

How Big is the Problem?

The Center for Disease Control (CDC) estimates that there are more than 80,000,000 cases of foodborne illness in this country each year. Approximately 65% of these or 52,000,000 of these cases are caused by restaurants and other types of food service establishments.

To put in perspective, there are a little over 1,000,000 food service establishments in this country, therefore, the average would be about 52 ill customers per establishment each year.

Nearly all cases of illness can be prevented by practicing good food sanitation techniques and by understanding how foodborne illness occurs.

Foodborne Illness Can Prevented

For each food service manager and worker to do their part in keeping the food they serve safe and of good quality they must:

- know the causes of foodborne illness
- use only high quality foods to begin with
- take good care of their health
- handle, prepare, and serve food carefully

Make the kitchen the source of delicious meals—*not FOODBORNE ILLNESS*.

Meet the Enemy

An Army of Microorganisms Waiting for the Opportunity to Contaminate Food:

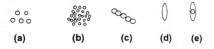

(a)   (b)   (c)   (d)   (e)

(a) single cocci; (b) staphylococcus; (c) streptococcus; (d) rod shaped bacteria: i.e. salmonella, campylobacter, shigella; (e) spore forming rod shaped bacteria: i.e. Botulism, Clostridium perfringins, Bacillus cereus.

SALMONELLA - a bacteria often found in raw meats, in and on eggs and especially poultry.
- spreads to other foods from cutting boards, utensils, and unwashed hands that have come in contact with meat, eggs, and poultry
- 2-6% of the general population are carriers of Salmonella
- causes diarrhea, cramps, dehydration, fever within 24-48 hours, symptoms lasting 2-6 days. Can be fatal to young, old and chronically ill persons.

Staphylococcus- A bacteria often found in nose, throat of humans and in infected cuts, boils, and burns

- spreads to food through direct or indirect contact with infected skin by coughing or sneezing
- causes nausea, violent vomiting, chills, prostration, and subsequent diarrhea within 2-4 hours, symptoms end in about 24 hours

Campylobacter - A bacteria found in raw meats, poultry, and other animal sources.

- spreads to other foods by cross contamination, unwashed hands and improper refrigeration
- causes diarrhea, bloody stools, cramps, fever and headache within 3 to 5 days
- symptoms last up to one week
- one of the most common causes of diarrhea in humans.

Clostridium perfringins -

- may be found in fresh vegetables, raw meats, poultry, gravy and stew
- spreads to food by way of air, dust, soil, sewage, human and animal feces
- symptoms include cramps and diarrhea within 12 hours
- symptoms end in 12-24 hours

Shigellosis -

- associated with foods such as potato, tuna, macaroni, chicken, and shrimp salads
- spreads to such foods by infected food service workers who do not wash their hands properly and often
- symptoms include cramps, diarrhea, bloody stools and fever within 24-72 hours and ending in 24-48 hours

285

Clostridium botulinum -
- usually found in the soil, therefore, found generally on foods in contact with soil such as vegetables
- becomes a dangerous poison when vegetables are improperly canned, or heated, cooled and reheated.
  Ex: rewarming baked potatoes, garlic in oil, or sauteed onions
- causes botulism: double vision, difficulty swallowing, speaking and breathing within 2 hours to 8 days depending on the dose
- botulism is often fatal

Enteropathogenic E-coli -
- found in pork, poultry, raw ground beef and lamb
- spreads to other foods through poor personal hygiene habits and can be spread person to person
- causes cramps, bloody diarrhea, low grade fever and eventually vomiting. Symptoms appear in 12 to 26 hours and may last up to 10 days.

Bacillus cereus -
- found commonly in soil, dust, spices, cereals, flour, starch, rice and baking products
- causes problems when large batches of food are prepared ahead of time and not cooled properly
- symptoms are mild and of short duration, diarrhea, vomiting, fever, nausea, cramps

Most foodborne illnesses (70%) are caused by bacteria, but illness can also be caused by foods contaminated with viruses such as:

Hepatitis A -a virus spread through the feces of persons infected with the disease or by way of shellfish that have been harvested from sewage polluted waters.

- spread to food by infected workers not washing hands after using restroom and by eating raw oysters from polluted waters
- lingering symptoms include jaundice, malaise and fever

Norwalk Virus - found in feces of persons infected with the virus.

- caused by eating ready to eat foods or undercooked foods that have been contaminated by unclean hands of infected person
- symptoms include sudden nausea, vomiting, cramps, and diarrhea and last about 24 hours

OR PARASITES, such as those that cause:

Trichinosis - a parasitic illness caused by the trichinae worm that is found, on occasions, in pork and wild game meat such as deer and bear.

- illness caused by eating undercooked pork or wild game meat
- the parasite in cyst form moves through the digestive system into the blood system and finally become lodged in the muscles where they mature
- symptoms include nausea, vomiting, diarrhea initially, then muscular stiffness, and fever

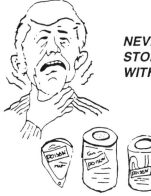

NEVER
STORE TOXICS
WITH FOOD!

Finally, chemical contamination of food is possible through careless use or storage of cleansers, pesticides and sanitizers which are responsible for approximately 10-20% of foodborne illnesses each year.

The following pie chart illustrates the various agents that cause outbreaks:

AGENTS IN REPORTED SELECTED*
FOODBORNE OUTBREAKS, U.S., 1973-1987

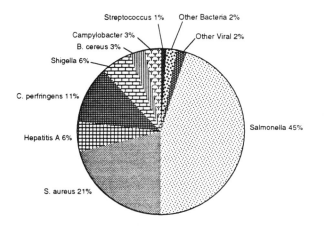

Streptococcus 1%   Other Bacteria 2%
Campylobacter 3%   Other Viral 2%
B. cereus 3%
Shigella 6%
C. perfringens 11%
Hepatitis A 6%
S. aureus 21%
Salmonella 45%

Food Vehicles in Outbreaks

Under the right conditions, any food can become contaminated to a level to cause illness. However, from 1977 to 1984 the most frequent food vehicles were as follows: Note pie graph for percentage breakdown.

1. Seafood (raw clams)
1. Meat (roast beef, ham, ground beef)
3. Poultry (turkey, chicken)
4. Salads (potato, chicken)
5. Chinese food (rice)
6. Mexican-style food (beans, meat)

The chart shows the types of food vehicles involved in bacterial foodborne illness outbreaks between 1973 and 1984.

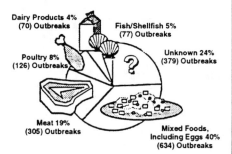

Dairy Products 4%
(70) Outbreaks

Fish/Shellfish 5%
(77) Outbreaks

Poultry 8%
(126) Outbreaks

Unknown 24%
(379) Outbreaks

Meat 19%
(305) Outbreaks

Mixed Foods,
Including Eggs 40%
(634) Outbreaks

Food Microbiology

Since most foodborne illnesses are caused by tiny microscopic living microorganisms such as; bacteria, viruses, and parasitic worms, it becomes important for you to have basic knowledge of these microbes.

Knowing what microorganisms are, what they need to survive and multiply, how they get into food, how they cause illness and how they can be killed, or controlled to prevent foodborne illness will go a long way in making prepared foods safe to eat.

Mircoorganisms comes from latin words— meaning small and organism—meaning living being. Microorganisms are, in fact, small living beings, and carry on the same life functions we perform to survive.

Microorganisms:
- take in food (nutrients)
- reproduce
- give off waste products

The significance of this is that:
- the nutrients they need are in those foods high in protein that were most implicated in outbreaks
- reproducing to large numbers (millions in a short period) is what causes us to get ill in most cases)
- the waste products given off may make us ill such as with staphylococcus foodborne illness and botulism

However, microorganisms have to be in the right environment to reproduce and subsequently give off waste products.

Microbial growth depends upon:

1. The correct temperature —
   45° to 140°
2. Proper pH — pH above 4.6
3. Moisture — Available water (Aw) above
   0.85
4. Oxygen availability

If these conditions exist, the microorganisms in the food will multiply to huge numbers in a short period of time causing illness in the person eating it.

How microorganisms get into foods can be answered by examining the sources of contamination.

Sources of Contamination

Contamination of food is possible through a number of routes, but primarily through the following:

1. People (food service workers are the primary source of contamination). Poor personal hygiene habits may spread contamination to food and 60% of the general population are carriers of infectious disease.
2. Equipment food contact surfaces, unclean slicers, cutting boards, grinders, pots and pans harbor millions of microorganisms.
3. Chemical — accidentally spilled on or added to foods.
4. Pest — cockroaches, flies, and rodents carry disease causing mircoorganisms on the feet and body that contaminate food when they crawl across it and eat. They can also contaminate surfaces where foods are laid.

5. Cross contamination — cooked or ready to eat products coming in contact with raw products.

   Examples:
   • Knife just used to cut raw chicken now being used to cut lettuce or cooked ready to eat meats
   • Storing raw meats above ready to eat foods in the refrigerator
   • Shredding lettuce on a cutting board that was previously used to cut raw meats.

Controlling contamination and its proliferation in foods are the key ingredients to successfully preventing foodborne illness.

There are two lines of attack:

1. Deprive the microorganisms of the conditions they need to survive and multiply, i.e. temperature control.
2. Cut off the routes microorganisms take to contaminate food, i.e. good personal hygiene, prevents cross contamination, dirty countertops, improper storage, pests, etc.

The remainder of this manual will discuss these control measures that are essential to preventing foodborne illness.

A. Personal Food Hygiene and Habits
B. Securing Foods From Approved Sources
C. Proper Food Storage
D. Proper Washing and Sanitizing of Food Contact Surfaces
E. Housekeeping
F. Rodent and Insect Control
G. Time-Temperature Controls to Prevent Foodborne Illness

Personal Hygiene and Habits

Personal Appearance

Personal appearance is a general indication of personal habits. A clean, neat appearance reflects understanding that personal hygiene is important in preventing food contamination. Also, personal appearance is important from a business point of view.

The Center for Disease Control had stated that foodborne disease outbreaks generally occur due to food handlers:

- being ill
- practices poor food hygiene habits
- practicing improper food handling techniques

Good personal hygiene habits include:

Proper Clothing

1. Wear clean, washable items of clothing. Also, when possible, food service workers should change into their uniforms after arriving at the food service establishment. This prevents contamination of clothing while traveling to work.
2. Wear hair restraints that effectively prevent hair from falling into food during preparation or service of foods. Also, a hair restraint is likely to remind us not to touch our hair. Remember, hairnets, hats, or similarly appropriate hair restraints must be worn by personnel in food preparation areas.
3. Avoid wearing excessive jewelry. Hollow type rings and loose jewelry are not only a source of contamination, but could also be a safety hazard.
4. Wear a clean uniform every day.
5. Wear comfortable, skid resistant shoes.

Personal Hygiene Habits

1. Cover coughs/sneezes with disposable tissues. Assure that hands are properly washed after coughing or sneezing to prevent contamination of foods.
2. A sink or sinks designated for employee handwashing complete with hot and cold running water, bactericidal soap and individual paper towels should be provided in convenient locations to promote proper and frequent handwashing. Handsinks should be provided in preparation areas, behind bars and in restrooms.
3. Employees should wash their hands before beginning work, after visiting the toilet, smoking, drinking or eating, after handling raw foods or after sneezing.
4. Apply first aid to any injury no matter how minor; do not work with foods while hands/ arms have wounds, cuts, boils, or burns.
5. Bathe or shower daily and use effective deodorant.
6. Keep fingernails short and clean. Avoid the use of fingernail polish and fake fingernails.
7. Don't work when you are ill.

Employee Illness

1. If an employee has a disease or is a carrier of an organism that is transmissible through food, that employee should not be working in the food service establishment. Both workers and management should be on the lookout for the following symptoms or ailments:

- nausea and vomiting
- diarrhea
- fever
- acute or chronic coughing
- sore throat
- boils
- exposed cuts, burns, or wounds

2. If the restaurant operator/owner suspects that an employee has a communicable disease that may be transmitted by food handling practices, the operator shall, by law, exclude that employee from working in the food service establishment.

3. The Kentucky Food Establishment Act and State Retail Food Code, Section 13, states the following regarding employee health. "No person, while infected with a disease in a communicable form that can be transmitted by foods or who is a carrier of organisms that cause such a disease or while affected with a boil, an infected wound, or an acute respiratory infection, shall work in an establishment."

Employee Practices

1. Use tongs, forks, etc., rather than hands to dispense ice cubes, butter, bread and other food items. Wear disposable plastic gloves if direct handling of food is a necessity and then throw the gloves away. One use only!

2. Pick up clean glasses and cups by the handle or sides.

3. Pick up clean utensils by the handle only.

4. Wash hands before handling clean dishware.

5. Observe the "No Smoking" rule while handling, preparing, or serving food or drink. Never smoke in food preparation areas.

6. Avoid leaning, sitting, or placing personal items on surfaces or in areas where food is prepared or served.

7. Use a clean cup or spoon each time food is tasted while cooking; do not taste food with the utensil being used to stir the food.

8. Consume food and beverages only in designated "break" areas and never eat or drink while you are working in the kitchen.

VERY IMPORTANT!

A. THE CUSTOMER ALWAYS OBSERVES YOUR PERSONAL HYGIENE AND HABITS.

B. NEVER ALLOW AN EMPLOYEE TO WORK WHILE ILL.

C. CONTINUALLY BE AWARE OF THE IMPORTANCE OF HANDWASHING. The American Medical Society (AMA) states that 40% of all infectious diseases could be prevented by proper handwashing.

WASH YOUR HANDS

The BEST way to stop disease is to wash your hands well. Use this method to make sure your hands are free of germs.

HOW:
- Use SOAP and RUNNING WATER.
- Rub your hands vigorously as you wash them.
- Wash ALL surfaces, including
  — backs of hands
  — wrists
  — between fingers
  — under fingernails.
- Rinse your hands well. Leave the water running.
- Dry your hands with a single-use towel.
- Turn off the water using a PAPER TOWEL instead of bare hands.

WHEN:
- When you come to the center in the morning
- Before preparing or serving food
- After diapering a child or wiping his nose or cleaning up messes
- And after you've been to the bathroom— either with a child or by yourself.

Proper Food Storage

Practically all foodborne illness outbreaks are the result, directly or indirectly, of inadequate refrigeration or improper storage of foods. Bacterial growth is most active in moist, warm conditions. Low temperatures provided by proper refrigeration slows down the growth of these bacteria drastically, while freezing temperatures (0° F or below) stop the growth of bacteria. Therefore, refrigeration at proper temperatures and proper handling keep food spoilage to a minimum and prevents foodborne illness.

Keep these perishable and potentially hazardous foods refrigerated until prepared and served:

FRESH	PROCESSED	FROZEN
• meat	• custards	• meat
• fish	• gravy	• fish
• poultry	• sauces	• poultry
• eggs	• cooked foods	• desserts
• dairy foods	(meats)	
	• foods prepared	
	in advance	

Recommended Refrigerated Storage Practices

1. Storage temperatures of 45° F or less are required for potentially hazardous foods. Specific temperature recommendations include the following:

   A. Produce   45° F or below
   B. Dry Foods   60-70° F
   C. Dairy and Meat   40° F or below
   D. Seafood   30° F or below

2. Thick, hot, potentially hazardous foods such as sauces, gravies, stew, etc. should be placed in shallow containers to an overall depth of no more than 4 inches to promote rapid cooling prior to refrigeration.
   Reason: Food at the center may retain enough heat to spoil or allow dangerous growth of disease causing bacteria.

3. If hot foods must be stored in large quantities, place containers in ice bath and stir to bring the temperature down quickly before refrigerating.

4. Cover food with a tight fitting lid or cover so that the food product is protected from spills, condensation, dust or cross contamination.

5. Allow adequate space between containers of food placed in refrigerators or walk in coolers to permit proper air circulation.

6. Store food in walk-in refrigerators at least 6 inches off the floor.

7. Provide at least one thermometer accurate to plus or minus 2° F in the warmest area of the refrigerators, walk in coolers and freezer units. Keep the thermometer in accessible and easily readable position.

8. Never store raw foods such as meat or produce above, over or adjacent to prepared or ready to eat foods. (Cross Contamination)

9. Keep refrigeration shelves clean, wipe up spills immediately.

10. Do not cover wire shelving with aluminum foil or other material. Covering shelves prevents proper air circulation and thus prevents proper cooling of foods.

11. Ice used for cooling packaged food or beverages should not be used for human consumption.

Refrigeration is necessary and very expensive storage. The amount of refrigeration space needed depends upon the number of meals served, type of service, and delivery schedules.

```
Recommended Minumum Refrigeration
    Space For Average Full Menu
  Restaurant—Not Including Beverage
     Cooling of Frozen Foods

Number of Meals    Recommended Capacity
    75-150            20 cubic feet
   150-250            45 cubic feet
   250-350            60 cubic feet
   350-500            90 cubic feet
```

Freezer Storage

Freezer storage is designed to be long term storage. Frozen food items, if promptly frozen upon arrival, may remain of good quality and safe for months. A constant temperature of 0° F or below maintains flavor and nutritive value while. At the same time stopping bacterial growth.

The less variation in temperature, the better. Therefore, avoid unnecessary door opening and never leave the door or lid open for any period of time.

Points to remember regarding Freezer Storage:

• Never refreeze foods that have thawed. Nutritive value, appearance, and texture suffer greatly from refreezing.
• Insist that frozen foods be delivered completely frozen. Inspect each shipment carefully and place in freezer immediately.
• Place old stock in front of new. Use it first. Rotate stock and purchase frequently.
• Realize frozen foods will not keep indefi-

nitely. Long periods of storage cause loss of nutritive value, loss of flavor, change in texture and color.
• When bringing frozen foods out of storage, never thaw them at room temperature. Only thaw foods:
  — In the refrigerator
  — During the cooking process
  — Under cold running water
  — In a microwave, if you transfer directly to cooking process
• Always label and date packages of foods placed in storage. Remember, foods cannot be stored indefinitely in a freezer.

Dry Food Storage

If possible, locate storeroom near the kitchen. An outside door is convenient for the delivery of foods. Remember the food storage room is not a janitors closet. Mops, brooms, chemical cleaners, and pesticides are to be stored elsewhere.

Dry storage areas must be:

• Well ventilated
• Dry and cool
• Free from insects and rodents
• Clean, orderly and well managed

Proper Ventilation
Ventilation is one of the most important requirements of correct dry storage. If a room isn't properly ventilated, the results are readily seen. The air in the room becomes hot, stale, odorous, moist, greasy, and smoky because of cooking, dishwashing, and other activities.

Also, water droplets and moisture will appear on walls. This can lead to bacterial and mold contaminated food products.

If these conditions are observed, have a professional look at your mechanical ventilation system and also seek natural ventilating methods.

Keep It Cool

The major cause of food quality deterioration and food spoilage is heat. Attempt to keep dry food storage room temperature between 60-70° F. Also, motors, compressors or heating units which can generate quite a bit of heat should not be located in storage rooms.

Control Insects and Rodents

Insects and rodents can cause a great amount of damage to food supplies and to the building structure. Plus these pests carry disease causing microorganisms and will scare away customers eventually.

Control measures you can take would include:
- Rat proofing building
- Inspect all shipments received for infestation
- If infested, refuse the shipment

WARNING: Do not keep poisonous pesticides in your food storage area and remember: Poisonous pesticides should only be applied by a trained certified pest control operator.

A clean, orderly well managed dry food storage room will:

- Prolong shelf life of food products
- Eliminate pests
- Make stock rotation much easier

The Importance of Proper Cleaning and Sanitizing Utensils and Equipment

Definitions

Cleaning - the removal of visible soil or matter from a surface by use of a cleaning agent such as detergent.

Sanitizing - also known as invisible cleaning, sanitizing by chemicals or heat kills disease causing microorganisms that still remain on surfaces after visibly cleaning.

Preventing Disease by Proper Dishwashing

It is a known fact that disease causing organisms can be found on utensils, plates, pots, pans and equipment that haven't been properly cleaned and sanitized.

Clean and sanitized tableware is also important from a business standpoint. Customers will be less likely to return to an establishment they believe is unclean.

Items such as utensils, plates, pots, pans, slicers, preparation tables, cutting boards are known as food contact surfaces.

Food contact surfaces shall be cleaned and sanitized, according to regulation;

- after each use, *example: utensils, plates, pots and pans*
- between processing of different foods, *example: cutting raw chicken on a cutting board, then cutting raw vegetables on same cutting board*
- following an interruption in use, *example: using meat slicer in the morning and continuing to use it after lunch without cleaning it*

Cleaning and sanitizing most of these articles can be accomplished in one of two dishwashing methods.

1. Manual Dishwashing
2. Mechanical Dishwashing

Manual Dishwashing

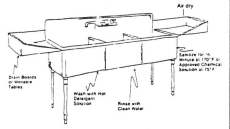

Manual dishwashing can be accomplished by utilizing a stainless steel three compartment sink with adequate sized drainboards. Also:

1. Sink compartments must be large enough to immerse all utensils and equipment to be cleaned and sanitized manually.
2. Each compartment must be supplied with hot and cold running water.

The 5 steps of Manual Dishwashing

Step 1 —
Pre-soak and pre-scrape equipment and utensils when necessary.

Step 2 —
In the first compartment, wash all utensils, dishes, and silverware in clean hot water between 110-120° F, which contains a proper dishwashing detergent.

Step 3 —
In the middle compartment, rinse with clean hot water.

Step 4 —
In the third compartment, sanitize (chemically) by submerging utensils, dishes and silverware for at least 30 seconds to 1 minute in at least 75° F water containing an appropriate concentration of an approved sanitizer.

Note: A list of approved sanitizers and necessary concentrations is provided in the Kentucky Food Establishment and State Retail Food Code Appendix A.

Step 5 —
Completely air dry all items on the drainboard.

Mechanical Dishwashing Method
SPRAY TYPE DISHWASHING MACHINE

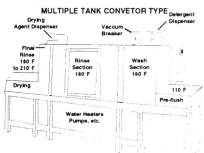

Step 1 —
Pre-wash in sink, preferably with overhead spray hose, to remove large particles of food. Soak silverware. Scrape, dishes and while doing so, discard chipped, broken or cracked dishes, cups or glasses.

Step 2 —
Stack utensils in the rack or tray properly. Rack silverware with handles down, cups and glasses inverted, places, and saucers stacked vertically with small stacked in front of larger ones.

Step 3—
In the wash cycle, the water must reach between 150-165° F and the cycle should last at least 20 seconds.

Note: If "baked on" food particles are being found on utensils or plates, it may mean wash temperatures are too high.

Step 4 —
Rinse and Sanitize
The rinse water cycle will not last long, but

the water should be at least 160° F.

The sanitizing spray rinse water temperature should be a minimum of 180° F (in line) and should last at least 10 seconds.
Note: Keep spray arms in machine free of food debris, straws, lint, and rust accumulation.

Many mechanical dishwashers in recent years utilize chemicals as sanitizers instead of high heat temperatures in the final rinse. Whatever machine you might have, remember to follow temperature requirements specified for that machine and be aware of proper maintenance.

Step 5 —
Air Dry
Let all items in rack remain on drainboard until completely dried. Using a towel to dry dishes just recontaminates them.

Step 6 —
Store Properly
THERE IS LITTLE SENSE IN SPENDING THE TIME AND EFFORT AND MONEY TO PROPERLY WASH AND SANITIZE EQUIPMENT IF THEY ARE STORED ON UNCLEAN SHELVES IN UNCLEAN AREAS UNPROTECTED FROM PESTS, AND OTHER CONTAMINATING SOURCES.

Finally, prevent contamination of clean utensils, dishware, and silverware by having dishwashing personnel take extra precautions not to contaminate clean utensils. Make sure that they WASH THEIR HANDS, AFTER HANDLING SOILED UTENSILS, AND BEFORE HANDLING CLEANED AND SANITIZED ITEMS.

Maintaining a Sanitary Facility

Keeping the entire establishment clean and sanitary makes for a more pleasant and safe environment for food service workers and patrons.

More importantly, it breaks the "chain of infection" creating a barrier between microorganisms and the customer.

The primary requirement of management is to assure that the food service establishment is "easily cleanable".

Therefore, management is responsible for providing the following:

• durable floors, walls, and ceilings
• equipment and work surfaces that have been approved for commercial food service use, which is easily cleanable
• adequate number of handsinks, three compartment stainless steel sinks, service sink and restrooms as required by regulation
• adequate lighting in all areas to assure safety and proper cleaning
• proper ventilation in all areas of the facility, but especially in the food preparation areas and dry food storage

Excessive grease accumulation and/or condensation on the walls and ceilings indicate inadequate ventilation exhaust systems.

Properly constructed, approved, installed and maintained ventilation systems will greatly reduce cleaning time.

The most important aspect of keeping a clean food service facility is proper supervision to see that the job gets done.

By creating a cleaning schedule, such as the one illustrated at the top of page 297, three objectives are assured;

1. It creates a chain of responsibility. Employees know what is expected of them.
2. Makes sure the job is done.
3. Makes sure cleaning takes place during slack business hours.

CLEANING SCHEDULE

Items	What	When	Cleaning Article	Who Cleans
Utensils	Wash-rinse-sanitize	After each use, following an interruption in use between preparation of different foods	3 compartment sink or automatic dishwasher used as prescribed	Jim Doe - Day Shift Jill Doe - Night Shift
Floors	Clean up spills	As soon as possible	Mop and bucket or broom and dust pan	All employees will wipe up own spills
	Damp mop entire prep area	Once per shift	Mop and bucket of clean water	Barbara Doe
	Scrub	Every Tuesday night	Brushes, detergent Scrubo	Pete the Scrubber
Walls and Ceilings	Clean up splashes	As soon as possible	Damp clean cloth	All employees clean own spills & splashes
	Major cleaning of all walls	January, April and October	Portable high pressure cleaning unit and foam cleaning unit	Contractor specialist

Control of Insects and Rodents

Not only can the presence of insects and/or rodents in a food service facility destroy customer relations, they can also destroy food and contaminate foods with microorganisms capable of causing disease.

The three most common pests in food service are the common house fly, German cockroach, and the common house mouse. All three routinely carry many of the disease organisms mentioned early on such as: salmonella, and shigella.

By keeping these three pests out of the foods service facility, you lessen the chance of foodborne illness.

The Tale of Three Pests

House Fly
Flies are attracted to garbage, decaying materials, human waste and food. The female lays her eggs (150 at a time) on these items as part of the reproductive cycle. Eggs will hatch into larvae (known as maggots) within 2 to 3 days in warm weathers and begin to burrow into and eat the decaying food or garbage. In 5-6 more days, the larvae will go through a dormant stage and then the adult fly will emerge. All of this happens in about 10 days and the female will lay about 3,000 eggs in a matter of weeks.

Because flies live and breed in garbage, sewage, decaying matter, and body waste, it is obvious they carry all kinds of germs (microorganisms). Flies pick up disease causing organisms on their body and then contaminate food when they land on it,

Flies are known to transmit about 30-35 specific diseases to man.

How to Control?

1. Keep them out of the facility. Use screening on open doors and windows, fly fans, make sure all outside doors are self-closing.
2. Take away their breeding places by keeping garbage in containers with tight fitting lids, having garbage picked up routinely (2 times per week is best), keep outside areas clean and free of debris.
3. By practicing good sanitation and keeping foods in storage in insect proof containers.

Cockroaches

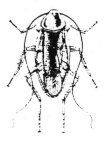

1. The German Cockroach feeds on human body waste, starchy foods, sweet foods and meat.
2. This particular roach potentially carries more than 50 different disease causing microorganisms on their hairy bodies and transport them to food when they touch it.
3. The German Cockroach may by found breeding in a particular environment to its liking; warm, dark, moist, well hidden areas with a food supply close by.

How to Control?

1. Keep all food storage areas clean and well lighted. Don't let food particles accumulate under shelves.
2. Eliminate their hiding places by caulking all cracks and crevices.
3. Inspect all incoming boxes and produce crates. Roaches or roach eggs may be hitch-hiking into your establishment. Be

extra careful to examine incoming egg cartons and boxes of single service items such as napkins, paper cups and paper or styrofoam plates. Discard all boxes as soon as emptied.

4. Finally, leave the chemical treatment to a licensed pest control operator.

Rodents

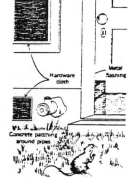

Just like the first two pests; rodents also potentially carry various disease causing organisms. It is estimated that there are over 250 million rats in this country and that they cost the food service industry several billion dollars in damage each year.

Damage in the form of food consumed, food contaminated and to actual buildings due to their need to continually gnaw.

The common house mouse is just as numerous and just as destructive.

Whereas, mice usually hitch-hike with food deliveries, the rat actually enters from the outside.

How To Control?

1. Build them out. As noted in the above illustration, concrete patching around pipes, metal flashing around bottom of exit doors and hardware cloth or steel wool will offer control.

2. Eliminate food and garbage that might be available to the rodent. Inside, keep all foods in rodent proof containers. Outside, keep all garbage in rodent proof covered containers and keep debris picked up off the ground.
3. Extermination - the old rat or mouse trap is the best. Place it near a wall with some peanut butter for bait and leave it undisturbed for a few days. Also, exterminators have multiple catch boxes that merely traps them.

No matter what the pest may be, always be sure to keep the inside and outside of your facility clean and sanitary, be alert to signs of pest activity before the problem gets out of hand, and let a reliable pest control company routinely service your food service establishment.

Time Temperature Controls to Prevent Foodborne Illness

Foodborne illness is caused primarily by bacteria that are allowed to multiply to large numbers in food.

As stated early on in this manual, microorganisms (bacteria) need the right environment to reproduce.

The necessary environment must provide; in most cases:
1. Oxygen
2. Proper pH
3. Moisture
4. Temperature between 45° F and 140° F

In food service, one can only take away one of these necessary ingredients: TEMPERATURE.

If all food service personnel can take extra precautions to keep potentially hazardous foods cold (below 45°F) or hot (above 140°F) foodborne illness would be prevented.

According to the food temperature chart provided, the temperature at which microorganisms grow best is called the DANGER ZONE. (40° F - 140° F). It is also important to note that refrigerating or freezing foods will not destroy the microorganisms, but only slow their growth. Then as those foods are thawed or left out of refrigeration, growth begins again when the food enters the DANGER ZONE.

As the temperature chart shows, only cooking of foods will kill those microorganisms responsible for disease.

There are three basic rules relating to time-temperature requirements that must be followed to prevent foodborne illness.

1. Keep potentially hazardous foods out of the temperature danger zone.
2. Pass through the DANGER ZONE as quickly as possible. In other words, be careful when heating leftovers.
3. Pass through the DANGER ZONE as quickly as possible. (Do not slow cook any food items.) There are some exceptions to the 140° F hot holding temperature requirement as noted on the temperature chart provided.

If one observes the principles during preparation, serving and, hot holding and refrigeration, foodborne illness and food spoilage may be avoided.

- Rare roast beef need only be cooked and held at 130° F
- Pork must be cooked quickly to an interval temperature of 150° F
- Cooked poultry, stuffed meats, and re-heated foods must be cooked quickly to a minimum of 165° F

Studies have shown that time-temperature principles are most often abused during the cooling of hot foods.
Foods must be cooled from 140° F to 45° F or

below within four hours. This is only possible if hot foods are poured into shallow pans not more than 4 inches deep, covered and placed in a refrigerator, preferably a walk in unit; or place containers of hot food in an ice bath. This allows for quicker cooling. Then place food in the walk in refrigerator.

The key to successful cooling or any time-temperature check is to use a metal stemmed thermometer scaled 0° F to 220° F. Check temperatures of foods being held in steam tables and those being cooked in refrigeration periodically to make sure foods are not in the danger zone for extended periods of time.

FOODSERVICE
CRITICAL TEMPERATURES
Temperature Danger Zone 45° - 140°

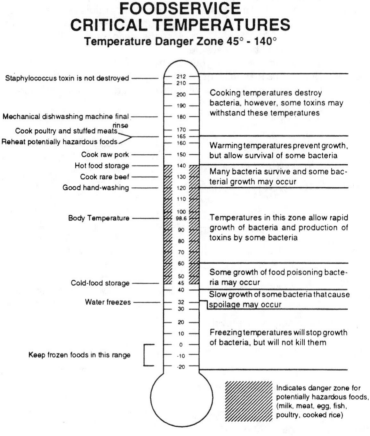

Fahrenheit Thermometer

U.S. Public Health Service Food Code: Management and Personnel

The following can be used in conjunction with Appendix C (Food Service Sanitation Manual) or independently as a training tool for foodservice workers.

Food Code

U.S. Public Health Service

1995

U. S. DEPARTMENT OF HEALTH AND HUMAN SERVICES

Public Health Service • Food and Drug Administration

Washington, DC 20204

Chapter

2 Management and Personnel

Parts

2-1   SUPERVISION

Subparts

Responsibility   **2-101.11   Assignment.***

The PERMIT HOLDER shall be the PERSON IN CHARGE or shall designate a PERSON IN CHARGE and shall ensure that a PERSON IN CHARGE is present at the FOOD ESTABLISHMENT during all hours of operation.

Knowledge   **2-102.11   Demonstration.***

Based on the risks of foodborne illness inherent to the FOOD operation, during inspections and upon request the PERSON IN CHARGE shall demonstrate to the REGULATORY AUTHORITY knowledge of foodborne disease prevention, application of the HAZARD Analysis CRITICAL CONTROL POINT principles, and the requirements of this Code, as it relates to the FOOD operation, by:

(A) Describing the relationship between the prevention of foodborne disease and the personal hygiene of a FOOD EMPLOYEE;

(B) Explaining the responsibility of the PERSON IN CHARGE for preventing the transmission of foodborne disease by a FOOD EMPLOYEE who has a disease or medical condition that may cause foodborne disease;

(C) Describing diseases that are transmissible through FOOD and the symptoms associated with the diseases;

(D) Explaining the significance of the relationship between maintaining the time and temperature of POTENTIALLY HAZARDOUS FOOD and the prevention of foodborne illness;

(E) Explaining the HAZARDS involved in the consumption of raw or undercooked MEAT, POULTRY, eggs, and FISH;

(F) Stating the required FOOD temperatures and times for safe cooking of POTENTIALLY HAZARDOUS FOOD including MEAT, POULTRY, eggs, and FISH;

(G) Stating the required temperatures and times for the safe refrigerated storage, hot holding, cooling, and reheating of POTENTIALLY HAZARDOUS FOOD;

(H) Describing the relationship between the prevention of foodborne illness and the management and control of the following:

(1) Cross contamination,

(2) Hand contact with READY-TO-EAT FOODS,

(3) Handwashing, and

(4) Maintaining the FOOD ESTABLISHMENT in a clean condition and in good repair;

(I) Explaining the relationship between FOOD safety and providing EQUIPMENT that is:

(1) Sufficient in number and capacity, and

(2) Properly designed, constructed, located, installed, operated, maintained, and cleaned;

(J) Explaining correct procedures for cleaning and SANITIZING UTENSILS and FOOD-CONTACT SURFACES of EQUIPMENT;

(K) Identifying the source of water used and measures taken to ensure that it remains protected from contamination such as providing protection from backflow and precluding the creation of cross connections;

(L) Identifying poisonous or toxic materials in the FOOD ESTABLISHMENT and the procedures necessary to ensure that they are safely stored, dispensed, used, and disposed of according to LAW;

(M) Identifying CRITICAL CONTROL POINTS in the operation from purchasing through sale or service that may contribute to foodborne illness and explaining steps taken to ensure that the points are controlled in accordance with the requirements of this Code;

(N) Explaining the details of how the PERSON IN CHARGE and FOOD EMPLOYEES comply with the HACCP PLAN if a plan is required by the LAW, this Code, or an agreement between the REGULATORY AUTHORITY and the establishment; and

(O) Explaining the responsibilities, rights, and authorities assigned by this Code to the:

(1) FOOD EMPLOYEE,

(2) PERSON IN CHARGE, and

(3) REGULATORY AUTHORITY.

Duties   **2-103.11   PERSON IN CHARGE.**

The PERSON IN CHARGE shall ensure that:

(A) FOOD ESTABLISHMENT operations are not conducted in a private home or in a room used as living or sleeping quarters as specified under § 6-202.111;

(B) PERSONS unnecessary to the FOOD ESTABLISHMENT operation are not allowed in the FOOD preparation, FOOD storage, or WAREWASHING areas, *except that brief visits and tours may be authorized by the PERSON IN CHARGE if steps are taken to ensure that exposed FOOD; clean EQUIPMENT, UTENSILS, and LINENS; and unwrapped SINGLE-SERVICE and SINGLE-USE ARTICLES are protected from contamination;*

(C) EMPLOYEES and other PERSONS such as delivery and maintenance PERSONS and pesticide applicators entering the FOOD preparation, FOOD storage, and WAREWASHING areas comply with this Code;

(D) EMPLOYEES are effectively cleaning their hands, by routinely monitoring the EMPLOYEES' handwashing;

(E) EMPLOYEES are visibly observing FOODS as they are received to determine that they are from APPROVED sources, delivered at the required temperatures, protected from contamination, unADULTERATED, and accurately presented, by routinely monitoring the EMPLOYEES' observations and periodically evaluating FOODS upon their receipt;

(F) EMPLOYEES are properly cooking POTENTIALLY HAZARDOUS FOOD, being particularly careful in cooking those FOODs known to cause severe foodborne illness and death, such as eggs and COMMINUTED MEATS, through daily oversight of the EMPLOYEES' routine monitoring of the cooking temperatures;

(G) EMPLOYEES are using proper methods to rapidly cool POTENTIALLY HAZARDOUS FOODS that are not held hot or are not for consumption within 4 hours, through daily oversight of the EMPLOYEES' routine monitoring of FOOD temperatures during cooling;

(H) CONSUMERS who order raw or partially cooked FOODs of animal origin are informed as specified under § 3-603.11 that the FOOD is not cooked sufficiently to ensure its safety;

(I) EMPLOYEES are properly SANITIZING cleaned multiuse EQUIPMENT and UTENSILS before they are reused, through routine monitoring of solution temperature and exposure time for hot water SANITIZING, and chemical concentration, PH (pH), temperature, and exposure time for chemical SANITIZING; and

(J) CONSUMERS are notified that clean TABLEWARE is to be used when they return to self-service areas such as salad bars and buffets.

2-2   EMPLOYEE HEALTH

Subpart

2-201   Disease or Medical Condition

Disease or   **2-201.11   Responsibility of the PERSON IN CHARGE to**
Medical   **Require Reporting by FOOD EMPLOYEEs and**
Condition   **Applicants.***

employer requires   The PERMIT HOLDER shall require FOOD EMPLOYEE applicants to
employee   whom a conditional offer of employment is made and FOOD
reporting of: EMPLOYEES to report to the PERSON IN CHARGE,
                      information about their health and activities as they relate to
                      diseases that are transmissible through FOOD. A FOOD EMPLOYEE
                      or applicant shall report the information in a manner that allows the
                      PERSON IN CHARGE to prevent the likelihood of foodborne disease
                      transmission, including the date of onset of jaundice or of an
health status   illness specified in ¶ (C) of this section, if the FOOD EMPLOYEE or
                      applicant:

employee is ill   (A) Is diagnosed with an illness due to:

                          (1) *Salmonella typhi*,

                          (2) *Shigella* spp.,

                          (3) *Escherichia coli* O157:H7, or

                          (4) Hepatitis A virus;

employee has   (B) Has a symptom caused by illness, infection, or other
symptoms of: source that is:

• intestinal illness   (1) Associated with an acute gastrointestinal illness such as:

(a) Diarrhea,

(b) Fever,

(c) Vomiting,

(d) Jaundice, or

(e) Sore throat with fever, or

• Boil or infected
wound

(2) A lesion containing pus such as a boil or infected wound that is open or draining and is:

(a) On the hands or wrists, unless an impermeable cover such as a finger cot or stall protects the lesion and a single-use glove is worn over the impermeable cover,

(b) On exposed portions of the arms, unless the lesion is protected by an impermeable cover, or

(c) On other parts of the body, unless the lesion is covered by a dry, durable, tight-fitting bandage;

employee
previously ill

(C) Had a past illness from an infectious agent specified in ¶ (A) of this section; or

activities

(D) Meets one or more of the following high-risk conditions:

employee at high
risk of becoming
ill:
• prepared or
consumed food
that caused
disease outbreak

(1) Is suspected of causing, or being exposed to, a CONFIRMED DISEASE OUTBREAK caused by *S. typhi*, *Shigella* spp., *E. coli* O157:H7, or hepatitis A virus illness including an outbreak at an event such as a family meal, church supper, or ethnic festival because the FOOD EMPLOYEE or applicant:

(a) Prepared FOOD implicated in the outbreak,

(b) Consumed FOOD implicated in the outbreak, or

(c) Consumed FOOD at the event prepared by a PERSON who is infected or ill with the infectious agent that caused the outbreak or who is suspected of being a carrier of the infectious agent, or

---

2-3   PERSONAL CLEANLINESS

Subparts

2-301	Hands and Arms
2-302	Fingernails
2-303	Jewelry
2-304	Outer Clothing

Hands and Arms   2-301.11   Clean Condition.*

FOOD EMPLOYEES shall keep their hands and exposed portions of their arms clean.

2-301.12   Cleaning Procedure.*

Except as specified under § 2-301.13, FOOD EMPLOYEES shall clean their hands and exposed portions of their arms with a cleaning compound in a lavatory that is equipped as specified under ¶ 5-202.12(A) by vigorously rubbing together the surfaces of their lathered hands and arms for at least 20 seconds and thoroughly rinsing with clean water. EMPLOYEES shall pay particular attention to the areas underneath the fingernails and between the fingers.

2-301.13   Special Handwash Procedures.*

After defecating, contacting body fluids and discharges, or handling waste containing fecal matter, body fluids, or body discharges, and before beginning or returning to work, FOOD EMPLOYEES shall wash their hands:

(A) Twice, using the cleaning procedure specified in § 2-301.12; and

(B) By using a nailbrush during the first washing to clean their fingertips, under their fingernails, and between their fingers.

2-301.14   When to Wash.*

FOOD EMPLOYEES shall clean their hands and exposed portions of their arms as specified under §§ 2-301.12 or 2-301.13 at the following times:

(A) **After touching bare human body parts** other than clean hands and clean, exposed portions of arms;

(B) **After using the toilet room;**

(C) **After caring for or handling SUPPORT ANIMALS as allowed under § 2-403.11;**

(D) **After coughing, sneezing, using a handkerchief or disposable tissue, using tobacco, eating, or drinking;**

(E) **After handling soiled EQUIPMENT or UTENSILS;**

(F) **Immediately before** engaging in **FOOD preparation** including working with exposed FOOD, clean EQUIPMENT and UTENSILs, and unwrapped SINGLE-SERVICE and SINGLE-USE ARTICLES;

(G) **During FOOD preparation, as often as necessary to remove soil and contamination and to prevent cross contamination when changing tasks;**

(H) **When switching between** working with raw **FOODS and** working with **READY-TO-EAT FOODS;** or

(I) **After** engaging in other **activities that contaminate** the hands.

2-301.15   Where to Wash.

FOOD EMPLOYEES shall clean their hands in a handwashing lavatory and may not clean their hands in a sink used for food preparation, or in a service sink or a curbed cleaning facility used for the disposal of mop water and similar liquid waste.

2-301.16   Hand Sanitizers.

(A) An alcohol-based, instant hand sanitizer lotion and a chemical hand SANITIZING solution used as a hand dip shall:

(1) Consist of, or be made up of, a chemical formulation **specifically listed for use as a hand sanitizer** in 21 CFR 178.1010 SANITIZING solutions or their components shall be generally recognized as safe as specified in 21 CFR 182-Substances Generally Recognized As Safe and 21 CFR 184-Direct FOOD Substances Affirmed As Generally Recognized As Safe; or

(2) Consist of, or be made up of, a chemical formulation that is not generally recognized as safe or listed for use as a hand sanitizer, and:

(a) Is followed by thorough hand rinsing in clean water or the use of gloves, or

(b) Is used only where there is no direct contact with FOOD by the hands; and

(3) Be applied only to hands that are cleaned as specified under §§ 2-301.12 or 2-301.13.

(B) A chemical hand SANITIZING solution used as a hand dip shall be maintained clean and at a strength equivalent to 100 MG/L(mg/L) chlorine or above.

Fingernails   **2-302.11   Maintenance.**

FOOD EMPLOYEES shall keep their fingernails trimmed, filed, and maintained so the edges and surfaces are cleanable and not rough.

Jewelry   **2-303.11   Prohibition.**

While preparing FOOD, FOOD EMPLOYEES may not wear jewelry on their arms and hands. *This section does not apply to a plain ring such as a wedding band.*

Outer Clothing   **2-304.11   Clean Condition.**

FOOD EMPLOYEES shall wear clean outer clothing. When moving from a raw FOOD operation to a READY-TO-EAT FOOD operation, FOOD EMPLOYEES shall wear a clean outer covering over clothing or change to clean clothing if their clothing is soiled.

2-4		**HYGIENIC PRACTICES**

Subparts

2-401		**FOOD Contamination Prevention**
2-402		**Hair Restraints**
2-403		**Animals**

Food
Contamination
Prevention

**2-401.11		Eating, Drinking, or Using Tobacco.***

(A) Except as specified in ¶ (B) of this section, an EMPLOYEE shall eat, drink, or use any form of tobacco only in designated areas where the contamination of exposed FOOD; clean EQUIPMENT, UTENSILS, and LINENS; unwrapped SINGLE-SERVICE and SINGLE-USE ARTICLES; or other items needing protection can not result.

(B) *A FOOD EMPLOYEE may drink from a closed BEVERAGE container if the container is handled to prevent contamination of:*

(1) *The EMPLOYEE'S hands;*

(2) *The container; and*

(3) *Exposed FOOD; clean EQUIPMENT, UTENSILS, and LINENS; and unwrapped SINGLE-SERVICE and SINGLE-USE ARTICLES.*

**2-401.12		Discharges from the Eyes, Nose, and Mouth.***

FOOD EMPLOYEES experiencing persistent sneezing, coughing, or a runny nose that causes discharges from the eyes, nose, or mouth may not work with exposed FOOD; clean EQUIPMENT, UTENSILS, and LINENS; or unwrapped SINGLE-SERVICE or SINGLE-USE ARTICLES.

Hair Restraints		**2-402.11		Effectiveness.**

(A) Except as provided under ¶ (B) of this section, FOOD EMPLOYEES shall wear hair restraints such as hats, hair coverings or nets, beard restraints, and clothing that covers body hair, that are designed and worn to effectively keep their hair from contacting exposed FOOD; clean EQUIPMENT, UTENSILS, and LINENS; and unwrapped SINGLE-SERVICE and SINGLE-USE ARTICLES.

(B) *This section does not apply to FOOD EMPLOYEES such as counter staff who only serve BEVERAGES and wrapped or PACKAGED FOODS, hostesses, and wait staff if they present a minimal risk of contaminating exposed FOOD; clean EQUIPMENT, UTENSILS, and LINENS; and unwrapped SINGLE-SERVICE and SINGLE-USE ARTICLES.*

Animals   **2-403.11   Handling Prohibition.***

(A) Except as specified in ¶ (B) of this section, FOOD EMPLOYEES may not care for or handle animals that may be present such as patrol dogs, SUPPORT ANIMALS, or pets that are allowed under Subparagraphs 6-501.115(B)(2)-(4).

(B) *FOOD EMPLOYEES with SUPPORT ANIMALS may care for their SUPPORT ANIMALS if they wash their hands as specified under § 2-301.13 before working with exposed FOOD; clean EQUIPMENT, UTENSILS, and LINENS; or unwrapped SINGLE-SERVICE and SINGLE-USE ARTICLES.*

Final Rule on the FSIS Pathogen Reduction and HACCP System for Meat and Poultry Establishments

Enclosed at the back of this book is a $3^{1}/2''$, PC-supported, floppy disk containing Appendix E. Appendix E contains the complete Final Rule on the FSIS Pathogen Reduction and HACCP System for meat and poultry establishments. This new regulation requires that

1. Each establishment develop and implement written sanitation standard operating procedures (Sanitation SOP's).
2. Slaughter establishments verify their process controls by using regular microbial testing.
3. Slaughter facilities and raw ground beef producers establish pathogen reduction performance standards for **Salmonella**.
4. All meat and poultry establishments implement a HACCP program.

An electronic version of this document is available on the Internet from the Federal Register at www.access.gpo.gov/su_docs/aces/aces140.html. Paper or diskette copies of this document may be ordered from the National Technical Information Service (NTIS), U.S. Department of Commerce, 5285 Port Royal Road, Springfield, VA 22161. For telephone orders or more information on placing an order, call NTIS at (703)487-4650 for regular service or (800)553-NTIS for rush service. Dial (703)321-8020 with a modem or Telnet fedworld.gov to access this document electronically for ordering and downloading via Fed-World. For technical assistance to access FedWorld, call (703)487-4608.

Index